a special gift

presented to:

Mary Ehy Bradley

from:

Mom & Dad, with all our love

date:

Jan, 18 2017

The LORD has appeared of old to me, saying:
"Yes, I have loved you with an everlasting love;
therefore with lovingkindness I have drawn you."
—Jeremiah 31:3, NKJV

The Women's Devotional Series

Love You More

I have loved you with an everlasting love . . .

Carolyn Rathbun Sutton

EDITOR

Pacific Press®
Publishing Association

Nampa, Idaho | Oshawa, Ontario, Canada
www.pacificpress.com

You can obtain additional copies of this book by calling toll-free 1-800-765-6955 or by visiting http://www.adventistbookcenter.com.

Library of Congress Cataloging-in-Publication Data

Names: Sutton, Carolyn, 1944- compiler.
Title: Love you more / compiled and edited by Carolyn Rathbun Sutton, with Ardis Dick Stenbakken.
Description: Nampa : Pacific Press Pub., 2016.
Identifiers: LCCN 2016019365 | ISBN 978-0-8163-5875-5 (hard cover)
Subjects: LCSH: Devotional calendars. | Christian life—Anecdotes.
Classification: LCC BV4810 .L68 2016 | DDC 242/.2—dc23 LC record available at https://lccn.loc.gov/2016019365

June 2016

About the Editor

Carolyn Rathbun Sutton
finds great joy in "being there" for other
women, especially those struggling to
find renewed purpose after a major life
setback. She particularly enjoys helping
women share with others their own
personal stories of God's faithfulness.

Scholarshipping Our Sisters
Women Helping Women

There is an aspect of this book that is unique . . .

None of these contributors has been paid—each has shared freely so that all profits go to scholarships for women. As this book goes to press, approximately 2,200 scholarships have been given to women in 127 countries.

For more current information, or to contribute to these scholarships, please go to http://adventistwomensministries.org/index.php?id=52. In this way you too can help fulfill the dream of some woman—or even yourself—to attend college or university.

General Conference Women's Ministries Scholarship Fund

The General Conference Women's Ministries scholarship program supports higher education for Adventist women globally. Recipients are talented women of vision who are committed to serving the mission of the Seventh-day Adventist Church.

Among Friends, published in 1992, was the first annual women's devotional book. Since then, proceeds from 22 of these devotional books have funded scholarships for Adventist women seeking to obtain higher education. However, as tuition costs have risen and more women have applied for assistance, funding has not kept pace with the need. Many dedicated women who apply must be turned down.

Recognizing the importance of educating women—to build stronger families, stronger communities, and a stronger church—each of us can help. Together we can change lives!

There are many ways to support our sisters, such as . . .

- Praying for women worldwide who are struggling to get an education.
- Telling others about the Women's Ministries scholarship program. (Materials are available to share.)
- Writing for the women's devotional book. (Guidelines are available.)
- Your gift or pledge to support women's education.

To make a gift or receive materials, send us a postcard with the following information. (Our address is on page 8.)

Name _____

Street _____

City _____ State/Province _____

Postal Code_____ Country _____

E-mail _____

To contact us:

Women's Ministries Department

General Conference of Seventh-day Adventists
12501 Old Columbia Pike
Silver Spring, MD 20904

Phone: 301-680-6636
Fax: 301-680-6600
E-mail: womensministries@gc.adventist.org
Web site: http://adventistwomensministries.org
Scholarship application and devotional book writers' guidelines are available at our Web site.

New Year's Day Baby

"Before they call I will answer;
while they are still speaking I will hear."
—*Isaiah 65:24, NIV*

It was the first day of the new year. As soon as I came into the obstetrics department where I worked, I knew by the sounds coming from one of the labor rooms that a baby was soon to be born. He arrived in time for breakfast—robust, healthy, and ready for his first meal. Midmorning the hospital chaplain, Danny Parada, came to visit my patients. After he had made his rounds he came to me and said that the mother who had delivered that morning had nothing at home but a box for her baby to sleep in. Her two- and four-year-old boys slept on the floor with blankets. "Do you know of any cribs the mother could have or borrow?" he asked.

"No," I told him, "but give me some time and I will make some phone calls." The first person I phoned was the director of the local community service center. I knew the center was not large enough to store any furniture, but sometimes the director was aware of things people were willing to donate. On the phone she told me she had just gotten a call about an hour before from a friend, stating that she had a daughter-in-law who wanted to give away a crib. When I phoned the daughter-in-law, she was delighted to find someone who could use the crib, and she was also willing to deliver.

The new mother was thrilled with the news I shared with her. When I asked her for her delivery address, she hesitated for a moment and then asked me if delivery could be postponed until she got home. Her husband was in jail. Fortunately, other arrangements were made for the successful delivery and setup of the crib. Later that afternoon the donor phoned me at work to ask if the new mother could use linens for the crib and a safety bumper. When I told her Yes, she asked, "Is the new baby a boy or a girl? I have some boys' clothing I'd be happy to donate."

"It's a boy!" I happily informed her, "and he has two other brothers at home. They can use *any* clothing you have to share."

In a matter of three hours God had arranged a chain of events to help a young mother with some very real needs. What a way to start out the new year! As you begin this new year with our loving and caring God, be mindful of ways and events He uses and puts in place to meet not only your needs but also the needs of others—through you.

Shirley A. Thomas

New Beginnings

Then He who sat on the throne said, "Behold, I make all things new."
And He said to me, "Write, for these words are true and faithful."
—*Revelation 21:5, NKJV*

Last night I changed my profile picture on Facebook. Previously I had a picture I had taken of a monarch butterfly. This time I decided to showcase another of my photographs, which was of a monarch butterfly in the chrysalis stage. You can actually see the monarch in the chrysalis! This morning, when I checked Facebook, several friends had left messages about my new profile picture. Some of them were, "Wow! New beginnings!" "God's handiwork!" "Beautiful!" "That's awesome! My wish for this new year is for God to make me a new creature."

If someone were to say to you, "Close your eyes and tell me what comes to mind when I say, 'new beginnings,' " what would you say? Here's my list: September—beginning of school. A baby. Morning. Waking up. Baptism. Butterflies.

Interestingly, I chose the picture of the monarch butterfly to showcase my photography skills. Then I realized what a fitting picture it was to start the new year with. It is so fitting because everyone in the world (I think) can relate to the life cycle of the butterfly. Each butterfly starts out as an egg. Then it changes to a caterpillar. The third stage is the pupa, and the fourth stage is the butterfly. In Bermuda alone there are six species of butterflies. Although some may differ in color or eating habits, they all go through the same lifecycle. What unfolds after the caterpillar stage is an amazing, beautiful creature that only God could make.

In Revelation 21, John shares the vision God gave him of a new heaven and a new earth. Why would we need a new heaven? In *Patriarchs and Prophets,* we read, "As the earth came forth from the hand of its Maker, it was exceedingly beautiful. Its surface was diversified with mountains, hills, and plains, interspersed with noble rivers and lovely lakes; but the hills and mountains were not abrupt and rugged. . . . There were no loathsome swamps or barren deserts."* Death, tears, and sorrow were nonexistent. These evils are now so much a part of this world that, to remove them, God must make all things new. I want to echo my friend and say, "That's awesome! My wish for this new year is for God to make me a new creature."

If He can do it for a caterpillar, He can do it for you.

Dana M. Bean

---

* Ellen G. White, *Patriarchs and Prophets* (Mountain View, CA: Pacific Press®, 1958), 44.

God's Security System

Be sober, be vigilant; because your adversary the devil, as a roaring
lion, walketh about, seeking whom he may devour.
—1 Peter 5:8

Recently, while visiting relatives in North America, we stayed in a neighborhood of beautiful homes. Expansive, well-manicured lawns, punctuated here and there by majestic trees and colorful ornamental shrubs, surrounded each home. The gardens sloped right down to the road. As a European, I was intrigued by the complete absence of any dividing hedge, wall, or fence between properties or even between the gardens and the road. Therefore, when fierce-looking, loudly barking dogs raced to the roadside to meet me during my early-morning walk, I became more than apprehensive. However, to my utter amazement and relief, they all stopped exactly at the edge of the road.

When I shared my amazement with my relatives, they told me that an invisible electric fence surrounded each property. The electric current, sent out by the invisible electric fences, reacted with a mechanism in the dogs' collars, giving the animals a low-voltage electric shock. It was this shock from their collars that brought the animals to the abrupt halt just where their property lines ended. This protective measure kept the dogs from harming people.

In God's eyes, we, His children, are far more precious than any stately home. He calls us His jewels (Malachi 3:17) and has paid an immense price to buy each one of us back from the enemy. To protect us, He has encircled us with an invisible fence. Not only does it keep us from harming those around us, but it also saves us from attacks from our spiritual enemy, the devil. Written in our hearts and invisible to others, God's law of love, His royal law—the Ten Commandments— is this protective wall around us. The commandments encourage us to treat others with the same love and compassion with which God treats us. At the same time, they restrain us from behavior that would harm others and subsequently cause much pain to us as well. For we would eventually reap a bitter harvest from the evil we are so often tempted to sow.

God did not give us His law to spoil our fun or take the pleasure out of living. He gave us His law to protect us. He longs for us to enjoy life to its fullest. May we all be able to say with King David, "O how love I thy law! it is my meditation all the day" (Psalm 119:97).

Revel Papaioannou

God Provides

And my God shall supply all your need
according to His riches in glory by Christ Jesus.
—*Philippians 4:19, NKJV*

My husband Dan and I were having one of those talks that few married couples enjoy having. It was the dreaded talk about finances. I was working part-time as church secretary, and my husband was working full time as a pastor. We were also sending our two children to a private church school. There just wasn't enough money to go around. The solution to our financial situation seemed to be for me to find a second part-time job. My husband and I prayed about this and trusted that God would help us.

A few weeks after our talk I was in a large department store purchasing a nightgown in the lingerie department. I felt impressed to ask the saleswoman if there were any job openings in the store. The woman said Yes—in fact, there was an opening in that very department. I applied for the job and was trained for it right away.

My new job became my mission field. I would pray before going to work that God would help me to be a good witness for Him. I met many women who had breast cancer and needed to find comfortable undergarments to wear after their surgeries. I was able to find them the items needed both in the store and in the store's online catalog. I listened to these customers' stories and told them I would pray for them.

One day a woman came to my department and asked if I had any pink camisoles. I told her I didn't have any pink ones in my department but they did have some fancy camisole-type shirts in the women's department. The woman came back to my register with a pink T-shirt to purchase. She told me she was purchasing the T-shirt for her mother. Mother's Day was a week away, so I thought the shirt was a gift for her mother. I told her I thought her mother would like the shirt because it was a pretty shade of pink. The woman then told me her mother had died, and this shirt was for her mother to wear with her suit in the casket. I immediately said, "Oh, I am so sorry—I will pray for you!" Tears came to both our eyes, and the woman said, "Thank you!"

God provided that job for me, not only so He could help my family financially, but also so He could provide encouragement for others through me. Encourage someone today.

Christa White Schiffbauer

Beautiful on the Inside

"Only I can tell you the future
before it even happens.
Everything I plan will come to pass,
for I do whatever I wish."
—*Isaiah 46:10, NLT*

I believe in miracles. I really do. They happen daily all around us. Some miracles are extraordinary, and others are quiet, like the sunset or the workings of the human body. Christ performed lots of miracles when He was on this earth. He walked on water, healed the sick, turned water into wine, and even raised the dead.

I was faced with a health issue a few years ago. At first I thought it would pass, but after discussing it with my doctor, I realized the problem had to be dealt with. The first two in-office procedures failed. Painfully so, I might add. I was so frustrated! Why did I have to be the one unable to get help through a simple procedure? Procedures for which I had to pay in full, by the way. Unbelievable! I decided to ask a friend, a medical doctor, for her advice. She suggested I see another doctor for a second opinion. I did and learned that my best option for dealing with the medical problem was to have surgery—my greatest fear.

You see, as a registered nurse, I work in a hospital operating room and know too much of what can go wrong during surgery. Thinking about these things turned me into a nervous wreck! *What if something goes wrong?* I thought. *What would my three boys and husband do?*

With the prayers and support of my family I did undergo surgery. During my first follow-up appointment my doctor came into the room smiling. In her hand were pictures of what she'd seen inside my body while operating. She said, "Shelly-Ann, if those earlier failed procedures had been successful, you would not be here right now. I do not know why they failed, but I am happy they did. The problem is now solved!" I looked at her and said, "I serve a risen Savior."

Back at home I again looked at the picture of my internal organs and thought, *I am a special creation of God. I am God's masterpiece. To be alive is miracle enough.*

Sometimes God beautifies our lives with answers in obvious ways. Other times He performs His miracles quietly. Only later do we look back and realize what He has done for us and, as in my experience, *in* us. What beautiful miracle has He done for you?

Shelly-Ann Patricia Zabala

Do You Know God?

"Though He slay me, yet will I trust Him."
—Job 13:15, NKJV

O ver the years, I have preached many sermons to my sisters. Messages I know God provided for them and for me. One of my favorites is titled "God Knows My Name; Do I Know His?" In the sermon, I show how in Psalm 139 and other Bible passages we see how intimately God knows us. Not just as a group but individually. He knows each one of us. But the question begging to be answered was, "How well do I know God?" And the answer was, "Not as well as I should."

I put that question to you today. Do you know God? How well are you acquainted with who He is?

I ask this of myself also, for my knowledge of God grows each day, but only if I am intentionally looking to learn more about who God is. There is much information in the Bible about God. James 2:19 says, "You believe that there is one God. You do well. Even the demons believe—and tremble!" (NKJV). So knowing about God is not something unique to us. Anyone can find out about God by reading the Bible. But to truly *know* God we must have an intimate relationship with Him. To know His heart of love, His desire that *all* be saved, including the drug addict and the man on death row; to know He loves us no matter our past or present. Such knowledge begins in the heart of the believer. It comes from a personal experience with God.

That's the way we need to know God. Yet we fall short of this knowledge so many times as we allow the distractions of life to block our view of God. A popular chorus written by Helen H. Lemmel says, "Turn your eyes upon Jesus, look full in His wonderful face, and the things of earth will grow strangely dim, in the light of His glory and grace."

When we turn our eyes to focus on Jesus, our knowledge of who He is increases. We see the love, experience His mercy and forgiveness, and accept the hope He gives for an eternal future.

So today, take time to turn your eyes and look at the One who loves you more than anyone who lives or ever lived. The One who gave His all, His life for you and me.

That is the experiential knowledge that allows us to know God.

Heather-Dawn Small

The Illuminator

Thy word is a lamp unto my feet, and a light unto my path.
—Psalm 119:105

While out on my walk one spring evening, I noticed that most of the houses along the route had path lights. The personal taste, creativity, and structural style of the homeowners were quite evident in the design and positioning of the lights. Some lined the walkway, while others extended up the steps to the entrance door. Several were placed along the edges of flower gardens, between the plants on the side of the house, or surrounding the bottoms of trees sporting beautiful foliage.

It was clear to me that a number of the lights were functional, whereas others were merely decorative. There were those that were strategically located to reveal tripping or falling hazards. Perhaps some were even situated intentionally to deter intruders. Whatever the reasons, the many styles of walkways and path lights were unique to the landscapes and personal tastes.

As I continued my walk, I thought about those lights. I then began to notice that some of the houses had no path lights, even though they all had an outdoor light positioned above or beside the entrance door. Others, like my home, had a light over or next to the back door. I pondered the different functions of the lights. The path lights along the walkway were foot lamps that showed only where to place your next footstep. On the other hand, the lights above or next to the door illuminated the entire path so you could see.

The psalmist David presented God's Word as both a lamp and a light. Scripture is sufficient to guide us through the cares and chaos of each day. At the same time, the Word guides us through the vicissitudes of our entire lives. It allows us to see our life's journey and set our course. When we hide God's words in our hearts, it becomes our most portable Bible.

How does this "life-light" shine? Paul tells us in 2 Timothy 3:16. He says that God-breathed Scripture teaches us doctrine and truth; it rebukes us and exposes our rebellion; it corrects us our mistakes and faults; it trains us in right living. We can take it anywhere, and it cannot be taken away from us. This guiding light is accessible all the time, permeating our thoughts, and regulating our lives. What remarkable provision our Father has made for us, illuminating life's pitfalls and guiding us along life's treacherous course. Take it with you today.

Florence E. Callender

He Listens to Details

Take delight in the LORD,
and he will give you the desires of your heart.
—Psalm 37:4, NIV

Lord, it's time for us to move again. I'm not asking for a big house, but I just want to ask You for one favor. The next place we move to . . . would it be possible to please give us an apartment or house on a street that has the name of a flower? I would really love that!"

My husband, on the other hand, was praying, "Lord, we need to move out of here. The rent here is going up like crazy. Father, You know the maximum amount we are able to pay for rent, so please help us to find the right place at that very price."

And in Jesus' name, we prayed.

During a women's meeting a week later, those present prayed for God to help our family find a new place. A couple of days later the women's ministry leader called my husband and said, "My husband and I would like to rent you our house." We checked the house out on the Internet, and oh my! It was huge! We'd seen smaller houses than this listed for much more than we'd be able to afford. Yet, to be polite, we agreed to go see the house.

Our sister from church welcomed us and started showing us through the big, beautiful house. Knowing we couldn't afford to live there (even while seeing all its benefits) felt like torture to us. After the tour we sat in the living room with the couple, and my husband asked the all-important question: how much rent were they asking for the house? Without hesitation the wife responded with the exact figure my husband had earlier prayed would be the reasonable amount for us to pay. The couple was asking not one penny more, not one penny less. God must have smiled at the expressions on our faces. "Would you like to pray about this?" asked our hostess.

"Sister," responded my husband, "we *have* been praying for this. We'll take it!" Later we learned that she too had been praying—praying that we would say Yes to their offer.

We said our goodbyes, got inside the car, drove a block away from the house that God had given us, and then stopped just to praise God! Screaming. Laughing. Crying with relief and amazement that He had provided a beautiful house at the right price—and on Magnolia Way!

Don't hesitate to tell God everything on your heart. He listens to details.

Sayuri Ruiz Rodriguez

Living With God One Day at a Time!

The LORD is my shepherd; I shall not want.
—*Psalm 23:1*

Even though you are a child of God, life will frustrate you. People will stand negatively in your way. You may lack adequate food, clothing, housing, and family support. You may be left to cry alone with no one to comfort you when you fail or cheer you on when you succeed. The enemy of our souls will do his best to discourage you after you have made the decision to walk with Jesus and live your life according to the Bible. I know because this has been my ongoing experience.

After I finished secondary school, an American couple promised to help with my university tuition at the University of Nanga-Eboko in Cameroon, the school they had advised me to attend. I began the nursing course in February 2011. But when the couple did not fulfill their promise, I was suddenly wondering how I was going to live, eat, and pay for my school fees. What should I do? Because of my lack of immediate funds, I was removed from class, forbidden to use and even enter the library for study, and unable to eat in the cafeteria. I was tempted to leave school and altogether abandon my hope of earning a degree. Yet where would I go? So I prayed, and determined to finish what God had enabled me to start—no matter what.

Since that personal decision to hold on to God in the face of destitution, the Almighty has shown me that all things are possible with Him. Yes, at times, I've had nothing to eat, but never for longer than a week. I've gone for more than a month without money. Yet when I have had a true need, God has always provided. Here at school my faith has grown. When I face a difficult situation, I know that *God* will solve it. When it's time to go for an internship, I call on *Him*. Whatever I need, *He* is my first and last option. That is why I am still here. I thank Him for strengthening me in times of hardship or sorrow. And He somehow puts just enough money into my school account at just the right times. Some of my tuition has come from the Women's Ministries scholarship fund.

I am learning to trust God and cultivate patience. Most of all, I am learning to listen to Him and live with Him during my fourth and final year of schooling. What a miracle! One day at a time. If you are facing troubles in your life, don't cry. Don't give up. Just persevere. God will take good care of you—one day at a time.

Flore Njiki

The Fall

For He will give His angels charge concerning you,
to guard you in all your ways.
They will bear you up in their hands,
that you do not strike your foot against a stone.
—*Psalm 91:11, 12, NASB*

A friend gave me a stained-glass piece for Christmas. Because my office has windows on two sides I decided to take it to work. As soon as I got to the office I pulled a chair and climbed on the credenza so I could display my new gift. It looked great up there.

I stepped down toward the chair forgetting I was wearing a long skirt. My boot caught in the skirt hem. My subsequent fall slammed my back into the filing cabinet, hitting with such force that the lock key broke in half. I slowly straightened up, praising God that I was OK. I was also grateful for my guardian angel who, I believe, helped break my fall.

That incident reminded me of another fall—Adam and Eve's fall in the beautiful garden called Eden. The consequences of their fall were much more serious than the results of mine. Instead of trusting God's word, Eve let the devil, in the form of a serpent, deceive her. Curiosity got the best of her. She ate the fruit and shared it with her husband, who joined her in the first sin. No guardian angel could have helped break that fall. What pain, ruin, and loss that first couple's fall in the garden has brought upon this world in the intervening centuries!

Yet, as with the pain of my fall being broken by what I believe was the intervention of a guardian angel, God already had a plan in place to intervene on His first created children's behalf. And on ours. You know the name of that plan: the Plan of Salvation.

The Father loves us so much that He sent His only Son, Jesus, to pay the price. The price not only for the first fall of mankind but also for every heinous sin that every sinner has ever committed since then!

But we must be willing to accept what God and His Son have done for us and to allow His Holy Spirit to revive us, helping us recover from the Fall. His Word tells us, "Because of his great love for us, God, who is rich in mercy, made us alive with Christ even when we were dead in transgressions—it is by grace you have been saved. And God raised us up with Christ and seated us with him in the heavenly realms in Christ Jesus." (Ephesians 2:4–6, NIV).

What redemptive intervention for our fall! Far beyond what any angel could ever do!

Sharon Long (Brown)

Before They Call

"Before they call I will answer."
—Isaiah 65:24, NIV

Have you ever seen a cardboard testimony? With a dark marker, on a rough-cut or torn piece of cardboard, one distills one's testimony down to the starkest bottom line. On the front side, life before Jesus; on the other, life after meeting Jesus.

Moved by several cardboard testimonies I'd seen on GodTube, I resolved to organize a cardboard testimony event for my church. I also wanted to participate with a sign of my own.

I played with several ideas, each dealing with a different aspect of my story. I kept returning to this one, feeling compelled from the start that it was the one: "Never Read My Bible" read the "before" side of my cardboard. "Give Bible Studies Now" read my testimony on the "after" side.

On the appointed Sabbath I took my cardboard-testimony-sharing turn with others. When finished, we all made our way to seats in the sanctuary.

I immediately noticed a couple I'd never seen before and knew I wanted to meet and greet them after church. I wondered how I might accomplish this, as we were seated some distance apart.

I needn't have worried.

As I kept an eye on them at the service's end and planned my strategy, they stood up. The woman looked around. I saw her spot me, do a classic double-take, and head in my direction at a trot. All I had to do was stand up and move into the aisle.

She reached me and, without preamble, said, "You give Bible studies?"

"I do," I replied.

"That's why I'm here," she told me. "I need someone to study the Bible with. I was sitting at home last night and felt absolutely compelled to be in church this morning. I couldn't *not* be here, the feeling was so strong. I looked up this church on the Internet. I hoped I'd somehow find someone who could help me. And you held up a sign! I can hardly believe it."

Sister, I thought but didn't say aloud, *believe it. This is just the beginning.*

And it was.

Carolyn K. Karlstrom

A Guardian Angel Named Nicki

The angel of the LORD encamps around those who fear him,
and he delivers them.
—*Psalm 34:7, NIV*

Mum and I love to sit down and chat over a cup of steaming hot tea. It's in these moments that I learn more about my childhood.

My brother is two years older than I, and we have always been close. Mum tells me my first word was my brother's name. After I had awakened from my daily naps, I would call out for my brother to come and take me out of my cot. As I got older, I would always run after him because not only did I want to play with him but I also thought I was able to do what he could do.

My family lived in a country town and owned a dairy farm across the road from our house. My four-year-old brother loved to spend hours there with the cows. I was still too little to be permitted to cross the road and go with him. One day my brother raced out the front door toward the farm. The front door didn't shut properly, so I slipped out behind him. I ran down the three front steps, down the pathway, and onto the road. Then, for some reason, I stopped in my tracks.

Perhaps I lost sight of my brother and didn't know which way he had gone. Perhaps I regretted coming after him. I don't know, and Mum doesn't know either. What happened next is what our next-door neighbor, Mrs. Boyd, related to Mum.

Regarding that long-ago day, Mrs. Boyd remembers hearing Nicki, her German shepherd dog, barking uncontrollably, if not with urgency. Mrs. Boyd went outside to see what was wrong with Nicki and spotted me standing in the middle of the road—directly in the path of a speeding car. She quickly raced toward the road, grabbing and pulling me to the side and out of the way of the oncoming vehicle. Then Mrs. Boyd led me back home to my very worried and grateful mum.

I know Mum has always prayed for me since I was born. And on that day especially God answered her prayers for my safety. He sent Nicki and then Mrs. Boyd to rescue me. I will always be grateful for their quick response. The angel of the Lord was watching out for me that day. God is looking out for you today as well. Let's praise Him for heaven's angelic watch care.

Jenny Rivera

A Miracle in 2013

Again I say unto you, That if two of you shall agree on earth as touching any thing that they shall ask, it shall be done for them of my Father which is in heaven. For where two or three are gathered together in my name, there am I in the midst of them.
—Matthew 18:19, 20

Camp meeting was over. On this Sunday I was waiting for my ride to take me home.

My roommate came into the room, sat down, and said, "It's a miracle. It has to be a miracle. A *miracle!*"

"*What's* a miracle, Rose?" I asked.

She stood up, briskly walked to the door, and quickly returned, repeating, "It's a miracle." She sat on the bed opposite me and quickly raised and lowered her leg several times.

"Oh, Rose, be careful of your leg," I said. I knew her hip was in a sad condition. The doctor had told her there was no possibility of her having a hip replacement because of the poor condition of her bones. Because of this she had been living on painkillers for four or five years.

Rose began sharing with me.

"In coming to camp meeting," Rose said, "I had determined to ask a minister to pray and anoint me. But now it's Sunday and our last day here. So I went to the small chapel near the lodge and was just praying. Suddenly people began to come in, and I felt I should leave." Rose continued, recounting that before she could leave the chapel, she was invited to stay and quietly wait out an anointing service for someone she knew.

While Rose waited, one of the ministers offered to pray for her. Rose told him that she couldn't kneel because of her medical problem.

"That's all right," the minister told her. He then offered prayer and anointed her.

Rose fell to her knees, stood to her feet, and picked up her cane. After resting in a lobby rocking chair, Rose walked back to our room—and she has been walking well ever since.

Rose's walker and cane are no longer in use. Truly God chose to honor the faith of one of His children and perform a miracle on her behalf!

"Trust in the LORD, and do good; so shalt thou dwell in the land, and verily thou shalt be fed. Delight thyself also in the LORD: and he shall give thee the desires of thine heart. Commit thy way unto the LORD; trust also in him; and he shall bring it to pass" (Psalm 37:3–5).

Muriel Heppel

21

Looking Back

"For I know the plans I have for you," declares the Lord,
"plans to prosper you and not to harm you,
plans to give you hope and a future."
—Jeremiah 29:11, NIV

At a very young age I recall my mother telling me that I was a beautiful, round-faced, smiling baby born in Cook County Hospital in Chicago, Illinois. Six months after my birth my mom left my dad and moved back to her home in Tchula, Mississippi, where her parents lived. She never returned to my dad. Some months after we moved, my brother was born, and we grew up in the home of our grandparents, where we received good Christian training. They taught us to repeat Bible verses and to give thanks before we ate.

Without support from her husband, my mother worked as a maid and on plantations to help support her family. We moved a lot within nearby cities where work was available. When Mother was away working, my brother and I took care of ourselves. We got into a lot of trouble; however, God always intervened and saved us from major injuries or tragedy.

At the age of ten, I gave my heart to God and was baptized in a small creek behind a little church called Mount Zion. I was terrified as I walked toward the water. The boy ahead of me went into the water smiling and came up smiling. I decided to try the same thing, but the smile refused to come. I went under the water without a smile and came up without one.

Some years later I graduated from high school and got married. God blessed my husband and me with four children and has kept us together for more than forty-three years. We are delighted that one of our sons is a pastor, and we praise God for that.

Our family has been through many ups and downs, heartaches and pain, trials and tribulations. Through it all we've come to realize that living a Christian life is not easy. However, we have learned to put our trust in God, no matter the difficulties. He has been with us all the way, and we are living witnesses of His unconditional love, grace, and mercy.

My greatest joy is meeting people and giving Bible studies. My dream is to finish college and open a senior care center. I pray that with God's help this dream will become reality. He has said He has plans to prosper me in hope and the future He has planned. I claim the promise. You can too.

Martha Shields

Never Give Up

Now this is the confidence that we have in Him,
that if we ask anything according to His will, He hears us.
And if we know that He hears us, whatever we ask,
we know that we have the petitions that we have asked of Him.
—*1 John 5:14, 15, NKJV*

Tell me about your mother," I asked my husband of three days. For our honeymoon, he had planned a tour of the area where he'd grown up. We stood looking at an overgrown lot, deep in the woods off the New Brunswick oil fields where his home had once stood.

He grew thoughtful. "Whenever I visited home, my mother told me how she prayed for me. I would tell her to save her prayers for someone who was interested. One afternoon, while I was having a beer and a cigarette, she told me she had been praying that someday I would give up those 'poisons,' marry a committed Christian woman, and follow God's commandments."

He drank heavily at the time, smoked two and a half packs of cigarettes a day, did drugs regularly, and gambled daily. His vocabulary was peppered with curses and crude jokes. Weekends were spent partying with a rough crowd. At times he was even an unwitting accomplice to criminal activity! He laughed and asked his mother if she'd been drinking his beer. He knew how many times he had tried to change his lifestyle but without success. "I know it's going to happen!" she had said. One month later his mother died without seeing any of the changes she had prayed for. It would be another three years before her son was ready to give up the life he had grown so sick of. For the first time, he knelt and prayed. And never drank again. He made an appointment at a drug rehab facility to begin his recovery back to health.

He began to believe that God had a plan for his life. When he prayed another prayer of surrender, God also helped him quit smoking, abusing drugs, gambling, and swearing. As his mind cleared, he developed a hunger to know God better. That was when our paths crossed, and he joined me in my Christian journey. Each of his mother's requests was granted. Tears of gratitude stung my eyes as I realized that the mother-in-law I have yet to meet spent years praying for me too. I am looking forward one day soon to meeting this faithful mother who prayed for us so persistently. Somehow I think she will be happy—but not surprised—to see us in heaven! Let's never give up trusting that God will answer what we pray within His will.

Vicki Mellish

One Blood

And hath made of one blood all nations of men
for to dwell on all the face of the earth.
—*Acts 17:26*

In retirement I have discovered crocheting. I've joined a group of women who eagerly search craft stores and thrift shops for one more ball of just the right color of yarn. I'm also learning the meaning of single and double crochet. Best of all, I've learned how to hold a crochet pin (also called crochet needle) without giving away the secret that I am a total novice. Now my family is finding polite ways to tell me they really don't need any more homemade scarves.

So I've chosen a new project, a granny stitch afghan. After a brief tutoring session from my aunt, I am on my own with a crochet pin, a ball of yarn, and a question mark printed on my face. I begin crocheting, at times having to rip out a mistake and then start again. I will soon have the first square for my afghan. As I create yet another triple crochet, I am amazed at how much my crochet yarn resembles God's family. He has made "of one blood all . . . men." One blood line, just like one ball of yarn. From Adam and Eve to our newest grandbaby, we are made of one common thread, so to speak. Making up God's great "ball of yarn," we are all human beings who smile, shed tears, make mistakes, and love passionately. We grandparents look at the families we've created and see that our descendants look surprisingly like us—our frames, our temperaments, and our flaws, such as a predilection for telling white lies.

Sometimes we don't like what we see in our families. But we recognize the yarn. We comb our family tree for answers. We tried so hard to keep the thread untangled and the stitches straight by setting the right examples. But between the perfect triple crochets in the yarn, a mis-stitch mars the perfection. Yes, I'm slowly mastering the new stitch, though I've made a few errors. Soon I'll complete another square for my afghan. Despite its flaws, my finished project will still look like an afghan. It will be beautiful. Likewise, with all our flaws God still recognizes us as family. We are His remnant, descended from our original parents, created in Eden "of one blood." So remember that if you are ever tempted to think you have strayed too far because of mis-stitches you've made, remember that our Creator shed His blood—having taken on human form—to redeem His family's flaws and failures. We're still His: one blood!

Annette Walwyn Michael

Righteously Indignant

The LORD is slow to anger.
—Nahum 1:3, NIV

t's not fair!" Melissa shouted, jumping up and down and pumping her fists in the air.

"What isn't fair?" I asked. By way of response, Melissa picked up a pillow and threw it across the family room, narrowly missing a cathedral candlestick.

"Janice and Jason are going to Disneyland with their granny. I don't have a granny to take me. It isn't fair." This was followed by more jumping and arm pumping. "I'm righteously indignant!" *I wonder where she heard that phrase,* I thought.

"You might want to be careful about that," I said calmly. "Vengeance belongs to God. It's less about life not being fair and more about each brain on this planet being different and not getting to do the same things. Besides, it's not like you to shout and throw things when you're disappointed." Melissa looked at me, puzzled. "Usually you talk out your disappointments," I explained. At this, Melissa slumped to the floor, the picture of dejection.

"You always have a choice in situations such as this," I continued. "You can choose to get angry and waste a great deal of time and energy acting mad, or you can be happy for Janice and Jason. After all, they didn't get to go to the Grand Canyon last year when you did."

Melissa retrieved the pillow and returned it to the sofa. "Good thing my aim was off," she said, "or I might have flattened your favorite candlestick and been grounded."

"No 'might' about it," I said. "Throwing a pillow because you were acting out anger or sadness would not be an accident."

I knew Melissa would need to work off the energy that had been generated by her temper tantrum. "Get your coat and we'll walk down to the fish hatchery," I suggested. "We can talk about some Bible stories of what happened when people acted out their anger inappropriately."

"Oh," said Melissa, "like when Balaam beat his donkey [Numbers 22:28], and when Cain killed Abel [Genesis 4:8], and when Jezebel got mad at Elijah [1 Kings 19:2]?" I nodded. As Melissa ran to get her coat, I heard her say, "It's not like me to scream and throw things. I talk out my disappointments—and every brain has some." I smiled to myself.

It would be wonderful if adults responded like this.

Arlene R. Taylor

Just Like Grass

The LORD has appeared of old to me, saying:
"Yes, I have loved you with an everlasting love;
Therefore with lovingkindness I have drawn you."
—*Jeremiah 31:3, NKJV*

I watched with keen interest as the workmen removed every blade of grass from the driveway and yard in front of my building, replacing the rich red soil with a snow white carpet of fine marl (crumbly mixture of clays and other materials). Following the thick layer of marl, a heavy roller was used to press the marl into place, followed by a light roller to seal the particles.

The final coat was the tarry black asphalt. What was the final product? A spanking new black driveway extending all the way to the front step of my building. The new driveway was black and clean, but I missed the grass and the earthy fresh smell after a shower of rain. All gone was the grassy patch and the beautiful red soil, or so I thought.

Six weeks later I ventured out for a midafternoon stroll and noticed fresh green patches of grass peeking through the asphalt. I was puzzled. Where did the grass come from? How could such delicate, fragile blades of grass penetrate the compressed marl and the asphalt? This should not be happening.

I was sure that no grass would ever grow after such harsh treatment of the ground. Asphalt should last for at least ten years. Well, so I had been assured. I was not seeing things; the grass was growing back in several places and had defied the odds.

Just like grass, God's love is persistent and will penetrate the hardest heart and most hardened nature. It can push through the most blackened life calcified from the ravages of sin. God's love penetrates the layers of guilt and hardened will.

Even when the conditions are not right or conducive for Him to love a person, He still loves unconditionally, and He loves always. John 3:16 assures me, "For God so loved the world that He gave His only begotten Son, that whoever believes in Him should not perish but have everlasting life" (NKJV).

I embrace the words of the songwriter who describes God's love as strong, pure, measureless, and enduring forever.

Oh God, thank You for Your penetrating love.

Gloria Gregory

Awesome

Jesus looked at them and said, "With man this is impossible,
but not with God; all things are possible with God."
—*Mark 10:27, NIV*

The church clerk kept on announcing, every Sabbath, the upcoming date for our church's harvest offering. I shuddered every time I heard the announcement because I didn't have enough money put aside for the offering. So, I prayed about it.

Then, out of the blue, I was called to substitute for a teacher at school. I earned fifty dollars, which strengthened my hope that we could help with the offering. The last Sabbath before the harvest offering deadline, a parent visited my church kindergarten class, handing me a check "of appreciation" for helping keep the little ones so their parents could enjoy the church service.

Dear friends, is God not awesome? Though others were able to give so much more, I was so very happy to be able to put—into the harvest offering—an envelope bearing our name and containing $150. I was not embarrassed. My husband had reminded me that we, as with the widow and her mites, had given all we could, and God would not look on our offering as insignificant (Mark 12:44). By the end of the day the harvest offering collection had risen to twenty-five thousand dollars for a new church building.

As we were saying goodbye, the women's ministries leader came from nowhere and gave me an envelope. She then vanished back into the crowd. At home, when I later opened the envelope, I found four hundred dollars! Confused, I phoned her for an explanation. She told me that the women decided to give me a little financial help because I do not work. I was stunned and grateful at the same time, realizing that no amount of thanks could show my gratitude.

Earlier that day I had given God all I had for the new church. Within mere hours He had replaced it—threefold. How could this be possible? I asked myself, *How does God do it?* He is full of surprises, and with Him nothing is impossible. I remembered His saying to test Him in this and to see if He "will not throw open the floodgates of heaven and pour out so much blessing" (Malachi 3:10, NIV). He is true to His word. I am glad I trusted Him.

Thank You, my awesome Father, my shelter in the time of storm. For I have tested You and learned that, despite my flaws, You will help me scale any wall. I am so grateful. Amen.

Mabel Kwei

Be Thankful

In every thing give thanks:
for this is the will of God in Christ Jesus concerning you.
—*1 Thessalonians 5:18*

Wednesday, January 20, 2010. What a busy day it had been! I planned to relax and watch my favorite television program at 6:30. At 6:20, the electricity went off. Checking with neighbors, I learned that the whole neighborhood was without power. Hoping it would soon be restored, we lit candles for light. The next morning I chafed at the inconvenience of trying to prepare a proper breakfast without electricity; we remained "powerless" fifteen hours later.

Though greatly inconvenienced, I recalled the poor victims of the catastrophic Haitian earthquake that had occurred only eight days earlier. Many still had no electricity nor food nor clean drinking water. Suddenly, I realized how many daily blessings I take for granted—especially compared to these earthquake victims.

One newspaper quoted Enazizi, sixty-nine, as saying, "I prayed constantly." Apparently this victim had been trapped under earthquake rubble. When the quake struck, she was in an informal church meeting in someone's home. Her vicar, who also was at the meeting, had been trapped nearby—close enough that they could converse. Rescuers did not find Enazizi for several days. By then the trapped vicar was no longer responding to her conversational calls. She realized he had succumbed, and she told the newspaper, "After that, I talked only to my boss—God, as there seemed to be no more human help."

Authorities say chances of victims surviving prolonged entrapment greatly diminish after the third day. Yet Enazizi's son, Maxime Xavier, never gave up hope that his mother would be found. He too was praying. Fortunately, rescue workers eventually found Enazizi and took her, in the back of a truck, to a hospital. Examining doctors determined she had suffered dehydration, a dislocated hip, and a broken leg.

Recalling this story during my fifteen-hour power outage, I realized two spiritual facts:

First, there is strength in hope.

Second, I am greatly blessed, despite any inconvenience in life.

God, forgive me when I whine about mere inconveniences. For my blessings I need to give You thanks every day, every hour, every minute, and every second. Amen.

Priscilla E. Adonis

Joschua

As an example of patience in
the face of suffering, take the prophets.
—James 5:10, NIV

Our wonderful little grandson Joschua was born with perfect, beautiful features—and a genetic anomaly, Morbus Hirschsprung (a life-threatening bowel condition). Within days of his birth, he had to have surgery to place a stoma. Blood tests revealed an infection and then subsequent leakage that required another surgery to patch up the hole.

We were fortunate to be close to the university hospital where Joschua was treated and spent many months. Yet the whole family was in shock, and our daughter's little family—including Joschua's brother, just eighteen months older than he—was under a huge strain. Joschua's parents took turns being with him at the hospital. They lived with the mental strain of not knowing if they'd lose their beloved baby. My husband and I helped with babysitting. And all of us trusted that the best doctors were in charge of the baby's case. Family, local church members, and friends around the world prayed for Joschua. He soon became the darling of the children's surgical ward and learned to be patient even during unpleasant procedures of care. Joschua has now undergone several life-saving surgeries, including a seven-hour colon removal procedure. One of our friends, a medical doctor, said that children who have a difficult start in life develop more stamina and are often more successful in life because they have learned to fight. Little Joschua is a great fighter, and maybe it is significant that his name means "Jehovah saves."

With so many people praying for Joschua, the question comes to mind: why did God not answer our prayers with a less radical result? I do not know. I just trust that God knows best. I have to be patient. When Christ comes again, I will find out the answers.

Our daughter and son-in-law have experienced amazing strength in this difficult situation. They say that although God did not work a miracle in Joschua's physical condition, He certainly worked miracles with *their* mental and physical strength. God helped them through this difficult time, and they could feel how the prayers gave them wings to soar even in the darkest of nights.

May their experience encourage you in difficult times as well, giving you patience, strength, trust, and wings of prayer to help you soar during your darkest nights too.

Hannele Ottschofski

Career Day Surprise Invitation

Do any of you have wisdom and insight? Show this by living the right
way with the humility that comes from wisdom.
—*James 3:13, GOD'S WORD*

It was a typical family dinner with my husband, daughter, and three granddaughters. The girls shared the ups and downs of their day at school and whatever else was on their minds. Ariyah—the youngest, the family chatterbox, and a second-grader—announced that her class was having a career day soon. In all my years of raising kids, I had never been invited to be part of a career day, although I would certainly have been happy to participate.

"Those days are always interesting," I remarked. "There is so much to learn about the many different careers parents and grandparents have."

"Yep," she replied, "it will be fun." Then, looking straight at Will, my husband, she announced, "Papa, I want *you* to come to our career day."

"Oh, nice, Ariyah," Will responded, grateful to be asked, I was sure. Although an accountant, he often wished he had considered being a teacher for one of the early grades. Now was his chance to interact with kids and to show Ariyah's class what someone in his profession did. He'd enjoy the challenge. I wondered why she hadn't asked me rather than him, but before another thought could go through my mind, Ariyah spoke again. "Yeah, Papa, I do want you to come to Career Day, but I want you to come as a clown!"

The snickering and hilarious laughter in the room was deafening. No one expected to hear those words! Will wasn't a clown, but clowning around and making people laugh was something he loved to do. Ariyah knew this all too well. A bit disappointed, he still realized that she had given acknowledgement that he brought giggles, joy, and happiness into her young life, a mini-vacation from the difficulties and sadness that she and her older sisters, Bianca and Kali, had experienced. I had experienced much happiness and hysterical laughter myself.

This career day invitation has remained an unforgettable moment, for the hilarity of it as well as the seriousness. Often we proudly tell others we are Christians and God fearing. Yet, is that how they see us? Our actions always tell the real truth of who we really are. Let us, on each day of this life journey, be sure that who we really are is what others truly see.

Iris L. Kitching

Kingdom Keys

"I will give you the keys to the kingdom of heaven.
What you lock on earth will be locked in heaven.
What you unlock on earth will be unlocked in heaven."
—Matthew 16:19, NIrV

Have you ever lost your keys? If so, you're familiar with the sense of frustration and inconvenience that the experience can bring. Keys are important because they give us access to our homes, vehicles, and offices. Although we may be the rightful owner or have authorized access, without keys we don't have what we need.

Likewise, God gives us spiritual keys—kingdom keys—that we don't want to lose, as they open up to us the deeper presence of God. Let's look briefly at seven of these keys, the first being the key of worship. We worship God for who He is, not for what He can do for us. Yet He often responded to repentant Israel's worship with healing and victory.

A second kingdom key is prayer. In prayer we open our hearts to God, and He honors our faith by unlocking heavenly resources for us. Through an angel, the prayers of the early church opened prison doors for the incarcerated Peter.

A third kingdom key is praise. Because God inhabits the praises of His people, this key invites God's presence into our lives. Praise is the language of gratitude. Paul and Silas used the keys both of prayer and of praise in a prison dungeon, from which God released them.

A fourth kingdom key is the study and knowledge of God's Word. This key dispels darkness and brings greater faith into our lives. It opens the door of Christ's victory so we can resist temptation and deception. Jesus used the Word of God against Satan in the wilderness.

The next two kingdom keys that open up heaven's riches to us are the keys of ministry and Christian fellowship. Dorcas ministered to the poor, and later Peter raised her to life after she had died. The key of ministry opens up the doors of comfort and encouragement for those who are oppressed. The resulting Christian fellowship helps them better understand the kind of love God has for them. This then puts into their hand the seventh key: their personal testimony. A personal testimony puts God's power on display. The Bible tells us we can overcome the enemy by the blood of the Lamb and the word of our testimonies.

Which kingdom keys will you use today?

Tamara Brown

These Things Shall Be Added

But seek ye first the kingdom of God, and his righteousness;
and all these things shall be added unto you.
—*Matthew 6:33*

Y ou've made *The Big Ten Winners List*," declares the big, bold, red-and-black lettering on the oversized envelope. Instructions inside advise the addressee to send in the grand prize winning number found somewhere in the maze of enclosed advertisements. It's a gimmick to lure the recipient into purchasing magazines and hoping for what is nearly impossible. To those who have a steady income, this notification may seem amusing and be easily tossed away. To those who already have all their wants and needs met, the ad may barely catch their eyes. To those who have a firm trust in God to provide all their needs, the ad holds no attraction.

There are so many, however, who are not able to work—they are sick or challenged in some other way. They may have limited ability to learn and an earning power that is minimal. Many don't "meet" society's standard in appearance, aptitude, or attitude, so they have a difficult time obtaining full-time employment as well. Therefore, an advertisement suggesting one can instantly win a sweepstakes prize may sound wonderfully attractive to people who have little and not much chance of obtaining life's bare necessities. Thus the big brown envelope with the large red letters inviting the recipient to send in an entry form, along with an order for a magazine or two, holds great appeal.

Yet there is a financial catch. The recipient of the ad is pressured to give up what one already has (for example, spend one's money for magazine subscriptions to better the odds of winning the sweepstakes). In doing so, one risks forever parting with a current sum of money for a one-time stab at a one-in-a-million—and improbable—chance of making it onto the Top Ten Winners List. Unfortunately, magazine subscriptions won't buy the groceries. A gamble like this is problematic at a spiritual level as well because it is, well, just that—a gamble. Someone who gambles probably isn't placing full trust in God's ability to provide for all of life's needs.

On the other hand, we never take a gamble when we first seek His kingdom through prayer and the study of His Word. We never take a gamble when we trust and claim His promises to provide for all our needs even as we wait on, and work for, Him.

Elizabeth Darby Watson

Milestones

I press on toward the goal to win the prize for which God
has called me heavenward in Christ Jesus.
—Philippians 3:14, NIV

On June 26, 1946, I filled my lungs with air for the first time and cried. My mother was elated. After my birth the milestones, as they do for most of us, came quickly: the first smile, the first tooth, the first word, the first step. I was incredibly and wonderfully made (Psalm 139:14).

Years passed, and the milestones of childhood quickly became the milestones of growing up. Entering the teen years meant I was no longer a child. I had more freedom and maturity for making decisions. My most important decision was to accept Christ as my best Friend and be baptized, remembering my Creator while I was still young (Ecclesiastes 12:1).

At the age of twenty-one, my career choice became another milestone for me as I praised God for life, forgetting not His benefits (Psalm 103:2). Then I took on motherhood and its challenges and now claimed the promises of Jeremiah 29:11–13, enjoying good health and financial security, and daily proving God's hand in my life. And how strange that fifty-year-olds seemed "old" to me though I still felt young, though mature, in my forties. Before I realized it, I reached the senior citizen milestone myself! I received senior discount privileges and enjoyed having to show proof that I was really fifty-five because God was preserving me (Psalm 97:10).

I now approach the biblical milestone of "threescore years and ten" (Psalm 90:10). I can declare that at every milestone I have experienced God's marvelous grace. Life has not been easy. My middle-income family lost the main breadwinner when I was only thirteen. Though I was just an average student who studied hard, my best Friend enabled me to receive scholarships for secondary, tertiary, and postgraduate studies. God has provided necessary and even extra funds so I could travel worldwide exploring His creation. Adulthood crises have provided evidence that God delivers—just when I have been about to cave in. And Christ's blood covers my imperfections. Even now I prepare for the most important milestone, the change of this mortal body to eventual immortality (1 Corinthians 15:54). I know that only with God's help will I make it. So I pray daily that He will take me through to this ultimate milestone.

Whatever your current milestone or challenge, God will help you through as well.

Cecelia Grant

It's Nothing Personal

For God wanted them to know that the riches and glory of Christ are
for you Gentiles, too. And this is the secret: Christ lives in you.
This gives you assurance of sharing his glory.
—*Colossians 1:27, NLT*

When I started raising Angora rabbits for their fiber, the last thing I expected to learn was a lesson in spirituality. But it happened almost right away. At about six months old, one of my two initial rabbits, a doe, began lunging and growling at me whenever I opened her cage to feed or pet her.

At first I was insulted, and my feelings were hurt. How dare she? I had treated her with nothing but kindness. I was so worried about this sudden change in behavior that I watched her continually for signs of rabies. Surely there had to be some medical explanation. Surely she couldn't hate *me*.

Gradually, as I got over the fear of being bitten, I persisted in trying to pet her (because I am nothing if not stubborn). I was amazed to realize that after her initial bluster she still longed to be petted.

Many rabbits later, I now know that female rabbits are often cage aggressive. I know that bad bunny behavior is not to be taken personally or countered with anything other than kindness. I have been scraped, scratched, pummeled, and bitten (once so hard that I almost landed in the emergency room, the victim of bunny-assisted suicide). Yet I continue to love all my rabbits—even the nasty-tempered ones—because I finally realized it was not personal.

And then a strange thing happened. This calmer reaction to unprovoked aggression began to carry over into my relationships with people. No one could have been more surprised than I. Being both French and Italian I was born with a hair trigger when it comes to reaction time.

Slowly a great truth dawned on me. When people attack us, are mean to us, or even betray us, we take it personally, but it's *not* personal. Not personal to us, anyway. They are being used as pawns by Satan to attack *Christ in us*. If you can grasp that essential truth, you will find yourself filled with compassion and patience the next time you are attacked, because those are the gifts Jesus gives us to offer those who are lashing out under Satan's goad.

Céleste Perrino-Walker

A New Beginning

And it shall come to pass, that before they call,
I will answer; and while they are yet speaking, I will hear.
—Isaiah 65:24

As I have shared in a previously published devotional, I found myself one evening pleading for the life of my husband, Michael, in the midst of a multi-level medical crisis in the Port of Spain hospital. Then God directed my attention to a plaque on the wall that read, "This Is Not The End of Anything, It Is Only The Beginning." Later that night, as I prayed with my husband, he gave his heart to Jesus. Years later, my husband—still trusting God with all his heart—decided he wanted an organ transplant. We prayed about going to Pakistan, which was our only option.

After corresponding with a doctor over there, my husband was accepted as a patient. Because my husband was a police officer, his association agreed to send the needed money directly to the hospital where the surgery would take place. However, my husband's new doctor declined to carry out the operation unless the funds were sent directly to his account. This was devastating news for us. Immediately we went to God. We prayed and prayed about this. After my further explanatory e-mail to the doctor, he agreed to perform the surgery on humanitarian grounds. God came through for us again.

The eight days we spent there were not easy for me. One night after the operation when Michael was still in intensive care, I was alone again in my room waiting for daybreak. I needed comfort from the Scriptures, but I could not find my Bible. The nurses gave me a Bible, and I opened it and read words something like, "If he is allowed to live, he will do evil." Sister, I closed that Bible and prayed like never before until it was daylight!

In the morning, I prepared to go visit my husband. As I opened the side table drawer to get the mask I had to wear into the intensive care department, there was my Bible! I concluded that God had wanted me to spend time in prayer.

This crisis was not the end for my husband but a new beginning. It has been five years since the transplant, and God continues to keep my husband in a bubble of protection. Every day I praise God for this miracle and for being my comfort and rock.

If you are facing a crisis right now, remember that God is able to turn what appears to be an end into a new beginning. Today He wants you to prayerfully trust Him and trust His plans.

Marilyn Thompson Marshall

Ask for a Miracle

"He performs wonders that cannot be fathomed,
miracles that cannot be counted."
—Job 5:9, NIV

My husband and I were so happy when we got married that we did not notice my mother's name was misspelled and had been partially obscured on the copy of my birth certificate. I later discovered it when that error kept me from obtaining an identity card as a married woman. In the notary's office (where we got married), I was told that the name could only be changed with proof of a better copy of the birth certificate. The problem was that the notary's office where I was registered was more than two thousand miles (3,219 kilometers) from where I lived. I did not have financial resources at that time to ask for a duplicate birth certificate, so I left things as they were.

Fifteen years went by. One day I had to do a re-registration at my job. It was necessary to show my marriage certificate. If I didn't, my salary would be suspended in sixty days. So I applied for a duplicate birth certificate, and I received it about fifteen days later. I went to the notary's office where we got married. This clerk said that, because of the many intervening years, the misspelling on the certificate could be cleared up only with a court order.

I left the notary's office, devastated.

I knew that the standard time period for an identity card replacement is usually forty-five days. I would not have time to get a court order and still obtain a new identity card. My husband encouraged me to go to the police station where they issue all state identification cards. There I could talk to the woman who authorizes new identity cards. As we arrived, we stopped under a large tree and prayed for God to work a miracle.

"You need a court order," a clerk rudely said. "Besides, you shouldn't have waited so long to do this!" I started crying. An arriving police department employee noticed my distress and asked why I was crying. I told her my story. She kindly told me not to worry, that the error had occurred in the notary's office, and that she would arrange everything. Two hours later we left the police station with my identity card showing that I was a married woman and with my mother's name perfectly legible.

What usually takes forty-five days to process, God had resolved in two hours!

When all seems hopeless, ask God for a miracle. He is able to work it out. Just trust Him.

Nilva de F. Oliveira da Boa Morte

Lord, Please Heal Me!

For he doth not afflict willingly nor grieve the children of men.
—*Lamentations 3:33*

I had been agonizing on the bathroom floor for two hours when my husband found me. "What is the matter? Why didn't you call me?" His questions poured out like a waterfall. We were visiting my brother, and I did not want to wake anybody. The pain in my lower back was unbearable; I had to drag myself because I could not walk. Unbeknownst to me I'd suffered a ruptured disk. Little did I know that I would be bedridden for the next eight weeks!

During those days I took refuge in God. He was my constant companion, just like with Jeremiah; the Lord was my refuge in the day of affliction. During the early hours before dawn, I would roll out of my water bed and slip into the bathtub filled with hot water. There I would spend hours talking to God, crying, sobbing, and begging for His help. My husband and I tried all kinds of natural treatments, but the only thing that helped was painkillers.

The time came for us to head to our new mission appointment. Somehow we packed up the whole house—with the help of family and friends—and then we set off for the beautiful island of Palau in Micronesia.

There I met Christina, a wonderful eighty-four-year-old woman, who invited me to become her prayer partner. Every morning we prayed at eight o'clock. Three months after our arrival in Palau, it was time for camp meeting. Everything was set up in the midst of great expectations. My responsibility as the technical director for video-recording the event brought more anxiety. The one thing I especially dreaded was the thought of going up and down the stairs—I prayed for strength. Early Sabbath morning Christina gathered her prayer committee. The women prayed that the Lord would bless the program and heal the pastor's wife—me.

On Monday morning Christina asked how I'd felt over the weekend. I responded, "Just fine. I have not taken any painkillers, and on Sunday I went on a boat ride to Jellyfish Lake, where I climbed the rock island and went swimming."

"Then you have been healed!" she exclaimed. Five months of agony were now gone—just like that! Many times I have wondered about the whole experience. It seems that through our afflictions, sorrows, and troubles God is trying to teach us some lessons that we will not otherwise learn. With God, there is always purpose in our pain. That thought brings me comfort.

Gloria Turcios

Redemption

God's free gift is not at all to be compared to the trespass
[His grace is out of all proportion to the fall of man].
—*Romans 5:15, AMPC*

Emitting ear-splitting squeals, the pig ran, legs pumping furiously, propelling him and his pendulous pot belly around the auction arena, two farmhands in hot pursuit. When he spun out at the next turn, he was captured and returned to the auctioneer's stand. Poor pig. It was the worst day of his life. However he had ended up at a hay auction, it wasn't turning out well for him.

"What am I bid for this frisky little rascal?" the auctioneer laughed, pointing at the hapless pig, which immediately lunged at his finger, teeth bared. The man snatched his hand back. "Guess that takes him out of the pet category!" he said, in a feeble attempt at humor. It was obvious to everyone that the "frisky little rascal" wouldn't be good eating, either. But something about the ill-tempered porker aroused my granddaughter Coramina's sympathies. She looked at her mom, eyebrows raised. Mom nodded. "One dollar!" Coramina yelled.

"Sold!" the auctioneer hollered back, not missing a beat.

That's how Spats was redeemed and came to ride to his new home in the trunk of a yellow Volkswagen Bug. They turned him out in a large green pasture behind the horse barn. He had his own stall, filled with fragrant hay he could burrow in and make a cozy nest. Grain, banana peels, and other delightful delicacies arrived twice a day, and he had a wading pool to cool off in on hot days. Pig heaven, right?

Then why did he spend all his time worming his way under the fence to get into the next pasture that had none of these amenities? He always kept a careful eye out, though, for Coramina and her little switch, quickly hustling back to the fence opening. He'd sometimes become stuck and get a swat on his behind. Squealing, "I do what I want! I do what I want!"* he'd squeeze back through, grunting belligerently with each step.

How very human of him! Like Spats, we too have been redeemed, though at an infinitely, fearfully, greater price. Like Spats, we have absolutely nothing to recommend us to our Redeemer's unfathomable love and extravagant grace; grace "out of all proportion" to our sins.

Oh, how He loves you and me!

Jeannette Busby Johnson

---

* Translation by Coramina, who now speaks fluent "pig-ese."

Power of the Sun

"You are the world's light—a city on a hill,
glowing in the night for all to see."
—*Matthew 5:14, TLB*

I am astounded at the number of solar-powered items available these days. I started out with one plain solar-powered light in my garden. As time passed, frogs, butterflies, and an owl have come to adorn the yard, along with an array of differently shaped solar lights that change color. It depends on how much the solar panel has charged during the day as to how long these lights continue shining into the night. Sometimes it's not very long after a dismal day.

I know for sure that the power of "the Son," who is Jesus our Savior, can work in our lives day and night. When we choose to give our hearts to Him, they too will be energized, so they may be shining lights, witnessing to others for Jesus.

On my window sill inside the house, I have a number of solar birds that light up the kitchen after dark; one changes color and chirps. But, the kitchen light must be off to see this happen.

Among these birds, I have a little chicken that flaps its wings when the solar panel is charged. For some reason this chicken always needed a bit of a push to get it flapping. However, a little monkey that waves its arms joined the chicken recently. When the monkey started waving his arms in the morning, it somehow activated the chicken.

My husband is as fascinated as I am, watching these two plastic solar creatures flap and dance all day.

This may be a simple observation, but this brings me to another thought regarding our influence on others as we walk life's road. Matthew 5:16 says, "Let your light so shine before men, that they may see your good works, and glorify your Father which is in heaven."

By obedience and love for Jesus our lives will reflect the example He has left for us. By our fruits we are known. Galatians 5:22, 23 says, "But the fruit of the Spirit is love, joy, peace, longsuffering, gentleness, goodness, faith, meekness, temperance: against such there is no law."

With these qualities, we can humbly help others to become activated in service for Jesus too. The monkey probably prompts the chicken by vibration. Our promptings, however, are of the Holy Spirit. May the power of the Son activate our lives today.

Lyn Welk-Sandy

I Did Not Get Anything I Asked For

On the Sabbath we went outside the city gate to the river,
where we expected to find a place of prayer. We sat down and
began to speak to the women who had gathered there.
One of those listening was a woman . . . named Lydia, a dealer in
purple cloth. She was a worshiper of God. The Lord opened her
heart to respond to Paul's message. When she and the members of
her household were baptized, she invited us to her home.
—Acts 16:13–15, NIV

A young Christian applied for permission to sell Bibles in the marketplace
of a small French city. Instead, civic officials sent him to a location on
the city outskirts. The young man, knowing hardly anyone would pass
by this remote area, still built his Christian literature booth, and trustingly put
His situation in God's hands. Not long afterward, a journalist noticed storks
gathering nest-building materials and settling in treetops of a forest near the
young Christian's booth. Because this was not a usual nesting place for storks,
the journalist wrote a short article about it in the city's newspaper. Soon crowds
of people came to see the storks. On their way to the forest, the people noticed
Bibles and Christian literature at the young man's nearby booth. He was able to
share with them about the Creator of storks and of the world, selling quite a few
Bibles in the process. The young man was thankful God had not given him what
he'd originally desired—a marketplace booth. God had given him what was best.

We are inclined to feel discouraged when we don't receive something for
which we've asked God. Faith, however, helps us believe God has a better plan
for us. Instead of giving up in discouragement when Paul didn't find a Philippian
synagogue in which to worship, he and his friends went to worship down by
a river. There he found a group of women gathered. One of them—Lydia, a
businesswoman—was so convicted with Paul's teaching that she and her whole
household were baptized. Right then, though Paul had not found his desired
synagogue in Philippi, he was able to start his missionary work and raise up the
first Christian community in Philippi. And this new little church became the
start of Christianity in Europe! As the poem of an unknown writer goes, "I asked
for everything so I could enjoy life. Instead, [God] gave me life so I could enjoy
everything. I received nothing I wanted, I received everything I needed."

*Thank You, God, for showing me I can trust You to give me exactly what is best
for me.*

Denise Hochstrasser

The Job

*And it shall come to pass, that before they call, I will answer;
and while they are yet speaking, I will hear.*
—Isaiah 65:24

Once I told God what job I wanted: a nine-to-five desk job where I could dress nicely and work with people in the nursing profession. Well, I got everything I wanted—down to the last detail. I should have been happy, right? But I wasn't—it was the most miserable job I ever had in my life. After two years of this, I had to resign this job to help out with a family matter. When the family situation resolved, I needed to look for another job. This time, however, I decided to give God complete control over where I should work. So I did.

One day I had to call the hospital regarding a friend's hospital bill. I also asked questions about inexpensive medications for which my friend was being charged large amounts of money. The person in accounts payable said, "Let me transfer you to Barb, the manager of the medical floor, and you can explain your concerns to her." In my conversation with Barb, she picked up that I was understanding medical terms she used. I explained that I was a nurse.

"Are you working now?" Her questions tumbled out. "Are you an RN or LPN? Would you like to be working and, if so, what shifts? Would you be willing to come to Saint Mary's and chat? I would like to meet someone who has gone way out of her way to help a friend." After a little chat together, Barb asked me to go to the human resources department and submit an application for an open position that she had. "We have a few other applications," she shared, "but I'll be in touch."

The next day at church Cindy, a friend who worked at Saint Mary's Hospital, told me, "Barb really likes you. She asked me to come up as a reference for you." She smiled sweetly as I wondered if there were more to the story. There was, as the following Monday a phone call informed me that I had gotten the job! The following Sabbath at church Cindy said, "When I went up to give you a reference, Barb told me she'd already decided to hire you."

When I stopped telling God what to do and gave Him permission to work on my behalf, He provided me with a wonderful job that I had for years. God did it all. I didn't even have to look for the job. I prayed. He did the rest. He knows what is best for each of us.

Marge Vande Hei

God's Faithfulness

Fear thou not; for I am with thee: be not dismayed; for I am thy God:
I will strengthen thee; yea, I will help thee;
yea, I will uphold thee with the right hand of my righteousness.
—Isaiah 41:10

Some years ago I returned to my homeland, Jamaica, after spending more than three years in Great Britain. I spent some time familiarizing myself with recent happenings in my country, because a lot of things had changed while I'd been gone. During this time I also went job hunting. The Lord blessed me with a suitable position of employment for which I was very grateful. After I'd worked with this company for a few years, management began reengineering one of our programs, making some of the organization's positions redundant. *I hope I won't be on the list of persons whose positions will soon be considered unnecessary,* I thought.

One fateful day, a few minutes before I was to leave work, the manager called me to the head office and handed me a letter of dismissal. Numbly I listened to his instructions. "You know our procedure is that you pack your bags and leave immediately." There was no time for proper goodbyes.

The Lord brought me through these fast changes and this difficult period. Since then He has opened many other doors for me. I have experienced His promise of faithfulness, giving myself to His care and submitting to His leading as I've prayed each day.

Christian vocal artist Dámaris Carbaugh sings a beautiful song titled "He's Been Faithful." It perfectly describes God's faithfulness in my life. I obtained the cassette album containing that song and played it again and again. I never tire of hearing or singing this song because it echoes the sentiments of my heart. So many times we have questions for which there seems to be no answer. But when we turn to the Lord in prayerful supplication, He is there for us. Even if He chooses not to give an immediate answer, He comforts our hearts and strengthens us.

God is faithful, and you too can prove Him daily. When we have faith, pray, read His Word, and trust Him for His grace, we need have no fear—whatever the outcome of our problems. All things are in His hands. As the Bible says, He does not change. He is the same faithful God today as He was yesterday. He promises to be the same tomorrow.

Will you join me in trusting God for His continued faithfulness?

Elizabeth Ida Cain

Why?

We are hard-pressed on every side, yet not crushed;
we are perplexed, but not in despair; persecuted, but not forsaken;
struck down, but not destroyed. . . . For our light affliction,
which is but for a moment, is working for us
a far more exceeding and eternal weight of glory.
—*2 Corinthians 4:8, 9, 17, NKJV*

A few days after Typhoon Haiyan devastated many islands in the Philippines, I attended a service held at one of the area Filipino churches in Toronto. "God Restores" was the theme for the program, which a number of governmental authorities and church leaders attended. The purpose of the meeting was to give support and hope to the many families affected and find ways to assist with the human needs caused by the devastation.

The question on all our lips was that three-letter word: Why? Why were so many children left without parents? Why were so many parents left without children? Why were so many left without shelter or food? And where was the Good Shepherd when the disaster occurred?

At times, believers have asked these questions since the fall of man. Adam and Eve must have stood over the slain body of their son Abel asking *Why?*

Tears flowed in our service as people recounted stories of loss. Yet tears of hope also flowed as Bible passages were read to bring solace to hurting hearts.

"Blessed is the man that trusteth in the LORD, and whose hope the LORD is. For he shall be as a tree planted by the waters, and that spreadeth out her roots by the river, and shall not see when heat cometh, but her leaf shall be green; and shall not be careful in the year of drought, neither shall cease from yielding fruit" (Jeremiah 17:7, 8).

Readings from Psalm 23 brought us additional promises of hope, protection, and restoration: "The LORD is my shepherd; I shall not want" (verse 1). Truly the Good Shepherd cares for His sheep. Growth and rebuilding would again occur in the Philippines.

We may never have the answers to all our Why? questions this side of eternity. Yet in times of loss, God will send His Holy Spirit in response to our prayers of pain and confusion. He will give us the faith of Job despite our losses. And, as with Job, we too will be able to say in the midst of our devastation, "Yet will I trust in him" (Job 13:15).

Sonia Kennedy-Brown

A Place for God

*"Then have them make a sanctuary for me,
and I will dwell among them."*
—*Exodus 25:8, NIV*

O h, Mother, I could give this gold bracelet!" exclaimed Sarah.

"And I wonder if they could use my little bronze horse," Nathan offered.

"I have a lot of blue and purple yarn," Mother mused, as the family gathered to discuss what they could offer to help build the sanctuary there in the wilderness.

After the Israelites had endured a lifetime of slavery and seen the devastation God's plagues had brought on Egypt, they were now surrounded by desert, but with a leader who had special instructions from God. Moses had spent time in the mountain with God, where he was given exact directions for the people to build a meeting place where God and they could connect. The Israelites were invited to make donations to the new tabernacle as their heart prompted them.

Each family could tell a story of pain from their years as slaves, and now living in tents with nothing to eat but manna, it was still easy to look at hardships and find things to complain about. Surrounded by the idol worshipers in Egypt, they hadn't really developed a relationship with God and hadn't learned to trust Him. However, two years after they left Egypt, the Israelites—in the spring of 1461 B.C.*—had an amazing wilderness sanctuary where they could go and know God's presence was there to meet with them.

Nearly two thousand years later on the Isle of Patmos, the apostle John was given a glorious vision of God's sanctuary in heaven. He was shown that in time to come God's Holy City will be brought to this re-created earth and, indeed, at that time, "God's dwelling place [will be] among the people, and he will dwell with them. They will be his people, and God himself will be with them and be their God" (Revelation 21:3, NIV).

We're a long time removed from the pain of the Israelites' experience and from that wilderness visual of God's presence. Sadly, we're not yet living on the new earth. However, we can build God a sanctuary in our homes where we can meet with Him and know He is dwelling with us! My sanctuary is a favorite rocking chair by the corner window. When I sit there with my Bible open and my head bowed I know I am meeting in God's presence. I can feel His smile as I join Him there.

Roxy Hoehn

---

* From Edward Reese, ed., *The Reese Chronological Bible* (1977).

No More Pain

Then I saw "a new heaven and a new earth," for the first heaven and
the first earth had passed away, and there was no longer any sea. . . .
" 'He will wipe every tear from their eyes.
There will be no more death' or mourning or crying or pain,
for the old order of things has passed away."
—*Revelation 21:1–4, NIV*

Every human being works toward reaching goals: buying a house, getting a good job, obtaining a car, getting into a good college. Goals are why many people work constantly, almost without resting. Unfortunately, in the blink of an eye, everything can be destroyed. I have witnessed this reality around me. I have seen evidence of it on the news as people, with pain and suffering, lose everything—especially in floods.

After five days of uninterrupted rain, Pernambuco was on high alert. Televised news reports showed the fearful force of the water after so many days of heavy rain. Several cities were affected, and thousands of people mourned the loss of their relatives and their riches.

Soon, members of our church district began to help others who had been adversely affected. We went from street to street asking for food, clothes, water, mattresses, bed sheets, and other essentials.

A few days later we went to the closest cities to deliver the donations. What we saw was shocking! Houses had been swept away in the flood waters. Those still standing were filled with the same mud that covered the streets. Survivors crowded into schools and shelters. A number had lost everything except their lives. Some were weeping because they had worked so hard to make some kind of a life for their families and themselves. Now the floodwaters had taken everything from them.

I prayed for the people there, asking myself what I could share that would bring them comfort. God reminded me of His promise that one day He will end all suffering and pain. I prayed for God to supply every need and soothe the brokenhearted. He was surely saying, "My children, have a little patience. I am here. Wait a little longer. You will be with Me forever in a place with no more crying, no more suffering, and no more pain!" Let these words comfort you.

Carmem Virgínia dos Santos Paulo

Touching a Life

*Let your light so shine before men, that they may see
your good works, and glorify your Father which is in heaven.*
—*Matthew 5:16*

Dressed for church one Sabbath morning in May 2001, I hurried down the hall of Brookdale Hospital in New York. Coming toward me from the opposite direction was a college classmate of mine whom I had not seen for a number of years. I called his name, and he stopped to greet me. "Why are you at the hospital?" he asked.

"I have cancer," I answered, "and am here for an injection to perk up my blood count, which dropped during chemotherapy treatment. Then I'm heading to church. And you?" He didn't seem to give me a clear response before we went our separate ways.

Nine years later my late husband and I met this same classmate at a university alumni function. I left the two men to converse and moved on to greet other friends.

At my mother's apartment later that evening my husband and I were discussing the events of the day and the many people we had seen. During our conversation, my husband said, "By the way, your college classmate indicated that he is interested in having you attend a seminar he is conducting on drug use and abuse. It seems that when he ran into you nine years ago in the hospital corridor, he was on his way to take care of some illegal drug business. He said his encounter with you was a turning point in his life. So he told God, 'Look what I am doing with my life, and yet I am OK, healthwise. This classmate of mine has not abused drugs, and yet she is suffering with cancer—but with such grace.'"

Then my classmate told my husband that he confessed his destructive habits to God. "Help me to do something positive with my life," he had prayed. Now he is conducting seminars for drug addicts and wants them to meet the person whom God used to help him out of his pit of sin.

As with this classmate, God allows situations into our lives to teach lessons that wake us up to our true condition. The effect this simple encounter had on my classmate reminded me that we never know who is watching us or how our lives might be affecting others. Today let us resolve to let God live through us—for His glory and to help point others to the way of the Cross.

Ruby H. Enniss-Alleyne

Returning Home

Then spake Jesus again unto them, saying, I am the light of the world.
—*John 8:12*

"I am the vine; you are the branches. . . .
Apart from me you can do nothing."
—*John 15:5, NIV*

When I was a teenager, Dad moved to a nearby town to work. The rest of us stayed with Mom so we could finish out the school semester. On Fridays we would all go and spend the weekend with Dad, making the twenty-five-kilometer (fifteen-mile) trip. In fact, I made this journey several times by myself and knew how to get there by taking the intercity bus. After it passed by some television antennas, I would ask the conductor to stop, get off the bus, take a trail in a gravel pit and soon see the ranch where my father worked.

This short trip made in daylight was a very easy one. But making the trip at night was another story. I'll never forget it. We learned on our first trip at night that there wasn't enough light to see our landmark, the television antennas. In the darkness we were frightened—and lost.

The bus stopped, and we disembarked. Yet again, because of the gloomy darkness, we could not find the trail at the gravel pit. Though near a main highway, we were still lost and didn't know where to go. Mom thought we should head toward a lighted neighborhood, take another city bus to the downtown area, and then get to Dad's ranch in a taxi. Of course, this would be at an inflated price. Tired and almost penniless, we finally reached Dad. How happy he was to see us! He had been so worried about our delay and welcomed us with open arms. He had everything ready for us. Once we were reunited, our earlier misfortune almost seemed funny.

It was through encouraging one another and finishing the trip in mutual strength that helped us reach our destination and the safety of our father's arms. Seeing our father's relief and joy made our hearts glad as well.

We are all part of God's family. We all have the opportunity to encourage one another, to point each other to the light, and to journey together toward the home of our other father. We have a heavenly Father who cares for each of us individually. He is watching over us and waiting with open arms, anticipating the day when we will be reunited with Him in our heavenly home. Let's not lose our way in the darkness of this world. Let's travel in the light of His Word. And when feeling lost, let's remember His welcoming arms at the end of our long journey home.

Sueli da Silva Pereira

Unequaled Love

For Christ's love compels us, because we are convinced
that one died for all, and therefore all died.
—*2 Corinthians 5:14, NIV*

Soon after my fiancé graduated with a bachelor's degree in theology, we got married and were sent by our church area headquarters to work in a small city in the countryside of Paraná, Brazil. Sertanópolis was the headquarters of a district with seventeen churches; therefore, my husband had to travel a lot. I felt lonely, especially because I was so far from my family, but I knew that God had chosen my husband and me for this ministry.

One morning we heard a faint meowing coming from our backyard, and we went out to see what was happening. We spotted a small yellow cat, gaunt and hungry, with big blue eyes. He had been abandoned. His bleak eyes seemed to say, "Please, look after me." We took him in, fed him, treated his ailments, and put him in a box to sleep. He grew larger and became beautiful. He was always by our side.

In the mornings when my husband went to the bakery to buy bread, the cat accompanied him and received warm bread as a reward. The church was not very far from our house, and one night, during the worship time, I was surprised when I saw the cat walking down the aisle, heading to the pulpit where my husband was preaching. People who were at the church observed the scene and asked, "How can a simple cat show such affection, such unequaled love, to a person and know where he is?" When we returned to our house, the cat was waiting at the gate. When our eldest daughter was born, he pointed to the spot where she was supposed to be placed, lifted his paws on the bed, and watched the newcomer. It was like giving her a warm welcome.

It is interesting to see how animals respond to the attention that is given to them. This makes us wonder if we respond to the love that God gives us. John 3:16 says God sent His only Son to die in our place and offer us salvation, "that whoever believes in him shall not perish but have eternal life" (NIV). Verse 17 continues, "For God did not send his Son into the world to condemn the world, but to save the world through him" (NIV). Nothing compares to the love God has for us and to the sacrifice He made. God loved us and gave us the ability to love others. But the most wonderful thing is that we can enjoy His love for all eternity, sharing with Him the joys of eternal salvation.

Maria Bellesi Guilhem

I Know How You Feel

Bear ye one another's burdens,
and so fulfil the law of Christ.
—*Galatians 6:2*

How often have you heard or even said "I know how you feel" when talking to someone in pain, in crisis, or in bereavement?

Recently I was hospitalized for two biopsies: one of my thyroid and the other of a mass in my chest cavity that involved going through the sternum. Before the biopsies could be done, I had to have a blood platelet transfusion, which got delayed for reasons unknown. After receiving the blood platelets, the biopsies were delayed and delayed until the radiologist on call could work it into his schedule. In the meantime I was not to eat or drink.

My meals were delivered on time but I was denied each one because *the biopsies would be done this morning, then this afternoon, and then evening.* But nothing happened. I went forty-three hours without food and water. I did have an IV solution dripping into my arm to keep me hydrated, but nothing satisfies like a hearty meal, especially when you're not sick.

When my friend Diane heard about my experience, she e-mailed this message: "If I had been sitting with you, I would have fasted with you, my friend!" This message hit home for me. She didn't say, "I know how you feel"; her message was, "I will suffer along with you." She went on to say how her teenage son had a similar experience as he was being monitored for a serious bone infection.

During the *looong* wait, he said, "Mom, what did you eat for lunch?" She told him that if he had to go without food, she could too. She added, "In the scheme of things, for me it was a little thing, but I think it meant a lot to him."

This experience has prompted me to think of more creative ways to demonstrate "I know how you feel" or to show "I care." Jesus, our prime example, showed He cared. He welcomed children to His side; He mingled with sinners; He touched the untouchable; He fed the multitude and provided "living water" to the woman at the well. He was a servant. He took His disciples apart for rest. He listened and He wept and much more. Above all, though sinless Himself, He died on the cross that we might have eternal life. I can't do all that Jesus did, but I can do something to show "I know how you feel. I care."

Edith Fitch

February 11

The Lilies of the Field

*Consider the lilies of the field, how they grow; they toil not,
neither do they spin: And yet I say unto you, That even Solomon
in all his glory was not arrayed like one of these.*
—Matthew 6:28, 29

As a military family, we are constantly relocating. Our family has moved five times over the last few years. Some locations we loved. Others we couldn't wait to leave. Some moves were seamless; others were trying. Each move came with a different set of challenges than we had encountered before. Yet through it all God has blessed us tremendously. So you would think that having moved so many times before, I would be prepared to handle our latest move. But I wasn't!

With a time constraint of three months, there was so much to do in such a little time. I made a to-do list. Each day I tackled my list. Instead of crossing things off, however, it seemed that more things were added. Eventually, God helped me complete the tasks on my list.

The day finally came for us to move, yet there were a few things left to be completed. Ever the perfectionist, I started wondering and worrying about what we were going to do. My husband assured me that everything would work itself out. I didn't have to worry. We prayed and embarked on a new voyage. It took us five days to drive across the country to our destination. God was with us along the way.

Once in our new home, things started falling into place except for one thing—I didn't have a job. Now what? My husband and I continuously prayed for guidance. We could use our savings to help support the family until I landed a job. During this time my faith was severely tested. I applied for every job I possibly could. I waited patiently for a call back. I got an interview, but no job. I watched in horror as our savings became depleted and wondered what would happen next. I prayed, cried, and pled for God's help. Five months later, I was still unemployed.

A week ago, my husband reminded me about Jesus' analogy of the lilies of the field and God's love and care for us. If God can take good care of the lilies that are here one day and gone tomorrow, why couldn't He take good care of us? Reflecting on this, I stopped worrying and am allowing God to fully care for us.

Though I have no job right yet, it is OK. God generously takes care of our daily needs.

Diantha Hall-Smith

A Shelter in the Time of Storm

The LORD shall preserve you from all evil;
He shall preserve your soul.
The LORD shall preserve your going out and your coming in
From this time forth, and even forevermore.
—*Psalm 121:7, 8, NKJV*

I was sitting at home in Zimbabwe with my four-year-old son and a young woman who babysat when I was at work. Outside, the dark rainclouds threatened a heavy downpour any minute. I turned on the lights because it was growing too dark inside to even read. As I sat back down, I pulled a book back in my lap—*Life Sketches,* by Ellen G. White, a remarkable writer and servant of the Lord. I quickly became engrossed in my reading.

Suddenly, from the corner of my left eye, I saw a fist-sized bolt of fire come through the window. It appeared to be heading straight toward my lap. My knee-jerk reaction was to raise my hands, still holding the book, which repelled the fireball toward the lightbulb in the ceiling above me. The fireball disappeared into the bulb, shattering it into a thousand pieces and disabling the house's electrical system. All this happened in a fraction of a second. Before I could take a deep breath, a thunderous roll followed and sent us all diving under whatever we could find for protection.

After what seemed like an eternity, we collected ourselves, thanking God that we were still alive. A few minutes later it dawned on me what the devil had planned! But the mighty power of an ever-present God, who never sleeps nor slumbers, foiled the devil's plan!

Those who live in Africa will agree that it is no uncommon thing for a whole family to be struck by lightning and their home burnt to ashes. On that stormy date in 1998, God graciously spared us that fate. Looking back today, I remember many other instances where the hand of God has dashed me to safety though the evil one was intent on destroying me.

So how can I fear? God is my very present help in danger! Though the devil is angry with us (Revelation 12:17), the everlasting hand of our God will always sustain us according to His will (Psalm 91). Job suffered both joy and pain, good and bad. Yet his choice to trust in God as his refuge during the time of storm spared Job for eternity.

Despite any storm in our personal lives today, we can trust Jesus to be our shelter.

Nokuthula Maphosa-Mutumhe

Who Was Jack?

Love is as powerful as death. . . .
It bursts into flame and burns like a raging fire.
Water cannot put it out; no flood can drown it.
—*Song of Solomon 8:6, 7, GNT*

Some years ago one of my hobbies was making placemats out of old greeting cards. My friends and I would get together and create our masterpieces. One day I decided to advertise that I needed assorted greeting cards and was overwhelmed with calls. On one card retrieval outing I filled up half of my car trunk with boxes of cards. In my spare time I sorted the cards by various occasions, colors, pictures, and sizes. Soon I had separate—and big—boxes of Mother's Day cards, Father's Day cards, Christmas cards, and get-well cards. Boxes for pictures of birds, animals, flowers. Shiny cards to catch one's eyes, and cards to use for borders on the placemats.

I began to notice that many of the very stunning, unusual cards were signed by someone named Jack. Inside these cards I found handwritten poems and words of endearment. The cards sparkled with touches of ribbon and bows. Instead of using Jack's cards for placemats, I began putting them into a separate medium-sized box, which was soon full. Who was Jack and who was the object of affection? Jack had obviously cared deeply for her. He missed her when they were apart. Somehow reading Jack's words of endearment made me feel a bit more special too.

Jack was a very special person to have given so many tokens of his devotion and love to his dear one. He had undoubtedly spent many hours picking out those special cards—just for her. I suspect that Jack thought about her throughout each day. I'm sure he longingly anticipated the expression on her face when she opened a card and read it. Not all his cards celebrated a special occasion, but all held reminders of his ongoing affection, care, and love.

Just as Jack's words of endearment drew me to save his cards, my heavenly Father's love notes to me—through His Word—draw me to Him. I know, from what He has left me through the prophets, the poets, and the New Testament writers, that He spends all day thinking about me. He yearns to catch my facial expression when I approach Him in prayer each day and then open His "card" to me. Our Father in heaven sends each of us, His dearly beloved, words of everlasting, powerful, and unquenchable endearment (see text above) throughout the Bible.

How has He expressed His love to you today through His Written Word?

Vidella McClellan

A Woman Won by Love

"Come, I will show you the bride, the Lamb's wife."
—*Revelation 21:9, NKJV*

Flirting has been raised to a science in recent years. Books and other tools abound to teach the ignorant. For example, a blogger named Donalgraeme created an acronym for what he called "the five vectors of female attraction." He wanted to concisely identify what traits in a man attract women. The vectors are these: *L*ooks, *A*thleticism, *M*oney, *P*ower, *S*tatus.

The LAMPS acronym has no doubt worked magic for many a man in fleshly pursuit of a woman. But would it work to win a pure woman, a real relationship?

I've recently studied the book of Revelation carefully while working on a music project called *The Lamb Wins*. I've come to believe the central motif of the book is the romance between the Lamb and the bride. It seems to me that the war between the Lamb and the beast is really the secondary war of Revelation. The primary war is the Lamb's death-defying struggle to win the bride's affections. It has been a slow, agonizing war—a cold war at times, fought in the silent disappointments of the Bridegroom. But finally He wins her.

I found it illuminating that it is *after* she bestows her full affections, *after* she is clothed "in fine linen, clean and bright" (Revelation 19:8, NKJV), symbolizing her full dependency upon Christ's righteousness, that Jesus returns. Then the White Horse Rider, in a mode of utter triumph and masculine virtuosity, thunders forth to vanquish the enemy. So what won the bride? Did Jesus use the vectors of Donalgraeme's LAMPS acronym? Let's see. Looks—she doesn't lay eyes on His physical self until the wedding. Athleticism—a lamb doesn't show much muscle. Money—the Lamb's beast-nemesis flashes much more money than He does. Power—the beast seems to have more power. Status—does dying on a cross sound like status?

The Lamb wins the bride's heart on something far more substantial than Donalgraeme's LAMPS. The Lamb has a lamp of His own. The goodness of God illuminates the Holy City, and "the Lamb *is* its lamp" (Revelation 21:23, NIV; emphasis added). That Jesus calls Himself the "Lamb" more than twenty times in Revelation is no accident. He refers to the aspect of Himself that ultimately succeeds in conquering the heart of His woman: self-sacrificing love. The Lamb wins His bride on the basis of His character of love, and a woman won by love is a woman won forever.

Jennifer Jill Schwirzer

A Wake-Up Call

And I saw another angel fly in the midst of heaven, having the everlasting gospel to preach unto them that dwell on the earth, and to every nation, and kindred, and tongue, and people, Saying with a loud voice, Fear God, and give glory to him; for the hour of his judgment is come: and worship him that made heaven, and earth, and the sea, and the fountains of waters.
—*Revelation 14:6, 7*

Just before dawn one late January morning, we were awakened by a loud call: *kuoo-kuoo-kuoo.* Then a pause, and the call again, and again. We recognized it as the call of a koel. During the winter these birds are silent, but as the summer sets in, the male koel becomes very noisy. Because koels are noisy and early risers, they make effective alarm clocks. As that morning dawned, "our" bird sensed the heat and started calling. Without fail, it promptly woke us up each morning at six thirty and with a sense of urgency before flying off with its mate to find food. This bird not only woke us up but also woke up our neighbor. It became our friend, and we in turn greeted it with a daily "good morning."

Summer heat in India usually takes a toll on lives each year. It was extremely hot that summer. Yet often in the middle of a hot day, we would hear the koel's call. We recognized its low-pitched start and the increasing volume, which reaches its loudest on the seventh or eighth *kuoo.* Then the call stops abruptly only to be repeated later. Though the bird itself was suffering from heat and lack of water, it still warned street dwellers of the heat wave's dangers.

The call of the koel reminds me of God's patient, consistent calling of His children, wanting their attention so He can warn them—warn them that sin's heat wave is increasing in its deadly intensity in these last days of earth's history. Many souls, dying in sin, need a call to the fountain of living water. Those who are spiritually asleep need to be awakened and made aware that time is quickly slipping by. The call of the koel also reminds me that we are to join God in His loud, urgent warnings to people of all nations. A heavenly judgment is taking place. People must know every name is under review by the heavenly Judge. We must also tell them the good news—that Jesus is their advocate who already paid the ransom for their sins with His blood.

Even today, as with the daily calls of the koel, let us faithfully call others to fall at the feet of Jesus and worship their Creator and Redeemer.

Birdie Poddar

Typos and Truth

Trust in the LORD and do good;
dwell in the land and enjoy safe pasture.
Take delight in the LORD,
and he will give you the desires of your heart.
Commit your way to the LORD;
trust in him and he will do this.
—*Psalm 37:3–5, NIV*

Sometimes I feel like I am a dyslexic typist; I can't even remember the last time I spelled "because" correctly the first time; it always comes out "beacuse." Or I add a *k* in the middle of any and all words. And other times I leave out letters entirely. What kind of condition is that? Sometimes it is frustrating, and other times it is just plain amusing. Like the time I typed a devotional title "In God We Trust" as "In God We Rust." As I looked at it, and chuckled a bit, I realized there was real truth in it. Something to which to give serious thought.

I fear that for many of us, when we first come to know and love the Lord, we have lots of enthusiasm for sharing God's love and a serious desire to study the Word—to know what the Word has to say to us. But then as time goes on, we begin to lose that first excitement—we begin to rust. When Jesus addressed the church at Ephesus, He said, "Yet I hold this against you: You have forsaken the love you had at first. Consider how far you have fallen! Repent and do the things you did at first" (Revelation 2:4, 5, NIV). We are urged to go back to our first love; instead of rust, we are invited to trust. Probably one of the more quoted Bible texts is "Trust in the LORD with all your heart and lean not on your own understanding; in all your ways submit to him, and he will make your paths straight" (Proverbs 3:5, 6, NIV).

How do we develop that trust? We do it day by day, spending time nurturing our relationship with God. I love to observe my grandchildren and see how they love and trust their parents. And I see that same trust carrying over to their love for and trust in Jesus. They don't doubt—they just know their needs are going to be taken care of. They pray about everything, and as their prayers are answered, their trust grows. During His sermon on the mount, Jesus urged the people not to worry about their food, their drink, their clothing because God would take care of them (Matthew 6:31, 32). If we believe Him, we will experience His care, and our trust will strengthen. As we look back over our lives, we can see many times when God stepped in on our behalf. In God we trust. Or in God we rust. The choice is ours.

Ardis Dick Stenbakken

Lessons on Light and Darkness

And this is the message [the message of promise] which we have
heard from Him and now are reporting to you: God is Light,
and there is no darkness in Him at all [no, not in any way].
—*1 John 1:5, AMPC*

I opened my eyes to the darkness of my room. I had ignored my alarm, and now I would be late for work. I jumped up when I remembered that I would have to prepare Grandma's breakfast and lunch before I left. Before I could think of my other duties, there was a song in my heart—"I Need Thee Every Hour." If I am open to God's leading, He frequently gives me a song in the morning—I love it when He does that. Many times the song sets the foundation for the lessons He will teach during the day. I quickly groped various objects in the dark trying to find where I had put my glasses. I had not turned on the light, and it took several attempts for me to find them in the dark. I quickly put my glasses on but, before racing downstairs, I stopped.

As I sang the words, "I need Thee every hour," it occurred to me that I need God not just every hour but also every moment of every hour. I need Him in order to be able to perform even the simplest of tasks—just as I needed the light to find my glasses without groping. God is light, and without Him we often have to make several attempts at what would be simple tasks if we just flipped the switch. We can turn on His light in our lives by reading His Word, praying, and praising Him. Then the light of His presence shines on any dark situation.

That morning I knew where the light switch was, but in my haste to get started on my morning responsibilities, I plunged into the darkness, which only increased the hopelessness of my efforts. I should have learned this lesson earlier. Only three months earlier, I ran downstairs in the darkness. Once downstairs I confidently and briskly walked . . . into a wall. I don't walk through the foyer anymore to go to the kitchen. And, most important, I now always turn on the light first.

Sometimes we need to change our path in which we're walking. We need to make a conscious effort to walk in light and not in darkness. Jesus has made Himself available to us. He is willing to shine His light on a myriad of lessons, ideas, and needs imprisoned in our current darkness—if we will just ask Him.

Marsha-Jay Dallas

What Goes Around Comes Around

You will always harvest what you plant.
—*Galatians 6:7, NLT*

In December 1992, just months after the Bosnian War began, we students at Belgrade Theological Seminary were asked to assist in preparing humanitarian aid. We willingly helped pack and load relief supplies for families in Sarajevo that had been devastated or displaced by the war. In a large, unheated room, we worked alongside representatives from ADRA (Adventist Development and Relief Agency) to box up soup, salt, flour, oil, toothpaste, gloves, warm socks, insulin, and tins of tuna or beans. ADRA makes no distinction between ethnic or religious differences. Families from three people groups at war with each other would get in the same line in the backyard of our church to obtain these precious packages.

Years passed, the war ended, and I got married and soon became the mother of a little girl. Although the war was long finished, religious freedom was still not always recognized. So when our daughter started school, my husband and I drafted a letter to the school board explaining why she would be in church on Saturdays instead of at school. We prayed fervently that God would direct the people who needed to make the decision about our daughter's education. Then we went to the school for the ruling. The principal spoke with us. She said, "Though a number of people on the school board were not sympathetic to your request, I defended your request because I have one connection with your church. During the siege of Sarajevo in wartime, your church—through the ADRA organization—kept my family alive with your boxes of provisions. Therefore, I am giving your daughter permission to miss her classes on Saturdays." For a moment, it all came back: the cold school rooms, the long hours packing relief boxes and loading them for delivery. That day we left the principal's office recalling the Bible promise, "Cast your bread upon the waters, for you will find it after many days" (Ecclesiastes 11:1, NKJV).

Whether we see instant results from our love-your-neighbor efforts or not, God makes Himself responsible for the outcome. We cannot see the effect our kindness today may have on someone tomorrow. So let's live our lives according to God's Word and leave the rest to Him. Besides, who knows? Perhaps today is the day that you will once again find your sacrifices—your shared "bread" of long ago—returning to you in the form of a blessing.

Aleksandra Tanurdzic

Called to Servanthood

"For even the Son of Man did not come to be served,
but to serve, and to give His life a ransom for many."
—Mark 10:45, NKJV

We live in a society that wants to be served. We hire housekeepers, nannies, and gardeners. We like drive-through service, and having others carry out our groceries or pump our gas. Because we want to "work smarter, not harder," we design machines to get the job done for us or to do our dirty work. We rarely stop to be a servant for others or even to notice the value of servant actions on our behalf. Yet God came not to be served but to serve. So what made us "greater" than God? What drives us to forget what the Son of Man was called to do?

Serving goes against our culture; it goes against our sinful nature. Who really wants to get up at three o'clock in the morning to help a feverish child, clean up their mess, change their diaper, and soothe them back to sleep? Wouldn't it be cruel, even illegal, negligence if a mother chose not to help her child? So, despite our comfortable beds, most of us choose to place our feet on the bedroom floor, lift our tired bodies from our warm blankets, and go to serve our child. Why? Because we love them. They belong to us. If they suffer, we suffer.

God did the same for us. Though He could have left us to self-destruct, He chose—the loving parent that He is—to hear our feverish cries, clean up our mess, and soothe us from this terrible world. The only cure for a fallen world is the Son of Man, made servant, to a world claiming it didn't need Him. To a world that could not look beyond its selfishness in order to recognize that their Creator and Savior was here waiting to serve them in a far greater manner than they could ever comprehend. He came to turn us from our selfish, greedy desires, to see the goodness of God, to share His story, and—most important to us—to lead us to servanthood.

"Each of you should use whatever gift you have received to serve others" (1 Peter 4:10, NIV). If we choose to obey and use our gifts to serve God by serving others and telling His story, God will make good on His promise: "[My word] will not return to me empty, but will accomplish what I desire and achieve the purpose for which I sent it" (Isaiah 55:11, NIV). We, the "church"—His body of believers, are His word in this fallen world. We tell the story; we say the message. And if we focus on obeying and sharing this message, God will do the rest.

Raquel Carrera

Waterbed Fascination!

For the eyes of the LORD run to and fro throughout the whole earth,
to shew himself strong in the behalf of them
whose heart is perfect toward him.
—*2 Chronicles 16:9*

Approximately eight months pregnant, I was shopping one day with friends and relatives in a large American department store. Everyone willingly assisted me with my nearly two-year-old daughter, who needed to be carried most of the time. I was grateful as I watched her go from one set of arms to another during this long day of shopping. Then at one point in the afternoon I turned to check on my little toddler but couldn't spot her anywhere! No one else knew when she had disappeared either. In horror I cried out, "Lord, help me please!" Everyone took off in different directions to search. For a moment everything turned pitch black and I couldn't see anything. Yet I kept running and crying out, "Please, Lord, You must help me! I need Your help now! Right now! I cannot live without her. Please, help me!"

Suddenly my vision cleared and I saw a store attendant in front of me. "Sir!" I cried out in desperation, "have you seen my little baby girl anywhere in here?" He turned and pointed to a far section of the store and said, "There is a little girl over yonder playing on a waterbed." I ran until I reached her. There she was, a most beautiful sight—my little girl, innocently jumping and laughing as her quick movements caused the water in the mattress to ripple. Completely fascinated with the waterbed, my daughter hadn't even realized she had been left alone.

The Bible tells us that the eyes of God constantly watch over us, His children, for He wants to work on our behalf. He becomes our strength in times of need. He shows Himself strong to those whose hearts are perfect toward Him. I am so grateful He was watching over my child.

I want to have a heart that is perfect toward God. How about you? Don't you long for that heart as well? It is possible. Desire it and work toward obtaining it from the hand of God. Be patient; it takes time. After all, sanctification is the work of a lifetime.

In the same way a child must take time to learn how to walk, so it is with the walk of the Christian. During this learning process the caring eyes of God are upon us. His hand is held out to steady us. He alone can rescue us when we start becoming fascinated by sin as my daughter was fascinated by the waterbed. Aren't you glad we can trust God to change us? I certainly am!

Jacqueline Hope HoShing-Clarke

Rest

"Come to me,
all you who are weary and burdened,
and I will give you rest."
—*Matthew 11:28, NIV*

anding in Kathmandu, Nepal's capital, was quite an experience. The plane had to find the best corridor to land between high mountains, and bad weather made it almost impossible to see the ground. Later, traveling by car through the countryside, I learned that Nepal is the land of hills. Land is a principal source of income and employment for a majority of households in Nepal. The hilly landscape is both a natural and cultural mosaic, shaped by geological forces and human activity. The hills, sculpted by human hands into a massive complex of terraces, are extensively cultivated. The women are part of the scenery. They carry heavy loads of rice up and down, doing a work that few men can do. Meeting the women in the villages, I asked them to allow me to try carrying one of their twenty-five-kilo loads (about fifty-five pounds) on my head as they easily do. They smiled, saying that I could not handle the weight. I insisted on trying, but I could walk only a few meters. When I asked how they do it, one of the women replied, "You do not feel the weight anymore as the years go by." When I asked if she was tired, she looked puzzled. I understood that perhaps this precious woman never had a chance to really know what rest is.

Seldom a day passes that I do not hear someone say, "I'm so tired I can hardly function." A major cause of weariness is the burdens we carry around: physical difficulties, emotional conflict, loss of loved ones, financial or business reversals, feelings of hopelessness. Whatever the burden, it may rest like a heavy weight on our shoulders, crushing us. You alone know what your burdens may be. The important thing is what we do about them.

If you are feeling compelled to do so much that you are physically worn out, you may be *driven* instead of *led*. Remember, you have to come apart from a busy routine before you come apart *yourself*. It may be tempting to do everything that everybody else is doing, to be involved in everything, know everything, hear everything, and be everywhere, but that isn't God's best for you. Be willing to "come." Spend time with God, and ask Him to give order to your day. What are you carrying today that doesn't belong to you? What worry, concern, burden, anxiety are you carrying that only Jesus can carry? God has a request to make of us today: "Come to Me, and I will give you rest." Take your burdens to Him. Let His presence refill and refresh you.

Raquel Queiroz da Costa Arrais

Every Person Is a Child of God

"I have summoned you by name; you are mine."
—Isaiah 43:1, NIV

Selina, my small daughter, went out to the front door and spotted many small ants on the steps. The ants seemed to be excited, swarming all over the steps. Some carried small sticks; others tried to help. Some ants would disappear and others seemed to appear out of nowhere to join the activity. "Look," said Selina suddenly. "A dead fly on top of the ants." I noticed that the ants were attempting to carry it off. Selina pointed at the ants and said, "Those all now come to bury it" (indicating a funeral).

Her childlike expression of thought caused me to start thinking. *Is it really like that? Are we humans like those ants? When a dear one is torn from our lives, do we just show up at the funeral to say good-bye? Yes, our presence indicates that the deceased person was valuable and precious to us. Yet did we express that same attention to them when they were still living?*

Selina's observation caused me to reflect that we have only a limited time on earth to show our regard for one another. Some of us have less time than others. So why wait until we lose someone? Can we not show others, while they are yet living, that their lives have value to us? Can we not demonstrate now the happiness they bring us?

That demonstration doesn't have to be a big celebration. We can enjoy a walk together. What about an informal breakfast with fresh rolls? Why not a "just because" telephone call or a bouquet of daisies? Or a "thinking about you" card after a long silence? Besides, when we are friendly and attentive, we earn the confidence of others. A small gesture of remembrance in daily life doesn't cost much time or expense. Every person has value. When it comes to people, there is no such thing as a "nobody" in this world.

Yet there is another more important reason to reach out to those around us while we have the opportunity. Dr. Ben Carson stated it well when he once observed, "Each human you meet is a child of God." God, in the Bible, states that He knows each of His children by name and loves them. That includes everyone around us. Should we not then pray to see others as God sees them? When we do, we will love them as He does.

Is there someone in your life that you need to tell today how special they are to you?

Sandra Widulle

A Woman God Can Use

"I know the plans I have for you," declares the LORD,
"plans to prosper you and not to harm you,
plans to give you hope and a future."
—*Jeremiah 29:11, NIV*

One Sabbath morning in the mid-1990s I awoke and realized this was Women's Ministry Sabbath. A woman would be preaching at my church. I really wasn't looking forward to listening to whoever would be speaking. I readied myself and my family and went to Sabbath School, then on to the worship service. Rose Otis, who was the editor of the women's devotional book at that time, was the speaker. I don't remember the exact title of her sermon, but her recurring theme was, "Lord, make me a woman You can use."

Despite my apathetic attitude when I walked into the sanctuary, I found myself repeating those words many times in the days that followed. Eventually it became part of my prayer each morning—even my theme, "Lord, make me a woman You can use." And God began to work in my life, but from a very different angle than I ever would have said I wanted, if I had been asked.

A year or two later, my husband came home from work one day and told me he wanted to go back to school and study accounting. A day later he informed me that God was calling him instead into the ministry. He began studying and, long story short, several years later, he became the pastor of a small three-church district in West Virginia.

I was *not* excited. I didn't want to leave my home. I didn't want to move to a new place. I was quite comfortable where I was. I didn't want to leave my friends and make new ones. I enjoyed the life I had. I was involved in my church. I homeschooled my children and was very involved in a homeschool group. I liked my life, and I didn't want to be a pastor's wife. I was not happy, and I let everyone, including my husband (and God), know it. But despite my whining and griping, things happened fast. We put our house on the market. Someone made an offer on it. We put an offer on a house of our own and had it accepted. All this in the space of eight days. God was not paying attention to my complaints.

Or was He? Through all the upheaval of moving, saying good-bye to friends, making new friends, and settling into a new job description, I continued to repeat, "Lord, make me a woman You can use," not realizing that was exactly what He was doing.

Kathy Pepper

Bible Stories

We have been made a spectacle to the whole universe,
to angels as well as to human beings.
—*1 Corinthians 4:9, NIV*

When I was a little girl, I believed the Bible was still being written. It seems silly to think of that concept now that I'm an adult, but growing up having no media, it somehow made sense. I had never watched a movie or television show, listened to the radio, or heard any stories that didn't come from the Bible at that young age. So when my cousin and I would play dress up, it was always to imitate what we knew—Bible characters. We would throw towels over our heads and wrap blankets around our bodies and pretend we were in days of old. Except I didn't know how "old" those days really were. For all I knew they could have been the generation before me. And every time I heard the phrase "living Word," I took it to mean that the stories were real and living all around us and God was deciding whose life would be written about next.

I remember lying in the grass and contemplating how it all worked and, more important, how I could get written into the Bible too. There were so many people in the world it seemed those who would be written about next would have to do something pretty spectacular to get noticed by God. After all, it was the most important book in the whole world! I sometimes grew concerned about the fact that there was already a Naomi in the book of Ruth, and wondered if two people with the same name could be allowed. I would think of Moses and his great feats and eventually came to conclude that, yes, I would do something spectacular. I would lead a great nation of people to Jesus just like Moses. I didn't know how or where, but it would happen. But I thought I'd have to start getting ready right away because it wasn't going to be easy.

Childhood imaginations are exquisite. I may have been two thousand years too late with my young plans, but my ideas were valid.

How different would our lives be if we knew there was a spot waiting for our story in the Bible? If we knew others would read our story, contemplate it, and learn from it? Would it be a story of courage, faith, and triumph? Or something else? The truth is we *are* being written about in a great book at this very moment: the book of life from the pen of Jesus. And others *are* watching and waiting to see what we will do next.

Naomi Striemer

An Unexpected Gift

My tongue is the pen of a ready writer.
—*Psalm 45:1*

We all love to receive gifts. Sometimes we are pleased with the gift, sometimes we are not. But as children of God, we try to appreciate the thought behind the gift and not the gift itself. The Bible states that "every good gift and every perfect gift is from above" (James 1:17).

As a child growing up in school, English was not my strong point. Even in college, I dreaded English classes. In fact, I decided my college major would be finance because sentence construction wouldn't play much of a role in a profession where I wouldn't have to write a lot.

After finishing college I got a job as a salary clerk at a government office. A couple months later I was placed in final accounts to do bank reconciliation. Shortly after that I saw an advertisement where my office was recruiting auditors. The salary package looked fabulous. How could I resist? I applied and got the position. Here began my long, arduous journey into an experience I refer to as "If-I-Had-Known-I-Never-Would-Have Land."

The job, as you might have guessed, required a lot of writing. I needed to know what to write and how to express my thoughts. I needed to pay close attention to details and technical competence. All these are skills I did not naturally possess. So you can just imagine how dreadful this experience was when I began it. My superiors at work did not make it any easier either. I was told I lacked the aptitude for auditing. But through persistence, great humility, and the guidance of the Holy Spirit, I began to make progress. After some years I excelled at what I did. Yet fear of (respect for) the English language remains. As a result, every time I take up a pen to write, be it at work or church, I am in deep prayer for God's guidance on what or how to write.

I have come to recognize that writing is a gift from God. My unexpected gift. A gift I have come to treasure. Always cognizant of the fact that without Christ I am and can do nothing, I thank Him for the ability I now have to write—as with this devotional. I thank Him for the opportunity to be able to share about His goodness in this fashion. I realize that the gifts God gives us—even the unexpected ones—can become sources of hope and encouragement to others.

Lord, thank You for my unexpected gift. Thank You for all the special gifts You have given each of us. May we use them today for You.

Thamer Cassandra Smikle

Capsized

Then spake Jesus again unto them, saying,
I am the light of the world: he that followeth me
shall not walk in darkness, but shall have the light of life.
—*John 8:12*

We were running late after a court date and would not be able to catch the public transport vehicle going from Port Real to Polillo. A companion suggested that we take a boat instead from Dinahican. We were a couple of hours late for the launch that usually crosses the ocean. If we didn't take what was available, we'd be delayed for three days getting home. The clear weather pointed to our getting home safely.

We boarded the only available boat. The boat was scheduled to leave at one o'clock that afternoon, but it did not leave until two o'clock. I never heard the reason, though I had noticed before embarking that more and more heavy cargo was being loaded—cargo such as big blocks of ice, galvanized iron, rolls of barbed wire, and pallets laden with construction plywood.

Rhona, my seatmate, and I were casually conversing when the engine started and the large craft headed toward the ocean. Without warning the boat suddenly tipped to the left and never righted itself again. In mere seconds it capsized, splashing us passengers into the dark waters and trapping us underneath the overturned hull. Midst the chaos of screaming passengers and visual obscurity I somehow saw a single ray of sunlight. I swam toward it and realized it might lead me out from underneath the boat. As I frantically swam, I heard the echoing cries of others, shouting out their panic and distress. Rhona, who was sinking, was rescued by Resty, another acquaintance, who pulled my seatmate from the water by her long hair. A young mother was able to save her nearly drowned one-and-a-half-year-old. Rescue workers later rushed the pair to a nearby hospital. We cried out encouragement for other endangered passengers to hang on to floating objects because we'd had no time to grab for life jackets. "Rescue is coming soon!" we'd call. I praise God that we were all eventually rescued and able to head to Port Real at four o'clock the following morning on a regularly scheduled launch.

As that ray of sunlight led me to an escape, so the Holy Spirit will guide us "into all truth" (John 16:13). And in those times when Satan would attempt to entrap us, we will follow the light of God's truth—and find the escape and freedom it brings (John 8:32).

Esperanza Aquino Mopera

God Has a Fire Marshal Too!

Before they call, I will answer;
and while they are yet speaking, I will hear.
—Isaiah 65:24

A terrible electrical storm exploded over us that Friday, August 12, 2011. As peals of thunder followed the rapid flashes of lightning, I quickly turned off our home's main switch in the breaker panel.

About fifteen minutes later, a friend who was sheltering in our home during the storm shouted, "There's a fire on the side of the house!"

When we ran outside we saw clouds of thick black smoke and snapping sparks billowing from an area under the eve above my bedroom window. This was the area where the electric company's service wires connected to our house.

It was time for quick action! The fire department was called as neighbors rushed over to see what assistance they could give. Then the fire simply went out. A few minutes later the fire truck arrived. The officers noted that the wires had been burned and the area under the eve and the wall where the wires had been connected was black with soot. However, our house had not experienced any serious damage!

"You are really lucky!" people kept saying to us.

"It isn't luck," I responded. "I am convinced that God sent His fire marshal ahead of the local fire department to put this fire out. And I praise Him for that and give Him all the glory!"

This experience caused me to reflect on some important truths. First, God makes our welfare His concern. My family could have become homeless that day.

Second, when we ask for God's protection each day in our prayers, He hears them.

Third, we should recognize that our material possessions are gifts from God to be used to bless others. At the same time, they are His to leave with us or take away (Job 1:21). He knows best.

Finally, all praise and honor belong to our awesome God who, in spite of the fact that we sometimes forget to pray in the moment of crisis, answers one way or another even before we call.

Let's ask God to watch over us today. Then let's thank Him for however He answers.

Carol Joy Fider

Screwdriver Miracle

For he will command his angels concerning you
to guard you in all your ways.
—*Psalm 91:11, NIV*

I was on my way to support a colleague at an induction ceremony. All was quiet until I crossed State Road 441. Just as I crossed over I heard a clanking sound coming from the direction of my right rear wheel. Immediately I turned into a vacant parking lot, from where I spotted an auto and body repair shop. I quickly got out of the car and examined the car with my inexperienced eyes. The tire was not losing air. I watched it and waited a few minutes. The tire pressure seemed to remain the same.

I breathed another prayer and resumed my journey to the program at a school fewer than ten minutes away. However, the clanking sound grew louder. Not only was it troubling; it was embarrassing! I kept driving. I arrived safely at the school's parking lot in good time, noise and all. Again I checked the tire pressure. All seemed fine.

After a beautiful induction ceremony, I asked the associate pastor to watch my tire and listen as I drove around the parking lot. He did, assuring me the tire was fine. It was definitely not losing air. He certainly heard the clanking sound, though. I thought I could complete the next little drive of my day, which would be to my church. I phoned my husband to alert him to a possible issue with the car should he need to come pick me up. Then I continued my trip on "wheels of prayer" accompanied by the ever-present clanking sound. I reached church safely with the tire still intact! By then my husband had called one of the church members, an auto mechanic, to come check the tire.

In my opinion, the mechanic uncovered a miracle. A six-inch, headless screwdriver had punctured the right rear tire. The top of the screwdriver, lodged into the tire rubber, had become sort of a plug that prevented any air from escaping the damaged tire. "What an amazing God!" the mechanic exclaimed. "I've never seen anything like it!"

"Praise God! Praise God!" I responded as he handed me the now dislodged screwdriver.

Sometimes God sends His angels to shut lions' mouths. Yet He is just as capable of shutting a tire puncture so that air won't escape until His daughter has reached a place of safety.

Thank You, Father, for Your unique plans to provide for each of our needs today.

Claudette Garbutt-Harding

The Broken Sole—Part 1

From the sole of the foot even unto the head there is no soundness
in it; but wounds, and bruises, and putrifying sores: they have not
been closed, neither bound up, neither mollified with ointment.
—Isaiah 1:6

I have a pair of shoes that I've worn for years. They've carried me through sandy beaches, jagged mountain hikes, walks on cobblestone streets, and just about every place you can imagine, including several trips overseas to such places as Romania, Norway, and Australia. They've gotten wet as I trudged through water, flattened or scrunched up as they've been packed in tight suitcases, covered with dust, dirt, and even a few paint drops. They are comfortable, worn, casual, broken in—and now they are just plain broken. The soles have split in half and, when I walk, I can feel the concrete, rocks, or dirt touching my feet. Yet, I still wear them, even though they are truly falling off my feet! Why would I do such a thing? Because they are *comfortable*—and because the manufacturer no longer makes them—yet the sole is no longer sound.

This makes me think of the verse found in Isaiah 1:6: "From the sole of the foot even unto the head there is no soundness in it; but wounds, and bruises, and putrifying sores: they have not been closed, neither bound up, neither mollified with ointment." Not a very pretty picture, is it? Yet it proves that it's not just the sole of a shoe that breaks sometimes. It's our *souls* that get crushed, broken, and worn. We are wounded and bruised by those around us at times and by circumstances or events in life that create unimaginable—and often unbearable—pain. Where has your soul traveled? Has it been crushed, covered with mud, and scourged by the rough path you've been traveling? What has your soul been through or endured to reach this breaking point?

It's in these times of pain that we become no longer sound, and sometimes our faith crumbles like the soles of my shoes. But it is in these very times that God is the nearest to us and will help us if we will only allow Him to do so. As Peter puts it, "Casting all your care upon him; for he careth for you" (1 Peter 5:7).

There's no hope for the broken sole of my shoe, but there *is* hope for you. Will you choose to let God mend your soul today?

Samantha Nelson

The Broken Sole—Part 2

For he maketh sore, and bindeth up:
he woundeth, and his hands make whole.
—Job 5:18

Over the past twelve years, I have had an opportunity to minister to many broken souls either through the Hope of Survivors ministry or at one of the congregations that my husband pastors. I've observed that, like me with my broken-soled shoe, sometimes people don't want to let go of something that clearly holds no value to them or is not helpful or healthful for them. I'm not talking about material things here; I'm talking about feelings, thoughts, attitudes, behaviors, and, sometimes, even people.

Why do some victims of domestic violence stay with their abusers? One reason is because it's "comfortable" for them. No, not in a good way and definitely not in a safe way. Victims may stay with an abuser because it's the only "way" they're accustomed to—a way that seems to be more comfortable to them than the thought of leaving and starting over. Facing the abuse one lives with is sometimes less frightening than stepping out into the unknown and beginning a new life free of abuse. Sometimes a woman will date a man who treats her poorly, perhaps belittles her in some way, yet she will either stay with him or find someone else who ends up treating her the same way. Why? Again, it's what she's used to experiencing. She doesn't know any differently. Her soul, however, is crushed and broken, and she needs to experience healing.

How does one overcome such self-destructive choices? By drawing near and ever nearer to the One who gave all so we might live. This verse in Job 5:18 is comforting: "For he maketh sore, and bindeth up: he woundeth, and his hands make whole." Did you catch that? God's hands make whole! That is the best news ever! We don't have to walk around with broken souls. We can experience wholeness and newness of life through Jesus. We can claim and experience the promise found in Psalm 34:18: "The LORD is nigh unto them that are of a broken heart; and saveth such as be of a contrite spirit." With a promise like that, I'd say it's worth getting out of our "comfort" zones to risk experiencing a life that only Jesus can provide.

What do you say? Are you willing to break out of your comfort zone and allow Jesus to replace your broken thoughts, feelings, and behaviors with His? I'm willing—and soon I may be willing to give up my broken-soled shoes too.

Samantha Nelson

Everything I Have

Then the LORD called Samuel. Samuel answered, "Here I am."
—*1 Samuel 3:4, NIV*

At the age of forty-three, my mother discovered she was pregnant again. My brother and I were already adults. Mother was very scared and almost went into depression, fearing the child would be born with health problems because she would be an older mother giving birth—especially after such a long interval of time, more than twenty years.

Mother was also afraid of the possible complications she could have during childbirth, but after a nice baby shower that she and I organized, a beautiful and healthy baby was born. Little Victor arrived midst a quiet and normal delivery.

He has grown into an energetic and intelligent boy who has also quickly become the darling of the family. His favorite song is "Mansion on the Hill." His favorite flower is the sunflower. I enjoy telling him Bible stories. He becomes excited when anyone in the family speaks about heaven and the earth made new. My little brother's interest in spiritual topics impresses me deeply. His childhood heartfelt choices are often lessons for the rest of us.

Once, on the way to church, Mother and Victor came across a little kitten. Victor, who is very fond of animals, took pity on the creature and asked to take it home. With the kitten meowing nonstop and Victor holding it close, he asked, "Mom, can we keep it?"

"You know that Daddy wouldn't allow that. Remember that you have an allergy," Mother replied.

Victor responded, "I've saved up a lot of money since last year. I can give it all to Daddy if he would let me keep this kitten!" About this time an acquaintance living nearby drove up with his daughter and stopped. Victor, desperate now for the kitten's welfare, approached the little girl and handed her the kitten. "This is a gift for you," he said. The little girl beamed as she accepted the kitten and began to cuddle it.

I do not know if she was allowed to keep the kitten or not. What impressed me, though, was that my little brother was willing to give up everything he had for the sake of a kitten that he wanted to rescue from off the street. Just like Jesus gave His all for us.

What about us? Are we willing to give our all for our Lord and the benefit of others?

Daniela Santos de Oliveira

Your Emotions Are Real and Valid

And about the ninth hour Jesus cried out with a loud voice, saying,
"Eli, Eli, lama sabachthani?" that is,
"My God, My God, why have You forsaken Me?"
—*Matthew 27:46, NKJV*

Have you felt pain to the extent that you thought you were about to see death face to face? Have you suffered the loss of a loved one? Or felt the loneliness of a broken relationship? Have you been abused or rejected by someone close to you? Have you been disappointed, deserted, or forsaken? Sometimes life's journeys through the darkest places of our emotions make us question the validity of our feelings and even our reason for living.

Yet we have only to look at the life of Jesus to understand that our emotions are real, and they are valid. He experienced all the feelings that we do (Hebrews 4:15). The same Jesus who stilled violent storms, healed the lame, and brought the dead to life again is the same Jesus who broke down and wept. He wept when His dear friend Lazarus died. Onlookers said, "See how He loved him!" (John 11:36, NKJV). He wept when foreseeing the destruction of Jerusalem and of its people who had rejected Him (Luke 19:41–44). On the darkest day of Jesus' life, He cried out from the cross, "My God, My God, why have You forsaken Me?" (Matthew 27:46, NKJV). Christ is God incarnate who knows what it feels like to see no light at the end of an emotionally dark tunnel. Truly Jesus understands our why, when, and how questions. Although He understood prophecy and the glorious unfolding of salvation's plan, He still cried out when reality struck. His emotions were real and valid.

Many of us feel guilty for expressing emotion in times of distress. Some even feel guilty for experiencing these emotions. We may wonder, *Is acknowledging my emotions misrepresenting God's character?* Yet Jesus, who never sinned, experienced the same emotions that we do. He understands them. King David recognized this when he prayed, "You understand my thought afar off. You comprehend my path and my lying down, and are acquainted with all my ways" (Psalm 139:2, 3, NKJV). God's Word validates our very real emotions. Moreover, it shows us how to deal with them—by taking them to the Great Healer of our hearts.

What emotions do you need to take to Him today?

Charmaine N. Williams Tate

Angels

The angel of the LORD encampeth
round about them that fear him, and delivereth them.
—*Psalm 34:7*

Have you ever wondered how many accidents you have escaped because God has sent angels to protect you? How many times have you been kept from danger and death because Jesus cares? Can you recall times when you have been led to make a certain decision only to discover that in so choosing, you saved so much that might have otherwise been lost?

Throughout Scripture, we see God's loving intervention in human life through His angels.

He is far from distant but is acutely aware and concerned about us.

We observe His love as He sends angels to direct Lot and his family to safety, saving them out of Sodom (Genesis 19:1–30). We see the Lord engage angels to encourage and strengthen His people when they are afraid, as He did for Jacob (32:1). God promised to send angels before His people in battle to drive out their enemies (Exodus 33:2).

We see the Lord send His angels to deliver messages to His people (Judges 2:1–3). Angels instruct people of their calling, as in the case of Gideon (6:11–24) and Samson (13:3–20). In His love, God employs angels to feed His servants during distressing times, as He did for Elijah (1 Kings 19:5–8). Mouths of lions are shut by His angels (Daniel 6:22).

Angels brought glad tidings of the conception of Jesus to Mary and Joseph and of John the Baptist to Elizabeth and Zacharias (Luke 1). Prison doors unjustly confining God's children are opened by angels, as for the apostles, Peter, Paul, and Silas (Acts 5; 12; 16). Angels have even spoken in order to direct the spreading of the gospel (8:26).

The truth is that God loves you so much that He even sends heavenly beings to keep guard over you. Live life joyfully, knowing that God sends His angels to be with His children.

Praise the Lord, O my soul! While I live, I will praise the Lord. I will sing praises unto my God while I have any being. What am I that you take knowledge of me or even think of me? I am like a breath; my days are like a fleeting shadow, yet You love me. You send Your angels to protect me. You give them charge over me. Thank You, Lord, for all that You have done for me. I praise You especially for the blessings I do not see (adapted from Psalm 91:11; 144:3, 4). Amen.

Tricia Wynn

The Prime Minister's Present

Three things will last forever—faith, hope, and love—
and the greatest of these is love.
—*1 Corinthians 13:13, NLT*

I advocate for individuals (including my own twenty-five-year-old son, Sonny) with severe developmental disabilities. My personal ministry for the past five years has been to facilitate the sending of encouraging letters and gifts to people. In 2011, we decided to send a copy of the newly released 2012 women's devotional book, *Renew,* along with a card, to the Canadian prime minister. We marked the return name and address as that of Sonny.

On December 5, after I finished some banking, I returned to our car. Sonny's dad, Ron, was talking on the phone to a Constable Smith from the Royal Canadian Mounted Police. I heard Ron say, "But, sir, our gifts and letters to Prime Minister Stephen Harper for the past five years have always been well received. My wife's advocacy for persons with developmental disabilities is tied to her personal faith and ministry." He handed me the phone to explain further.

It seems that the recycled bubble wrap envelope in which I'd sent the copy of the devotional book had also contained some white powder! The police had tried to identify the substance but couldn't. Because Sonny could not answer the official's questions, his support worker, Doug, had referred the constable to Sonny's parents for further questioning. Sadly, I could not remember where I'd obtained the envelope!

For an anxious hour, Ron and I waited as the substance was further analyzed.

An official phoned us back saying, "Though we've not been able to identify the white powder, we did ascertain that it is nothing harmful." He further assured us that no one was in trouble and that Sonny's personalized book and Christmas letter would be delivered to the prime minister. Later that day I remembered where the envelope came from, so I quickly left a message on Constable Smith's answering machine: "The envelope came home with Sonny from Camp Joy, along with the enclosed painted plaque portraying Christ with an open Bible and the text about loving God first and then loving one's neighbors." And that's exactly what Sonny had been trying to do.

Like Sonny, let us also resolve to love someone for Jesus today.

Deborah Sanders

Christ in Us

To them God has chosen to make known
among the Gentiles the glorious riches of this mystery,
which is Christ in you, the hope of glory.
—Colossians 1:27, NIV

Many times I've wondered about the expression in today's text: "Christ in you." It's been only in the recent few years that I've finally come to understand what it really means.

There are some women in the Bible that I could name who, I believe, had God living in—and through—them. Elizabeth, the elderly mother of John the Baptist, was one. When her husband told her—or rather wrote down for her—what the angel had said to him (that she would give birth in old age), there was no hesitation in her at all. She didn't doubt. She didn't complain. What a woman! Of course, God never makes a mistake, and He chose the right woman for the job. I admire Elizabeth and her faith and dedication. She brought up the son that God gave into her care so that he was the perfect forerunner for Christ's ministry on earth.

So, how can we also have Christ in us? Here's how I believe it's possible: A daily spiritual experience will be the basis of everything we do and say as Christian women. I am a routine kind of person, so my days usually start the same way. Not much changes from day to day. In the book *Steps to Christ* we read: "Each morning consecrate yourself to God for that day. Surrender all your plans to Him, to be carried out or given up as His providence shall indicate."*

When we are organizers, it's not easy to change our plans. Often we are not used to having to wait for things to happen. We want things done ASAP! But if we want to have Christ living in us and through us, we've got to learn to surrender everything about our lives to God to manage. Sometimes that's hard. I need to wait to find out what God's will is for me for any particular moment.

If we want to have Christ in us we need to fill ourselves with His mind and let Him work in and through us.

Being in Christ and Christ being in us doesn't happen by accident. It happens because we commune with Him on a regular basis. We give Him our will, and His will comes to us in place of our wills, projects, and plans. May "Christ in us" be the deepest desire for our hearts!

Erna Johnson

---

* Ellen G. White, *Steps to Christ* (Washington, D.C.: Review and Herald®, 1956), 70.

Love Lessons From Suzie-Cutie!

"On the day you were born your cord was not cut,
nor were you washed with water to make you clean,
nor were you rubbed with salt or wrapped in cloths.
No one looked on you with pity or had compassion
enough to do any of these things for you.
Rather, you were thrown out into the open field,
for on the day you were born you were despised."
—*Ezekiel 16:4, 5, NIV*

We call her Suzie-Cutie, our sweet little niece. She's a clown, that girl. She loves making people smile and laugh. But the first day of Vacation Bible School (VBS) she also made me cry.

I was giving some little girls a tour of the church before VBS started. I stepped inside the interpreting room while the girls stayed outside in the hallway still listening to me. Suddenly a homeless woman walked into the church and came down the hallway. After she passed by, the little girls made faces. I too had caught the strong odor of dried urine and perspiration on the woman's clothing. The girls started checking one another to find out who was smelling so bad. I noticed what was happening and asked the girls to come into the interpreting room with me.

"What you smell is odor from the homeless woman who has no place to bathe. I know it smells bad, but please don't make mean faces," I counseled.

"We shouldn't make mean faces," Suzie interrupted me, "because she's still special—even if she does smell." After our little tour ended, the girls went off to play. The homeless woman kept walking around the church. Oh, my! I could hardly bear to be near her for more than a minute at a time. A short while later, the girls ran past the woman and must certainly have caught an unpleasant whiff of body odor. Yet Suzie suddenly stopped, turned around, and came back to the woman.

"Excuse me, Lady," she said. Both the woman and I turned to look down at her. What would she say next? She looked at the woman, smiled, and said, "You are beautiful!" Tears filled the eyes of the woman.

"Would you repeat that?" the woman asked. Suzie repeated her words.

That's how Suzie-Cutie made me cry the first day of VBS.

Oh, Lord, no matter how stinky we are, You still find us beautiful. Help us love as You love. Please give us Your heart of love for others. Amen.

Sayuri Ruiz Rodriguez

Darkness

For thou wilt light my candle:
the LORD my God will enlighten my darkness.
—*Psalm 18:28*

Many years ago we would take our summer campers from Camp Texico for a tour of Carlsbad Caverns National Park in southeastern New Mexico. Park rangers would guide the tours through the caverns. At one point in the tour the guide asked us visitors to sit on benches alongside the trail. "I'm requesting that everyone remain perfectly silent," he said, "while I turn out all the lights for sixty seconds in this section of the cavern. This will help you understand what the first cavern explorers experienced when first entering this cave with just a candle or a lantern." It is amazing how long this one little minute can seem when you are surrounded by complete darkness, not being able to see your hand in front of your face—even if it is touching your cheek. I found myself amazed that early explorers were able to map parts of these huge caverns with just small lanterns as a light source. All they could see was whatever was just around them. They never experienced the wonders we see today, thanks to a vast system of well-placed lights that illumine the cavern formations.

I recall the first few seconds of being almost surprised by the thick blackness when the guide turned off the lights. The darkness into which we were plunged began to take on an oppressive heaviness. Even seated beside friends, shoulder to shoulder, I began to feel utterly alone and forsaken. When the cavern guide again turned on the bright display lights, my eyes took a few moments to adjust. I experience something similar at bedtime when I turn out my light. I find myself in utter blackness for the first few seconds. Yet as my eyes begin to adjust to the sudden loss of light, I begin to see other light. The light of the moonbeams coming through the window. A streetlamp. The warm glow of the nightlight. Soon these other light sources help my eyes make out the silhouette of a chair in the corner of the room, or the frames of pictures on the wall, or the outline of the door leading to the hallway.

God's love is our light in the darkness of this world through which we are traveling. It not only reveals pitfalls but also illuminates hope and comfort and blessings along the way.

Won't you join me in thanking Him for the light of His love? Won't you join me in praying for the wisdom and the will to walk in the light He so graciously provides?

Mary E. Dunkin

The Midnight Miracle

"Therefore I say to you, whatever things you ask when you pray,
believe that you receive them, and you will have them."
—Mark 11:24, NKJV

On March 10, 2014, my daughter reached the age of fifteen months. Not only was this a special day, it was also time for her to get another vaccination. I soon realized that I had misplaced her immunization card, which I must present at the hospital. I looked everywhere, finding only the things I kept with the card, but no card.

I gave up the search on this particular morning and resumed it when I returned from work. Without a clue of where the card might be, I began to get worried and agitated because of the importance the hospital attached to this card. Also I did not want my carelessness to keep my baby from being immunized. I spent several hours searching for the card before going to bed.

Suddenly I remembered in my sleep that the card was still missing. This woke me up, so I got up again around 11:00 P.M. to continue the search for the card. Thirty minutes later I recognized that I really needed to sleep, so I went back to bed because it was obvious that I would never find the card by my own efforts. Before I went to sleep, I remembered that I could pray about whatever I desired and believe that God would hear me. So I whispered this simple prayer to God: "You are able to do all things. Please help me find my daughter's immunization card."

Thirty minutes after that, my brother came into my room and handed me the card, explaining that he had found it under one of the chairs in the sitting room. Alas, it was the only chair I did not check in my confusion. Wow, this was my midnight miracle!

In all this experience, God was trying to make a point, which became very clear to me the next morning. It happened when I opened my women's devotional book the following morning and read "The Sunset Miracle" by Cheryl Henry-Aguilar. In this devotional, Cheryl explains how she providentially found her daughter's missing shoe. I realized that God was trying to say to me, as He did to Cheryl some time ago—and to all of us at one time or another: "I answer prayer, even when you are dealing with a missing piece of paper—like an immunization card."

So what are you missing in your life today? Even spiritually? It may not matter to others, but it matters to God. Tell Him about your need for a miracle. He will help you find it.

Mofoluke I. Akoja

The Mistype

What man is there of you, whom if his son ask bread,
will he give him a stone? Or if he ask a fish, will he give him a
serpent?
If ye then, being evil, know how to give good gifts unto your
children, how much more shall your Father which is in heaven
give good things to them that ask him?
—*Matthew 7:9–11*

For I know the thoughts that I think toward you, saith the LORD,
thoughts of peace, and not of evil, to give you an expected end.
—*Jeremiah 29:11*

Back in the late 1990s when I wrote my still unpublished book, *The Secrets of Positive Womanhood (A Fresh Look at Bible Women)*, I wrote a sentence somewhere in the middle of the book that—thanks to my dyslexia—got mangled.

What I intended to write was "God made us so we could love Him."

What I wrote was "God made us so He could love us."

I sat there, looking at that typo, and the Holy Spirit instructed me that God *had* made us so He could love us. God is love. Love needs a receptacle. So God made us to receive His love.

What a wonderful realization! Realizing God made me so He could love me has changed my entire outlook on life and how I live it and react to what happens in my life.

Think about it: God made us so He could love us.

When frail, broken human beings love, we do everything we can to protect, nurture, and support whom or what we love.

Yet how much more does God, working in our favor, love us!

When no one else realizes who or what we are—when no one else appreciates us—God is there, casting His love all around us, and it will never, ever go away.

Christ Himself made us this promise when He uttered the memorable words, "Lo, I am with you always, even unto the end of the world. Amen" (Matthew 28:20).

Beloved heavenly Father, thank You for Your love. Thank You for caring about me, who I am, and what I do. Thank You for always being there for me. Please help me to appreciate Your love and accept Your guidance. May I always share this insight and this love from You with others. Amen.

Darlenejoan McKibbin Rhine

The Battle in the Mind

We take captive every thought to make it obedient to Christ.
—*2 Corinthians 10:5, NIV*

'm accustomed to singing. Yet, given the rare opportunity to speak . . . now that really tempts my ego. One particular Sabbath morning in church, all I could think of was my well-written congregational prayer. My wording hit on all the important topics with just the right mix of down-to-earth language and flowery accents to grab people's attention and focus it on what I was trying to say to God. Don't get me wrong; I am sure God helped me write that prayer. Yet that morning I just couldn't get *myself* out of my head. All I could think of was *me* and how people would be impressed with *my* prayer. Frankly, this was an old bad habit based on Satan's lie that I *needed* people to think I was smart. Now I grew sick of those thoughts.

Though I was sitting in a pew, I was running around inside my head. Running around like a frantic little girl with a cut finger, screaming for help. *Oh, God, I'm such a self-centered mess. I'm so unworthy. I don't deserve to say the prayer.* I kept chastising myself and begging for forgiveness. Even the thoughts I was using to battle my sin were still focused on *me*. The habit of self-centeredness was a deep rut in the pathways of my brain.

Finally, in my heart, I cried out to God, *Father, help me. I know it is my fault that I have permitted my brain to run in these selfish ruts for years. Please heal me and set me free.*

Then a voice in my head said, *Be still and know that I am God.* It was as if the Father had scooped me up and held me tight and said, *Hush now, calm down; I've got you.*

For the rest of the service I was relaxed and peaceful, in a state of mind about Him and not me.

Scripture and modern science agree that what we believe, the ideas engrained in our minds, is what makes or breaks our lives. In our physical brain, we can have ruts of bad habits and memories. But we can allow those ruts to atrophy and die with purposeful neglect as we quit feeding the lies and quit replaying old "tapes." At the same time, we can build up new brain pathways that are full of God's truth and love.

I know now that it is never too late for me to learn to take every thought captive, to reject lies, to choose carefully what I let in, and to saturate my mind with the Word of God.

Merrilou Wilder Inks

David and Goliath

"You come against me with sword and spear and scimitar,
but I come against you in the name of the LORD of hosts."
—*1 Samuel 17:45, NABRE*

I stopped next to the hospital suite door, listened, and smiled. Fifteen-year-old David is telling the story of, well, David and Goliath. He shares the story with great detail to the point where in my mind's eye I can see the sling, the stone, and the battleground. David's suitemate is fourteen-year-old Ben. Today, after many signatures, consents, and consultations, David will donate bone marrow to Ben, who has non-Hodgkin lymphoma. I walk into the room as David is explaining how Goliath falls, with sound effects to emphasize the victory. David is not ill. They met in the hospital waiting room when David was visiting his grandfather; Ben was there for treatment. Sharing similar sports interests and attending the same school, the friendship grew quickly. When the discussion of Ben needing bone marrow treatment came up, David volunteered to be tested, and the mouth swab indicated he was a matching donor. The approval process took a long time. A bone marrow transplant was the best option for Ben.

I walk to the waiting area. Both families are anxious, hopeful, but sad. Ben's illness will not go away, which makes the times he is in remission more precious. We head to the chapel to pray. There in the small room everyone speaks to God. It is there that tears surface and the reality of the surgery arrives, like an unwanted guest. As I walk the parents to David and Ben's suite for a brief reunion, I see them compose themselves and try to look prepared. *But who can prepare you for the next turn where you enter the room and see your sons with IVs, in white gowns and white linen beds, and a small pillow to rest on?*

During the surgery I stand in the private viewing gallery. I remember the beautiful painting of Jesus in the operating room. *I know He's there now.*

Sixteen hours later I walk past the recovery room, peek in, and see them both asleep. *David will be in pain when he awakens.* I enter quietly and pray by David's bedside, and then pray by Ben's. As I open my eyes I see Ben watching me. In a hoarse voice he says, "If David wakes up before I do, tell him I said thank you for running toward my Goliath." Tears slide across the corners of his eyes as he falls asleep. I step back and see the bigger picture.

Dixil Rodríguez

The Better Way

"Because you did not obey the voice of the LORD
nor execute His fierce wrath upon Amalek,
therefore the LORD has done this thing to you this day.
Moreover the LORD will also deliver Israel with you
into the hand of the Philistines."
—1 Samuel 28:18, 19, NKJV

So Samuel said: "Has the LORD as great delight in burnt offerings
and sacrifices, As in obeying the voice of the LORD?
Behold, to obey is better than sacrifice, And to heed
than the fat of rams. . . . He also has rejected you from being king."
—1 Samuel 15:22, 23, NKJV

God's directives in His Word are there for our good and should be obeyed. The tendency for us humans is to want to do things, or have things, our way. In other words, we say, "My way or no way!" Have you watched toddlers lately? They want their own way most of the time. This trait is inborn and can be changed only by the transforming power of the Holy Spirit.

The history of ancient Israel has always fascinated me. Sometimes I look at their behavior critically and accuse them of being stubborn and ungrateful. King Saul, Israel's first king, is a prime example of wanting and doing things his way. Yet when I look at myself in the mirror, I realize I am the very reflection of those Israelites in so many ways.

Israel's problems included disobedience, willfulness, pride, a tendency toward manipulation, and ingratitude. Any one of these sins can lead to ultimate destruction.

Many hardened criminals started out by performing one small, but apparently insignificant, "crime." By repeating this act, however, the person developed an evil habit. By practice, the habitual act became reinforced. This habit, among other unfortunate choices-turned-habits, led to a way of life. And this led to problems with society and with the law.

When small sins go unchecked, they lead to more grievous choices and actions that bring pain to man.

God will not force us to obey Him. His grace allows us freedom to choose—obedience and eternal life, or disobedience and eternal death.

The question for us to ask ourselves, dear sister, is which will I choose? What is one sin problem (attitude, behavior, habit) I can give to God today, asking for His help to choose the better way?

Kollis Salmon-Fairweather

Living the Mission

Then I heard the voice of the Lord saying, "Whom shall I send?
And who will go for us?" And I said, "Here am I. Send me!"
—Isaiah 6:8, NIV

Halfway around the world, I breathe in the tropical warmth and musty smells. The small blue waves juxtapose to ramshackle hovels and the giant city dump, giving new meaning to "Beachfront Property." Small bronze bodies stare and hide as Westerners walk their small atoll. Skirted teenage girls play invisible volleyball in a court decorated with graffiti. Weathered adult faces smile warmly, for they know we are part of the visiting medical team that has come to Ebeye to provide much needed specialty ear care.

Inside the clinic, I am gratified to be a part of the audiology team that has come to test people's hearing. A beautiful sixteen-year-old girl comes with her mother seeking treatment. The girl was born permanently deaf, and our inability to help her hurts my heart. They smile in resignation, yet they will return hopefully whenever the Ear Team comes back to their island (a one- to five-year wait).

An aged, stooped gentleman shuffles in, nearly unable to communicate because of hearing loss. This time the Ear Team can help. The old man's face breaks into a joyful smile as his new hearing aids give him the renewed gift of hearing. "Kommol tata!" he emotionally exclaims again and again, hugging each member of the audiology team before walking out. Walking tall.

On our final day, the islanders treat us to a show of their appreciation. A cappella singing. Clapping. Marching. Giving us handcrafted tokens of love. They give speeches. We cry. They pour out their appreciation. We feel humbled to have been a part of this. For two weeks already they have loved us. We know the Marshallese live in poverty, but they don't live without hope. So we experience irony in real time: we have come to give, but they give back to us even more. And the common denominator is Jesus, our Savior. He is the reason, despite any challenging circumstance, that we can all cherish this life and look forward to the next.

This short-term medical trip has changed me, deepening my compassion, renewing my commitment, expanding my joy. It has challenged me to live each day with a sense of the mission to which God calls me.

Donna Reese

All Aboard, Jesus!

"These things I have spoken to you, that in Me you may have peace.
In the world you will have tribulation; but be of good cheer,
I have overcome the world."
—*John 16:33, NKJV*

I am writing this devotional on the last day of our honeymoon. I'm in a library enjoying quietude after seven days aboard a colossal luxury ship that carried us to Malaga, Rome, Corsica, Florence, Pisa, and Valencia. It's hard to believe one week has passed since we heard that welcome cry, "All aboard!" This ship was fully booked, so now the staff is exhausted. We guests felt as if we were in downtown Manhattan. Throughout the week the throngs of guests made even dining difficult. So I'm now enjoying the quiet. We chose the late departure program, which allows us access to the ship until 3:00 P.M. Our flight home doesn't depart until 9:30 P.M., which allows us ample time to relax and even have lunch before we head to the airport.

All around me the ship is getting a complete makeover. The stewards are stripping beds, sterilizing rooms, emptying garbage, and putting welcome notes in each room. The kitchen team is working diligently to prepare a fabulous buffet to make a great first impression on the incoming guests. The cleaning crew is vacuuming, and the staff is wiping down every possible surface, especially the glass elevators. The entertainment group is enthusiastically rehearsing. The cruise director is working on the itinerary that will entertain the almost 3,000 women, men, and children. The staff and crew have three hours to turn the ship over, three hours to make the ship appear as if they have been prepping for these guests for weeks. Outside this quiet library, the frenzied staff is scurrying about everywhere.

I think of Martha and how my life (and that of the ship's staff right now) is often one of frenzy: work, household chores, and meal preparations. Peaceful times are few and far between. I need to learn that this is *not* what Jesus wants for me. Too often Martha—and I—haven't asked Jesus to be part of what we're doing. Then I reflect on how Mary, Martha's sister, found peace at the feet of Jesus. I too need to reach toward Him for that sweet and promised peace. And for joy in my sorrows, relief from my burdens, and hope for my tomorrows.

As frenzied Martha learned, the most important things—like Jesus—must come first. So let's slow down, look to Him, and then extend a heartfelt invitation: "All aboard, Jesus!"

Sharon Michael Palmer

Metallic Blessings

And I will make them and the places round about my hill a blessing;
and I will cause the shower to come down in his season;
there shall be showers of blessing.
—Ezekiel 34:26

Our family had gathered in Florida at my brother's tiled-roof apartment for yet another birthday event. The relatives arrived that Sunday afternoon, and the get-together was off to a wonderful time. The group mingled and did all the activities expected for such an occasion.

It was then getting late. All had to go back to their homes to prepare for work on Monday. The cumulonimbus clouds darkened. Thunder clapped as Florida's flashing lightning accompanied the weather festivities. The bellowing thunder caused trembling to the mind, body, and spirit. Lightning continued to present itself in bolts and jolts. White sheets of rain descended.

The storm made leaving the party impossible. Guests had to stay together for an extended visit. We shared stories from childhood, especially those that occurred during rainy days and nights. A few of the stories and jokes were new to some of the folks.

As we laughed and teased one another, we became aware of the rain starting to make a musical, metallic sound reminiscent of the rain-produced sound we had heard growing up in the Caribbean. A unique sound of rain falling on the zinc-roofed houses there. A rainy day sound that is unfamiliar in Florida.

I smiled because the musical, metallic sound reminded me of so many blessings, times of family togetherness, family bonding, and good nights of peaceful sleep. Yet the familiar brassy tone caused some questioning among us, namely, "Why is the falling rain on the tile roof overhead producing a *metallic* sound?"

Our brother Ray responded, "An aluminum baking pan blew over from a neighbor's apartment and perched itself right beside my patio. I left it there because I enjoy hearing that sound every time it rains. It lulls me to sleep at night."

That overturned pan was truly a metallic shower of blessing to all of us during the storm that day. It reminded us of home and also of our Creator preparing another home for us, an eternal home.

Will you not count today the blessings God has showered torrentially on you?

Pauline A. Dwyer-Kerr

For the Joy

Looking unto Jesus the author and finisher of our faith;
who for the joy that was set before him endured the cross, despising
the shame, and is set down at the right hand of the throne of God.
—*Hebrews 12:2*

You're pregnant?" several family members chorused to my niece.

"Yes." The new mother's eyes glowed. Then she looked directly at me. "I needed to tell you before dinner . . . because I need to sit where I can get to the bathroom quickly. Just the smell of food can start me retching." During the family dinner, my niece jumped up and headed to the bathroom, but that was far from the end of her misery. Throughout her pregnancy, she struggled with nausea. She knew she needed to eat, but nothing tasted good. Her head ached, her back hurt, a joint in her lower back or hip went out, so it hurt to walk, lie down, or stand. She tossed in bed, weary, but wide awake. It was a long nine months.

Then hard labor and a difficult birth. Exhausted, the new mother longed for rest, but the healthy baby boy was an energetic soul who slept little before he was ready to nurse again. The first weeks were a nightmare of exhaustion punctuated with the delight of the miracle that had Mom's slight nose, Dad's long legs, and his own set of healthy lungs. Days became months. Mom and Dad thrilled as their son grew and glimpsed the wonders of his world. They marveled at the miracle their genes and their God had created. Recently, we got the news that this child will become a big brother. Mom looked tired. "How are you doing?" I asked.

"Worse than last time," she muttered. Then a smile lighted her tired expression. "But it will be worth it." Even as she held her baby bump and looked a little green (like it wouldn't take much to make her lose her lunch), she pointed to little Mr. Energy jetting through the room. "He's such a joy! It will be so-o-o worth it!" In that instant, I glimpsed Another's heart. On the cross, Jesus looked down through time. He saw me. He saw you. And He told Himself, "It will be *sooo* worth it!" "For the joy that was set before him [He] endured the cross"—the pain, the shame, the disgrace. "For the joy" of being with you and me. I pray for my niece and think of her difficult first pregnancy and her willingness to endure another . . . for the joy before her. I ponder Jesus' love. If I understand even an inkling of His love for me, how can I help but love Him?

Helen Heavirland

Your pH Balance

*Do you not know that your bodies are temples of the Holy Spirit, who
is in you, whom you have received from God? You are not your own;
you were bought at a price. Therefore honor God with your bodies.*
—1 Corinthians 6:19, 20, NIV

I, along with many others, have gone on a diet like that of Daniel and his three friends. You can read their story in the first chapter of the book of Daniel. This adapted diet, which I am following, revolves largely around fruits, vegetables, and whole grains while avoiding meats, dairy products, rice, and artificial sweeteners. Because the diet is Bible based, its benefits are thought to include a clearer mind and a closer walk with the Lord.

As you can imagine, my thoughts on the first few days of the diet revolved around one main question: What *can* I eat? Friends' e-mails and text messages containing recipes helped very much with the answer to that question.

Then one day when I was at work, a thought struck like a ton of bricks: *If you focus on the purpose of the fast, which is to honor and draw closer to Me, the food will come more easily. You are concerned about the physical food, but should you not be concerned about your spiritual food?* Immediately I sent this Spirit-inspired thought in an e-mail to my friends who were also on the same diet, sharing with them what God had shared with me.

I thought about the pH balance (a measure of the acidity or alkalinity) in every human body. The lower the pH reading on a scale from zero to fourteen, the more acid in the body; the higher the pH reading, the more alkaline. A neutral or healthy pH balance on this scale is around seven. This fact holds particular interest for me because, in the Bible, the number seven represents perfection. Because our bodies are the temples of God, we should do our best, nutritionally, to keep our pH level balanced. Unhealthful sugars, for example, throw off this balance, bringing down the alkaline level and increasing the acidity, which makes one more susceptible to disease.

Spiritually speaking, I think of pH as representing the potential powerhouse we can be for God if we maintain good balance. Indulging in sin, of course, weakens our spiritual immune system, making us less capable of honoring God with our lives. The best way for a Christian to build up spiritual alkalinity is through spending time with God each day and ingesting His Word.

Sabrina Crichlow

What a Filly!

The LORD hath appeared of old unto me, saying,
Yea, I have loved thee with an everlasting love:
therefore with lovingkindness have I drawn thee.
—*Jeremiah 31:3*

Princess is the name of a filly my husband gave to me. Duchess, the mother of the animal, had a lineage of nobility. The filly's tawny coat and flowing, fluffy mane reflected this noble line, as did her free and spontaneous spirit.

We often visited Princess in the morning or evening. Visiting Princess was like therapy to me as I stood admiring her and watching her graceful movements. Somewhat skittish, she wouldn't allow us to get too close at first. However, my husband is a good trainer and soon earned her trust. As he would gently handle her, I would yearn for the day when I could do the same. One day we left home early to pay a quick visit to Princess. I was so happy that my husband had taught me the secret to being able to pet her silky coat. I would lean over and wait as Princess came toward me and began sniffing my head. Having this new trust interaction with my beautiful creature thrilled me deeply even though, much to my disappointment, she would not yet let me caress her with my arms as I longed to do.

Then tragedy struck. Princess had an accident, fracturing a leg in the process. When I saw her lying on the ground, my heart broke. I dropped to my knees and cradled her beautiful head. With great sorrow I caressed her and put her face in my lap. Sobs shook my body with inexpressible sadness. She had to be put down. I felt so empty. How I had longed to hold her and cuddle her when she was well! But she would not let me.

My tragic last few minutes with Princess remind me of how many times Jesus has yearningly extended His arms to embrace and hold us. Yet, with our sense of freedom and independence, we do not give Him our attention. Sometimes we outright reject His loving embrace. I remember how He wept over Jerusalem, expressing the sorrow of a mother hen whose chicks would not come under her protective wings. Let us not grieve our Lord. He wants to give us the divine touch of love that we so desperately need. He wants to wipe every tear from our eyes and lead us soon to a place of peace with no more death, weeping, or pain.

Today let His kindness attract you and His everlasting love hold you close.

Marialva Vasconcelos Monteiro Chaussé

Seek Ye First

*"But seek first the kingdom of God and His righteousness,
and all these things shall be added to you."*
—*Matthew 6:33, NKJV*

Not long ago I chose to go to bed later than I should have, resulting in only four hours of sleep that night. As usual, I arose early to get through the hustle and bustle of getting ready to leave for work. I could tell on my way to work that I hadn't had enough sleep. Neither my body nor my mind was happy with me. Not only did I feel physically exhausted and sluggish, I also felt mentally disconnected from reality as I began my shift at work. My perception was skewed and my reflexes slow. I didn't have my usual alertness or efficiency as I struggled to prioritize my workload. My energy level was at zero—most unusual for me.

This got me thinking. Not only is my physical and mental well-being vulnerable to unwise schedule choices, but my connection with God is broken if I don't nurture it carefully. It should not be a burden for us to make positive choices that keep our bodies and minds functioning at their highest potential. Neither should it be a burden to make choices that maintain a relationship with God.

Just as my body needs rest in order to find renewed strength and energy, my soul needs a time of daily rest in the renewing presence of my God. No bad choice I make can make God ever love me any less than He does. However, if I let the day go by without spending even just a bit of time in His presence or in His Word, or reflecting on Him and who He is, my spiritual perceptions, discernment, and reflexes will be slow at best. I start to feel that lack of renewal and refreshment that I would have received had I started out my day resting in Him.

God, however, does not abandon us to our poor choices—even the ones that leave Him out. His Holy Spirit of love and power continues to seek us out even after we have neglected Him and grown immediately weak in our own strength. We sense Him knocking on the door of our hearts, inviting us back into a prayerful relationship with Him for the rest of the day. What love and what faithfulness! And what second chances!

Let us purposefully start and end each day in the presence of God. Let's put first things first by letting Him be the Lord of each new day. Then everything else will fall into place.

Taylor Bajic

German Chocolate Brownies

Weeping may endure for a night,
but joy cometh in the morning.
—*Psalm 30:5*

My husband, Norman, had made a special birthday request. He wanted a German chocolate cake. He makes very few food requests and is usually happy with anything I prepare. I fancy myself to be a good cook, but pies are my specialty. In my trusty old Betty Crocker cookbook, I soon found a German chocolate cake recipe that seemed divine. I decided to make the nutty frosting first. That was accomplished without a hitch. Next I began to assemble the ingredients for the perfect cake. Butter and sugar in one bowl; carefully sifted dry ingredients in another. As I returned the unused ingredients to the kitchen cabinet, I glanced at what I was putting back. Was it baking powder or baking soda? Which one had I actually used? I said a quick prayer that the cake would turn out just perfect because it was for Norman's birthday.

When I later opened the oven door to remove the baked cake, it had risen only about half as much as it should have. Just then Norman came in from the yard. I began to weep and said, "I can't even make a decent cake for you."

He said, "Let me taste a little piece." I cut off a small bite. He tasted it and sweetly remarked, "It's not too bad; tastes kind of like brownies. Go ahead and frost it; it will be fine." I did so but would not be comforted.

After a quick phone chat with my daughter, Julie, I showered and went to bed early. But in my dreams I could visualize our Sabbath lunch guests trying to politely choke down my less-than-perfect cake. Still depressed the next day when we arrived home from church, I noticed a white box setting against the garage door. "Go out and get it, honey," I said to Norman. "Someone has mailed you a present." Peering inside, he saw this handwritten note on one of the cardboard flaps: "From the cake fairy—made from scratch. We even basted our own nuts. Happy Birthday, Norman." It was signed by our daughter, Julie, and my granddaughter, Olivia.

Little had I realized that our phone conversation the preceding evening would result in the return of my joy. When I served the cake after lunch, my sister commented that it was lovely. I hastened to tell her it was not my cake but one my loving Lord had sent me in order to put a smile on my face and my husband's too. How has God put a smile on your face today?

Rose Neff Sikora

Through *Whose* Eyes Do I See Me?

Oh yes, you shaped me first inside, then out;
you formed me in my mother's womb. I thank you, High God—you're
breathtaking! Body and soul, I am marvelously made! I worship in
adoration—what a creation! You know me inside and out, you know
every bone in my body; you know exactly how I was made, bit by bit,
how I was sculpted from nothing into something.

—*Psalm 139:13, 14*, The Message

Women spend their lives seeking approval. *Does this dress make me look fat? Am I dressed appropriately? Did I do things right?* It seems we never find the answers that give us the comfort and confidence we seek. What is a Christian woman to do? Where should she go to find the answers? Today's verse helps us with the answers. God knew us—long before anyone else ever saw us. Our mothers who carried us in their bodies for nine months; the doting family who saw us when we were born—God knew us before any of that. God created us as marvelous and His divine creation. He defines who we are and, more important, how we view ourselves. We tell the world we are Christians, and we are our own worst critics! How can we worship in adoration when we don't like ourselves?

Consider this quote: "The Lord is disappointed when His people place a low estimate upon themselves. He desires His chosen heritage to value themselves according to the price He has placed upon them. God wanted them, else He would not have sent His Son on such an expensive errand to redeem them."* Look into the mirror and *smile*—God wanted you just as you are because He sent His Son to redeem you!

God knows everything about us, even the number of hairs on our heads (Matthew 10:30). He collects all our tears (Psalm 56:8), knows what we do as well as what we are, and even knows what we think about (Psalm 139:1–5). Should we expect anything less from our Creator (verses 13, 14)?

Sometimes we don't let people get to know us because we are afraid they will discover—or already have discovered—something about us they don't like. We pull back, fearing rejection. That can't happen with God. He knows us completely and still He accepts and loves us.

When you fear (or actually face) rejection from others, remember that God made you and has already accepted you, exactly as you are. So let's look at ourselves through *God's* eyes.

Wilma Kirk Lee

---

* Ellen G. White, *The Desire of Ages* (Mountain View, CA.: Pacific Press®, 1940), 668.

Forgiveness

"Blessed are the merciful,
For they shall obtain mercy."
—*Matthew 5:7, NKJV*

Have you ever been wronged or hurt by someone? Have you ever wronged or hurt someone? I personally feel worse when I have done the wrong or hurt than when I've received it.

Sometimes we don't see what we have done to others. We feel our actions are warranted or that they were not done with malice. That may be the case. Yet the truth of the matter is that the wrong occurs when the person you are dealing with perceives your words or actions as a wrong directed against her.

I've been baffled for several years as to why someone I love never would answer the phone when I called or never called me when I sent messages to do so. After a while I just gave up trying to make contact. However, I didn't stop thinking about, praying for, or loving this person. But I backed off because I don't believe in invading anyone's space. I never could figure out what I had done to cause this situation. But remember, wrong is often about perception.

Yesterday I had a breakthrough. When I phoned this person on a new number I'd received from a mutual friend, the individual answered the phone. Perhaps they never answered before because the number I was calling and texting was no longer valid. Perhaps the individuals through whom I'd earlier sent invitations to call me had forgotten to deliver my messages. In the grand scheme of things, it does not matter. I still don't know what I did or didn't do, but I am open to finding out so I can ask forgiveness.

Whether you are the doer or the receiver of a wrong, forgiveness is always in order to restore relationships. Forgiveness is giving love when there is no reason to; no reason, except for the fact that the love of Jesus lives in your heart. After all, "it is no longer I who live, but Christ lives in me" (Galatians 2:20, NKJV).

Today, tell someone you are sorry, even if you feel you are right. Tell someone that you forgive them, even if you feel they were wrong. Today, tell someone that you love them—and mean it. Reach out like I did. You may be pleasantly surprised. I know I was! "For if you forgive other people when they sin against you, your heavenly Father will also forgive you. But if you do not forgive others their sins, your Father will not forgive your sins" (Matthew 6:14, 15, NIV).

Barbara J. Walker

God Teaches Through Our Children

For we walk by faith, not by sight.
—*2 Corinthians 5:7, NKJV*

My ten-month-old daughter slept quietly and peacefully next to me in the early morning hours. She had been stirring off and on peacefully for a few minutes, and I quietly watched her breathing and took in the blessing that she and her brother are in our lives. Then she stirred more intensely, made a little cry, and turned over toward me with her eyes still closed. I pulled her close to let her nurse.

Without opening her eyes, she just wrapped her arm around me and became peaceful once again. She sighed, safe and secure in the complete trust she had that I was right there and not anywhere else.

As I watched her nursing, still with her eyes closed, it made me think about how God is also right there for us. Sometimes it's easy to get lost in the present circumstance and forget that He is right there. I sometimes try to take care of things on my own. If only I would turn my eyes upward and trust, He is there to fulfill whatever need I have if I would let Him. I might not see Him right there beside me, but He is right there just patiently waiting for me to simply turn to Him!

When I turn my thoughts to God with my needs, problems, troubles, and cares, He isn't in another room. He isn't out taking a walk, and He isn't taking a phone call. He and His angels are all around me, ready to take my requests and hear my prayers. Day and night, God waits and is ready to hear every single prayer and request that any of us have. Whether it is praise or petition, when we reach out to the Lord, He hears!

Since that morning with my baby girl, whenever I awaken—even if it is at night—I talk to God about whatever is on my mind. I've also found that if I pray when I place my head on the pillow each night, sharing with God about every little thing on my mind, I usually fall asleep before I finish my prayer!

It is such relief to be able to just reach out anytime or anywhere and be able to trust that God is there, even if my eyes are closed.

Reach out to Him—He is never far away!

Ericka J. Iverson

God Fulfills His Promises!

For God so loved the world, that he gave his only begotten Son, that whosoever believeth in him should not perish, but have everlasting life.
—*John 3:16*

As a twelve-year-old orphan, I accepted Christ. Having no money for university studies after high school, I asked God for a husband who would also be a pastor. He answered my prayers, and I married thirteen years ago at the age of twenty-two. The next few years I mothered eight children, four of them being my own. Once I enrolled at a university but quickly stopped my studies, feeling my children's education was more important. When my husband left for a time to further pursue his education, he left our family in charge of a minibus business so that we would still have an income during his extended absence. Trouble soon found us. The minibus business failed. Unexpected divisions among in-laws tore us apart and left us helpless. They took my four children. I was perplexed by all the turmoil that had so quickly descended on our family. I had nothing on which to fall back in order to support my family. I was afraid my husband would quit his studies in order to come home and look after us. I prayed that he would somehow be able to finish the studies that he had begun. Oh, how I prayed!

Six months after our many losses, all my stepchildren were able to escape their relatives and return to me where they felt safe. God provided one day at a time. Staff members at the school my children attended began giving them small jobs to do and paying them—much more than the wages they were expecting. This helped pay their school fees. I worked hard to raise a garden for our food. Once again I dared to hope I could continue my education and enrolled in a university. Once again I had to drop out for financial reasons. I continued to pray and even fast for God's guidance. God answered. I was able to apply, through the women's ministries department of our church organization in Uganda, for a university scholarship. My application was accepted, and I was able to go back to school! Oh, the grace of God! When I finish my studies, I will be a family counselor, especially for women and children.

From my own difficult experience, I want to encourage you to never lose heart, even when resources are tight and the going is rough. The Lord always hears our prayers. He has ways to provide for our needs that are unknown to us. His ways and His timing are always the best.

Tumusiime Betty Tenywa

Fly the Love Flag High

Beloved, if God so loved us,
we ought also to love one another.
—1 John 4:11

I grew up in Jamaica, the country of my birth. Although I am from a very large family, I was raised by a great-aunt as an only child. It was so difficult leaving home after my fourth birthday to go live in the city. As I grew, I learned that many of my siblings had migrated to England in the sixties to seek a better life. At the time, England was known as "the mother country," being the seat of the British Commonwealth. After retiring in the summer of 2008, I was able to fulfill a lifelong dream of flying to England to visit my family.

From where I sat on the plane during that night flight in August, I had a commanding view of the most awesome sunrise. I was still contemplating the story of Creation and the greatness of our God when the plane landed at Gatwick Airport. Someone met me and took me to my sister's home in Manchester. She was ecstatic to see me. My nephew, with whom I would spend a part of my vacation, asked me what my greatest desire was for this trip. I told him I wanted to visit London and see Buckingham Palace, where the Queen resides.

He and his family drove me from Leeds to London. We traveled by train to see the palace, among other attractions. When we arrived at the palace, my nephew's wife remarked, "The Queen is not at home." When I asked how she knew, she answered, "When the Queen is at home, the flag flies at full mast. When she is away, the flag flies at half-mast."

Immediately I started singing a little chorus (whose composer is unknown) that came to mind: "Love is the flag flown high from the castle of my heart, for the King is in residence there." I taught it to my two little grandnephews, who loved it very much. As I sang, I thought about the position of the flag displayed in front of Buckingham Palace. In this context, a new meaning came into the words I was singing. If the King of heaven resides in our hearts, then the flag of His love will fly high on His behalf through our words and actions. Jesus said, "Ye are the light of the world. . . . Let your light so shine before men, that they may see your good works, and glorify your Father which is in heaven" (Matthew 5:14–16).

I encouraged my family to let the King of heaven live in their hearts, letting their love be the flag that proclaims Him to others. Do our behaviors show He is residing in our hearts too?

Cynthia Case-Walters

Free

"So if the Son sets you free,
you will be free indeed."
—*John 8:36, NIV*

I am very fond of things that are free. The air we breathe is free. Prayer is free. Internet sites list free items (and, yes, I have called people, gone to their homes, and picked up interesting items simply because they were free—much to my husband's dismay). A while back a television personality gave away a free chicken dinner on a particular television show. Someone told me about it, as well as how to print out a coupon from the Internet for that chicken dinner. Even though I am a vegetarian, I wanted that chicken dinner in the worst way—because it was free.

I reasoned that I would give it to someone else and save them some expense on a meal. My father's not a vegetarian, so I dialed my mother and arranged a day when I could drop off this free meal. As I drove into the parking lot of Kentucky Fried Chicken I noticed a woman sitting on the curb. When I opened my car door, she dashed across the parking lot, stood by me, and started yelling loudly.

"I need you to buy me food!" she demanded. "I'm hungry and have nothing to eat!" She kept on yelling as I headed toward the door. My instant reaction was to ignore her because she was yelling. When I reached the door, she walked back to the curb and sat down. There I was standing at the counter holding my coupon and looking at the menu. It was then it dawned on me—I had just passed up a God moment. I walked back out the door, noted her dejected countenance, and asked, "Are you still hungry? Can you come in here?" She walked with me to the counter, and I pointed to the menu and said, "Pick out anything you like." The cashier looked a little shaken because the hungry woman was clearly unkempt. Had this woman prayed for someone to help her? And then, when so many people ignored her, had she grown desperate and demanding? I don't know.

God did give her a free meal, yet mine, now, was no longer free because I still wanted to keep my promise of providing a free meal to my father. So was this extra cost worth it to me? Yes, of course it was. And I'd do the same thing again if given the opportunity.

Jesus extends gifts—free—to everyone all the time, including the gift of eternal salvation. In fact, Jesus Himself said, "So if the Son sets you free, you will be free indeed."

Now that's a gift we cannot afford to pass by!

Diane Pestes

Livin' Above Your Raisin'

I can do all things through Christ which strengtheneth me.
—*Philippians 4:13*

I used to live up a *holler* (a small valley between hills) on six acres in southern West Virginia. It was a different culture; it took some time getting used to the dialect and meanings behind people's words. "Stay for supper" didn't always mean to eat a meal with whomever you were visiting; it was just a polite way to let you know that it was time for you to leave so they could have supper. A *poke* was a brown paper bag; a *press*—a coat closet. My family and I so enjoyed learning more about these lovely folks.

Up our holler lived a group of folks who were all related. These neighbors viewed us skeptically at first, though they were always friendly. Over the more than twenty years that we lived there, these neighbors became like family as we shared everyday life events—sickness, deaths, births, forest fires, floods, gardening. Mutual support in good times and bad. One of these families had eight children, and we spent many hours with them—babysitting, playing with their children, learning about their hunting dogs and horses. One day the wife told me that her husband accused her of talking "city-fied." Because she was a country girl, she shouldn't be using words that were not part of their everyday language.

We learned the expression "livin' above their raisin'." It had nothing to do with a dried grape, a raisin. It was used to describe people who had achieved or gained status above their poorer upbringing. They were livin' above their raisin'. More education, higher income, or a better house might be indicators that someone was livin' above their raisin'. They had achieved something or improved over earlier conditions.

How about you and me? Are we livin' above our raisin'? Have we connected so solidly with Christ that we are now acting more like Him than we were previously? Is our sweetest thought of Him? Do we love His Word? When people hear our story, will they say, "She's livin' above her raisin'"? Only Jesus can bring us up from the lower level to the higher plane; only Jesus can take our messy lives and set us on that upward path toward heaven. We are all born sinners; we all need improvements on the old life. So it's wonderful news that we can all live above our raisin' with the help of Jesus Christ.

Valerie Hamel Morikone

The Crumpled Heart

They did not conquer by their own strength and skill, but by your mighty power and because you smiled upon them and favored them.
—*Psalm 44:3, TLB*

One day when I was doing some substitute teaching, I watched twenty-five first-graders stream into the classroom from their outdoor recreation. I got them settled and then read them a story titled "Chrysanthemum." It told of a little girl who loves her name until her peers at school begin to make fun of her. Her classmates do not realize how much their words hurt her. The purpose of the story was to help children understand how their words can affect others and that we should weigh our words before we speak them.

After the story, I discussed with the children what made Chrysanthemum hurt and also what could have been done to prevent or stop her hurt. To illustrate my point, I used a large smooth red paper heart. I said, "This paper heart is like your own heart." Then, crumpling the paper heart in my hands, I said, "This is what happens when people say and do mean things that hurt us." A student helped me flatten out the heart again as we tried to smooth out the stubborn wrinkles my crumpling it had caused. Students could see that there would always be evidence of the damage done to that heart because wrinkles remained in the paper heart. The wrinkles represented the scars that our words can leave on the hearts of others. Suddenly, one little boy had a bright idea. "Teacher," he said, "if we use a lot of pressure with our hands we could get the heart to look like it did before." So he set to work applying as much pressure as his tiny six-year-old hand could apply. The rest of the class watched with eager interest while some even cheered. However, in his effort to repair the heart, the little boy accidentally made a hole in it.

Many of us have also had our feelings hurt and our hearts broken. Perhaps we have suffered this pain from a friend or in the betrayal of a broken marriage or relationship. Perhaps we, in our own efforts to help others, have also caused pain. Often we depend on the advice of others for relief or run to the Internet for a quick fix, trying to relieve the pain ourselves. Like my little student trying to work out the wrinkles, we try to heal ourselves, leaving God and His will out of the picture.

Today let's trust God's wise ways to heal and restore our wounded and broken hearts.

Georgina George

The Salad Bar

What counts is whether we really have been changed
into new and different people. May God's mercy and peace
be upon all of you who live by this principle and
upon those everywhere who are really God's own.
—*Galatians 6:15, 16, TLB*

The dining room at Downtown Rescue Mission is passably clean, though the floor always seems a little sticky to me. On any given Saturday, volunteers like me will ladle food onto several hundred plates for men, women, and children. So I guess it's no surprise that things get spilled a bit in the rush. I'm standing at the far end with a man I haven't met before. He's a new resident in the program, meaning he's taken an affirmative step to end his problem with substance abuse.

We've been assigned to the salad bar, so we chit-chat about the local football team while filling Styrofoam bowls with lettuce and grated carrots. I'm always wondering how to share my faith in situations like this. They don't actually need our help to serve the dinner. We go because we want to represent Jesus somehow. But the "somehow" part is always the rub. I can't think of a single thing he and I have in common, except for the fact that we are both past sixty.

He's talking nonstop and, blessedly, comments from me don't seem to be required. He's despondent about his failure to put drugs completely behind him. The lost opportunities and burned bridges are like a haunting. It's a tough reality to face, and it strikes me that he faces it again and again every day. And then, as if recognizing he has unwittingly dominated the conversation, he turns to me and says, "You look like you must have had some success in life."

It was clearly a question. I had to answer him . . . but what could I say? Happily, the Holy Spirit does not experience system slowdowns. The words came into my mind instantly. "Well, I've done OK," I responded as I turned to face him. "But as you've been talking, it occurs to me that we wrestle with the same problem. I have control issues too. You say you've lacked control in your life. Well, my need for control is so strong it causes all kinds of problems. We're at opposite ends of the self-control spectrum, but guess what? It's just as hard for me to accept the gift of God's grace as it is for you. We both need divine assistance!" It wasn't the answer he expected, but it seemed to resonate. We hugged and filled up more bowls.

In my mind's eye, the sea of glass is level . . . we all need redeeming grace.

Linda Nottingham

Born for Music—Part 1

I will sing to the LORD all my life;
I will sing praise to my God as long as I live.
—*Psalm 104:33, NIV*

My father, the late Wayne Hooper, was born for music. From an early age he, growing up in a musical family, had a God-given talent for singing with excellence and maturity. He loved the Lord and later committed his life to composing and arranging sacred music for the glory of God—though, with his talent, he could have easily been drawn into secular music, especially during the impressionable years of his youth. Dad is probably best known for singing thirteen years with the King's Heralds quartet for the Voice of Prophecy radio ministry. He was often at the piano developing some original tune into a new anthem or harmonious arrangement.

During Dad's retirement he compiled a database of all his music and was surprised to discover he had arranged and composed fifteen hundred songs, including the well-known anthem "We Have This Hope," which he composed during my senior year in high school.

I remember the sound of music—vocal and instrumental—coursing through our house during my school years. Our family choir consisted of Dad singing baritone (though he had a wide singing range from tenor to bass), Mom singing soprano, me singing alto, and my three brothers alternating on tenor, baritone, and bass as their voices changed and matured. Our family looked forward to evening worship as we sang together while expanding our knowledge of music, sight reading ability, and vocal techniques—always coached by Dad.

As a result, singing in small groups and choirs throughout my life has been a joy for me and an important part of my worship and praise experience.

Yes, my father was born for music. Sacred music. On that point he was very clear. I remember his frequent quoting of Psalm 98:1: "Sing to the LORD a new song! For He has done marvelous things" (NKJV). I also grew to love Psalm 104:33: "I will sing to the LORD all my life; I will sing praise to my God as long as I live" (NIV). Dad left me—and countless others—the legacy of music. A legacy that is really a gift we can render back to God.

What legacy will you leave your posterity? For what have you been born? To what can you say Yes, thereby inviting God's thoughts, power, assurance, and guidance into your life? He will weave His words, melodies, and purposes into your song to be a blessing to others.

Jan Hooper Lind

Born for Music—Part 2

"The LORD your God in your midst,
The Mighty One, will save;
He will rejoice over you with gladness,
He will quiet you with His love,
He will rejoice over you with singing."
—*Zephaniah 3:17, NKJV*

My music-loving dad, the late Wayne Hooper, used to encourage me to sing a sacred song in my head whenever I was feeling stressed or having difficulty sleeping at night. He shared that doing so would bring comfort, calm anxiety, and let God quiet me with His love.

I have experienced many nights awaking at three-thirty for the day and longing for God to quiet my heart with His love. How desperately I seized the comfort of this promise during the heartache of a broken marriage, as the single mom of grade-school-aged children, and while seeking to regain confidence and find my purpose again! God sustained me during sorrow as my beloved dad was dying from metastatic bone cancer. I relied on deepening trust in God's strong arms when my dear younger brother recently died from liver failure complications—just one year after a transplant. While sitting at my brother's bedside in an intensive care unit for thirty-two days, I constantly lifted up to God my silent prayers—and songs. In turn, He comforted through the lyrics of "Turn Your Eyes Upon Jesus" and "We Have This Hope."

I believe God created each of us with a musical and spiritual ear. He speaks to us through sacred lyrics and beautiful melodies, lifting our spirits while molding our character as we experience a deepening relationship with Him. Praying the words of familiar songs helps build our faith as God once again assures us that He cares about the details of our lives. Through those prayerful words we invite God's power into our days and His peace into the long night hours. In fact, God promises to join us in our singing. "He will rejoice over you with singing."

Imagine that! God rejoicing over *us* with singing, with His clear, rich, mellow, multi-octave tones, thoughtful phrasing, and trumpet-like—yet tender—notes. Always drawing us closer to Him. God created us to respond to His singing. To *His* music. He invites us to live our very lives as a song that will witness to others of His love and grace.

So won't you select a favorite song right now to lift your spirits whenever you next face a challenge or want to minister to someone? After all, you too were born for music.

Jan Hooper Lind

Giving Thanks in All Circumstances

In every thing give thanks:
for this is the will of God in Christ Jesus concerning you.
—*1 Thessalonians 5:18*

From an early age I often heard my parents use the words "grateful" and "thankful" until they became embedded in my memory. Unfortunately, I developed an attitude of ungratefulness, but thanks to God, my parents never gave up on me. Whenever teaching opportunities arose, my parents reminded me to say Thank you whether we were at home or away. During family worship time, I often heard "Thank You" in my father's prayers as he gave thanks to God for his family. When my mother hugged us at bedtime, she said, "Thank You, God" for us.

Once during my first year in college, I was hurrying to class when someone loudly called my name. It was my roommate approaching me. Holding out her hand, she said, "Here's your favorite writing pen from the set your parents gave you when you graduated from high school. I thought you would worry that you had lost it, so I decided to run and find you." Her words immediately brought to my mind what my parents taught me on being grateful and showing gratitude. I said Thank you and gave my roommate a sincere hug. College days have been replaced by retirement days. Yet from that time until now I have resolved to give thanks in all situations, realizing that gratitude is a highly priced virtue in the sight of God.

In both the Old and the New Testaments of Scripture we find individuals who gave thanks in various circumstances. The healed Samaritan leper who came back to say Thank You to Jesus (the only one to do so out of the ten lepers healed) (Luke 17:12–18). The prophetess Anna of the tribe of Asher who, though having been a widow for eighty-four years, still served God night and day fasting and praying—and was grateful to see the Baby Jesus (Luke 2:36–38). I, a widow as well, remember thanking God for permitting my late husband to return home safely from World War II. I saw him work as a church elder and carry other responsibilities until God took him to rest.

God is worthy of our praise. Let's join together as grateful women thanking Him for past and present blessings as we realize that being grateful doesn't cost anything. God admonishes us to be thankful (1 Thessalonians 5:18). He tells us that in everything we should give thanks. For this is the will of God in Christ Jesus concerning you and me.

Annie B. Best

Blooming for Christ

My brethren, count it all joy when you fall into various trials,
knowing that the testing of your faith produces patience.
But let patience have its perfect work, that you may be
perfect and complete, lacking nothing.
—*James 1:2–4, NKJV*

When you get to be my age, most people dread birthdays! One birthday card states, "I thought you were going to pot, but you just keep blooming." Getting older is more often associated with the feelings of fatigue and the aches of aging than with the abundant life that God wants us to experience. In spite of aging, I continue praising the Lord because again and again I've experienced His healing power. And regardless of how old I get, or the condition I'm in, I have chosen each day to bloom for Him.

The car crash that killed my mom and tore my foot off my leg bone was my first major experience with suffering. But God arranged for the best orthopedic surgeon in the county to be on call that night, so even though it's highly unlikely I'll ever climb Mount Everest, I can walk.

Then seventeen years later, while I was taking a routine treadmill test, the doctor suddenly stopped the test and scheduled me for open-heart surgery the next day. What a shock to learn I had a congenitally defective aortic valve, when all my life I thought I was healthy!

On Friday the thirteenth—this past June—I was varnishing shelves while standing on a safe three-rung step ladder. I finished the shelf, held on to the handle, and went down one rung. Thinking I was at the bottom, I stepped off the ladder, only to discover I had one more rung to go. The fall on that hard tile floor resulted in a shattered femur bone just below the hip. Pain? I'd rather have three more children than ever experience that kind of pain again! After surgery to insert rods to hold my leg together, physical therapy, and time—once again I've experienced God's healing.

I've known all my life the Bible says we should be joyful when trials come because it helps us develop character. I used to selfishly pray, "God, please don't let anything bad happen to me. There must be another way I can develop the character You want me to have without suffering." Now, on the other side of a whole lot of suffering, I've changed my prayer: *Lord, regardless of what suffering I might have to endure, don't let me go to pot—just give me the strength and courage to keep blooming for You.*

Kay Kuzma

God Is Able

Jesus looked at them and said,
"With man this is impossible,
but with God all things are possible."
—*Matthew 19:26, NIV*

Several years ago I flew from Brisbane, Australia, to Sydney, where I was scheduled to catch a flight to Guam for a speaking commitment. I would have ninety minutes in Sydney to claim my bags, find my way to the international terminal in another building, recheck my bags for the next flight, go through airport security, and locate the departure gate to board the plane to Guam. Unfortunately, the flight from Brisbane did not leave when scheduled. It was half an hour late departing, so I began to ask God to allow me to get to Sydney in time to catch my connecting flight. After an hour of anxiety, I finally released my plans to God and reminded myself that He could get me to Guam if it was in His plan.

Minutes later I praised God when the plane's captain announced over the intercom that he had made up fifteen minutes of lost time during the flight. Then as we neared Sydney the intercom came on again. We heard the unwelcome announcement that planes were backed up at the Sydney airport and that we would be in a holding pattern for fifteen minutes. *Still,* I thought, *I might have time to get to my connecting flight—just barely.* Fifteen minutes of circling the airport turned into thirty minutes, then forty-five. I again relinquished my plans to God.

When the plane finally landed, I had only thirty minutes before my next flight. By this time I was resigned to missing it. Then the miracles began to happen. First, I almost immediately found my bags on the carousel. Then a kind passenger directed me to the international terminal, which was just one building away, through a parking garage. Several aisles in the parking garage were blocked off, so I asked a man how to get through the garage to the terminal. Instead of directing me, my guardian angel (as I called him) led me into the next terminal, up the elevator, and to the counter where I needed to check my bags. To my surprise, the attendant informed me I still had time to check my bags and catch the flight. After that, I sailed through security and arrived at the gate just as my flight began to board.

This remarkable experience strengthened my faith and reminded me once again of the futility of anxiety and that, truly, nothing is impossible for the Lord.

Carla Baker

Jerby's New Face

The LORD looked down from heaven upon the children of men.
—*Psalm 14:2*

Jerby, a seven-year-old boy, is the youngest of five children who lives in the beautiful island paradise of Palawan, Philippines. He was born with a deformed face and unable to breathe normally through his nose. Other complications made his life miserable. Jerby's family was destitute and unable to seek medical attention for him. Then a miracle happened!

A medical mission group of specially trained physicians, nurses, and auxiliary personnel from the White Memorial Medical Center in Los Angeles, California, came to Palawan. Jerby was chosen to be among the fortunate ones to be cared for.

The hospital team performed on Jerby a series of major surgeries, which necessitated drilling through his skull. As a result, Jerby is now in vibrant health and growing both physically and spiritually. He stands tall with his head up high—a silent testimony of God's goodness to him. Jerby loves attending church and is learning more about Jesus and exhibiting Christian traits to young classmates.

I came to meet Jerby and his family when recruiting children for our neighborhood Vacation Bible School. His parents are so thankful for the success of his medical care but did not have a chance to personally thank the medical mission group that provided the miracle of healing before they returned home. We assisted Jerby's family in extending thanks to his health-care providers.

Presently Jerby is experiencing the true essence of Christian love. His parents have opened their home to our Vacation Bible School and branch Sabbath School, where neighborhood children meet under their tamarind tree.

A wonderful opportunity to share the gospel in their community has opened up as a result of the care and compassion of trained and dedicated medical personnel from America, prompted by the Holy Spirit.

Indeed, the Lord still watches over all His children, particularly the less fortunate among us. He sends His love through the Christian benevolence of His chosen and willing messengers. Only time will tell the final result of the little good deeds we do each day. As Jesus Himself said—if we do good to the least among us, we have done it unto Him.

Zeny Marcelo

Hear My Cry!

Hear my cry, O God. . . .
From the ends of the earth I call to you,
I call as my heart grows faint. . . .
I long to . . .
take refuge in the shelter of your wings.
—*Psalm 61:1–4, NIV*

Sitting on the tour bus, I silently watched the Italian landscape roll by. All of a sudden, Geoff, my husband, leaned forward, put his hand on his forehead, and cried, "I have the worst heartburn!" Alarmed, I asked if he was all right. He didn't answer. Still hunched over and in severe pain, he drank water and swallowed charcoal tablets. Finally, after a few minutes, the pain subsided. As he sat up and expressed his desire to continue his Rook game, I noticed his pale face and shirt drenched in sweat. I worriedly asked, "Are you sure you're all right?"

"Yes, I'm fine," he said, trying to reassure me.

As I settled back into my seat, I tried to relax. Another five minutes passed when my husband grabbed the seat in front of him, crying out that his heartburn had returned. Without hesitating, a concerned friend advised Geoff that he should go to a hospital. When my husband, a physician, agreed, I knew this was serious. Immediately my mind froze, and all I could utter was "Help, God!" As the panic mounted, a nurse sitting behind us placed her hands on my shoulders and said, "Margie, let's pray." I grabbed her hand as a lifeline. Immediately, I felt God's loving arms enfold me as I listened to her calming words asking God for guidance and protection.

As the bus driver wound his way through the streets trying to find the nearest hospital, Pastor Quiroz came and wrapped his arms around Geoff and began praying in earnest. Upon our arrival at the hospital ten minutes later, the doctors evaluated Geoff and determined that he was having a heart attack. Again I prayed, "Help, God!" The next six hours were a blur as my husband finally received the necessary angiogram and two stents that opened up his left anterior descending artery. Nine days later, we returned home. I was overwhelmed with gratitude that my husband was alive!

Reflecting on that time, I have realized more fully that God cares for each one of us on a very personal level. As my husband's heart had grown faint sitting on that bus, our faith in God had an opportunity to grow and be strengthened under the wings of God's love.

Dear God, hear my cry. Help me to trust in the shelter of Your wings.

Margie Salcedo Rice

April 8

Spring Surprise at the Apple Tree

In You, O LORD, I have taken refuge. . . .
For You are my strong refuge.
My mouth is filled with Your praise
and with Your glory all day long.
—*Psalm 71:1, 7, 8, NASB*

The fragrance of spring is already in the air: blue sky, sunlight flooding through the old orchards in the hills around my village, bees humming. I take advantage of this wonderful day to go for a walk in the orchards, humming a tune as I go.

Suddenly I discover that one of the old apple trees has a hole in its trunk. Long ago a branch must have been cut off. Now, that part of trunk seems to be hollow. I walk over to the tree to examine it. Peeking into the hole I find myself eye-to-eye with a nearly featherless, partially grown starling chick. Chirping loudly, it hops expectantly into the entrance of the hole. Suddenly understanding that I am neither its mom nor dad, it closes its bill and freezes in place. We stare at each other.

The little fellow appears to gulp in surprise. I imagine it thinking, *My mistake, though it was nice to meet you. But I'd better return to my nest.* The little chick shakes off its paralysis. It slowly hops backward down into the tree trunk, disappearing from view. I can't help smiling. We were both so astonished at our unexpected encounter. With a grateful heart I lift my eyes to the blue sky. *Thank You, Father, that You have shown me one of Your little treasures.* I am certain God enjoys His little treasures too. He is the Almighty Creator of the universe who loves the smallest details of His creation, such as this little hidden starling chick down in the tree trunk.

Just as the trunk of that tree provided security, protection, and safety to the little bird, so God Himself is our security, protection, and safety. Whatever discouragements we may be facing in life right now—with their accompanying confusion, perplexities, or frightfulness—we can turn over everything to God. In the surrounding arms of His power, our heart and mind can be assured that He is our fortress. He is our safe haven and our home.

I continue my walk, humming "You Are My Hiding Place," followed by "Be Still, My Soul."

Why shouldn't our souls be at rest and at praise when we are surrounded by so much evidence of God's unchanging love in our own places of personal refuge and retreat?

Jaimée Seis

Triumphant in Adversity

He giveth power to the faint; and to them that have no might he
increaseth strength. . . . But they that wait upon the LORD shall renew
their strength; they shall mount up with wings as eagles; they shall
run, and not be weary; and they shall walk, and not faint.
—Isaiah 40:29–31

The year 2006 was filled with work and study. I had an examination and, while preparing for it, fell ill. The heavy workload and exam pressure were not the only stressors; my mother was sick, and my sister was diagnosed with a brain tumor, which only added to the already mounting stress. Then one morning I was jolted out of my sleep by an earache, pains in my head, and convulsions in my left leg—shattering any hope for further studies.

As the weeks progressed, reading and using the telephone became major challenges. Then, home on my back for six months, I experienced severe bouts of exhaustion and, sometimes, depression. I ate, showered, and listened to music at night when sleep eluded me. Quietness was my solace as I prayed, hoped, and waited for healing.

The song "God Will Make a Way" became my mantra. God was preparing me for what was to come: the loss of Mother in January 2007 and of my sister two years later. In fact, I lost seven family members over an eleven-month period. Talk about adversity! I paid several visits to Brother Job. Holy Writ says, "He was a truly good person, who respected God and refused to do evil" (Job 1:1, CEV). Though rich in family, livestock, and servants, Job was struck by Satan's attacks. He lost all his children and virtually all his earthly goods. When Job's wife saw his affliction, she told him to curse God and die. Yet Job never, for a moment, gave up on God. Instead he silently hoped, waited, and trusted God for deliverance. Solomon declares, "To every thing there is a season, and a time to every purpose under the heaven" (Ecclesiastes 3:1), while Job's response was "All the days of my appointed time will I wait, till my change come" (Job 14:14).

Whatever you are going through right now, just wait patiently for your "change" to come. Yes, your change will surely come in God's season and time. Keep your trust in God—no matter what.

That was Job's secret to being triumphant in adversity. Let that be your secret too.

Bula Rose Haughton Thompson

What to Do?

"Call to Me, and I will answer you,
and show you great and mighty things."
—*Jeremiah 33:3, NKJV*

It was Sabbath morning, and I was preparing to tell the children's story in church that day. I had a story prepared with lots of visual props to show the children. While quickly checking e-mail, I found a message from my friend Joyce way up north in Idaho. Recent cold weather caused the hot water line to her washing machine to freeze and burst—totally flooding one end of her house. The laundry room, kitchen, dining room, and living room had been inundated.

Her latest e-mail now shared how the disaster team had gotten the water out. However, everything was going to have to be replaced, even the kitchen cupboards, the walls, the carpeting, and the floor (also the ceiling over her basement). The work wouldn't be complete for about three months. Joyce had to camp out in her bedroom. Her spirits were good as she described how things were coming along. Joyce shared how, on Friday when the workmen arrived to clear the asbestos from the walls and ceiling, they told her they would have to work late that day in order to complete the job. If they did not get it done that day, they informed her, it would be two more weeks before they could return. Joyce replied that they would have to leave by five that afternoon because her Sabbath started shortly after that. The workmen just shook their heads and said there was no way. "I will pray that you can finish by five," she said.

During the course of the day, more workers showed up to help because they had run out of work on their site. By four o'clock (a whole hour before they needed to be finished), the asbestos insulation had been completely removed, and the cleanup was done!

Joyce had honored God by sharing her beliefs with those workmen, and God answered her prayer in a most remarkable way.

Reading her e-mail, I was impressed that morning to change my children's story from what I'd planned. Instead I would share about Joyce's experience. Not only did the children enjoy the story, but the adults did as well. Many prayers went up for Joyce that day.

Oh, Father God, help me to always be willing to stand up for the truth and to share what I believe with others. Amen.

Anna May Radke Waters

Abundant Life

I will arise and go to my father.
—Luke 15:18

The story of the prodigal son usually stresses the selfish attitude of one son or of the other. Recently, I revisited this story, paying attention to how it might relate to me.

As in that parable, my heavenly Father has given me an inheritance. Talents. Spiritual gifts. How will I use them? Will I use them for God, or will I use them up in selfish or worldly pursuits? We know that God-given talents and spiritual gifts can be hidden under a bushel (Matthew 5:15) instead of promoting the kingdom of God. And what about the gift of health? At birth, most of us are perfect and healthy—a God-given inheritance to be sure.

Unfortunately, health is easily squandered. We can do so by eating what God's Word has forbidden (such as fermented drink and unclean foods [see Leviticus 11]). At the other end of the spectrum, we can squander our health by not eating enough of what God provided as a healthy diet or by consuming too much of the things He allowed after the Flood to replace the herbs and fruits that had been washed away.

Another way to squander our health is by too many late nights and early mornings without enough sleep in between. Choosing not to exercise moderation in either work or play also contributes to the wasting away of one's health-inheritance. If we, like the prodigal son, squander our God-given health, we may end up having to live with the "pigs" of diabetes, heart disease, cancer, or chronic fatigue.

As with the prodigal, we too can "arise" and return to our heavenly Father, asking His help out of our bad habits and desperate situations. He will direct us to better health, showing us how to search out information about making positive lifestyle changes. He will give us the self-control we need to get back to the original plan He had for us when He first created humankind. As for not enough rest, God has already built in a weekly rest plan for us (Hebrews 4:1–8). He planned for us a weekly 24-hour period to rest *from* stressful daily work and rest *in* Him.

God's original plan was for us to live eternally. Why wait until we run out of health-inheritance? Our Father is waiting, watching for us to turn around and come back to Him for help. He is excited to accept His repentant prodigals and give them abundant life (John 10:10).

Beth Versteegh Odiyar

The Fragrance of Life

Now thanks be to God who always leads us in triumph in Christ, and through us diffuses the fragrance of His knowledge in every place. For we are to God the fragrance of Christ among those who are being saved and among those who are perishing. To the one we are the aroma of death leading to death, and to the other the aroma of life leading to life. And who is sufficient for these things?
—*2 Corinthians 2:14–16, NKJV*

Frequently God chooses to speak to us through His creation.

Once while watching bees buzzing around and enjoying the bright spring colors, my friend felt impressed to purchase some lemon-scented air refreshers for her home; the fragrance filled every part of her home.

Later, while I visited my friend, the lemon fragrance reminded me about another scent that long ago filled a different house. It happened the day Jesus Christ accepted an invitation from a Jewish leader to join him and his friends for a meal. The Scriptures tell this story:

> And when Jesus was in Bethany at the house of Simon the leper, a woman came to Him having an alabaster flask of very costly fragrant oil, and she poured it on His head as He sat at the table. But when His disciples saw it, they were indignant, saying, "Why this waste? For this fragrant oil might have been sold for much and given to the poor."
>
> But when Jesus was aware of it, He said to them, "Why do you trouble the woman? For she has done a good work for Me. For you have the poor with you always, but Me you do not have always. For in pouring this fragrant oil on My body, she did it for My burial. Assuredly, I say to you, wherever this gospel is preached in the whole world, what this woman has done will also be told as a memorial to her" (Matthew 26:6–13, NKJV).

It is absolutely wonderful to see God at work through nature, which points us back to Him.

How much more wonderful that God blessed an unselfish act done in His name so that it became part of the gospel story! Paul says that we too can be "the fragrance of Christ" among those who are perishing. Whom will you anoint today with the fragrance of God's love?

Yan Siew Ghiang

Communion Bread

"I am the bread of life. He who comes to Me shall never hunger."
—*John 6:35, NKJV*

With a long wooden pestle in a wooden mortar, I thumped wheat into gritty flour. Flour I needed—when it was my turn at this African mission station—to make unleavened Communion bread. Then with an old mission field hand-me-down recipe and a heavy wedding-gift rolling pin, I leaned over the narrow kitchen counter and smoothed the large clumps of flour-salt-peanut oil mixture into thin layers. A wayward grain of coarsely ground salt on my tongue activated salivary glands and made me anticipate the upcoming Communion experience.

My expectation grew as my oil-tipped fingers gently pushed the caramel-colored dough into corners of the cookie sheets. I anticipated my thumb and forefinger, twenty-four hours from then, grasping an earth-scented wafer from the serving platter. And I anticipated how, at the end of the sermon, its "wheaty" flavor would take the edge off my gnawing hunger. So I worked the dough and hoped I was making enough to service eight staff families and more than one hundred fifty students.

Every time I caught the sweet-pungent scent of moist wafer dough baking, phrases would float in and out of my mind: "I am the bread of life. He who comes to Me shall never hunger" (John 6:35, NKJV). "Take, eat: this is my body" (1 Corinthians 11:24). I'd wonder, *What does all that mean—really mean—for me in* everyday *life?* Beside my open Bible one chilly morning, the kerosene lantern cast new light on ancient words: "He who comes to Me shall never hunger." I read the words again. There it was—the simple, yet deep, answer to my longtime question!

Comes to Me. Communion bread is about fully opening up myself to relationship! "What food is to the body, Christ must be to the soul. . . . Christ is of no value to us if we do not know Him as a personal Saviour."* The symbol of the wafer is also about my spending time with Him throughout *each* day. It's about my approaching Him in prayerful meditation of His Word. It's about making subsequent wise choices as I expend the renewed, Bread-bestowed nourishment and energy into the nitty-gritty details of my everyday life.

Shall never hunger. The symbol of holy bread also promises that, in exchange for my opening of the heart, Jesus will satisfy my soul's deepest hunger. In close relationship. Always.

Carolyn Rathbun Sutton

* Ellen G. White, *The Desire of Ages* (Mountain View, CA: Pacific Press®, 1940), 389.

Purge Me With Hyssop

Purge me with hyssop, and I shall be clean:
wash me, and I shall be whiter than snow.
—*Psalm 51:7*

For a long time, this verse did not really register with me, until my husband and I lived in Coventry, England, for two years. He was studying for his master's degree, and I stayed at home with our three-month-old daughter. This was the first time I had used a washing machine to do my laundry; in my home country I did it all by hand.

In an effort to avoid damaging both the machine and the clothes, I was very careful to separate the clothes according to the washing instructions. Delicates. Whites. Colors. Woolens. I also diligently followed the temperature settings for each load. Sometimes I soaked my daughter's clothes in detergent before putting them in the machine.

One day as I was sorting my laundry, it dawned on me that God treats me just like I treat my laundry! Sometimes He recognizes that I'm in a delicate place and need a gentle spin. Other times, I've fallen so low I have to be washed at the hottest temperature. But all the time I realize that God wants me to come out clean after He's done with me. After the washing I may be hung in the shade, out of the direct sunlight. After all, He doesn't want me to lose my color. Sometimes God may even lay me flat to dry as I would my woolen things.

Afterward, He irons out the wrinkles with a cool iron or at the higher setting for linen. Always with the desire to make me the person He wants me to be. Always with the gentle care of the Master Cleaner. I needed to learn to wait patiently on Him as He worked to make me better, rather than complain and grumble. His ways of cleaning us up are full of purpose.

Thank You, Lord, for Your hyssop. Thank You for the washing machine. Wash me with hyssop and I will be clean.

Mukatimui Kalima-Munalula

Saturday Night in Jerusalem

"This will be a Sabbath day of complete rest for you,
and on that day you must deny yourselves. This day of rest
will begin at sundown on the ninth day of the month
and extend until sundown on the tenth day."
—*Leviticus 23:32, NLT*

When I read, "When the Sabbath was over, Mary Magdalene, Mary the mother of James, and Salome bought spices so that they might go to anoint Jesus' body" (Mark 16:1, NIV), I was surprised at the thought that stores would be open Saturday night. I wondered what Saturday night would have been like in Jerusalem or any other town or village in Israel.

When I was thirteen years old, our family moved to the little town of Goodrich, North Dakota. Saturday night was the biggest night of the week, when everyone—farmers, townspeople, kids—went to town. They might have been there to shop, or to meet friends and drive up and down the short little main street, but they were there. The stores were all open, the lights were on, and the town buzzed.

But what do you suppose Saturday night was like in Palestine? Did people count the hours and minutes until the sun went down so they could do what they had wanted to do all day and thereby miss the rest and benefit of the Sabbath? In Old Testament times there were three main issues about which the prophets warned: idol worship, keeping the Sabbath, and issues of justice and compassion. Well, the people got rid of their idols, made innumerable rules about keeping the Sabbath, and continued to ignore justice and mercy.

When Nehemiah returned to Jerusalem after a leave of absence, he discovered that the people were profaning the Sabbath once again. "Then I commanded that the gates of Jerusalem should be shut as darkness fell every Friday evening, not to be opened until the Sabbath ended" (Nehemiah 13:19, NLT). Then he discovered merchants "and sellers of all kinds of goods" (verse 20, NIV) waiting outside the walls for the Sabbath to end so they could enter the city; he threatened them with arrest (verse 21). But obviously Saturday night was a prime time for buying and selling.

I'm glad the stores were open for the two Marys and Salome; sometimes we imagine their world was entirely different from ours. But it wasn't—human nature has not changed. We need the risen Savior as much as they did, if not more!

Ardis Dick Stenbakken

What Are You Discussing?

He asked them, "What are you discussing together
as you walk along?" They stood still, their faces downcast.
—Luke 24:17, NIV

Sometimes when my heart is full of pain, I come to a stop and can't move on. The following Bible story—shared from the viewpoint of a participant— counsels me to share everything with Jesus, to take it to the Lord in prayer, so I can continue the journey with Him.

* * * * *

Our hope for the conquering Messiah has been dashed to pieces. How could we have misunderstood Jesus so completely? The women are clearly more distraught than we are and see illusions of an empty tomb and angels who claim Jesus lives. Steadily, we plod the road to Emmaus with our backs to Jerusalem, away from possibly seeing the risen Savior.

"What are you discussing?" asks another traveler. Cleopas halts abruptly. Seriously? Is this man the only visitor in Jerusalem who does not know? Sorrow overwhelms: for the loss of our dear friend Jesus, for the lost dreams of a restored Israel, for the lost time spent following the hoped-for Messiah.

Always the Shepherd, Jesus cannot bear to lose one sheep, so He searches for us, inviting us to share our hurts and fears. The stranger asks again, "What things?" Encouraged to rehearse the story, we resume the journey with him.

When Cain is troubled, the Lord comes to him and asks, "Why is your face downcast?" (Genesis 4:6, NIV). God wants us to unburden our hearts to Him. It gives Him permission to minister to us. The Lord counsels Cain, "Sin is crouching at your door; it desires to have you, but you must rule over it" (v. 7, NIV). The stranger focuses us on God's Word. He helps us master despondency, and we grow hopeful again. Scripture foretells of Jesus Messiah who dies to save. The dream is not dead; the Savior lives. The traveler appears to continue on his journey as we arrive home, but unwilling to be separated from his comforting presence, we beg him to enter in and break bread with us. Even if we don't see clearly, Jesus fully reveals Himself when we invite Him to be Master of our hearts, to be host at our table.

How do I channel this intimacy, this burning heart? Does it propel me along the road to the New Jerusalem? Do I breathlessly tell others that Jesus lives, that we have hope and a future? Or do I stay at home to savor the meal alone?

Rebecca Timon

Nothing but the Blood of Jesus

Forasmuch as ye know that ye were not redeemed with corruptible things . . . but with the precious blood of Christ.
—*1 Peter 1:18, 19*

Even now, I can see her in my mind's eye, a confident-looking teenager. She was intelligent, had great plans for the future, and appeared focused with a desire to excel. Gradually, however, my student's attendance at classes became very sporadic. I inquired, "What is the matter with you? I have not seen you very often in classes these days."

"I'm having some problems," was her answer. I told her I was concerned and she could talk to me. So Veron (not her real name) told me she was seeing figures on the walls in her room at night, and she was made uncomfortable by a strange presence. In addition, for inexplicable reasons, her knees would hurt and her feet would be unable to bear her up. Veron's "sightings" became more and more prevalent, and her attendance at classes less and less frequent.

One night while at prayer meeting, I heard what sounded to me like wails and screams coming from another part of the church building. My curiosity was aroused, and when the pastor said there was a young woman who was having some problems and had been brought to the meetings for special prayer, I realized it was my student. Immediately I left the main sanctuary and joined the prayer warriors, the first elder, and the pastor to pray for Veron.

When I entered the room, what I saw was a spectacle: a strong, Samson-like man sat on the floor attempting to hold the struggling, slimly built Veron, who was thrashing around uncontrollably, a menacing grimace on her face. Her wails and shrieks filled the room as individually we prayed for God to break the stronghold of the demons over this young woman. Each person interceded with God for deliverance. The mention of the blood of Jesus seemed to send the devil into a frenzy, and Veron would appear to pass out at each mention of covering by Jesus' blood.

We continued to pray. Invisibly the blood of Jesus was applied. Gradually the snarling and distorted facial expressions ceased until Veron became quiet and her stiff body became limp, a peaceful expression on her face. We continued to ask God to intervene, applying the blood of Jesus. The forces of darkness were put to flight. Veron then committed her life completely to Christ, and she had no more nightly visits from the devil. How precious is the blood of Jesus!

Hyacinth V. Caleb

April 18

Hummingbirds Versus Songbirds

"But whoever drinks the water I give them will never thirst.
Indeed, the water I give them will become in them
a spring of water welling up to eternal life."
—John 4:14, NIV

Each morning when I read my devotional, I sit in front of a large window that reveals our wooded backyard. My chair is positioned in the perfect spot to view an amazing variety of birds that come to my feeders.

One day nature brought me an insightful object lesson. I observed the tiniest ruby-throated hummingbird zoom in for a taste of the sugary nectar I had placed in one of the feeders. Just as he was ready to place his long, slender beak into the hole of the feeder, another hummingbird swooped in to get his share. There are four places on the feeder where hummingbirds can perch and enjoy, but those little fellows had to be territorial and fight it out! They fluttered and swooped and assertively chased each other for the next thirty minutes, never once partaking of the nectar that was available to them.

In comparison, I observed a frenzy of activity at my songbird feeder. What a variety of birds! Cardinals, nuthatches, chickadees, finches, sparrows, and even a large woodpecker. They either occupied the feeder at the same time or took turns. If the woodpecker took up too much room, the chickadees would get out of his way for a while and then return. The nuthatches would just move over and make room for the woodpecker. They all cooperated—coming and going or making room for one another. And they were all getting to enjoy their share of the feast. The hummingbirds, however, continued to exhibit a lesson in futility, spending their time and energy challenging each other—never once partaking of the life-sustaining nectar before them.

There are so many lessons in this observation of nature.

First, good comes through cooperation. No one wins if we become territorial and think only of ourselves.

Additionally, I couldn't help thinking that God has provided the gift of life for us through Jesus Christ. Are we going to partake of the living water He has provided for us? Or are we going to try to spend much of our lifetime defending our selfish ways? If we choose the latter, we will end up like those little hummingbirds. The "nectar" will be there for us, but we will not be nourished.

Bev Owen

God Listens to Us

" 'He will wipe every tear from their eyes.
There will be no more death' or mourning or crying or pain,
for the old order of things has passed away."
—*Revelation 21:4, NIV*

During my childhood, I was very attached to my father, who was a pastor and worked with evangelism. As an evangelist, he spent much time away from home, but when he came, every fifteen days, he would bring a treat for me and my siblings. That generated a lot of expectations.

In 2002 I went off to college. That year was very good with many blessings. But 2003 would hold a big surprise.

At first, everything was fine. During July, I went home and had pleasant moments with my family, but I soon had to return to school to continue my studies. Before I returned to school, my father proposed an idea to me. He asked me to pray early each morning and read from an inspirational book by Ellen G. White. At the same time each day, though we were apart, my father would also be in prayer and reading as well. I agreed to his proposal and began to read and pray each day at dawn when he did.

This arrangement, however, did not last long. In September of that same year, I received news that I never wanted to hear. My father had died of a massive heart attack.

That is when a most beautiful story between God and me began to unfold. My father had often said to me, "I will not always be with you, but the Father in heaven will always be with you."

And indeed it was so.

When I was told about the loss of my father, I literally felt a hug from God. He whispered in my ear, "The world can make you cry, but just cry out. I am here." This promise has stayed with me all the time.

God's miracles did not stop there; He enabled me to comfort my mother.

I am so grateful God and my father were such close friends. God knew I would suffer greatly, so He prepared me—through the words of my father. Now I await the big day when I will meet my father again and we will never have to be apart.

That can be our hope when we know God.

Rosângela Carniato Camargo de Oliveira

That Still, Small Voice

Be still, and know that I am God.
—*Psalm 46:10, NKJV*

My husband and I decided after our second child was born to move to Palm Bay, Florida, to be near my parents. However, he would remain in New York for a while to work so we could save up money to get our own home.

Soon I started my new job. Though my parents helped with the kids, I sometimes had to place the kids in daycare, which became very expensive. We decided to take the children (Sasha, two, and Ryan, twelve months) back to New York to stay with my husband and his mother for a time because his mother didn't work and could care for the children.

Our flight to New York was very stressful. Sasha threw up all over herself, and Ryan wouldn't stop crying and pulling on his ears. I thank God that the stewardess provided the help I needed. Finally we landed, and my husband was right there as soon as the plane door opened to help with the kids. When we arrived at the apartment building, I noticed that some of the apartments had guardrails at the windows. My mother-in-law's apartment on the thirteenth floor did not. A few days after we arrived, something happened that shook me to the core of my being.

I was on the phone in the kitchen when I clearly heard a voice in the room saying, "Turn slowly and look to the window." No one else was in the kitchen with me except the kids, yet that voice was very clear. I slowly turned to the window only to see that Ryan had climbed on to the windowsill of the unexpectedly open window, risking a possible thirteen-story fall! I slowly put down the phone and calmly walked over to the window so as not to startle him, and I safely lifted him down.

What if I had ignored the voice? What if I had screamed and rushed to the window, startling him? The voice I heard was a calm, clear voice that allowed me to react calmly.

Do you know *that* voice? Elijah on the mountain, while waiting for the Lord, thought He was in the strong wind, but no. God was not in the wind or in the earthquake that followed. Nor in the fire that followed that. The Lord manifested Himself to Elijah in a "still small voice" (1 Kings 19:12).

My sisters, I pray that you will hear that still, small Voice in your life, and when you hear it, you will know whose it is. Don't hesitate to respond to it.

Dorett Alleyne

The Master Artist

The foundations of the wall of the city
were adorned with all kinds of precious stones.
—*Revelation 21:19, NKJV*

The artist works vigorously with the stiff brush and sawdust to clean the linseed oil and flux from the intricate pieces of colored glass lying on the workbench. Lead and solder hold them together. She carefully raises the large panel perpendicularly to the bench and rests it there, brushing away all the particles that cling to it. Summoning extra strength, she lifts the panel in front of her and holds it toward the window where the sunlight is streaming in.

The light flows through her finished work and illuminates the myriad colors she has incorporated into this portrayal of Christ's second coming. Her heart rejoices at the beauty she could only imagine while the work still lay on the dark bench.

As the artist gazes at this new piece of artwork, she can't help comparing the process of the creation to what Jesus has done, and is still doing, in her life. She's been on the Master Artist's workbench for many years. She has felt the strain as He cut and chipped away at the broken pieces of her life to make them fit His perfect pattern. She has felt the burning heat as He drew all the pieces together and held them there with bonds not to be broken before cleaning away the remaining dross.

Studying her work, she can't help recounting the promises of the Master Artist to come, claim, and install in His own home the masterpiece on which He has lavished so much loving care. She remembers the description of this place where she will soon be taken. Walls of jasper. Twelve foundations, each made of a different precious stone, with the light from within shining through with untold brilliance. Beauty beyond the wildest imagination. Then it occurs to the artist that the reason the Master Artist is so qualified and adept at His work is that He once lay on the bench in the workshop Himself. He endured the cutting and burning process, even to the point of death. He knows what is required to bring forth a perfect work of unparalleled beauty.

As the artist thinks on this, her heart is broken and amazed at the love the Master Artist has poured into His work. *Oh, Jesus, forgive me for the resistance I show sometimes to Your artisanship. Thank You for Your loving patience. Amen.*

Sylvia Stark

Jesus With Skin On

*"The king will answer, 'Whenever you did it for any of my people,
no matter how unimportant they seemed, you did it for me.' "*
—Matthew 25:40, CEV

My daughter Rachel has a compassionate heart. She attracts the downtrodden at her school the way some people attract stray animals. They seem to sense that in her they will find a champion. Almost every afternoon she's got some kid in tow who needs a ride somewhere. One of her friends even called her for a ride late one night when he was wandering around intoxicated in the freezing cold. Rachel doesn't have her license, so all the lifts she gives her friends are via me, her father, or her brother. One evening her friend Zach called her and asked if she could give him a lift home from work because he had a migraine and didn't feel like walking home in the cold. I was still working so I told her to ask her brother. When no flurry of activity ensued, I tracked her down and asked what her brother had said. "He won't do it," she told me, "and I don't have any money to pay him to do it, either."

I like to think she was exaggerating. I hope my son isn't quite that mercenary, but I didn't have the energy to find out, so I simply told her to get her coat and we'd go give her friend a lift. On the way home after our good deed, Zach texted her saying, "I don't believe in God, but God bless you folks. It was really nice of you to give me a ride home." I jokingly told Rachel to text him back asking, "Who do you think sent us?"

I used to believe that a good deed wasn't worth doing or a conversation worth having if it didn't somehow hammer in the gospel message. Yet the truth is, every act of kindness, every listening moment, every expression of sympathy and caring *is* the gospel message. We don't have to find a way to wedge Jesus into acts of outreach—He's already there, in us. When we do anything to help someone else, we are Jesus with skin on to them, representing Jesus to them in a way they can see, hear, and touch. Even the most hardhearted person responds to Jesus at some level because even the demon possessed recognize Him.

We never mentioned God to Zach, yet his thoughts obviously went to God as a response to our act of kindness. God will never waste an opportunity to reach any soul; through every word and act, let's give Him as many as we possibly can.

Céleste Perrino-Walker

Redeeming the Time

And I will restore to you the years that the locust hath eaten.
—*Joel 2:25*

Nowadays Michael can be found at his grandma's house. Anything he can do to help around the house he willingly does. He takes her shopping, he takes out the trash. He does small repair jobs for her. I sometimes find myself getting a little jealous. Michael spends most of his holidays with his grandmother.

There was a time when Michael thought only of himself. He spent most of his life from his fourteenth to his twenty-eighth year in juvenile correction and prison. Year after year he got into trouble.

For many years Michael's grandma didn't get to see him. This was hard on her. She loved her grandson very much, and she always loved it when both Michael and his little brother could spend summer vacation and holidays with her.

As a family we prayed together, trusting God that when Michael did get released from prison he would have a change of mind and accept God as his personal Savior.

Many years later Michael finally did get released from prison. He was now a grown man. His little brother was a young man now. His baby sisters were teenagers, and his grandmother was now eighty-five years old and had Parkinson's disease. Even though Michael missed so many years being with his family, God redeemed the time for him, restoring all the time that he'd not had with his grandmother and family. Michael has given his life to God; he is in school and working. The relationship between him and his grandmother is better than it has ever been.

The Word of God tells us He will restore what the devil has stolen from us (Joel 2:25). As with Israel of old, God heard the prayers of Michael's grandmother and of his family that prayed every night. God saw the tears Michael's mother cried. God knew the hurt his family was going through. God said, "For I know the thoughts that I think toward you . . . , thoughts of peace, and not of evil" (Jeremiah 29:11).

Let's thank God that He redeems the lost years for those who call upon His name.

Avis Floyd Jackson

Behind the Appearance

"You are masters at making yourselves look good in front of others,
but God knows what's behind the appearance."
—*Luke 16:15*, The Message

During the summer months, Mark, a young college student majoring in computer information systems, was hired to assist our departmental support staff with various projects. He was assigned a workspace near me, one primarily set up for someone who needed to make a few phone calls or to have a quiet spot to work in for a short while.

Considering Mark's training and exposure to the latest technologies, he must have been surprised, even disappointed, with the nine-year-old desktop computer in his workspace. Often the computer would suddenly shut down. Mark patiently restarted it each time and even did some troubleshooting, building on his professional skills.

One day he casually mentioned he could rebuild the computer. I was impressed. He was knowledgeable, conscientious, and dependable—a great worker. Still, I could imagine frustration with the computer when trying to do the work requested.

I brought up the issue of the malfunctioning old computer to administration. After all, we had all-in-one computers barely two years old. Within days a newer loaner computer was delivered, an all-in-one! Personnel in the technical support department soon realized, however, that this computer also had problems. After many calls for assistance, one techie took the computer to work on it. An hour later it was returned, the problem solved.

"Is it the same computer?" I asked Mark later that day.

"I don't know," he responded. "It looks the same on the outside; maybe the inside is different. Something could have been swapped out."

The computer was now working well.

What about us? Do we, like some computers, look pretty good on the outside but have something terribly wrong inside? Do we seem OK, but something within is defective? What will it take for us to function properly? Thankfully, our Lord knows what's behind our appearances. He can reboot us as needed or rebuild us again in His likeness. May we allow His Spirit to work in us daily so we will always be what is pleasing to Him and to others.

Iris L. Kitching

The Red Mark

*"For though you wash yourself with lye, and use much soap,
Yet your iniquity is marked before Me," says the Lord God.
—Jeremiah 2:22, NKJV*

One night a few years ago, after arriving home from a dinner party, I discovered a red mark on the front of my lovely white shirt—probably from some of the food I had consumed. I quickly soaked the shirt in cold soapy water. However, two hours later the stain was still there. I decided to soak it in very hot soapy water overnight. The following morning I rushed to the bathroom hoping to see my shirt free of the stain. The stubborn stain was still there. I then remembered I had stain remover somewhere in the house. I sprayed the solution on the stain, and then again soaked it in hot soapy water. After a few hours I looked, and the stain was gone. I was so happy but regretted that I had not thought of the stain remover before wasting a lot of time.

That's what we do with sin. We may have a relationship with the Lord, but there may still be bad attributes that we hold on to—such as anger, jealousy, an unforgiving attitude, arrogance, or stealing small things at work. Our sins may include ingratitude, arguing, being a bit cruel or hard to please. The list can go on and on. In our hearts we know that's not what God desires in us. Each time we behave badly we promise ourselves we will not do it again, but a few days down the line, we burst into a fit of anger, become arrogant, or vow not to forgive someone.

Sin, like the stubborn stain on my shirt, needs something stronger than our willpower to purge it from our lives. Let us always remember what Paul wrote: "For the good that I will to do, I do not do; but the evil I will not to do, that I practice" (Romans 7:19, NKJV). There is a force within us that wants to do good, but poor choices often prevail because our nature is sinful. David recognized this reality when he wrote, "Behold, I was brought forth in iniquity, and in sin my mother conceived me" (Psalm 51:5, NKJV).

Most marks that we place on ourselves—whether makeup or dirt stains from working outside—we can wash off. However, only Jesus can remove the stains arising from our sinful natures with which we were born.

Let us ask God to forgive our sins and to change us. Only His blood can remove the stains from our hearts. He is waiting to hear from us.

Peggy S. Rusike Edden

The God of Physics and Beauty

Dost thou know the balancings of the clouds,
the wondrous works of him which is perfect in knowledge?
—Job 37:16

And the foundations of the wall of the city were garnished
with all manner of precious stones. The first foundation was jasper;
the second, sapphire; the third, a chalcedony; the fourth, an emerald;
the fifth, sardonyx; the sixth, sardius; the seventh, chrysolyte;
the eighth, beryl; the ninth, a topaz; the tenth, a chrysoprasus;
the eleventh, a jacinth; the twelfth, an amethyst.
—Revelation 21:19, 20.

Whenever someone asks me about my job, I respond, "I teach physics." I often receive, in response, a puzzled look, as in, "How can you like that subject, so full of boring laws and regulations?" But now I ask you, have you ever considered that without these laws, we would not be here on planet Earth? We'd simply fly around without touching the ground, since the law of gravity would not exist. However, God created this law during the Creation week (Genesis 1), along with all the others needed for order and structure with the sole purpose of ruling our existence. Not even one tiny essential detail was left out of this process.

Amazingly, our God of laws (as studied in physics) is also our God who loves array and aesthetics. Simply put, He also created—and loves—beauty. He took time to form the first woman, Eve, and made her exceedingly beautiful, designing every inch of her body. God's love of beauty was evident throughout sacred history in the high priest's breastplate (Exodus 28:17–20) and in Solomon's temple, so full of beauty and splendor. And our ultimate place to worship Him for eternity will also be in the midst of gold, gemstones and geometry, brilliance, and beauty!

I'm looking forward to heaven, where we'll worship God in the midst of precious stones. I'll learn new laws of physics while basking in the beauty of the New Jerusalem. I try to imagine the twelve gemstones of the Holy City's foundation, each one of a different color.

And physics will explain the perfection that we are seeing and enjoying with Him, our God of beauty, order, symmetry, and loving laws.

Will you not join me in worshiping Him? For only He is worthy to receive glory, honor, praise, blessings, wisdom, strength, and power! Amen! See you there!

Marli Ritter-Hein

A Lesson From Noah

Like as a father pitieth his children,
so the LORD pitieth them that fear him.
—*Psalm 103:13*

It had been a good weekend spending time with my middle son, Norris; his wife, Kimberly; and my two grandchildren, Noah (one and a half) and Gianna (nine months). Together we'd gone "bye-bye" to church, to the children's water park, and to the riverfront fireworks display ("let's go bye-bye to see the big lights"). Now it was time for us, the doting grandparents, to make the long drive from Ohio back home to North Carolina. The distance in my mind seemed to stretch even farther than the actual distance because I was leaving my family once again.

I noticed little Noah watching as his father prayed for our trip to be safe. I wondered what was in my grandson's mind. Was he wondering, *Another good-bye? Another adventure? Another trip?* After the prayer he grasped *his* two one-dollar bills that Great-grandmother Hughes had sent for his second birthday. He grabbed his little diaper bag. Next he took my hand and placed it on the doorknob. This little man wanted to go bye-bye too.

All the grownups smiled to see such an independent streak. Was he planning on going bye-bye to North Carolina, or was he planning on just leaving home with his essentials? I turned the doorknob and followed him out the front door. Noah did not walk toward our Ford truck. Instead he headed straight toward his non-motorized red wagon (complete with a door that opened). He resolutely put his dollar bills on the wagon seat, put his diaper bag on top of the money, opened the wagon door, got in, and sat down. "I guess I'll have to pull him somewhere," said his father, exchanging amused glances with us. And that is just what happened. As we drove away from our amazing family, we saw our dutiful son, Noah's father, pulling the wagon up the street on the sidewalk as Noah went "bye-bye."

That incident reminded me of our total dependence on our heavenly Father even when we don't realize it. We have our own jobs, money, vehicles, and personal items. Yet we are as dependent on God for guidance and direction as my grandson was dependent on his earthly father just to move the wagon. Let us not forget our dependence on our loving heavenly Father. He will never guide us wrong and will constantly be with us to lead if we let Him. He is coming one day to take us to that final "bye-bye" destination—to heaven and eternal life.

Charlotte Verrett

You Are More Valuable Than Sparrows

"Are not two sparrows sold for a penny?
Yet not one of them will fall to the ground outside your Father's care.
And even the very hairs of your head are all numbered.
So don't be afraid; you are worth more than many sparrows."
—Matthew 10:29–31, NIV

From his bedroom window, I watched my grandson Nikolas get on the school bus for what would be his last school bus ride in Lisle, Illinois. He and his mom were moving away to sunny California. She had invited her dad and me to assist with the transition. I was happy for her new job but not the relocation so far away. As I stood gazing out his window, I reminisced about the years Nikolas had spent with neighbors, church family, and friends. He would leave them all behind. Suddenly my attention was drawn to the nearby pond on which two ducks were cruising nonchalantly in the water without a single care in the world. As they swam back and forth, a ripple effect flowed out to the edge of the pond. I watched as the process repeated itself. In the trees nearby, two little birds chirped their springtime melodies of praise to God. Looking further, I saw an animal swimming in the pond, seeming to enjoy the serenity of the moment.

Right before my eyes were God's creatures going about their business without a concern about what they would eat or where they would sleep.

On the contrary, I was overwhelmed by worry, fear, sadness, and many questions bombarding my mind about Nikolas' future and new neighborhood. Would he find a Christian school? Would he be in a church that would help develop his character? Would he adjust to this transition? My main concern was how far away he was moving—our future visits would be much less frequent.

I felt God had wanted me to linger at Nikolas's bedroom window for a reason: to catch a glimpse of His creatures enjoying their beautiful surroundings without worrying about anything. Every day they go about their work, flying here and there without a thought that they might fall to the ground or be eaten by the neighbor's cat lurking stealthily in the bush.

It was then that I recalled the Bible verse about the sparrows. If God cares for little birds, how much more He loves and cares for my family and me. We are of much more value to Him than little birds.

Shirley C. Iheanacho

Not Good Enough—God's Enough

Trust in the LORD with all your heart and
lean not on your own understanding.
—*Proverbs 3:5, NIV*

Awonderful university in Tennessee was robbing me of my firstborn. My precious boy had grown up, and it was time for him to leave our Florida home.

It was a bittersweet time for me. I was proud of the young man that he'd become, and I was excited that he was ready for college.

However, somewhere deep in my heart, some troubling questions tugged at me. *Did I love this child enough? Have we said all there is between mom and son? Does he know that life had never been sweeter until his first smile lodged in my heart?* I had many questions and a few regrets.

I could have praised him more and criticized him less. I shouted his mistakes while I whispered his successes. My only son was leaving, and there were things I needed to say.

We drove to his favorite Mexican restaurant, just the two of us. I used that time alone with him to chat, as we'd done many times before. I told him that he was my miracle, a gift from God.

Then I apologized for not having always been the best mom.

Before I could continue, my child reached out for my hand and said, "You've done great, Mom. We are all right!"

I needed to hear that. My precious young man was all right. He was kind, honest, and godly. I had not been good enough as a mom, but God's grace had been more than enough.

I can't comprehend how God was able to turn a tiny boy into a strong man in spite of my mistakes, but I don't have to understand. I simply have to trust that the Master Craftsman has been—and is—shaping my child into a man of God.

This fact is good enough. It's not my "enough" but, rather, God's "enough."

Dear Lord, today my prayer is for the young mother who struggles to grow her children. I pray as well for the older mom who wishes she could go back to do it over again. Please remind these precious women that Your perfection covers their blunders. Remind them that Your grace is more than enough for their children. Amen.

Rose Joseph Thomas

Grace—Not Coupons!

For the grace of God has been revealed,
bringing salvation to all people.
—*Titus 2:11, NLT*

Because of his grace he declared us righteous and gave us
confidence that we will inherit eternal life.
—*Titus 3:7, NLT*

My favorite department store featured an outstanding sale one weekend, and I was lured by the advertisements. When I got to the store on Sunday afternoon, the last few hours of the sale, I was pleased that there were still shoes on sale in the size and style I needed.

Upon paying for my treasures, I noticed my store receipt showed that if I came back the next weekend, I could save even more money. So that's what I did. However, I didn't focus on the date of this second sale, so when I got to the store, I discovered I was a day early.

Naturally, I went back the next day and found more bargains.

On my store receipt this time was *another* worthwhile sale scheduled to be in effect in a few days. I thought, *This is enough. No more sale shopping—right now.*

All during this time I was carrying sale coupons in my car for specific grocery store items. I let one or two expire but took advantage of a couple more. Every time I pay for something at that store, there is also a coupon attached to my cash register receipt. Sometimes the coupon is for more of the same items I have just purchased. Other times the coupon is for something I don't need or want. Often I have to evaluate the coupon, which is usually a name brand item, against the price of a generic version of the same product.

The store is trying to hook me, so I have to shop carefully.

In addition, offers for a myriad of goods and services arrive in my mailbox. Should I switch brands or places to shop and take advantage of these new bargains? By the time one considers the bottom line cost and the effort made to make the changes, there really is no cost savings. I've learned I must read fine print and the "exceptions" very carefully.

Oh, how thankful I am for God's grace! It isn't valid on only certain days of the week or for certain hours of a day. God's grace doesn't expire. I don't have to keep a file of the conditions under which His grace is effective. For in the words of that old hymn, God's grace is truly greater "than all our sin" (Julia H. Johnston, 1910).

Barbara Huff

Let's Have a Bible Study

Study to shew thyself approved unto God, a workman that needeth
not to be ashamed, rightly dividing the word of truth.
—*2 Timothy 2:15*

One of the things I disliked most about school was studying for an exam—usually because I left all my studying for right before the exam. You can imagine the pain and distress of trying to fill my head with a semester of schoolwork in a few nights. And therein lies the reason I disliked studying. I tried to do too much in too short a period of time.

Experience and some wisdom eventually taught me that in order to succeed, and remember what I learned, I needed to do a bit at a time. Each evening I needed to take time to go over what I had learned in school that day. By the end of the semester I had already learned most of what was taught and needed only to revise the work for things to flow back into my mind.

Is it the same with God's Word? Truthfully, there was a time in my life when going to a Bible study group was a nightmare for me. I always found I did not know what people were talking about. My knowledge of the Bible was very limited.

How could that be when I had grown up in the church, attended every evangelistic meeting my church planned, studied my Bible study guides each week (well, I tried to read it all on Friday evenings), and learned long passages of scripture while attending our church youth program through the years? Yet I still found myself limited in my knowledge of the Word of God.

This frustrated me because the Bible seemed so big and like too much to study until I remembered: a bit at a time. So rather than putting the Bible aside because of my frustration at how little I knew of what there was to know, I began to read a bit at a time. As the years have passed, my knowledge of God's Word has improved. I would not call myself a Bible scholar, but I know so much more than I did ten years ago, five years ago, or even one year ago.

Don't be discouraged by how much there is to know in God's Word. Remember, it's divided into books, chapters, and verses. Take a bit at a time and depend on the Holy Spirit to teach you and strengthen you as your knowledge grows.

The day will come when we will be tested. I want to pass. What about you?

Heather-Dawn Small

In Desperate Need of Oil

"Be filled with the Holy Spirit."
—*Acts 9:17, NKJV*

I bought my first sewing machine about ten years ago, and yet, I remain a novice sewer, and I am afraid that the occasional work I produce testifies to that sad reality.

My sewing takes place in fits and starts—as time and creativity allow. After having moved house and everything that goes with it recently, I decided to make a small article of clothing for my daughter. So, I dusted off the fairly newly purchased sewing machine (which sewed so beautifully in the store). I am not very good at following patterns, so I decided to create my own masterpiece, with a few hints here and there. I could hardly wait to start and complete the project—quickly. It was going to be a piece of cake. My fabric was cut and ready, and my sewing machine and instructions were ready to go! Or so I thought.

For some reason, this fairly new (and fairly expensive) sewing machine refused to cooperate with me. It did not produce the results I wanted. The thread kept breaking! I changed the needle, changed the thread, changed the tension, and re-threaded (more than once). Still, the thread remained unmanageable! All the while, I heard a noise that did not sound quite right.

A tiny voice reminded me that the machine probably needed some oil. No, I didn't feel like oiling the machine. That would take too long. I was afraid I would not put the parts back properly; I had a project to complete. I would fix it the way I knew how! Besides, a constantly breaking thread had nothing to do with oil, right?

Cluck-cluck-cluck, then *snap!* Not again! OK, against my "better" judgment I decided to oil the machine. I didn't expect it to fix the problem, though.

I applied the oil; then, ah, the machine operated so smoothly! No more strange sounds. No more broken thread. I never would have thought that oil could make such a difference!

Lord, I have so much to learn! I am sorry for assuming, time and time again, that I have a better way. Forgive me for trying to operate without the oil of the Holy Spirit. Without You, Lord, I sputter and struggle, and I often snap. Help me to be filled and be led by Your Holy Spirit today. I really need You! I do! Amen.

Belinda Solomon

God's Faithfulness

Praise the LORD, all you nations; extol him, all you peoples.
For great is his love toward us,
and the faithfulness of the LORD endures forever.
Praise the LORD.
—*Psalm 117:1, 2, NIV*

In 1993, the United States went into an economic recession, which affected hospitals and health care systems. Middle management positions were realigned, and people holding those positions were laid off as various departments downsized and streamlined. At the same time, hospitals froze the hiring of nurses, making it difficult to get a job. I was an employee in middle management and was laid off. Losing my job created uncertainty in our family because we had children in a Christian school and our oldest daughter was in college.

In desperation, I pleaded with my husband to get a second job. Instantly the telephone rang. As soon as I picked up the receiver and said hello, someone at the other end of the line asked, "Is this Edna?"

"Yes," I affirmed.

The person continued, "I am dean of the Department of Nursing at Victor Valley College. You were recommended by the dean of the San Bernardino Valley College. We need your expertise in pediatrics very badly. Can you come right now? We will wait for you." *Was I hearing correctly?* I wondered.

I agreed to drive to the college, almost forgetting that an accident a few months back had made me afraid of freeway driving. Fortunately, my oldest daughter was home from school and gladly agreed to drive me to the college.

My daughter and I were amazed to discover both the dean and her assistant anxiously awaiting my arrival. Without much ado, they offered me a job! This job sustained the education of my daughter until she finished a bachelor of science in nursing at Southwestern Adventist University. Great is God's faithfulness!

God promises in Malachi 3:10 that if we will test His faithfulness, He will pour out blessings beyond measure. Have you tested His faithfulness? He will fulfill His promise in Isaiah 65:24: "Before they call I will answer; while they are still speaking I will hear" (NIV).

Even as unworthy as we are to receive His mercy, grace, and faithfulness, He notices every tear that drops from our eyes. Because He is worthy to be praised, we can give Him honor and glory, for His love, mercy, and faithfulness endure forever.

Edna Bacate-Domingo

Helen's Hope

" 'He has sent Me to heal the brokenhearted,
To proclaim liberty to the captives
And recovery of sight to the blind,
To set at liberty those who are oppressed;
To proclaim the acceptable year of the LORD.' "
—*Luke 4:18, 19, NKJV*

Helen was admitted to the hospital on my shift. After assessing her needs, I explained the medications and tests that would be required. Her response was gentle, and she was clearly grateful. I sensed something special about her and her husband, Neville. By the next morning the medications were having their effect and Helen was ready to go home. As I discharged her, she proudly announced that she had not smoked for two days!

My passion for lifestyle medicine was aroused. Because they both smoked, I asked Helen and Neville for permission to help them both quit, and they immediately agreed. I spent about half an hour with them. They were so grateful and expressed how empowered they felt by this new understanding. Helen said, "I wish I had videotaped your advice, to share with my friends and family!"

"Well," I explained, "I have hosted a series of four episodes on quitting smoking that you can watch—video-on-demand. Perhaps that will suffice?" They were both excited as I explained how to access it via the Internet and how to find the Hope Channel. Helen deduced that if I worked for a Christian network, then I must be a Christian. We suddenly and joyfully realized that the "something special" we had all sensed about one another was that we were all believers. They accepted my offer to pray with them, and forming a small circle, we claimed the promise that "with God *all* things are possible" (Matthew 19:26; emphasis added), acknowledging that above all things, God's wish for Helen and Neville was for them to "prosper and be in health" (3 John 2). Their faith strengthened as they realized Heaven was on their side in the battle ahead!

As I rose from prayer, I became aware that the patients in the other three hospital beds in Helen's room had quieted, possibly listening through the flimsy curtain that separated us. Already Helen's new hope was witnessing to others. My ongoing prayer for Helen and Neville is not just that they gain victory over nicotine but that their lives will be transformed by truth that will radiate to the rest of their family.

Nerida McKibben

Peace That Passes All Understanding

Peace I leave with you, my peace I give unto you:
not as the world giveth, give I unto you.
Let not your heart be troubled, neither let it be afraid.
—John 14:27

For a long time, one of my wisdom teeth had a cavity that the dentist filled and refilled. After nearly four years of my babysitting this troublesome molar, part of it broke off. I still wasn't convinced that the remaining part had to be taken out. I strongly believed there was an alternative to extracting it. I prayed hard for God to reveal that alternative. By the time I was in the last trimester of pregnancy with our second baby, nothing could calm the pain of the toothache. I resolved to have it worked on after the baby came.

After the baby came, I still lingered in my decision to remove the tooth. In fact, I begged one dentist to fill it even though I knew that was not the solution. She complied. The filling settled next to a nerve that caused more severe pain. I rushed back, begging the dentist to remove the tooth. To my shock, she told me she was not authorized to remove it. I visited several dentists only to learn I had a special kind of wisdom tooth requiring a surgical extraction—a surgery that would involve cutting into the jawbone to reach the roots growing sideways.

The dental specialist explained the possible side effects. I could be numb for six months. The injection to relieve pain could interfere with breastfeeding. In fear, I began to cry, insisting, "I don't think I'm ready." The doctor agreed. I went home with my infected wisdom tooth but with an upcoming appointment to extract it.

Again I prayed for a miracle, but this time I begged God for peace and His presence if I must indeed go through with the surgery.

The day of the surgery my family and friends were praying for me. I knew God would answer all those prayers.

The surgery was difficult, but I had so much peace knowing the Lord was with me. And, yes, the surgery was a success.

Do you need peace for a distressing situation in your life? Go to the Peacegiver and ask. And "the peace of God, which surpasses all understanding, will guard your hearts and minds through Christ Jesus" (Philippians 4:7, NKJV).

Lynn Mfuru Lukwaro

Going Places

"Let not your heart be troubled; you believe in God, believe also in Me. In My Father's house are many mansions; if it were not so, I would have told you. I go to prepare a place for you. And if I go and prepare a place for you, I will come again and receive you to Myself; that where I am, there you may be also."
—John 14:1–3, NKJV

Don't you love to go places you've never been before? Traveling can be a lot of fun, and sometimes you never know when or where you might go or what you will find, especially if you travel by car as my husband and I do.

I lived in Texas most of my life. I am a Texan, and I love it. It's a great place to live. I never thought I would leave it to move to another state.

Then I married Frank.

Frank was raised in Texas. He knows what a great state it is. But for many, many years he had lived in Idaho. Frank did not want to move back to Texas. Guess who had to move? None of my friends could believe I would do such a thing.

"What? Move from Texas to Idaho? No way." But I did.

Since my move to Idaho, Frank and I have traveled to a lot of places and states I had never been to before. New mountains, valleys, lakes, birds, and wildlife. It's been quite a wonderful and exciting experience.

We have another trip planned too. It's to a place we've never been before but have been anticipating for a long, long time. We've heard a lot of good things about this place. But this trip will be different, for we aren't going to take anything with us. We're not even going to drive the car. On this special trip we are going to fly. This time we're going to heaven!

We will be going places and seeing things we've never seen or experienced. From what we have read about heaven, it will outshine all the breathtaking scenery that impressed us so much down here. Up there we plan to do a lot more traveling. That is where we will make our home. And we are excited.

Moving again—this time to heaven, and it seems we cannot wait. We're longing to enter the city's pearly gates. Why not make plans to go with us!

Donna Sherrill Lewis

A Curve in the Road

For our light affliction, which is but for a moment, is working for us
a far more exceeding *and* eternal weight of glory.
— *2 Corinthians 4:17, NKJV*

On August 24, 2014, at 3:20 A.M., Napa, California, experienced a 6.0 earthquake. The quake was felt for many miles around, including our little village of Angwin, which sits on Howell Mountain. After the shaking was over, we settled back down in bed thinking that all was well again. At 8:30 that morning, as we'd previously planned, we left on a camping trip up north.

That afternoon when we got settled in an RV (recreational vehicle) park, I checked our voicemail on our cell phone. Our renter had called to say that what little water he was getting from our well was brown. He wondered if he should get someone to check our pump. We soon learned the quake had disturbed the sediment in hundreds of wells. We were told to wait till the dirt settled again and the water cleared. That meant getting bottled water for drinking.

On arriving home I talked to someone who told me where we could get good, constantly running spring water from a pipe—free. It was located next to a road near the top of our hill just a couple of miles away at a curve in the road. My husband and I set off to find it. After going down the hill about halfway and not seeing the pipe, we turned and headed back up the hill.

Suddenly, there it was—the water pipe next to a curve in the road. We had missed it coming downhill because the pipe was just around the sharp curve. We had focused our eyes on the road ahead instead of watching for details along the way.

Days later I was thinking about this experience. In life's pursuits, we have our plans, goals, objectives, and hopes in mind. We think we know where we're going and what we're going to do. Yet life doesn't always happen according to our expectations. We don't always clearly notice the bends in the roads because we're focused on what lies ahead. So we pass by important details. However, as time passes, we can look back over the roads we've traveled and, with God's help, gain a clearer perspective concerning the possible need to turn around and go in a different direction to fulfill His purposes. God is good at helping us reassess our journeys. We can trust the Lord to sustain us through every curve in life's road.

He promised, "I am with you always, even to the end" (Matthew 28:20, NKJV).

Donna Voth

Misty

The Lord God hath given me the tongue of the learned, that I should
know how to speak a word in season to him that is weary:
he wakeneth morning by morning,
he wakeneth mine ear to hear as the learned.
—Isaiah 50:4

I hurried down the school hallway, anxious to get started on the day's drug testing for the school bus drivers. A young woman sat patiently outside the doorway of the room we would use for testing.

"Good morning! Are you ready to use the bathroom?" I asked her.

"I just had a Coke, so I think I'll try and go," she responded.

Unfortunately, the Coke had not provided adequate hydration. "Why don't you get a couple bottles of water, and then you should be able to use the bathroom."

Her response was not favorable, as she did not like to drink water. Misty proceeded to tell me how she had been sick with an upper respiratory infection but had little money for physician care. While I was encouraging her and sharing ways she could combat her infection by drinking more water, she interjected that she was also a smoker. We were discussing tobacco cessation when she began to share about some of her life stressors. "Do you remember about a year ago when a young boy stabbed his mother to death?" she asked me. "That was my aunt, and I was the one that found her." Her eyes began to tear up as she related more. "This all brings back memories of abuse by my father. I feel my aunt's spirit is trying to tell me something." Praying for divine guidance, I reassured her of God's willingness to help us when we ask for His help. I asked her if she'd mind my praying with her. She readily agreed. Wrapping our arms around each other, I prayed earnestly for God to protect her from Satan's assaults and to strengthen her in all the ways she needed. With tears running down her cheeks, she thanked me before leaving.

A random drug test was where God fulfilled His promise from my earlier time with Him that morning. The promise was that I would "know how to speak a word in season" to a weary soul and to offer comfort. If we neglect spending time with God each day, we may miss the blessing we need in order to help those with pain and need in their lives. When we do take time with Him, however, He will teach and equip any of us to hear Him and then speak as the learned.

Sandi B. Cook

Persevering Potter

So I went down to the potter's house,
and I saw him working at the wheel.
—Jeremiah 18:3, NIV

I have admired many a handmade clay pot. They remind me of the Bible's illustration comparing us to wet, unformed clay—and to Christ as our persevering potter.

As with Israel of old, how continually we need to submit to the hands of the heavenly Potter! In order to form character in each work of clay, Christ presses, flattens, and molds. This process often causes us pain that we sometimes don't understand. Yet, with care, Jesus continues forming each one of us according to the aim and purpose He has determined for our lives. He is imprinting us with His own character, forming us into vessels of honor that will bring praise and glory to Him.

Have you ever seen a potter work? As a dedicated sculptor, the potter focuses untiringly and perseveringly on the work he or she is shaping. The potter puts the clay on the potter's wheel, keeping his or her hands on the unformed lump. Without the potter's hands on the clay, it could never be anything other than a shapeless lump. However, our loving Creator not only forms us; He also brings His life into our lifeless being. We become vessels shaped by love and care. He brings us into fellowship, and we please Him as we submit to the formation process.

Unlike a human potter working a lump of clay for just a short period of time, the heavenly Potter keeps His hands on us for a lifetime. What perseverance! We partake of His life through the daily reading of His Word. Through frequent prayer we realize how dependent we are on Him for everything we are and everything we do. For without Him, we truly can do nothing (John 15:5).

What should delight our hearts is that the heavenly Potter does not give up on us, even when we don't allow Him to form us as quickly as He would like to. And during those seasons when the human clay—our hearts—might grow hard, Jesus still patiently works, refreshing and softening the brittle human vessel with the oil of forgiveness and grace. Do not look at yourself today. You are still a clay pot in the making. Rather, look at God, the persevering and perfect Potter. Each time we submit to Him, He forgives the sins of our past and begins forming us anew. And in His hands we become living vessels for His honor and glory.

Maria Raimunda Lopes Costa

Answered Prayer, Big and Little

Pray for each other.
—James 5:16, NIV

My most memorable answer to prayer occurred many years ago.

A friend in college informed me that she dearly wanted to go on a particular mission trip. The cost of the trip would be two thousand dollars, which I knew she didn't have. Nor did I. The Lord impressed me to pray for her.

As I prayed, I felt that God would make a way for her if I asked some of my wealthy family members for their help. So I chose four of them and prayerfully wrote letters, asking each one if they would be willing to contribute $500 apiece. Three of them responded positively, and others gave all but the last $125 of the needed sum. The deadline drew near for the money to be turned in. At the last moment the remaining $125 arrived in the mail—unsolicited! My friend's trip was a great success and very worthwhile. That was a big answer to prayer.

Perhaps as with you, I have found that it is often easier to help someone in need than to desire something for myself. Yet each of us has needs too.

Recently I gave one of my best Bibles to a friend who didn't have one. I also had a bookmark that would go perfectly with the gift of the Bible. However, I couldn't find it. I prayed. Jesus answered my prayer and showed me where to look to find the bookmark. Compared to praying for two thousand dollars, this was a small request. Yet Jesus cares about small requests too. Just the other day I asked my husband to drop off some items at our church while I was getting my hair done. This errand would take only a minute or so because the church was just a few blocks away. When he arrived at the church he was surprised to see one of our female members pounding on the back door trying to get in.

"Can I help you?" he asked.

Relieved to see him, the woman responded, "I need to retrieve some important papers I left inside the church earlier. But I don't have my church key with me. Just before you drove up, I was praying here in the parking lot for help."

My husband—with his key—was able to come to her rescue.

Let's follow the Bible's admonition to pray faithfully for one another's needs.

Frieda Tanner

When We Were a Family

And be kind to one another, tenderhearted,
forgiving one another, even as God in Christ forgave you.
—*Ephesians 4:32, NKJV*

Today is my father's seventy-fifth birthday, so I call him. I feel it my duty because I'm his daughter. He's lonely and friendless. We never mention that my own birthday is in eight days and that he neither sends me presents nor calls me. I try to honor him, my father, as the Bible says to do, but it is almost always hard.

My father is delighted to hear from me and talks for two hours and ten minutes, stopping at the hour mark to ask how the children are. He can't remember their names right off the bat, even though my daughter is named after his mom. Other than that, our conversation is nearly a monologue bouncing between two subjects: his broken leg and how much his mother did him wrong.

I'm pretty sure his leg will heal.

His mother, my grandma, Grace, was my MIP (most important person) growing up. It was because of her tender love in my life that I came to know the Lord. So I weary of hearing my father tell me all the ways she let him down when he was growing up in New York City. She didn't put him in school until forced to by the authorities when he was nine or ten. They moved a lot around the city, so he could never make friends. She made him empty out ash cans in the tenements where she was the superintendent. Even her turning to religion upset him and unbalanced his teenage world, he says.

As I listen to his complaints, I don't bother bringing up all the ways he let me down when I was a kid. But it does come to mind in the conversation, especially when he starts a story with, "When we were a family . . ." For a long moment, I don't hear anything else he says. It has never, ever, entered my mind that once we were actually a family. My memories kick in at five years of age when my mom left him because of his alcoholism.

We don't talk about that. A long time ago I said I forgave him and he owes me nothing. The Lord did that for me, and I'm trying to do that for my father. So I call him on his birthday and am left with many conflicting emotions. I keep praying for more than his broken leg.

Lisa DeGraw

All Glorious Within

And he said unto me, My grace is sufficient for thee:
for my strength is made perfect in weakness.
—*2 Corinthians 12:9*

My college years were memorable. I still cherish the friendships and experiences of my stay at Union College. Rees Hall, the women's dormitory, was home away from home, and it was there that I found a very beautiful mosaic hanging in the lobby. It simply read, "King's daughters all glorious within, fashioned after the similitude of a palace." I pondered the excerpt gleaned from the psalmist. How appropriate that the awesome mosaic should hang where young women pass by—women who come from different homelands, backgrounds, and social standings—that they might be influenced by its inspiration. I hope it shaped the woman I've become because I've never forgotten it. For me, it is a humbling thought that the King of the universe considers me his daughter! Imagine! Me, a member of His royal family! How cool that is!

The "all glorious within" part is where it gets a little tricky. As daughters of the King we have much to live up to. Much is expected.

Many of us are fascinated by the royal family of England. We are "royal watchers," expecting more from them than the average Brit. We enjoy their pomp and traditions. We want them to act royally and keep the royal image spotless. But they are also human, and at times the sons and daughters of the king and queen tarnish the crown. As in *Downton Abbey*, a popular television drama, we watch the regal moves of the lord and lady of the manor. We are intrigued by the grandeur of the estate. The daughters, who are becoming more modern women with the changing times, carry themselves in a way befitting the magnificent castle within which they reside. But as circumstances would have it, their lives are not always as beautiful as the Abbey. Perhaps that makes for a riveting story, but it is not what we want for ourselves.

As daughters of the heavenly King, we aspire to be worthy. The good news is that it isn't all that difficult, really! As we approach the throne of God to ask forgiveness, He is happy to make us clean again. He extends His grace as needed. His strength is made perfect in our weakness. And more good news—His grace is sufficient for all!

Bernadine Delafield

Graduation Day

Therefore I say unto you, What things soever ye desire, when ye pray, believe that ye receive them, and ye shall have them.
—Mark 11:24

It was June 1986, and graduation day was rapidly approaching. I had just passed my nursing finals by the skin of my teeth, but I had no money to pay my balance to graduate. I didn't know what to do. I owed Oakwood College (now Oakwood University) $1,264. Where was I going to get the money? I knew my family didn't have it, but I knew my heavenly Father owns "the cattle upon a thousand hills" (Psalm 50:10)!

I bowed on my knees and prayed, asking God what *He* would have me to do. I knew He had not brought me this far to leave me. I claimed Mark 11:24: "What things soever ye desire, when ye pray, believe that ye receive them, and ye shall have them."

It was graduation weekend. I went to the registrar's office that Friday to see if there was anything they could do about my being able to receive my diploma. I was told I had to pay the money, and there was nothing they could do. I would be allowed to participate in the graduation activities on Friday night and Sabbath. In order, though, to participate on Sunday—graduation day—I had to have my yellow marching card and be financially cleared.

My family arrived in town for my graduation. I participated in the activities on Friday and Sabbath, but I still was not cleared for graduation.

On Sunday I got up and went to the campus chapel in Carter Hall and prayed that God would show me what to do. I told Him I knew He had not brought me this far to leave me. I felt impressed to speak with the college's vice president of finance, Robert Patterson. I arrived at his office at nine that Sunday morning.

He was there! He called me into his office after speaking with the dean regarding my situation. Then, to my surprise, Mr. Patterson signed my clearance sheet and told me to go out and make our school proud!

Graduation started at ten thirty, and I got my yellow marching card at ten fifteen!

I graduated from Oakwood that day, and I know beyond a shadow of a doubt that there is nothing too hard for God.

Deniece G. Anderson

A Good Woman

A good woman is hard to find, and worth far more than diamonds.
—*Proverbs 31:10,* The Message

I cannot count how many times, after a concert, I've had women express to me that they admire the way I'm using my gifts for God. It is often very quickly followed by, "I've never discovered what my talents or gifts are! But I wish I could, so I could use them to bless others and God." This thought baffles me. So many wonderful women lose their self-esteem by comparing what God has given them to what He has given others.

My mom is a classic example of this syndrome. She has been a mom her entire adult life. First, she was a single working mom struggling to survive in her late teens and twenties. And then, she became a stay-at-home mom after marrying Dad while in her thirties. She raised my brother and me. In my eyes, and God's eyes too, she has countless talents and gifts, but her greatest has always been her capabilities as a mom. The lessons and morals she instilled into my heart are priceless. The sacrifices she was willing to make for her children have always amazed me. It truly is a great skill to work selflessly for little-to-no praise, keeping a good home, making meals, cleaning messes, and training young minds. It's a job that comes with a heavy responsibility, requiring time and patience.

Today, because her children are all grown up, my mom can explore her many other skills, such as art and painting. Yet whenever she looks back in time as though her life has held little meaning, I quickly remind her that hers was and is a life filled with the greatest purpose—motherhood—that some women may ever have, a purpose highly valued in the courts of heaven.

We are all given different talents and gifts. Not everyone will be a mom and not everyone will be a singer or a preacher. Yet everyone has something great and meaningful given them by God. Perhaps it is the art of being a good friend, a good listener, a great cook, a volunteer, a smiling face, a smart businesswoman, a good gardener, a kind heart, or the best hugger.

Whatever your gifts and talents, they are needed in this world. As with my mother, you hold a very special God-given place in this world that only you can fill. With God as your strength, you will be more than capable of filling that special place, for "the woman to be admired and praised is the woman who lives in the Fear-of-God" (Proverbs 31:30, *The Message*).

Naomi Striemer

Who's Allelon?

Owe no one anything except to love one another.
—*Romans 13:8, NKJV*

Earth's probation will soon screech to a halt when Jesus comes with His glorious retinue of angels, and I must testify that we are not ready. In particular, one standard has been ignored, neglected, even despised among us. The standard of which I speak applies to the churched and the unchurched, to every nation, kindred, tongue, and people, and to man, woman, and child. It makes or breaks every individual life, relationship, family, community, nation, continent, and planet. The Bible speaks of it more than any other standard, and yet many who claim to follow the Bible regard it with indifference. Some of them even defiantly ignore it, in the name of keeping the standards!

Jesus stated it explicitly three times, Paul stated it twice, Peter stated it once, and John stated it six times. Countless additional times, all Bible writers say it implicitly. Jesus and Paul put it forth as a summary of all law, revealing its overarching, all-encompassing nature. In His great signs-of-the-end sermon in Matthew 24, Jesus said many of God's people would engage in the direct opposite of this command when they betray and hate one another (verse 10).

The standard, as you may have guessed, is "love one another." In Greek it's *agapeo allelon*. The sheer number of variations of this "love one another" command reveals its quintessence to spiritual life. We talk often about *agape*, but not as much about allelon. Yet the New Testament uses the latter almost as much as the former! "One another"—allelon—helps us better understand *agape*, because agape can't be experienced apart from allelon. Countless expansions of the "love one another" command pepper the New Testament letters. Among other things, we should prefer, edify, admonish, receive, care for, forbear, and esteem one another. Cold formalists, arrogant legalists, unprincipled compromisers, and bold-faced pagans alike fail to measure up to this standard. Because we already fall short, let's fall all the way down on our faces before God today, admitting that we don't love one another as Jesus has loved us.

Who's allelon? God is allelon. God is all about "one another." And God will live in us if we receive Him.

Jennifer Jill Schwirzer

A Little Child Shall Lead

You have taught children and infants to tell of your strength.
—Psalm 8:2, NLT

Our daughters and grandchildren from California were visiting my husband and me in Colorado. We had just spent a fun day in the mountains and had walked around shops in the town of Estes Park, which is a quaint little town right at the entrance of Rocky Mountain National Park. The children were tired and hungry and ready to get back home. But it was late Sunday afternoon, and traffic was heavy coming back from the mountains. We were inching along, stop and go. An occasional grumble or complaint sounded from the back seats. We heard the usual: "When will we be home?" "Are we almost there?"

Suddenly, we heard a siren. While we were stopped at a traffic light, a police car sped around us. As we started slowly on our way again, we could see many blinking lights ahead. Apparently, there had been an accident. Now the children were suddenly very quiet.

As we approached the blinking lights, we saw a car in the ditch and a police car at the scene. Just a short distance down the highway was another, more serious, accident. The ambulance attendants were loading someone onto a stretcher. Yet another short distance away was a motorcycle accident. Someone was lying on the ground surrounded by emergency workers.

The children were very quiet now when a shy little voice from the back seat said, "I think we should all bow our heads and close our eyes—well, all except Mommy because she is driving—and say a prayer for all those poor people in the accidents." So we did just that, and eight-year-old Charlotte prayed a simple but beautiful prayer asking Jesus to be with those people, to help them not to be hurt very badly—and for everybody to be OK.

We were all tired and anxious to be home and perhaps somewhat impatient at the delay. Consequently, none of us adults in the car had said a thing about praying for the accident victims. I thought, *Well, a little child shall lead them.*

No wonder Jesus said we should all become like little children if we would enter the kingdom of heaven (Matthew 18:3). The simple faith and trust of a child and the willingness to share our faith in the way that Charlotte did is something we should pray for today—and every day.

Sharon Oster

Committed to Rejoice

Then shall the virgin rejoice in the dance, both young men and old together: for I will turn their mourning into joy, and will comfort them, and make them rejoice from their sorrow.
—Jeremiah 31:13

When my father died quite suddenly and violently in an accident, I was crushed. You see, he had been drinking that day and, in attempting to cross the busy street, was hit by a car—then run over by another. I saw the body, and the image of it still haunts me four years later. What really disturbs me, though, is the fact that I question his spiritual state at his death, since I'm not certain whether he had time to make his life right with God.

During the days of the wake, I listened as the various people insisted on rejoicing even in death and that we shouldn't be sad and mournful when people die. All I wanted to do was scream at them to shut up. What did they know about how I felt? At that moment I was angry with God for allowing my father to die like that and for me not having the assurance that I would see my father again. What was there to rejoice about? I couldn't even summon the energy to call out to God. I was in a dark, deep pit, and the one person who could get me out of it was the One I turned away from.

Yet I had to admit that the Bible abounds with exhortations to rejoice and praise and give thanks. It does not make any distinction as to when. Paul says we are to "rejoice evermore" (1 Thessalonians 5:16). The book of Psalms is full of songs of praise sung during times of extreme stress and anxiety. Why do they do it? Why sing when you want to cry and give up? David and Jeremiah (see Lamentations 3:22, 23) realized the *power* of rejoicing in times of sadness.

There is untold power in our praise. Rejoicing is not just about saying "Thank You" and "Glory, hallelujah." It's a state of mind, a conscious decision one makes that says emphatically, "Lord, no matter what, I trust You and know You are in control." When we can proclaim as Job did, "The Lord gave, and the Lord hath taken away; blessed be the name of the Lord" (Job 1:21), we set in motion a chain of events that causes the devil to flee from the presence of God in us. We arise out of our situation not just alive but victorious.

Seems easy? Never! I have come to appreciate that God doesn't do easy. Whatever He does do, however, He does in love and He does well. So commit to rejoice evermore!

Greta Michelle Joachim-Fox-Dyett

The Eleventh-Hour Blessing

Every man according as he purposeth in his heart, so let him give;
not grudgingly, or of necessity: for God loveth a cheerful giver.
—2 Corinthians 9:7

I did not usually make it a habit to drop large bills (twenty dollars or more) into the offering plate during a Week of Prayer offering collection. However, this was a special week at the New Covenant Church in Savannah, Georgia. The congregation listened attentively as a well-known evangelist, Robert Connor, presented the message on that particular Wednesday evening. During the call for the offering, the speaker asked each person to give the largest bill in their purse or wallet that night. My largest bill was twenty dollars. The speaker prayed fervently that the Lord would bless those who gave by giving their offering back to them, doubled, and within one week's time. I placed my twenty-dollar bill in the offering plate.

The week passed quickly and another Wednesday evening prayer service rolled around. When the elder called for testimonies, members began to give testimonies as to how the Lord had blessed the offering they had given the previous week during the Week of Prayer. Some had given as much as one hundred dollars. I sat quietly because I had not witnessed any special monetary blessing. Boy, was I in for a surprise!

After I returned home, I heard a knock on my front door while preparing for bed. Opening the door, I greeted a very good friend who was not a member of my church. Therefore, he was not aware of the evangelist's special prayer over the previous Wednesday night's offering. My friend said, "The Lord told me to give you this." After having said this, he stood there and proceeded to write a check. Stunned, I took the check written for the amount of seventy-seven dollars! My friend said the check was to show appreciation for "all of your help." My blessing had come at the eleventh hour. And not only was it doubled; it had been more than tripled! At prayer meeting the next Wednesday, I was the first one to stand, telling of my unexpected blessing.

Yes, my sister, God loves a cheerful giver, and He cannot be beat when it comes to rewarding your faith, your faithfulness in giving tithes and offerings, and your cheerfulness in returning His own to Him. Prove Him. You will not be disappointed!

Beatrice Banks

Property Taxes

And it shall come to pass, that before they call, I will answer;
and while they are yet speaking, I will hear.
—Isaiah 65:24

Upon returning home after running a series of errands, I stopped at the entrance of the driveway to retrieve my mail before proceeding to the garage. Surprisingly, there was a bill from the county for payment of property taxes. My property taxes were always paid through my lender from my escrow account. *Why did I receive this bill?* I wondered. *Right when I'm in the process of working on a project that surfaced unexpectedly and that has drained me financially?* After the initial shock I began to pray for guidance.

Because it was only minutes past 3:00 P.M., I thought I might have a chance to speak to a specific representative prior to the end of her nine-to-five shift. So I called to discuss the matter with her. Unfortunately, I was coerced into speaking to several of her coworkers from various departments and placed on hold at intervals before being directed to her voicemail.

Thank God for His words of encouragement: "Be careful for nothing; but in every thing by prayer and supplication with thanksgiving let your requests be made known unto God" (Philippians 4:6). So I slept well that night, though I recalled a time in life when I would not have slept a wink for worrying about which corners to cut in order to pay my taxes on time.

I began to thank God again for the funds He had provided for the replacement of carpeting upstairs as well as some other expensive, but necessary, projects and replacements. My emergency money had been depleted and all within less than a year's time.

The next day I repeatedly phoned my lender but in vain. Though tempted to be anxious, I continued thanking God for His promise of peace (verse 7) and His admonition to "pray without ceasing" (1 Thessalonians 5:17). The third day the representative whom I had tried to reach finally returned my call.

Jesus once instructed Peter to pay taxes with money found in a fish's mouth (Matthew 17:27); this time, though not with money from a fish's mouth, God still made provision—with the help of the representative—for the payment of my property taxes through my escrow account as usual.

God will sustain and give you peace through any ordeal you are facing today. Praise Him.

Cora A. Walker

The Attitude You Choose

Finally, brothers and sisters, whatever is true, whatever is noble,
whatever is right, whatever is pure, whatever is lovely,
whatever is admirable—if anything is excellent
or praiseworthy—think about such things.
—*Philippians 4:8, NIV*

I recently read that a positive attitude can be the chain-reaction catalyst for positive thoughts, events, and outcomes. Several months ago I found myself, at 2:00 A.M., preparing to fly out of Vietnam's Ho Chi Minh City airport. I had just met with women from churches in the country. My heart was full of joy and gratitude, not only for the way God had led in the meetings, but also for the ten *nón lá* (conical-shaped hats) I was bringing home. The nón lá is distinctive in the Vietnamese woman's national costume and provides protection from sun or rain, collects rainwater, and can serve as a basket or bag.

As I presented my passport at the airline counter, I noticed the agent was having difficulty finding my name on the passenger list. He walked away and returned an hour later, saying, "Sorry, madam, you are not allowed to return home. Your documents are not listed in the system. You have to wait for a miracle." I returned quietly to my seat and starting praying—not for a miracle but for an attitude of praise in this complex situation. In my distress, I rejoiced that God is in heaven and I am His child. He knows what is best. My fears subsided. Peace came to my heart, and I was able to wait in hope. After another hour, the man behind the counter turned to me and said, "You are lucky. Washington responded and you are free to board. Your name is on the list." I ran to the gate singing and praising God for the blessing.

As you plan the day ahead, consider this: What will your attitude be today? Will you be fearful, angry, or worried? Will you be bitter or pessimistic? If so, it would be good to meditate on what Paul is saying to us today. Think about what is right, lovely, admirable, and praiseworthy. Think optimistically about yourself and your future. Give thanks to the One who has given you everything, and trust in your heart that He wants to give you so much more. Remember: the greater part of our happiness or misery depends on our thinking, and not on our circumstances. A miserable heart means a miserable life; a cheerful heart fills the day with a song (Proverbs 15:15).

Raquel Queiroz da Costa Arrais

Can You Smell That?

"I will give peace in the land, and you shall lie down,
and none will make you afraid."
—*Leviticus 26:6, NKJV*

My husband and I live in the country with dogs, cats, a bird, and goats. Every evening we look forward to worship, thanking God for His blessings.

In the cooler months of the year, we use propane to heat our home. One autumn day I thought I smelled fumes. "Can you smell that?" I asked my husband. Not wanting to have something serious happen, I called the gas company. They sent someone to the house to check for leaks, but none were found.

The following year, the same thing happened. This time I went to the company and explained that I smelled fumes in the mornings after the house had been closed up. "Well," said an employee, "we'll send someone out to check it again." Several days went by and no one came (I suspect they might have thought I was a worrier). My husband, who is legally sightless, began sniffing around but couldn't smell any fumes. Then I noticed we were using more fuel than usual that winter. So, I decided to stop by the company, pay my bill, and tell them again.

One of the workers, whom I personally knew, was there. I told him my concerns. He said he would be out the next day. During worship, my husband thanked God for my timely arrival at the gas company earlier that day. The next day, when I told the visiting gas company worker about our abnormally excessive gas consumption, he went straight outside and checked the gas gauge. "My gas reader went crazy," he reported back. "That means you had a bad leak. I turned off your gas and will be back at eight o'clock tomorrow morning with help. Be careful not to even turn on your electric stove tonight—the leak is bad." When the workers arrived the following morning, they found the leak under the house.

After they had repaired the leak, they showed me the old pipe, which had a big hole in it. I asked to keep it. To me it was a testament of God's love and protection to us who loved and worshiped Him. Truly He had fulfilled His promise: "He shall cover you with His feathers, and under His wings you shall take refuge; His truth shall be your shield and buckler" (Psalm 91:4, NKJV).

Elaine J. Johnson

He Is Always With Us!

Always be joyful in the Lord! . . . The Lord is near.
Never worry about anything. But in every situation let God know
what you need in prayers and requests. . . . Then God's peace,
which goes beyond anything we can imagine, will guard your
thoughts and emotions through Christ Jesus.
—*Philippians 4:4–7, GOD'S WORD*

As women, we go through different seasons in life. Through each season, we are always learning new lessons. Thankfully, through each transition and change in our lives, we serve a God "who does not change like shifting shadows" (James 1:17, NIV).

My husband is a pastor, and we have lived in several different places in our life together. As a result, our daughter is always on the move; she cannot settle down in a single place for very long. Recently she moved to South Korea to teach English for a year, as well as to decide what she wants to do for graduate school. She is a very determined young woman, but being in a foreign land is not always easy. She has faced a lot of challenges along the way. She has a great support system in her family and in the many good friends God has placed in her path over there. She has also embraced the culture and the people, and her joy is so infectious that someone recently told her they wanted to catch her spirit for themselves. But as great as all this is, we cannot always be there for her, and even the dear friends she leans on heavily can let her down. As a result, she has increasingly learned how to become closer to the One who will never leave nor forsake her (Deuteronomy 31:6). Sooner or later in life we will all need someone to hold our hand through whatever changes this world may throw at us. Our family and friends can be a great support but may still disappoint us at times. But Jesus Christ never fails. He is "the same yesterday, and to day, and for ever" (Hebrews 13:8). As the song says, He is a constant friend who notices the needs of a sparrow. So why would He not watch over me?

Imagine what joy we would have if we would only learn to lean wholly on Jesus through all of life's seasons! As David wrote, "Cast your cares on the LORD and he will sustain you" (Psalm 55:22, NIV).

My prayer is that we will realize, even in this changing world, that "no power in the sky above or in the earth below—indeed, nothing in all creation will ever be able to separate us from the love of God that is revealed in Christ Jesus our Lord" (Romans 8:39, NLT).

Judith M. Mwansa

Hair and Heart Disease

"People judge by outward appearance,
but the Lord looks at the heart."
—1 Samuel 16:7, NLT

Now nearly lost in the darkening recesses of memory and laughter is a phrase my son *meant* to use in an assigned essay for school: "a friend of my mother's hair." Now, in one sense, he was right on the money. My hair *does* need a friend. In fact, it needs all the friends it can get, as a string of disillusioned beauty salons will attest. Given the limp, fine texture and natural straightness of my hair, I have reduced it to stubble that I can shake dry in a jiffy along with the least shaggy mutt on the block. Out on the open road with the car windows down, stray strands flutter without blinding me or requiring a comb at my destination. All those well-coifed beauties should be so lucky!

But alas for me, I have more serious health and beauty issues than this superficial flaw. I suffer from heart trouble. Too often I display the classic symptoms of heart disease. Unrecognized by medical clinicians, these symptoms require the intervention of the Great Physician, who scrutinizes not my disheveled outward appearance but my heart with its spiritual plaque and character arrhythmias. The apostle Paul diagnoses this condition: "I have discovered this principle of life—that when I want to do what is right, I inevitably do what is wrong. . . . Oh, what a miserable person I am! Who will free me from this life that is dominated by sin and death? Thank God! The answer is in Jesus Christ our Lord" (Romans 7:21–25, NLT). Jesus sacrificed His life to arrest my heart disease, ennoble my motives and actions, and restore my beauty of character. His prescription for cardiac rehab—time in His Word and in communion with Him—is truly life-transforming.

"So, what do you think?" Paul asks. "With God on our side like this, how can we lose? If God didn't hesitate to put everything on the line for us, embracing our condition and exposing himself to the worst by sending his own Son, is there anything else he wouldn't gladly and freely do for us? . . . The One who died for us—who was raised to life for us!—is in the presence of God at this very moment sticking up for us. Do you think anyone is going to be able to drive a wedge between us and Christ's love for us? There is no way!" (Romans 8:31–35, *The Message*).

That's even better news than coarse, curly hair! And a lot better than heart disease.

Andrea Kristensen

A Sense of Danger

"I am with you always, even to the end of the world."
—Matthew 28:20, TLB

I had some trials at work. Being a manager and younger than most of those I supervised, I carried some challenges. But I noticed an emerging pattern in the timing of these challenging encounters at work. They came after times of spiritual refreshing in my life. The first challenging encounter came right after the Sabbath when our church's "Pentecost and More" program that year was uplinked from Kingston, Jamaica, where I live. I was thrilled to attend the uplink event where baptisms from our part of the world (Inter-America) were simulcast.

Three days later trouble struck at work. A month later—after another spiritually rich weekend I enjoyed with women from my church—the problem at work re-emerged. The situation at work reached the boiling point after a powerful women's ministries prayer and fasting session I'd been led to organize. The Holy Spirit had been manifest in the words and ministry of the women's ministries director during the session. Bonds were broken, and souls were set free.

At work the following week, "all hell broke loose," as the saying goes. As with Elijah, I went into a fit of fear, depression, anxiety, and wanting to flee. I could find nowhere to hide. I feared I was going to be murdered. Starting the next Friday evening, I prayed all weekend—until I passed out that Sunday night. On Monday, when I was back at work, a staff member came to me and commanded, "Go move your car." She also demanded that I change the time I leave work. That evening I had an unspeakable sense of fear. For much of the night, I was gravely uneasy and greatly feared the nocturnal sounds that I thought were indications of my approaching demise. I prayed until I fell asleep.

Awakening the next morning, I felt as if everything were new. I wondered if I had experienced the resurrection. I gave God thanks for His mercies. Then the same women's ministries director who had ministered to us at the earlier prayer and fasting session phoned me. She shared that she had sensed I was in trouble and had started praying. "I'm calling," she said, "to announce that it is over. God has triumphed." I was speechless, as I had not spoken with her—or with anyone else—about what was happening at work.

I know God leads in our lives and no weapon formed against us shall stand. When in Christ, we are more than conquerors (Isaiah 54:17; Romans 8:37).

Keisha D. Sterling

Focus

Looking unto Jesus the author and finisher of our faith.
—*Hebrews 12:2*

stood in one corner of a university gym, watching an instructor teaching a class of enthusiastic, wiggly ten-year-olds how to do a half turn while jumping on the trampoline.

"See the exit sign on that wall straight ahead?" the instructor asked.

"Yes!" the kids eagerly responded, eager for the fun to begin.

"Now look all the way behind you," the teacher continued. "See the poster up there on that wall?"

"Yes!" they all chorused, swiveling their heads to look around behind them to the opposite wall.

"Good!" said the teacher. "Now, when it's your turn, I want you to start jumping and, when you're ready to turn around, first look at the exit sign right in front of you, then turn your head and look at the poster all the way behind you."

One by one, each student tried the new maneuver.

Even though they had never done it before, when they followed the simple instructions to look straight ahead at the exit sign, then turn to look straight behind them at the poster, their bodies made the turn smoothly and easily.

Simply changing the focus of their gaze allowed them to effortlessly turn their whole body in the opposite direction.

In that experience, I saw again a lesson the Holy Spirit is patiently teaching me in ever deeper ways:

We move in the direction that we're looking.

When we look at past failures, we move toward self-condemnation. When we look at present difficult circumstances, we move toward discouragement.

But when we're looking at Jesus, we're moving toward joy. Toward a future and a hope. Toward safety and comfort and victory.

Dear God, may I take every step, pray every prayer, and live every moment looking unto Jesus, the author and finisher of my faith. Amen.

Kelly Mowrer

In His Presence

For his Spirit joins with our spirit
to affirm that we are God's children.
—*Romans 8:16, NLT*

I t had been a very stressful week for me, and I needed to feel Jesus' love in my soul. I wanted to rest by the wayside and be comforted by Him. Sitting quietly in my favorite chair with my Bible open, I began to pray. I wanted to sense His nearness.

I closed my eyes and prayed, "Lord, please comfort and calm my soul."

Then in an instant, Jesus' peace filled my heart. Oh! The love and comfort I felt in moment! Just what I needed! He let me know He was with me always, and I enjoyed the warmth of His presence.

It felt so wonderful, even though it was only for a brief moment, a moment that said so much without words; a moment that will be with me the rest of my life.

Blessed am I, for I received the comfort I needed from my Lord! I opened my eyes and was in awe of the way it had happened! I felt so loved and cared for by my Lord!

I share this experience for God's glory, to let His children know that He is there for them in many different circumstances. What He has done for me, He will do for you.

Thank You, Jesus, for Your comforting arms. I feel so special and blessed by Your presence in my life. I long for the day I'll be with You for eternity. Jesus, You truly are the Christ who cares. Love, Dianne.

Dianne Murphy

Answers on the Way

For I know that my redeemer liveth, and that he shall stand at the latter day upon the earth: . . . in my flesh shall I see God: whom I shall see for myself, and mine eyes shall behold, and not another.
—Job 19:25–27

I wonder, if Job had been a woman, what name could she have had? What kind of woman would she have been? One thing is for sure: she would have risen from those trials victorious in Jesus' name with faith and strength that only God's purifying fire can produce. In this day and age, there are modern women who, like Job, stand every day, facing affliction. They too may wonder, *Can it get any worse?* There are women who beg God for answers because they themselves don't know what the future holds. They need to find strength to face the next day.

Have you ever felt as if you were the only person on the planet facing a certain pain? Have you lamented the fact that you had no one with whom to share your frustration? No one, that is, who would truly understand?

Remember, though, that God is there to hear our frustrations and receive our pain. He is always ready to give us peace and, eventually, understanding that His ways are perfect—even if we don't understand them right now. Furthermore, God will give us the wisdom to deal with situations of pain—both now and in the future.

Today I have a special burden—and compassion—in my heart for women around the world who, like me, want to be mothers. But we just can't seem to get the pregnancy part in motion. On days when this very personal situation weighs heavy on me, I struggle to keep a smile on my face. I pray for God to help me keep faith and keep focused on Him, who gives true strength. Some days the devil tries hard to make me angry, to the point of giving up even on God. But I know that my Redeemer liveth! And He will not leave me in despair.

So today I feel the need to reach out and encourage readers who might be going through this, or a similar, experience. For God will come through for us in His way. He will continue to shine His light on us so that we may reflect it upon others who are struggling. Most important, God does answer prayers. Don't lose hope. God will give you the answers you need, and the end result will far surpass your expectations. It will be in His time, not ours. And He is able!

Yvita Antonette Villalona Bacchus

Sometimes I Do Dumb Things

Ye are of more value than many sparrows.
—Matthew 10:31

It was one of those harried Friday mornings with three appointments almost back to back. My mind was preoccupied with other things, but I felt I was organized and would get through the day with all missions accomplished.

On my way out the door I chatted briefly with an unknown visitor in the condo as I carried two large bags of garbage to drop in the dumpster. I locked the door and put the keys in my pocket. When I got to the car I placed my purse on the trunk, priding myself for "using my head" so I wouldn't accidently drop my purse in the dumpster as I wielded the bags inside. I wouldn't have a minute to spare to fish my purse out of the bottom of the dumpster if such an event happened.

I found a parking spot close to the doctor's office. I reached across the seat to grab my purse but it wasn't there. Then it dawned on me; I hadn't picked it up off the trunk. What should I do? I didn't have time to go home and retrace my steps because my appointment began in three minutes. I phoned my sister who lives in the same condo and got no answer.

During this trauma I was breathing a prayer for a miracle. A brief moment later, my sister walked in with my purse. I couldn't believe my good fortune. She didn't stop to explain anything, so I would have to wait. I praised the Lord for His goodness.

My next stop was at the post office, and whom should I meet but the stranger I had spoken to when I left the condo!

She told me the rest of the story. She saw me drive by with my purse on the trunk. She tried to get my attention, but I was concentrating on the traffic as I edged out of the driveway onto the busy street. She retrieved my purse from the center of the driving lane. Now she was in a quandary, wondering how to get it back to me. Just at that moment she met my sister leaving the condo, and all was resolved. I hugged the woman and thanked her for being part of a miracle in my life that day.

My God who sees the sparrows fall also steps in when I do dumb things. I cannot thank Him enough for the value He places on me.

Edith Fitch

The Power of a Prayer Circle

I will contend with him that contendeth with thee,
and I will save thy children.
—*Isaiah 49:25*

One little "church in the wildwood," located in the Pacific Northwest, has become famous for its powerful prayer circles. People phone in from everywhere with prayer requests. I was one of these who asked for prayer as the following story attests.

During Operation Iraqi Freedom, Paul Lee, a younger family member and medical doctor, was stationed in the Middle East. His war-torn area came under attack several times. Once he was asked to move to another room for lodging, but twenty-four hours before he was to move, mortar rounds completely demolished what were to be his new living quarters. The two medics who still lived there were on duty in the medical clinic at the time and were, therefore, spared.

On another occasion, just outside of Paul's clinic, a large car bomb exploded, leaving a crater in the road sixty feet deep. Many Iraqis were injured and brought to the clinic. The fifteen months of Paul's deployment saw some of the bitterest fighting of the conflict. As a result Paul witnessed much death and suffering. During one severe battle he found himself holding a teenage soldier in his arms, consoling and praying for him. The young man eventually died. Two other times Paul had similar experiences. These heart-wrenching incidents brought on a deep sadness. When it was possible, he retreated to his room to fight the onset of depression.

One time, when we phoned Paul, he had been in bed for days, depressed and struggling with the harsh realities of war. He felt he could not bear to see one more battle-ravaged body with missing extremities or other life-altering injuries. In addition—as a doctor—Paul felt he had a responsibility to help save *every* soldier's life. After all, he had taken the Hippocratic oath. Yet death was too often the end result of severe battlefield injuries. His inability to save every soldier's life brought him a sense of desperation. How our hearts hurt and agonized for him!

During these fifteen turbulent months, though, faithful prayer circle members of the little church in the wildwood were praying for Paul. Each week his name was listed in the church bulletin, and people prayed. Over time Paul began to experience restoration and rejuvenation.

Sister in Christ, form a prayer circle, and then watch for miracles! God has promised to contend with the enemy and save our precious loved ones in His time and in His ways.

Patty L. Hyland

What's in Your Garden?

For as the soil makes the sprout come up and a garden causes seeds
to grow, so the Sovereign LORD will make righteousness and
praise spring up before all nations.
—Isaiah 61:11, NIV

Sometimes God gives us extra peaceful days. Yesterday was like that for me. It started with my helping serve in a local soup kitchen. From there I went to church and helped out in a children's Bible study class. My heart felt blessed. I reflected that because the Lord is in the business of serving, our partaking in His service to others does something special to our hearts. It's all about Jesus, as I heard in a song at church yesterday morning.

When I got home later, I spent the rest of the day pretty much outside. Out in nature is a lovely place to be. It brings such peace to my soul. I never tire of gazing at all the different plants. I walk from one garden to the next just looking at them. They constantly change, grow, and produce. I noticed some string beans that are ready to be picked, and yellow and baby tomatoes starting to form.

I also spent time with my pets. They love to be petted and gently talked to. They want my human touch and enjoy my company. It pleases me to be among them as well. I noticed two lovely peacock feathers on my front porch, as if God had left me a gift. *Daughter, these are for you,* I imagined Him saying to me. Looking intently into the color and pattern of these feathers, I admired such fine artwork. I found a metal vase that'd been sitting outside and placed the feathers in it. I placed the vase strategically on the windowsill of my back porch for all to see.

Sitting in the rocking chair with Peaches, our dog, at my feet, I noticed two Carolina wrens investigating the back shed for possible nesting places. Their last nest had been destroyed by one of our cats. I moved a bird box high into the rafters of the shed and hoped the wrens would discover it. I feared they would not come back after their loss (and wouldn't have blamed them), but here they were—warbling their hearts out and flitting from one spot to another. They actually went to the same cardboard box they built their nest in before. They are happy, and so am I.

Thank You, Lord, for the privilege of being surrounded by Your creation, so peaceful and stress-free.

Do you have a "garden," a calm place where you can retreat from the stresses of life? What can you find as a place of personal retreat that will bring you closer to God?

Rosemarie Clardy

Waiting on God

"All the days of my hard service I will wait for my renewal to come."
—Job 14:14, NIV

You prepare a table before me.
—Psalm 23:5, NIV

As a young, new breastfeeding mother, I had challenges meeting the needs of my new baby. She cried often, and I would try to nurse her as often as she cried. But she didn't latch on as I had expected she would. The process was frustrating for her and physically painful for me. Sometimes I cried right along with her. I was capable of supplying what she needed, but we first had to learn to work through the process together. I truly wanted to nurture this impatient little treasure God had given to my husband and me after nine long months of anticipation.

Like my new baby daughter, I have sometimes cried out to God to meet a need—and to do so right away! I have asked Him for a certain job that I thought would be best for me. As with my baby who had to learn how to wait on my help in order to have her hunger need met, I've cried out to God many times about my work needs because a family move has once more left me with without a job. I've had to hunt for jobs several times as a result of my pastor-husband being reassigned to different localities.

I found the job-hunting experience to be both frustrating and frightening. Yet, despite my frustration and fear, God was already working on my behalf, patiently waiting for me to calm down and follow His lead.

Sometimes we, even as His children, cry out to God to feed us, though He has already set a table before us. We just can't see it yet through our tears of pressing fear and frustration. Sometimes in my life I have asked the Lord for a certain job or position that I thought would be best for me. I have not always gotten the job I thought I really wanted, but I always got what God knew was best for me—at the right place and time. He was teaching me to wait on Him.

As with my newborn daughter, God was aware of every detail of my needs and of my life. Sooner or later I could look back and see He was giving me time to learn, as I had given my crying newborn the time and help she needed in order for me to be able to meet her needs.

God tells us to wait on Him and be of courage. He promises not to withhold any good thing from His children. Waiting on God may be a lengthy process, but it has its eternal rewards.

Betty Glover Perry

I Thought You Was Going to Die

"This blood is poured out for many to forgive their sins."
—Matthew 26:28, NCV

Scotty threw his arms around my legs and screamed, "Please don't go, Mommy, please don't go!" I picked him up and hugged him, explaining that I would not be gone long and that Daddy would be here with him and his little brother already soundly napping. My husband took him from my arms, but Scotty continued to scream, calling me to come back as I left our camper. I headed across the camp meeting grounds to donate blood at the bloodmobile. This was my first time to donate, and Scott's inconsolable crying rang in my ears and added to my anxiety.

I was back at the camper sooner than any of us expected. I had not met the criteria for blood donation. Before I opened the camper door I could hear Scott crying in complete desolation. As I stepped into our camper he jumped from Dave's arms and once again wrapped his arms around my legs.

"Oh, Mommy," he sobbed, "I thought you was going to give *all* of your blood! I thought you was going to die!" His relief was almost palpable. At five years of age, he did not understand what "giving blood" meant. He just assumed I was giving my lifeblood so that someone else, whom he did not know, could live. Only his joy at once again seeing me could erase his tears of misunderstanding.

As he grew he would begin to learn more about the blood that was given so someone else, someone that he did not know, could live. The story of the Cross would become more than just a story. It would become a precious life-saving gift offered to everyone. And most of all, he would come to understand that the gift of blood was for him, so that he could live eternally.

The words Scott heard with every Communion service would take root in his heart: "Then Jesus took a cup and thanked God for it and gave it to the followers. He said, 'Every one of you drink this. This is my blood which is the new agreement that God makes with his people. This blood is poured out for many to forgive their sins' " (Matthew 26:27, 28, NCV).

The promise of the life-saving blood is for you! "For you know that God paid a ransom to save you. . . . It was the precious blood of Christ, the sinless, spotless Lamb of God" (1 Peter 1:18, 19, NLT).

Ginny Allen

Serious About Answering Prayer

Hear my prayer, LORD;
let my cry for help come to you.
Do not hide your face from me
when I am in distress.
Turn your ear to me;
when I call, answer me quickly.
—*Psalm 102:1, 2, NIV*

Throughout my twenty-three years as a Christian, I have learned that, despite trials and hardship, we become strong when we rely completely on God, the One who makes no mistakes.

At the time I got a divorce request, I was unemployed with two small children and dependent on the legal system to resolve civil and financial issues. Though I felt like giving up, something inside me said, "Courage! I am with you." Imbued with divine power, I raised my head and went in search of my dreams.

One morning, however, even though I'd found a job as a day worker, an eviction notice arrived because of late rent. I fell down and cried to the Lord for help. Soon—that very morning—my neighbor who was moving to the capital offered us his place to live in. In return, I would take care of his property. God put us into a 360-square-meter (3,800-square-foot) house! I thanked God but reminded Him we still had no food in the pantry. Once I finished praying, a dear sister knocked on our door, telling me, "I was in the market when I heard a voice saying, 'Take groceries to Rosana's house, for they are without anything to eat.'" She gave us so much food that it barely fit in our pantry. To God be the glory!

Time passed and I got a good job. After my father died, my mother came to live with me, and we decided to buy a piece of land and build a small house. From her savings, she put a down payment on property for a small house. With funds still owed me from the divorce, I built an unfinished house. Again I called on the Lord. A few days later my brother phoned and said, "Sister, I learned that you need to finish your house. I will help you finish." Gratitude filled my being. God does not fool around when it comes to answering prayer; He takes it seriously.

We must trust the Lord, and He will do the rest. We need to combine our faith and effort. Above all, we need to rely on divine help, believing that we can make it through any need and trial through Him who strengthens us.

God is faithful. Be strong and remember that God whispers in your ear today, "Courage! I am with you!"

Rosana Nieton Andrade

June 3

Loving Our Friends in Tough Times

Carry each other's burdens,
and in this way you will fulfill the law of Christ.
—*Galatians 6:2, NIV*

Michelle and I met in college. Together we compared notes, studied for tests, and enjoyed an occasional latte break. We recognized our friendship as a gift from the Lord. Indeed it was, but God had plans to strengthen our bond through upcoming trials.

Shortly before my last year as a college student, I despairingly ended a relationship with a man who I sensed was not God's best for me. Not long afterward, Michelle phoned me. "I'm coming over to pick you up. We need to go have some fun downtown."

Forcing myself to go along, I didn't anticipate having much fun. Yet somewhere in the midst of the simple outing, my spirits lifted. Michelle's thoughtful invitation became a turning point in my walk with God. Accepted by one of His daughters, I could turn to my heavenly Father to receive His healing.

Before long, I found myself in the position to carry a burden. Michelle and I had made weekend plans to enjoy a pizza. On our way Michelle was involved in a car accident. Driving directly behind her, I cringed as I watched my friend's shiny red vehicle smash into another car. Quickly pulling over, I ran to stand beside my friend. Although shaken, we both rejoiced that she and the other driver experienced no injuries. Later that evening we read Romans 8:28 together: "And we know that in all things God works for the good of those who love him, who have been called according to his purpose" (NIV).

Whether we are in college, at work, or raising children, the Lord faithfully brings supportive women into our lives to share our journey. Fun and lighthearted friendships certainly have their place in life. Yet relationships grow roots as we share the cup of suffering with each other. None of us escapes life's inevitable challenges and heartaches. Yet we please God by following Christ's example of loving our friends at all times. As Christ demonstrated His love for us by going to the cross to die, we also must prepare to love others in hard times.

Dear Lord, thank You for the women who grace our lives. We acknowledge You as the giver of all friendships. Equip us to lovingly minister to our friends in their times of need. Amen.

Bronwyn Worthington

Ask

Ask, and it shall be given you; seek, and ye shall find;
knock, and it shall be opened unto you.
—*Matthew 7:7*

My son was getting married. The wedding colors were teal and gold. I decided to ask the bride-to-be, Marsha, what color she wanted me to wear. Teal was her answer. Teal! What color is that? Where would I find an outfit of that color?

I decided to ask my friend Charlotte, who loves to sew, to make a solid teal outfit for me, and we went to the fabric store.

As we entered the store I asked the Lord to help us find a teal-colored fabric. Charlotte first advised me to pick out the pattern for the outfit. We sat down at the pattern table and started looking through the pattern books. An older woman eventually sat down beside me. I finally selected a pattern I liked. I showed it to Charlotte. This pattern book was unfamiliar to Charlotte (it wasn't the usual Simplicity or Vogue brands). Charlotte didn't know where to find how much material I would need.

The woman beside me asked what size I needed and showed Charlotte exactly where to find how much material she would need to make the dress.

Next I needed to find the fabric. I stated out loud that I didn't know what teal looked like. The woman came to my rescue again. She had me follow her to the thread section. She picked a teal (a greenish-blue color) spool of thread and gave it to me. It was very pretty. I thanked her.

Charlotte and I went in search of the teal fabric. Toward the end of the row Charlotte found a fabric the exact color as the thread with an exquisite gold pattern. We bought it.

It wasn't until I got home that it hit me. The fabric was *teal* with *gold* pattern. How cool is that! My God is awesome. First, He sends a woman to help us. Second, He gives me a fabric that has the exact colors of the wedding. He gave me more than I had asked Him for.

Jesus said, "Ask, and it shall be given you; seek, and ye shall find; knock, and it shall be opened unto you" (Matthew 7:7).

The first word of this verse is *Ask*.

Women, always ask. Talk to the Lord about everything—no matter how small the request.

Ruth Cantrell

Oatmeal. Not Again!

"You will have plenty to eat . . .
and you will praise the name of the Lord."
—Joel 2:26, NIV

In August of 1993, I was looking forward to embarking on a new adventure. I was going as a student missionary to Rwanda. Upon my arrival, I was immediately embraced by several missionary families. They helped me adjust to a new way of life. One of the things I had to get used to was speaking in French. Although I had studied this language for years and understood it, I was not able to speak it fluently. I also had to learn about the culture and customs of the people. And, I had to get used to bumpy roads and living alone.

One of the other—and main—things I had to get used to was the food. Now, I love different kinds of food, so learning to eat something new was all right with me. I soon learned that it would be cheaper for me to purchase food from the market instead of from the store. This meant that my choices for breakfast were very limited. I remember Mrs. VanLanen taught me how to make oatmeal for breakfast.

I had eaten oatmeal back home, when I was young, with my ma. But I didn't like it. Now here I was in a different country, and I had to survive. So I tried oatmeal again. After eating it for a couple of weeks, I realized once again that I was not enjoying it. I am *not* a lover of oatmeal. The thought of eating oatmeal for breakfast most of the time was not appealing. I needed to figure out a solution to this dilemma, and fast.

When I asked Mrs. VanLanen if there was another way I could use oats for breakfast, she showed me how to make granola. After that it was granola, tofu, or eggs for breakfast, and I became a happy camper.

This experience reminds me of the time when the Israelites were in the wilderness. They complained that they didn't have the rich foods of Egypt. They started to worry about food. Instead of trusting God, they started complaining and grumbling again. Then when God gave them manna to eat, they complained that it was not enough.

David reminds us to be grateful and to praise God: "Bless the Lord, O my soul, and forget not all his benefits" (Psalm 103:2). God may not send manna, or oats, but He will send what we need. However we get our food, it is because God is providing it for us. Let us give thanks!

Dana M. Bean

My Purpose

"Yet who knows whether you have come to the kingdom for such a time as this?"
—*Esther 4:14, NKJV*

One day Luiza, the seven-year-old daughter of a dear childhood friend, sat next to me and asked me to tell her a story. From a book, I read to her the story of Amy Carmichael, a Christian missionary to India who cared for orphans and preached Jesus.

When I finished reading the story, I told Luiza that God had a purpose for Amy's life and that He has a special purpose for each of us. Her eyes bright, Luiza looked at me and asked, "What is *my* purpose?"

I was clueless concerning God's purpose for that child's life, so I told her that maybe her purpose had something to do with something she enjoyed doing—such as handing out books about Jesus. Disappointed, Luiza asked: "That's it? That is my purpose? Only that?"

Her truthful response—and her willingness to do harder things for God—touched me. I assured her that one day God would completely reveal His purposes for her life. Since then I have been praying for God to honor the faith of this little girl and someday make known His plan for her. I am certain she will fulfill it with all her heart.

This makes me think of those who spend an entire lifetime studying, dreaming, working, having fun, and living out routines, yet without really dedicating time to examine if they are fulfilling God's specific purposes for their lives. I'm not simply referring to the work we do in ministries at our churches. My question is, Are we really asking God to help us see the big picture—His dream for our lives?

Queen Esther prayed and fasted before God revealed more specifics about His purposes for her life. When she was sure of God's will, she found the courage to accomplish His purpose even though it meant putting her own life at risk. Amy Carmichael did the same. And so can you and I.

Along with little Luiza, I desire to fulfill God's purpose for me more than anything else. What about you? Today are you willing to seek His purpose for you and then, by His grace and in His strength, fulfill it?

Kênia Kopitar

Bursting Through the Clouds

And Jesus said, I am: and ye shall see the Son of man sitting on the
right hand of power, and coming in the clouds of heaven.
—*Mark 14:62*

Have you ever thought about the kingdom of God bursting through the clouds? What a glorious day that will be!

I had the opportunity to spend the summer in Atlanta (or as some say, "Hotlanta"), Georgia. My routine, at least on most days, included early morning meditation and prayer walking.

One particular morning I was inspired by the cool temperature, the refreshing breeze, and the many sights and sounds of nature.

I gazed at the scampering of the squirrels, the mist of water on every blade of grass, and the rich greenery of the trees reaching for the sky. I noticed the fragrant flowers opening their petals to receive their morning strength.

Then I beheld it—a spectacular, bright yellow and orange sun bursting through the sky; for an instant, it seemed to move the trees and birds aside to make space for itself! I lingered to take in the beauty of this moment and captured the memory in my brain like a camera capturing a photograph.

The rising sun in the east immediately filled my mind with thoughts about that magnificent day when Christ will burst through the clouds and receive His people, a glorious appearance seen by every eye.

My heart was overwhelmed at the thought of this wonderful day. What a blessed hope this is, shining like the sun in our hearts!

May we enjoy the beauty on earth as we wait for Christ's coming. May we do good works as we prepare our hearts to meet our Savior and King, Jesus.

Don't you want to be there? I do. And along the lines of Jeff Wood's song "Side by Side," we can plan to meet one another in heaven and, in the meantime, fervently pray for one another to be there.

Ella Clark-Tolliver

Be Still

Be still, and know that I am God: I will be exalted among
the heathen, I will be exalted in the earth.
—*Psalm 46:10*

The year 2014 was a tough year for me because I lost two of my sisters that year. Also, June 8 was especially difficult—it was the anniversary of the birth of my dear little son, David. He would have been forty-six that year. Born prematurely, he developed hyaline membrane disease (known as respiratory distress syndrome, common in premature babies). David didn't survive long, and I didn't have a chance to hold him before he died.

Recalling all this sadness that day made me long for the time when I will hold David. My hope lies in Jesus, who will reunite families and friends when He returns to take us home. That evening I had an unusual experience. I posted it on Facebook the next day to encourage others. It read, "June 9, 2014—When I was getting ready for bed last night, only the nightlight in my bathroom was on. I had been looking up into the sky and praying and thanking God for His grace and mercy. The moon was almost full and had been shining brightly. Then clouds covered its shiny radiance, suggesting lurking storms. I felt sad and shut out."

My Facebook post continued: "Praying with my eyes open, I asked God to please hear my prayers. I asked if He would cause the moon to come out again, just for me, before I finished my prayer and went to bed. If it did, I would know—without a doubt—that He was listening to me. I softly whispered my request as I looked into the dark sky where the moon was supposed to be. In less than a minute, the moon's glow appeared from behind the dense clouds. I was happy with just the glow and thanked God for His mercy and goodness. Then suddenly the moon came out in full array. I was so excited! I know I had tears of happiness in my eyes. It wasn't even five minutes before the moon was gone again and the sky completely dark again. I finished my prayers and said good night and thank You to my King."

I concluded my post: "I slept like I haven't slept for a long time. No kind of medication or herbal teas needed. Just slept with God's love in my heart and mind. In those moments with just God and me, I learned a lot. I wanted to share this experience with you."

"Be still," God reminds us, "and know that I am God." Be still before Him today.

Judith Fletcher Norwood

Quake 2014—Part 1

Give thanks in all circumstances.
—1 Thessalonians 5:18, NIV

W hat a mess!" cried Melissa, a neighbor girl. An understatement if ever there was one. "And look! The windows in the family room, they're gone!" The sight was not completely unexpected.

The epicenter of the August 24 Napa earthquake was barely three miles from my house. What wasn't on the floor was askew on the walls or tumbling out of drawers. I began to tremble (the body's way of adjusting to shock) as tears trailed one another down my cheeks, unbidden.

Melissa tugged at my hand. "What are we going to do?" I stood immobile in the kitchen. Dimly I realized that it wasn't so much the piles of smashed glass and broken dishes littering the tile floor that my brain and body were reacting to—that was only *stuff*. It was that my home, the place I returned to both in mind and in body after travel, no longer felt like a refuge. It was a disaster zone.

Trying to pull myself together, a bit of brain-function research flashed into mind: fear and gratitude cannot coexist simultaneously in the brain. *Well*, I thought to myself, *here's an opportunity to put that research into practice.* Immediately I began to give thanks. Consciously. Aloud. "I'm grateful we were not here when the quake occurred and that the house is still standing. I'm grateful no one is hurt. I'm grateful that windows are replaceable. I'm grateful—"

Melissa jumped in: "There was no fire, friends are coming to help us clean up, the dishwasher wasn't unloaded so we still have some dishes and glasses, and the fridge only walked three feet into the kitchen and not all the way into the family room." She giggled. "The few pictures still left on the walls are askew, though. Really *askew*!"

I laughed, too, celebrating Melissa's opportunity to use a new word! Two minutes of gratitude. Barely 120 seconds, and already I had begun to feel more calm and centered.

"Hey, you've stopped shaking," said Melissa.

"Yes," I acknowledged. "*Choosing* to be grateful changed everything."

"Is that why the Bible says to be thankful?" asked Melissa.

Nodding, I thought to myself: *The antidote for fear and shock is clearly spelled out in Scripture: "In all things give thanks."*

Arlene R. Taylor

Quake 2014–Part 2

Giving thanks always for all things.
—*Ephesians 5:20*

Melissa and I stood looking at the earthquake mess—and it was a *mess*! Gingerly stepping around shattered glass, broken lamps, toppled furniture, we went through the rest of the house. In my office, far more books were in a mess on the floor than had remained on the shelves. In the bedroom, brass candlesticks and other decorative items had fallen from high shelving onto the bed.

"Wow!" exclaimed Melissa. "If you'd been in bed you might have gotten hurt! Those candlesticks are *heavy*." She paused. "So how did being thankful make you stop shaking?"

"Researchers have found that when you think about someone or something that you really appreciate and experience the feeling that goes with the thought, the parasympathetic calming-branch of the autonomic nervous system is triggered. This pattern, when repeated, provides a protective effect on the heart. The electromagnetic heart patterns of research participants became more coherent and ordered when they activated feelings of appreciation."

"OK, then," said Melissa, pulling on plastic gloves. "Let's clean up this mess."

And as we swept and shoveled and loaded "stuff" into garbage bags and bins, Melissa sang, "Thank You, Lord . . ." Four and a half hours later the house was at least livable.

In the weeks that followed, I learned that the fastest way to find tiny shards of broken glass that the vacuum cleaner had missed was to walk around the house barefoot. Almost daily there were other things for which to give thanks, as well, as we learned about the structural damage to many homes in the area. I had to replace only the refrigerator. Melissa's assessment was that "it must have died from the shock!"

At her next visit, Melissa said, "You always say to look for the silver lining in every dark cloud. Did you find one for the earthquake?"

"Yes," I replied. "I have found a silver lining: I'm using this earthquake as an opportunity to de-clutter and simplify." (I should have done that long ago!)

Scripture is a manual for everyday living, and brain-function research is validating Scripture's admonition to give thanks continually with one's whole heart (see Psalm 9:1, 2).

Arlene R. Taylor

The Missing Briefcase

"So do not fear, for I am with you;
do not be dismayed, for I am your God.
I will strengthen you and help you;
I will uphold you with my righteous right hand."
—Isaiah 41:10, NIV

I had a briefcase I wanted to send to a friend in India. So I went to my rather messy storeroom to get it—but couldn't find it. During the following weeks I searched for it in the storeroom whenever I had time. The shelves. The cupboards. Even the pile of stuff on the floor. But, I still could not locate the briefcase.

One day a visiting pastor friend from India came to my office. He had come to attend some meetings and do some traveling and would be returning to India in two weeks. He knew my friend in India and would be happy to return to get the briefcase from me for our friend.

In the meantime, frustrated in not being able to find the briefcase, I gave up looking for it, and asked a friend in the office if I could have his briefcase, which was exactly like mine. I told him I'd give him mine when I found it. He reluctantly agreed. However, I was a bit unhappy with this arrangement because his briefcase was used and looked a bit worn out compared to mine, which was practically new. I was glad that, at least, I could send a briefcase back with the pastor, knowing my friend would appreciate it very much and make good use of it.

When I knew the pastor would soon be by to pick up the briefcase, I decided to search diligently for it one more time. Earnestly I prayed as I went back down to the storeroom to check again.

As soon as I walked into the storeroom I went straight to the pile of stuff on the floor. Though I had searched in this area before, I reached for the topmost bag on the pile. To my utter joy and surprise, there was my briefcase—inside the bag! It looked so nice and so new, and now I'd found it just a few days before the pastor would come to get it.

I knew this discovery was a miracle, because I had looked in that same place several times before and I had not found it. I immediately thanked God for hearing and answering my prayer. My faith was strengthened.

Even in such a small matter, our loving God is so mindful of our desires and so kind to hear our prayers. Let us always be faithful in trusting Him!

Stella Thomas

Jesus Loves Me Too!

I . . . will draw all men unto me.
—*John 12:32*

No one was in the room, but from the distant corner in sweet babylike tones came four little sing-song words: "Jesus . . . loves . . . *me* . . . too." Mr. Nobody, the parakeet, had figured out that he could draw anyone— from anywhere in the room—over to his lonely corner cage by tilting his adorable little bright blue head and parroting this phrase.

I just had to have a parakeet too and set about learning what techniques produce the most talkative birds. One directive consistently came through: have only one bird, for when excluded from their own kind, they join the human world in order to have a relationship with *something*. Eventually, however, I settled on two birds that would sing in favor of one that would talk. We also discovered that hummingbird feeders that suction to our glass windows—and are positioned at eye level across from the breakfast nook—draw tiny flaming jewels to work their tapered beaks into their "baby juice" just inches from our eyes. These birds, too, enjoy community.

The solitary bird that speaks to gain attention reminds me that most of us could name someone within the sisterhood of our community, church, or workplace whom we might consider socially starved. Perhaps she feels her own attempts to reach out have fizzled. One church sister once told me that as she walked out of church alone, the elder on door duty shook her hand, saying, "Happy Sabbath!" at the same time he was already reaching for the hand of the person behind her. She told me she'd thought, *I don't need you to shake my hand. I'd rather have a hug from your wife.*

The lonely human heart longs for something to fill the vacuum. When parents and other adults do not spend time with their children and young people, noticing them and providing meaningful dialogue and activities, are they actually starving the social natures of the children and young people? Will the children and young people reach out for recognition in other ways as did that little bird who talked? Will they reach out in ways that are unhealthy or engage in spiritually harmful pastimes to fill the vacuum in their hearts?

Also, when we don't reach out to sisters around us, noticing them, affirming who they are, and involving them in our activities, are we starving them as well? Let's remember that by our kindness and attention, we can assure them—even demonstrate—that Jesus loves *them* too.

Janet Lankheet

Seeds

A sower went out to sow his seed: and as he sowed,
some fell by the way side; and it was trodden down,
and the fowls of the air devoured it.
—Luke 8:5

Not long ago I entered a market and saw a display of seed packets. I thought I could plant something that would not be too much work. So I chose an envelope of watermelon seeds and an assortment of poppies. I knew people who had buried kitchen scraps and then found plants growing on the site. Some of these plants produced a harvest of things just as good as those grown in a proper garden. So, even though I do not have a green thumb, I sowed my seeds—according to the instructions—expecting the same miracle. I watered them and watched. Finally, I grew tired and forgot them and never got my watermelons.

As for the poppies, I planted them in a large pot to bring color to the area. *They will bloom in all colors,* I thought, remembering the picture on the envelope. I watered them more often than I did the watermelon seeds. One day I noticed, with disgust, that ants had built a volcano-shaped anthill in the center of my poppy "garden." As I poured poison over the mound, I assumed the ants had already devoured my poppy seeds—though I kept watering the pot in case some seed remained.

One day I saw that two small green leaves had appeared in the pot. A few hours later, I noticed a small spot of purple. Could it be one of the poppies I had planted? Would I really have flowers? Yes! Time revealed they were flowers! But not poppies. Rather, petunias. Soon purple petunias cascaded down the sides of the pot, brightening the garden. What an unexpected result from the seeds I'd planted! Watermelon seeds did not grow like sheer magic (especially when I stopped watering them), and the flowers I thought would be poppies were something else.

As we go through life we are always planting seeds. We have expectations for them. We often believe that what we sow will emerge just as we had imagined. Yet the harvest of what we have planted in the hearts of others may surprise us. We may be disappointed or surprised with the results, yet our responsibility is simply to plant. I want to keep sowing—not only seed in my garden, but also love in the hearts of others. The results I can leave with God. "And let us not be weary in well doing: for in due season we shall reap, if we faint not" (Galatians 6:9).

Leni Uría de Zamorano

God Answers Prayer

*"He shall call upon Me, and I will answer him;
I will be with him in trouble;
I will deliver him and honor him."*
—*Psalm 91:15, NKJV*

My travel itinerary would take me to two different countries, neither of which was my home country. One required that I have a visa prior to entry. I had a limited number of days during which I could apply for a visa before traveling to the visa-free country. Though the visa was to have taken only a week to process, it was somehow delayed. So I had no visa when it was time to leave on my trip.

I had to leave my passport behind in order to have the visa stamped in it. Because I could travel without a visa to the visa-free country, I left my passport behind and planned for it to be sent by DHL (an international express mail service) for processing at the embassy. Of course, this was risky because doing this put me in the other country without my primary international identification document. Yet I had no other choice.

I was to leave that country on a Sunday. As the departure day approached, we waited, counted the days, and prayed. Wednesday arrived. Thursday arrived. Yet still there was no word from the visa agent. Now I had no passport to enable me to extend my days should my visa application be delayed once again.

Friday arrived. And so did word from the visa agent that my visa had been granted! Now, however, sending my passport by DHL on Friday would mean it would arrive on Monday—one day too late for my scheduled departure date. This was very tricky. As a group of leaders, we prayed fervently and fasted for the intervention of the Holy Spirit in bringing about a solution to my dilemma. Eventually, my husband was able to travel to deliver my passport and go back home the same day. The Lord had listened to our cry and helped in this situation.

I would like to testify that there is nothing more important in this life than prayer. Prayer is our connection with God, especially in crisis. It is our strength and bridge to heaven. When we begin to call upon His name, we will surely find Him. His promise is that He hears our prayers.

Dear Lord, thank You for the ministry of the Holy Spirit, who unites with us in our petitions and intercedes on our behalf. Thank You for not leaving us alone in the battle of life because all of heaven is on our side.

Caroline Chola

A Special Bond

"Behold, I stand at the door and knock.
If anyone hears my voice and opens the door,
then I will come in to him, and will dine with him, and he with me."
—*Revelation 3:20, WEB*

I have the cutest grandson who soon will be turning two. I love him so much. When I see him, I want to hug him, hold him, and coo to him. There is no better feeling in the whole world than when he reaches his little arms out to me. We spend time talking and sharing. I can't understand very much of what he says, but that doesn't really matter much because our bond is so special. We spend a lot of time looking at pictures on my phone or on the camera. (I can't delete them, even though they've been on my computer for a long time, because he likes them so much.) Sometimes we color, read books, or play with cars; we always have a lot of fun.

But sometimes when I reach for him, he turns his head away and buries his face in his mommy's shoulder, or he runs and hides behind her leg, not wanting anything to do with me. This rejection crushes me for a moment. I have to back away and give him time to warm up to me again. Soon he usually warms up, and we can have our time together again. Yet, on occasion, he doesn't warm up to me. When that happens, I have to be an outside observer—watching but not touching—and we miss out on our bonding.

The last time he turned from me I thought about my relationship with Jesus. How many times has Jesus had to back away from me and wait for *me* to be ready to spend time with Him again? How many times have I crushed His heart when I chose to run to some worldly distraction instead of running to Him for comfort? How many times has He stood knocking at the door of my heart and I wouldn't let Him in? Instead, I left Him watching but not touching.

I don't want to treat Him like that because I lose out on so much when I'm not spending time with Him. I lose out when I fail to reflect on His goodness to me and on His many blessings in my life. Even when my words and thoughts are garbled and don't make sense to anyone else, He understands. I sense Him smiling at me, just like I smile at my grandson when he babbles his thoughts to me. Every day now I try to tell Jesus I want to know Him better.

Jesus is your friend too. God the Father is your daddy. They want to spend time with you. Will you reach out to them today and experience that special bond that nothing can surpass?

Mona Fellers

Peace Amid Gunfire

You will keep in perfect peace
those whose minds are steadfast,
because they trust in you.
—Isaiah 26:3, NIV

'd had a wonderful weekend of prayer fellowship at church. We'd just finished a Week of Prayer, which included a Communion service Friday evening. When the Sabbath afternoon youth program finished, some teenagers and young people decided to watch a movie at church, and I agreed to participate. As soon as the movie finished we got ready to leave. While a friend and I were putting away the equipment, some of the young people stood outside, visiting. Suddenly the uncle of one of the teens arrived. Breathlessly he said, "Go to your homes immediately! An armed man is driving around the area threatening whomever he passes." The man took his nephew and another young man to their houses.

"Please, everyone," I said, "let's all go to our homes. And don't take any shortcuts." While I was talking, a friend's cell phone rang. A woman, who lives on the street where our church is located, reported, "I just saw an armed man in a red car. He is menacing people."

As our church group left in twos and threes, I noticed that the only person who was going to go back alone was me. Everyone else who had been at the event left with others. It was not late, so I began walking. After I'd taken a few steps, God touched the heart of my friend Vasty. "Let me come with you to your house," she offered. "In fact, let's both ride my bike to your place to get there sooner. Then I can ride home quickly from there."

I accepted her offer. We started cycling toward my home. As we left the church and turned the bike into another street, we saw a group of people who suddenly began to run—as if in desperation. Then we heard gunshots. Overcome by fear, I said, "Lord, help me!"

Vasty said, "Don't look back! Ride nonstop. Just follow the path home. Now go! Go! *Go!*" Her words brought me a sense of assurance and encouragement. My fear went away.

Vasty left me at my home and continued on her way. Minutes later she phoned to say she had arrived safely and was OK. The Lord helped us trust in Him for our protection.

Thank You, Lord, for wanting us to depend on You and rely on Your protection. Thank You for Your care and for friends who help us in difficult situations—and give us comfort.

Carmem Virgínia dos Santos Paulo

What Is *Peculiar*? Do I Meet the Criteria?

Don't copy the behavior and customs of this world,
but let God transform you into a new person
by changing the way you think.
Then you will learn to know God's will for you,
which is good and pleasing and perfect.
—Romans 12:2, NLT

I had a flash of thought at 1:00 A.M. on a Sabbath morning and had to look up the word *peculiar*.

Merriam-Webster.com defines it a couple ways: (1) "characteristic of only one person, group, or thing," and (2) "different from the usual or normal."

All of my Christian life I have heard that God's followers are to be thought of as a "peculiar people." That statement has often caused me to cringe—with images in my mind of a group of somewhat cult-like individuals. The details this image entailed seemed, for the lack of a better word, uninviting. So I've wondered, *What does it mean to be peculiar in this world—in relationship to the living example that Jesus set for us?*

Ah! A revelation of sorts smacks me square in the gut. Jesus was peculiar. In fact, Jesus was a breath of fresh air to people living in their own "spiritual" captivity. Jesus broke the norm. The church leaders, most of them, didn't understand Him. They didn't appreciate the way He would not submit to their rituals and their traditions. Jesus was special, odd, and possibly seemed, at times, a bit eccentric. Jesus, the Savior of the world, who sat in the home of a Gentile, was the epitome of peculiar. He was the One who stood among the crowds and preached—not laws and rules and tradition, but—God the Father, heaven, and amazing grace. He *loved* sinners.

So what *is* peculiar in this world? I believe that it means living a life cloaked in the *grace* of Jesus. I believe that a person who understands the *peace* that passes *all* understanding will be viewed as peculiar. This world does not understand the pure love of Jesus—the love that will never fail us.

To be a person who loves like Christ Jesus in a world that is hurting and at constant odds with itself, now *that* is a peculiar person. And I am good with that. Count me in.

Joey Lynn Norwood Tolbert

The Awakening

And he shall see his face with joy.
—Job 33:26

And they shall see his face.
—Revelation 22:4

I discovered the lump in my breast in my late teens. My doctor said it appeared to be a benign noma and we'd just watch it a while. Five years later my breast began to hurt, so I went back to my doctor. His examination discovered the small lump had grown significantly in the few months since my yearly exam. He sent me directly from his office to the hospital and scheduled surgery for the next morning.

That morning when the nurse awakened me I was very frightened because I knew that if this suddenly growing tumor had turned cancerous the doctor would remove my breast. About 6:30 A.M. the nurse gave me a shot. "To relax you," she said. "We won't put you under until just before you go into the operating room at seven." But it seemed to take forever for them to come back to put me "under." The nurse came by and I asked her, "What time is it?"

She laughed and said a time that didn't register in my foggy mind. Then, as though she were speaking to someone else, I heard her say, "She's coming out of the anesthetic now. She's been asking the time every time I checked on her for the last half hour. Surgery went well. The tumor was a noncancerous noma."

I opened my eyes to see who she was talking to. There, looking down at me with love in his eyes, was my dad. He had taken off work to be with me when I awoke from my terrifying surgery! Now, more than fifty years later, I often think of that reassuring moment when I opened my eyes and saw my loving dad smiling down at me in the recovery room.

Not all of us will be alive when Christ returns. Some of us will find our guardian angels with us as we rise from our graves, just like that recovery room nurse was with me. And when we look up we shall see our Savior, smiling down at us with reassurance and love. We are told, "We will not all sleep, but we will all be changed—in a flash, in the twinkling of an eye, at the last trumpet. For the trumpet will sound, the dead will be raised imperishable, and we will be changed" (1 Corinthians 15:51, 52, NIV). If we are faithful but not among those living when Christ returns, our angel will awaken us with those of the first resurrection. Oh, what joy!

Darlenejoan McKibbin Rhine

Witnessing for Jesus

For God so loved the world,
that he gave his only begotten Son.
—*John 3:16*

I was talking with one of my many nephews one day, explaining to him what God requires of a Christian. My dear nephew does not believe in Christianity. He believes it is a belief system used to control people. I explained to him that to be a Christian means to accept Christ as one's personal Savior, and to be in a loving relationship with Him that will draw us into doing His will.

As my nephew and I continued our conversation, I explained to him that to be a true Christian is to follow God's will because we love Him and because His Son, Jesus Christ, loves us so much He died to save us from our sins.

Christians must have a very close relationship with Christ in order to obey His will. Making choices to obey—in God's strength—is an ongoing process. In fact, it is the work of a lifetime. (The Bible refers to this process as sanctification.) We can do all things only through Christ who makes us strong (Philippians 4:13).

I explained to my nephew that the way to obtain strength in Christ is to talk to Him through prayer. We listen to Him through the study of the Bible. We ask for the Holy Spirit's guidance to know what God's will and purpose is for our lives.

My nephew said he believes only in Jehovah. I pointed out that Christians believe in Jehovah as well. God has many names, and Jehovah is one of His names. It means Lord. I showed him the name Jehovah in the Bible (Exodus 6:3; Psalm 83:18; Isaiah 12:2; 26:4).

During our conversation my prayer was (and still is) that my nephew will someday understand that we can do nothing to save ourselves. Self-disciplined obedience to God's law cannot save us. Only the shed blood of Jesus can forgive and cleanse our sins.

I shared with my nephew that the only thing we can "do" toward our own salvation is simply choose to give our heart, our will, our life to God. We have nothing in ourselves to merit His grace, for, as the Bible points out, our "righteousness" is as dirty rags in God's sight (Isaiah 64:6). I pray that my family and friends will know the love of Jesus for themselves.

With love, we can witness for Jesus to those around us, but only God can save.

Moselle Slaten Blackwell

Cost of Reconstruction

"I will give you a new heart and put a new spirit in you; I will remove from you your heart of stone and give you a heart of flesh."
—*Ezekiel 36:26, NIV*

Several years ago I had both knees replaced. First, I had the right knee replaced, and it was a miracle. In just a few weeks, I was able to return to teaching. The pain was gone and I felt that I was as good as new.

Then came the left knee replacement. It was a nightmare. Never-ending pain forced me to curtail many activities. When I could stand no more, I consulted a new surgeon. We set a date for reconstruction. The big day finally came. I had a new knee. The surgeon was pleased with the outcome. Because of drug allergies there were few remedies for my intense pain. But I mastered my rehabilitation exercises, and medical personnel told me I was ready to go home.

My daughter, Patti, had come to stay with me for the first part of my recovery. She filled my days with encouraging smiles. I thought I was doing very well. Then Patti had to leave. I struggled through pain-filled hours trying to remember to take my medication, to exercise, and to complete my tasks about the home.

Those first few weeks after surgery reminded me many times that reconstruction is much more serious than construction. Indeed, at that point, I still had many more weeks of discomfort before I would be able to move freely again. My experience has reminded me of what God promised to Ezekiel and all others willing to listen: He will give them a new heart. A knee cannot compare to a heart, but the principle is the same. My surgeon promised to remove my faulty knee replacement and install a reconstructed one. God, however, promises to remove our stony hearts and replace them with hearts of flesh. He will give us a new spirit. I must be willing to have my old selfish ways sliced off and a new caring me grafted in.

What will that look like in everyday life? Instead of filling just my cupboards, I will help fill the food bank cupboards. Instead of expecting others to pass out literature, I will be a part of that outreach. Instead of saying, "I can't do anything," I will choose to let God use me in ways that will bless others. That is the cost of heart reconstruction—though it's not about the work I may do. What it *is* about, is living out Christ's commitment: "Not my will, but yours be done" (Luke 22:42, NIV). Our personal cost of reconstruction will be someone else's blessing.

Patricia Cove

The Leaning Boot

Casting all your care upon Him,
for He cares for you.
—1 Peter 5:7, NKJV

There come seasons in our lives when we plummet into despair and become discouraged. We become so overwhelmed by, and enslaved to, the cares of this world, that we forget God's words of solace: that we should cast all of our cares upon Him, for He cares for us.

One Tuesday morning I was preparing for work, still recovering from the flu. The cares of my world rushed upon me with the force of a tsunami and reduced me to tears of helplessness. Cares such as mounting bills, family, work pressures, high accountability, and exhaustion. Feeling like I couldn't carry on, I leaned my head on the wall and cried out in silent tears to my heavenly Father.

I had to finish dressing for work, however. In my closet, I have boots, supported by inner boot holders, standing up against a wall. I reached down and picked out my pair of black. In the vacuum left by the boots I'd removed, a brown boot, previously standing next to the black boots, slowly leaned over into the vacated space and against the next pair of boots.

Startled, I instinctively pushed the brown boot back, perplexed that it should even move. After all, that was the purpose of the boot holders situated inside each boot—to keep them upright. But right after I pushed back the brown boot, it slowly leaned over onto the next boot.

Then I knew. God, in His infinite compassion and love for me, had just vividly yet gently reminded me to lean on Him. He would be my solace, my inner strength, the supplier of all my needs. A sense of peace swept over me. I was filled with thanksgiving and praise to God.

Friends, we serve the Almighty, who is, as Psalm 24 says, the "King of glory," "strong and mighty," "mighty in battle," the "Lord of hosts." God is our watchful, loving Shepherd who knows our every need and promises to supply all our needs according to His good will and pleasure.

Jesus says in Matthew 6:26: "Behold the fowls of the air: for they sow not, neither do they reap, nor gather into barns; yet your heavenly Father feedeth them. Are ye not much better than they?"

So, be encouraged today, have faith in God, and lean on Him.

Cynthia Best-Goring

Surprises From Our Heavenly Father

I will bless the LORD at all times:
his praise shall continually be in my mouth.
—*Psalm 34:1*

For my special birthday and Christmas presents in December 2012, my daughter Cheri and son-in-law Jeff gave me a trip to Scotland with them in late July 2013. Before touring Scotland, as was our plan, we would allow ourselves a bit of extra time, to try to locate the house where my father was raised before coming to the United States at the age of eighteen or nineteen. We had only a 3 x 5 inch (7.6 x 12.7 centimeter) black-and-white photo of the house in Uddingston, not far from Glasgow.

In June, we had our first surprise. Jeff found out that the wife of his boss is Scottish. Her brother Steve and family still live in Scotland and—of all places—in Uddingston. In early July of that year, Steve made a business trip to the United States. It was arranged for him to meet Jeff at the radio station where Jeff worked. Jeff had questions concerning transportation to and around Uddingston. At that time Steve offered to take the day off from work, after our arrival in Scotland, to pick us up at our hotel and help us locate my father's house. He took a copy of the picture of the house and exchanged contact information with Jeff. It seemed that God definitely planned this surprising turn of events.

True to his word, Steve met us at the hotel the morning of July 24. As we drove, he told us that at first he had no idea where this house was. Then he showed the picture to his son, who knew exactly where the house was, as he had friends who lived on the adjoining property. It was exciting to drive outside of Uddingston down a narrow country lane. At the end of the road—in a clearing next to the river Clyde—stood a two-story, red sandstone blockhouse. The very one I'd seen only in a picture. (The name of the house had been changed from Clydeside to Greyfriar House because the last inhabitants had been Greyfriar monks.) Though the house was vacant and padlocked, what a thrill it still was to see the house where my father and his family had lived before migrating to the United States in the late 1920s!

Our heavenly Father orchestrated this happy, exciting surprise for us so that we could visit the home of my earthly father. God enjoys doing wonderful things for His children. Because of His constant concern for our welfare and happiness, should we not continually praise Him?

Patricia Mulraney Kovalski

What a God!—Part 1

*The steadfast love of the LORD never ceases; his mercies never come
to an end; they are new every morning; great is your faithfulness.*
—*Lamentations 3:22, 23, ESV*

The Wailing Wall in Old Jerusalem attracts thousands of believers and tourists every day. The ancient wall (known also as the Western Wall, standing 187 feet—almost 57 meters—high on the western side of the Temple Mount in Old Jerusalem) has been a site for Jewish prayer and pilgrimages for centuries. People write their prayers on pieces of paper and insert them into the crevices in the lower blocks where joints between the stones have eroded. Many believe that this is a special way to have their prayers answered. In fact, people of various religious beliefs have left prayers in the wall. Interestingly enough, people can also e-mail, fax, tweet, and text prayers to place in the wall. One can also pay for some of these services with a credit card as well as make donations to help keep these services going.

While these services provide much needed employment for some, this interesting prayer setup reflects some of the unbiblical concepts out there about who God is and how He interacts with those whom He has created.

Far from Jerusalem's Wailing Wall, I grew up amid a mixture of other superstitious beliefs: Taoism, Confucianism, and animism (the belief of spirits inhabiting objects). The beliefs around me were so varied, so unstable, so inconsistent (depending on who you talked to), that I was very confused as a child listening to the interpretations of what was happening in our everyday life. Devout prayer was also very much a part of that worship, with offerings to the myriad spirits and the gods who were as fickle as the human beings who served them. Some people around us prayed regularly; others, not at all until a crisis hit them. I remember devotees busily offering *joss sticks* (a kind of incense often burnt in Eastern religious practice) morning and night to the altars. Special feast days called for special offerings such as chickens, ducks, or pigs (depending on one's financial ability) and visits to the temple. As a child, I enjoyed the fact that after offering the food to the gods, you got to eat it yourself!

Yet God desired to reveal to me, little by little, who He really is. He wants to do the same for you—today. Let us always be watchful and eager to learn more about who God is.

Sally Lam-Phoon

What a God!—Part 2

"But You are God, ready to pardon,
Gracious and merciful,
Slow to anger, abundant in kindness."
—Nehemiah 9:17, NKJV

The myriad belief systems—and gods—surrounding me as I grew up made it hard for me to figure out exactly what the gods were thinking. It seemed that they kept us humans guessing as to what was going on behind the scenes. The various beliefs of these religions also kept us in the dark concerning what caused so much misfortune and illness in the world. Many people expended much effort and money to appease the spirits so they would cease hurting humans with their mischievous pranks. Different temple priests sometimes offered "answers" to our questions, yet these conflicting interpretations confused us even more. The inconsistency and lack of a unified belief system left many of us worshipers in doubt and fear.

Hence, when I met Jesus, the Christian God, through the influence of the parochial school I attended, His love and compassion—His willingness to die for me so I could be saved—was a gospel truth that thrilled my soul. What a God!

Later, through Bible studies at a Christian church, my knowledge of God was deepened, and further insights into the character of God drew me to make a decision to join the church. It was wonderful to learn that my God does not play any tricks on me. He is consistent and committed to giving me joy, peace, and an abundant life—for I have surrendered my life to Him.

Over the years as a Christian, I came to appreciate God's unchanging love for me, though my love for Him has had its ups and downs. After almost fifty years of walking with Him, I have learned to trust Him completely, relying on His promises to be fulfilled. He has given me confidence and security even in an uncertain world. He has buoyed up my spirits. He has given me the deepest joy, even in the midst of life's storms. I don't have to pay another human being to intercede with God for me or to tell me what God wants of me. He has given me His sure Word with its power, strength, and guidance for my everyday life—whatever comes my way.

Yes, my God is on my side. He wants what is best for me. He forgives my sins when I fail Him and realigns my will with His. He takes me places in life where I'd never dreamed of going. He encourages me. He promises me His power, His love, and His grace. What a God!

Sally Lam-Phoon

He Is Able

By the word of the LORD the heavens were made,
their starry host by the breath of his mouth. . . .
For he spoke, and it came to be;
he commanded, and it stood firm.
—*Psalm 33:6–9, NIV*

I recently watched an interview with Marcos Pontes, the first Brazilian astronaut. In this interview, he said that his religious faith and belief in God increased after his space trip. It is impossible not to believe in the existence of God after having contemplated the immensity of the universe. It is wonderful to contemplate nature and each perfect detail that only a living God has the power to create. Isn't God's power wonderful? He is so powerful that He need only speak words to bring things into existence!

I want to remind you that this same power that established the worlds in space and filled the earth with beautiful things is still accessible to us today. The Bible shows that this power has served not only to create but also to heal. When Jesus walked on this earth, He spoke to the lepers and they were healed. By His voice demons were cast out. Jesus spoke to the storm and it ceased. So let me say it again: this power is at your disposal today.

What things would you like to see changed in your life? The same power that created the world can create new life in us. The same power that healed people still effects cures today. The same power that cast out demons has strength to expel our anxieties. The same power that calmed the storm can calm the storms of life. It replaces insecurity, discouragement, and despair with peace. God's power can transform us. So often, when we look at ourselves, we see many imperfect actions. Yet God's power, through Christ's sacrifice, has done everything to make us better people—people with willpower to overcome bad habits.

Friend, what would you like to ask God to change in you? In 2 Corinthians 5:17, we read, "Therefore, if anyone is in Christ, the new creation has come: The old has gone, the new is here!" (NIV). God can take away a bad temper and habits that harm our health.

King David prayed, "Create in me a pure heart, O God, and renew a steadfast spirit within me" (Psalm 51:10, NIV).

May these biblical promises be your prayer today. Remember that God has the power to create in you a pure heart, full of love and kindness.

Meibel Mello Guedes

Tithing and Trust

"Bring the whole tithe into the storehouse, that there may be food in my house. Test me in this," says the LORD Almighty, "and see if I will not throw open the floodgates of heaven and pour out so much blessing that there will not be room enough to store it."
—*Malachi 3:10, NIV*

My financial life was in shambles. Due to bad decisions and poor judgment, I had ended up bankrupt and starting over. I lived paycheck to paycheck while the cost of living, unexpected car repairs, and other bills just kept adding up. To make matters worse, my conscience was bothering me about tithing. I had been raised to believe that tithing was essential. But a couple of years before this point I had allowed myself to stop paying tithe because (I reasoned) I couldn't afford it. I was a single mom and money was tight. I'd planned to stop tithing just for a little while. I would get back to it when things got better. I rationalized that this made financial sense and God would understand. But the "little while" stretched into a couple of years. Things hadn't improved; in fact, they grew much worse. Now my conscience was convicting me that I should start paying tithe again. Yet I was still convinced I couldn't afford it.

One night I had a long struggle with God. With no peace in my heart, I kept arguing that I just didn't have enough money. It was as close to an actual conversation with God as I had ever had—not audible but so very real. God urged me to trust Him and pay tithe, reminding me it wasn't my money anyway. I countered with a balance sheet of my income and expenses and then gave in. It was presumptuous to argue with God. I said, "OK, I will pay tithe."

I have come to understand that paying tithe is not about the money. It's about trusting God to take care of us. God owns all the money in the world. We pay tithe to be reminded where our support truly comes from—not because God needs the money. It's also about trusting God to do what He says He will do.

The very next month after I began paying tithe, I received an unexpected and generous bonus at work. Paying tithe has now become my joy every month, and my financial life is entirely different. God has indeed blessed me abundantly—no matter what I've gone through.

I urge you, as well, to trust God for your financial needs. Pay your tithe. Test Him. See if He won't take care of you too. I guarantee He will!

Jeanene MacLean

God Is Always in Control

The LORD says, "I will make you wise and show you where to go.
I will guide you and watch over you."
—*Psalm 32:8, NCV*

Have you ever noticed how just one day can change your whole life? Maybe you get a phone call asking if you would like to move to Hawaii. Or an invitation to do mission work in Russia. When a new grandchild is born, you receive that happy announcement: "She's here!" And life changes for you from that day on.

There are some calls you don't want to receive. Calls from a police officer or the hospital or the morgue. Maybe a child phones to tell you they have chosen an alternative lifestyle. Perhaps a spouse calls to say he isn't coming home again. Just that quickly our lives can change.

Recently, I received a phone call I didn't ever want to receive. Don, my husband, was calling to tell me he had totaled my car. That's never what you want to hear. But, praise the Lord, my husband was spared and OK! A car can be replaced, but a husband—not so much!

The more we talked about the accident the more we saw God's hand in that event. There were no cars around him as Don drifted off the side of the road, hitting snow and ice. Over-correcting had put him in a spin, and he hit the snow bank on the other side of the road. This impact flipped the car three or four times before it landed upright again. All the windows were broken out, letting the snow pour inside the car. However, Don had no scratches, cuts, or bruises when it was over! Later he said he felt like someone had held his head, as he hadn't even strained his neck. Though his glasses and sunglasses flew off, they were easy to find in the snow. After the accident, cars quickly stopped and strangers helped. A retired couple were the first to stop. They stayed by while the ambulance and police came. When everything was all taken care of, they offered to take Don home, a very kind offer because the incident happened about two hours away from home! In getting acquainted with the kind couple, Don discovered the woman had just written a children's book about an angel with big feet. Don definitely felt as if that woman was his angel that day!

It's amazing how God puts the right people in our path when we need them. I am so thankful God guides and watches over us—and is *always* in control! Of course, I am especially grateful He has allowed my husband to live out more of his "threescore and ten" years.

Louise Driver

Wake-Up Call

Peter said to Him, "Lord, why can I not follow You now?
I will lay down my life for Your sake."
—John 13:37, NKJV

"Watch and pray, lest you enter into temptation.
The spirit indeed is willing, but the flesh is weak."
—Matthew 26:41, NKJV

Of course, I'll pray for you!" I confidently assured my friend concerning her upcoming worship presentation on Morning Manna, a weekday call-in prayer conference. "You can count on me to be your silent prayer partner!" I affirmed. The day before my friend's conference presentation, I wrote "Morning Manna" on a yellow sticky note and posted it conspicuously on my desk, so I wouldn't forget. I wrote "Morning Manna" on the palm of my left hand, so I'd remember to set my alarm for the 5:30 A.M. conference call. Before going to bed, I placed the conference call number between the alarm clock and the telephone and drifted off to sleep.

The alarm clock beeped shrilly at five twenty-five the next morning. I turned on the light, slipped out of bed, and downed a glass of cold water to wake myself up. Shivering slightly in the chilly predawn air, I dialed the conference call number and resumed prayers for my friend and her presentation.

As I joined the call, a thought interrupted my initial move toward a chair: *I can just sit up in bed. That would be much more comfy!* Settling against bed pillows, I put the phone on speaker mode and pulled the still-warm blanket up under my chin. I relaxed hearing the friendly voice of the conference facilitator and luxuriating in the special music as I joined my intercessory thoughts with the participants' praise reports. I closed my eyes for the prayer of praise and opened them—an hour later—totally missing my friend's presentation!

All day long I labored under a burden of disbelief, chagrin, disappointment in myself, and loss. I'd planned so carefully, yet I'd still missed out. What had gone wrong? Peter kept coming to mind. *Hmm.* Peter with the bold declaration to have Christ's back—even to the death. Peter with the heavy eyelids as he slipped into a Gethsemane snooze instead of watching unto prayer when Jesus yearned for his support. Like well-intentioned Peter, I'd also carelessly checked out.

That morning my failure—my drowsy self-indulgence—was an abrupt wake-up call. *Lord, today help our willing spirits vanquish weak flesh so that we'll be faithful promise keepers.*

Carolyn Rathbun Sutton

Tagged

Inasmuch as ye have done it unto one of the least of these
my brethren, ye have done it unto me.
—Matthew 25:40

A friend of ours left a message on the telephone to inform us that his wife, whom we had visited in the hospital a few days before, had died. He said also that arrangements for the funeral had been made, the date was set, and he expected us to be present.

Of course, we knew that was the least we could do, as we were considered a part of the family.

As we visited the family on the day of the funeral, the funeral director apparently ordered that each vehicle outside be tagged in order to be recognized as part of the funeral procession. As the grieving family proceeded to the church, we noticed that our car had been tagged. We had unintentionally lined up with other vehicles and now had no choice but to go forward.

While we waited in the car for the procession to start, we heard people approaching. Suddenly someone opened the door of our car and let two persons in (obviously, mourners).

What's going on? my heart asked. *Who are these people? How can they do this?* We learned these two individuals—strangers to us—were relatives of the deceased. They needed a ride. Our car was selected to take them because it had been tagged.

Soon we would learn that what had taken place was customary practice in that society. Fortunately for us, this was a secure situation, and all went well. Our riders gave us no cause for alarm or fear.

Furthermore, although we had no choice in the matter at this point, we were able to provide a most helpful service. Finally, we had the privilege of meeting some new people and learning something about their lives.

We were in the right place at the right time and were tagged for service.

How do we relate to people God uses to increase our awareness of the blessings that can be ours when we are willing to experience the privilege of service?

Fall in line. Let yourself be tagged for God's service today.

Quilvie G. Mills

A Christian Reincarnation

For the Lord himself will descend from heaven with a cry of command, with the voice of an archangel, and with the sound of the trumpet of God. And the dead in Christ will rise first.
—*1 Thessalonians 4:16, ESV*

Once I dreamt that my mother had died. Then, unfortunately, through a series of shocking events, she really did die seven months after that dream. Then, seven months after her death, I again had a dream—this time that she was still alive. Waking up from that dream was difficult because it reminded me of the painful loss. Yet I believed that God in His goodness was giving me the hope of seeing her again.

Before my mom's first memorial, God blessed my husband and me with the news of a baby on the way. My Hindu friends were excited. Their belief in reincarnation brought about comments such as, "Your mom is a fighter; she is coming back to us." Although my sister and I are fourth-generation Christians, the thought sounded sweet. The ultrasound results confirmed the baby was a girl. "A baby girl is an affirmation to your Hindu friends, I guess," my husband said with a chuckle. Even my mom's dog, on multiple occasions, would lay his head over my tummy.

Soon after my ultrasound, I had to attend a conference in Los Angeles. My husband had never been to California, so we decided to make it a road trip through San Francisco via Yosemite National Park. Being bored on the journey, I started reading all the signs we would pass. One sign read "Happy Feet." At that, my husband immediately asked concerning our baby, "Is she kicking?" After that, whenever the baby kicked, our theme song was, "Happy Feet is kicking." So soothing was the name that I started posting pictures on Facebook with the caption "Happy Feet." My sister was dumbfounded and looked at me in horror, asking, "Did you know that at work they used to call Mom 'Happy Feet'?" For a moment, I lost strength in my legs and felt weak.

Little Happy Feet was soon born, and interestingly she looks just like my mom.

Though my mother is now resting in Jesus, I believe God gave me the second dream to assure me that I will see her again after the resurrection. What joy that will be! Reuniting with our loved ones by the grace of God. Let's thank the Lord and trust Him to see us through.

Suhana Benny Prasad Chikatla

What a God!

When I said, "My foot is slipping,"
your unfailing love, LORD, supported me.
When anxiety was great within me,
your consolation brought me joy.
—*Psalm 94:18, 19, NIV*

As I sat, dejected and teary-eyed, at my desk on July 1, 2010, I felt all alone and useless. My husband had been killed suddenly in an automobile accident nearly six months earlier. No longer did I have a purpose for living. My identity and self-worth suffered immensely. Life seemed to have lost its meaning.

As I sat there in despair, the phone rang. It was my niece. "Auntie," she said, "this morning I read the devotional you wrote that was published in this year's Women's Ministries devotional book on today's date. I needed what you wrote. Thank you!" Not long after that a friend called to tell me that my same devotional, titled "My Comforter," had also encouraged her. God had sent me two hugs! I felt humbled and affirmed—just what I needed at that time. *Perhaps I am worth something,* I thought. *At least I can write an encouraging devotional.*

Isn't that just like God to know us so well He sends hugs at just the right time? What a blessing and comfort to realize we have a God who knows what kind of boost we need and when we need it! He also knows the most effective way to do it.

At other challenging times in my life, while facing situations that didn't seem to resolve, I've experienced hugs that only I could have recognized. Sometimes the encouragement exceeded anything I could have imagined.

I have often experienced God's hugs in the form of Bible promises. For example, He promises we won't have to carry more burdens than what we are able to bear (1 Corinthians 10:13). I take great courage in that promise. His Word lets us know He is near at all times. Another of His promises is that He will never fail nor forsake us (Joshua 1:5). Knowing God is always available and just a prayer away is in itself reassuring and comforting, especially in times of pain and loss.

That July day God affirmed, through the hugs He brought me, that I am invaluable to Him. In fact, all of us are invaluable to God. Nothing in our lives is too hard for Him. He invites us to come to Him when we are joyful, sorrowful, angry, or emotionally bankrupt. He is there to give us a hug. He is eager to see us through anything we encounter.

Marian Hart-Gay

My Disposition

The name of the LORD is a strong tower;
The righteous run to it and are safe.
—*Proverbs 18:10, NKJV*

My mother and my nine-year-old brother attended a world church conference several years ago. While there, my brother needed to use the restroom. Mom could no longer take him into the women's restroom with her, so off to the men's room my brother went with strict instructions to meet Mom outside. After waiting outside the restroom and seeing men coming and going—with no sign of my little brother—Mom became concerned. She approached one man and asked if he had seen a young boy in the restroom. "Yes," he replied. "It looks like he will be out shortly." Mom waited but there was still no sign of my little brother. Suddenly, she dashed into the men's room and found my brother playing in the water at the sink. Naturally she demanded that he come with her but was also very relieved that he was safe. Later Mom told me that during her prayerful deliberation about whether to enter the men's room, she felt a "force" influencing her to go in search of her little boy.

Mom's story made me wonder, *Should we not also allow the "force" of the Holy Spirit to develop our walk with the Lord? Are we looking for Him in every single situation of our lives?*

I know I have a disposition, a tendency, to react impulsively to situations. I know there are times I should have waited before acting on things. But when I allow the Holy Spirit to be the moving force in my life, I have a *spiritual* disposition. Instead of reacting, I can respond in faith, resting in the wisdom of God. "The Spirit Himself bears witness with our spirit that we are children of God, and if children, then heirs—heirs of God and joint heirs with Christ, if indeed we suffer with Him, that we may also be glorified together" (Romans 8:16, 17, NKJV).

In other words, since I am a child of God, His Spirit is within me and continually draws me closer to Him. I am entitled to all that He has—and is—because He died for me. The psalmist writes, "And those who know Your name will put their trust in You; for You, LORD, have not forsaken those who seek You" (Psalm 9:10, NKJV). Jehovah-Jireh, one name for God, suggests He will always provide for us.

I pray that we all will continue to learn to walk with a spiritual disposition. In doing so, we will follow the Spirit's promptings to turn to God and His help in every time of need.

Margo Peterson

But Grammy, It's My Birthday!

"I know what I'm doing. I have it all planned out—
plans to take care of you, not abandon you,
plans to give you the future you hope for."
—*Jeremiah 29:11*, The Message

Our grandson Anthony decided to work a summer job in Huntsville before going back to high school in Atlanta. His brother, Andrew, came along to keep my husband and me company. By the middle of the summer our whole family had made plans to take a vacation to Niagara Falls. In just a few days, Anthony would be seventeen years old, and his supervisor suggested that he could take off for the special day. I reminded Anthony that he had only been on the job less than two weeks and it didn't seem appropriate to take time off this early. Anthony insisted that it was fine because his supervisor was already impressed with his work ethic.

On the morning of Anthony's birthday, July 3, everything seemed fine. Anthony and Andrew stayed at the house with my husband, who was resting in bed, while I ran errands. While out, I received a call that would change our lives forever. It was a call from Anthony. "Grammy," said Anthony, "something happened to Poppy!" Anthony had already called 9-1-1. Within minutes, I arrived home and found my husband sitting on the edge of the bed, feeling weak. The rescue workers arrived. After evaluating him, they advised a trip to the emergency room.

As we arrived at the hospital, my husband looked at me but could not speak. A nurse frantically shouted, "Oh, no! Your heart rate has dropped to thirty!" My husband was having a mild heart attack and seizures. Though never having had heart problems before, he was admitted to the hospital, where he stayed for six days. We notified family, friends, and prayer warriors to go into immediate action for my husband's healing. God is so wonderful and always on time. Over the next few months, we saw improvements in my husband's health.

Reflecting on the situation, I see that Anthony and Andrew celebrated July 3 by being instrumental in saving their grandfather's life. While I was more concerned about work ethics, God already had everything planned according to His will. The promise of Jeremiah 29:11 became more meaningful to me through this experience. I praise God for His timing and care.

Lord, give us hearts that always let You lead in our lives.

Vivian E. Brown

The Well That Has Never Run Dry

These are wells without water, clouds carried by a tempest,
for whom is reserved the blackness of darkness forever.
—2 Peter 2:17, NKJV

The drought was fierce and long. Harrison and his family had to abandon their beachside home on Putput, New Ireland, Papua New Guinea, and flee to the mountains to find water and food. The creek that ran by their homestead had dried up. They survived each day by drinking coconut juice and eating the cool kernel. Soon the coconuts also began drying out, so the family ate the sprouted nuts and chewed the husk for water. They moved deeper into the forest in search of anything edible. Some days they ate ferns and wild yams cooked in bamboo over fire. Harrison regularly went to the sea to catch fish to supplement their diet. During this difficult time, he continued to praise God for their life and encouraged his family that God would sustain them and provide for their needs.

Several months passed. Finding water was now critical. They sat under a dried tree by the seashore and shared stories from the Bible about people for whom God had provided water in difficult times—Hagar and Ishmael, the children of Israel in the desert, and the woman at the well needing the water of life. Suddenly everything around them went deadly silent. *Is a storm brewing?* the family wondered. In that instant of stillness, a deafening roar exploded in the silence, so close they felt the ground tremble.

"What was that?" queried Harrison, his eyes wide. He walked one hundred yards (about ninety-one meters) in the direction of the noise and, to his amazement, saw a large, gaping, freshly formed hole in the earth. Upon closer inspection, he realized he was looking at a newly "dug" well full of fresh, crystal clear water. A quick taste confirmed that it was not salty water. Joyfully he ran to announce the miracle to his family. They all sat by the well and praised the Lord, taking turns to sip and savor the longest drinks they had had in a long time.

Harrison dedicated, to God's use, that well, which has never run dry. Today residents of Putput enjoy the school that Harrison also built there. The campground at Putput provides a welcoming place for women's retreats. That miracle well continues to be a blessing to many!

Likewise, when God works a miracle in our hearts, He turns the drought of sin into a spring of living water. May we bring the water of life to someone today.

Fulori Sususewa Bola

July 5

A Poor Reflection

"For the LORD does not see as man sees; for man looks at the outward appearance, but the LORD looks at the heart."
—1 Samuel 16:7, NKJV

When we moved to Florida, one of the things we knew we wanted was a house with an in-ground pool. Therefore, we barely considered the homes without a pool. Finally, our search narrowed down to two homes. One had hide-away doors that made you feel as if the back patio area was an extension of the living room. We loved the openness of the space, but there was no pool. The second house was smaller, but it had a pool. We purchased the home with the pool.

We love our new home. Having a pool, however, has taught me many lessons.

First, maintaining a pool is a lot of work. Our pool is covered by a pool cage, yet we still spend time skimming leaves and other material off the surface of the water. This is a daily job; otherwise, by the weekend, it would be rather disgusting. Unless cleaned, the pool is unusable.

Second, maintaining a pool takes time and attention. We have to pay attention to the water level to make sure it doesn't drop too low or go too high. If the level gets too low, it can burn out the pool pump motor. If it gets too high, the water can overflow and flood the patio. Not having the right water level can also render the pool unusable.

Finally, we have to check the pH balance of the water (levels of alkalinity and acidity). If we don't check or we fail to utilize the proper chemicals, the water will turn an interesting shade of green that my girls refer to as "pea soup green." This too makes the pool unusable.

Having a pool and *maintaining* a pool are two different things. Just like *professing* to be a Christian and *being* a Christian are two different things. I call myself a Christian, but unless I maintain my relationship with God, I am fooling myself. If I don't put in the time to read and study my Bible, my spiritual life gets low, and I make decisions without God's guidance—a sure recipe for disaster. Finally, if I don't pray and allow the Holy Spirit to cover my sinful nature, God's reflection in my life, when people look for it, will be murky. This, like how an un-maintained swimming pool is unusable, will render me non-useful as a Christian.

The needs of my swimming pool daily remind me of my need to live in Christ so I can be a transparent source of clean, refreshing, living water—which clearly reflects His love.

Tamara Marquez de Smith

Yolanda

I will say of the LORD, "He is my refuge and my fortress;
My God, in Him I will trust."
Surely He shall deliver you from the snare of the fowler
And from the perilous pestilence.
He shall cover you with His feathers,
And under His wings you shall take refuge;
His truth shall be your shield and buckler.
—*Psalm 91:2–4, NKJV*

In 2013, Typhoon Yolanda visited the Philippines and made landfall in the East Visayan provinces. This created untold havoc, destroying properties and killing thousands of adults and children. Many shelters, schools, hospitals, and other important service buildings were unable to function because the typhoon knocked them down.

Tents and other temporary shelters were so overcrowded that infectious diseases spread fast among the occupants. Even health providers were heavily affected. The limited supplies of food and water added to the worsening situation. Blocked roads made the transporting of essential commodities difficult—especially when it came to reaching remote areas. The death toll increased daily as a result of these conditions. Besides the great number of listed deaths, there were thousands of missing family members, friends, and neighbors. Even three weeks after the initial devastation, some corpses were still unidentified and scattered in many places, causing an unbearable odor. Survivors of this calamity, however, were thankful for both the local and the overseas assistance they received. Government, nongovernmental, individual, and private organizations all pulled together to make a positive difference in the lives of the people caught up in overwhelming destruction.

Our next-door neighbor's huge mango tree fell on their house and ruined it, but thankfully, nobody was hurt. Though we lost a smaller mango tree, our larger one stood firm, thereby not endangering our house. This tree reminds me of something else that stands firm: God's promises to His faithful children. The Bible reminds us that current trials that seem unbearable to us really do serve to strengthen our faith and prepare our souls for salvation (1 Peter 1:3–9).

More than ever, I am aware that our hearts must be prepared to meet Jesus at any time. I know the Lord will help us. We can trust Him to lead us to be ready to follow Him home.

Esperanza Aquino Mopera

Anxiety-Busting Faith

Do not be anxious about anything, but in every situation, by prayer
and petition, with thanksgiving, present your requests to God.
And the peace of God, which transcends all understanding,
will guard your hearts and your minds in Christ Jesus.
—*Philippians 4:6, 7, NIV*

One of the problems that seem to plague women is anxiety. We're anxious about our children, our marriages, our finances, our jobs (or lack of). You name it; we experience anxiety over it.

Recently, I read a statement by the well-known prayer warrior George Mueller, and it grabbed my attention: "The beginning of anxiety is the end of faith." The *end* of faith! Put another way, when we pray with an anxious, doubtful spirit, we are not praying with faith. This hinders God's ability to answer our prayers. Thankfully, Mueller continued his statement with a wonderful assurance: "And the beginning of true faith is the end of anxiety."

For many years, one of my loved ones had a problem that stemmed from his childhood and greatly affected his adult life. I prayed for him daily, each time giving God all the details of the problem. At the end of my prayers, I was so depressed from rehearsing the seemingly insurmountable problem that I dragged myself through the rest of the day. I began to avoid prayer time because it was so depressing. Even though I felt that I was leaving the issue with God, in reality I was weakening my own paltry faith by dwelling on the details. Only after I understood that I was praying *without* faith did I change my prayer. I stopped presenting God all the details and simply reminded Him of my concern; then I left it up to God to work out the answers. I was no longer depressed and anxious about the issue. In a remarkably short time I began to see major changes in my dear one's situation. God worked in ways that I never dreamed of. Now I give Him all the glory because I know I had nothing to do with it except to believe.

Ellen White wrote, "Our heavenly Father has a thousand ways to provide for us, of which we know nothing."* *Nothing!* God is not limited by our finite thinking. He has all the resources of heaven at His command. So why do we worry and lack faith? The answer to anxiety is to strengthen our faith by focusing on God's extravagant love and limitless ability to solve *all* our problems. Why not accept His loving invitation: "Come to me, all you who are weary and burdened, and I will give you rest" (Matthew 11:28, NIV).

Carla Baker

---

* Ellen G. White, *The Desire of Ages* (Mountain View, CA: Pacific Press®, 1940), 330.

Wrong Flight

Whoever gives heed to instruction prospers,
and blessed is the one who trusts in the LORD.
—*Proverbs 16:20, NIV*

I have traveled a lot lately—to different cities in North America, Europe, and Asia. I have gone through various airports and security checks and seen all kinds and sizes of luggage. Furthermore, I am always fascinated watching people as they rush to and fro trying to meet their flights.

One nice summer day, as I walked to my commuter plane parked a little ways from the terminal, I noticed there were several planes on the tarmac ready for boarding. I made sure I went through the correct gate that had my posted destination and boarded the plane. After settling in my seat, I thanked God for bringing me this far and breathed a prayer for safe and smooth travel back home.

Because of a lack of bin space, some carry-on bags were checked in as passengers boarded. As the flight attendant welcomed everyone to the flight for Baltimore, two women stood up and said, "But we thought this plane was bound for Atlanta!" Apparently they had been busy chatting and didn't notice they had walked through the incorrect gate and boarded the wrong flight! Needless to say, our flight was delayed as their bags were unloaded and transferred to the correct plane.

I reflected on this incident as our plane taxied for takeoff. How many times have we been so distracted that we failed to recognize where we were headed? Do we allow our distractions to keep us from spending time with our Lord? As we go through our journey in life, let us pray for guidance and leading so we can stay on track and keep focused on things that will help us grow in our walk with God. I wouldn't want to miss out on meeting my Savior face to face because I got too busy enjoying the pleasures of this world.

My prayer is that we will not lose sight of our ultimate destination as we go about our daily lives. Let us be steadfast in our faith as we travel toward that heavenly kingdom that Jesus is preparing for you and me.

Rhona Grace Magpayo

Printer Problems!

"I am the vine, you are the branches. He who abides in Me, and I in him, bears much fruit; for without Me you can do nothing."
—John 15:5, NKJV

Recently, I wanted to print a document in color. As my laptop is normally connected to a simple black-and-white printer, I disconnected it and plugged it into our color printer. I pushed the usual key commands to print, but nothing happened. I tried again—two more times—but still nothing printed. I suddenly realized I hadn't changed the default setting from the black-and-white printer to the color printer. Sometimes computer details like that elude me! As soon as I changed the setting, out popped three lovely color copies of my document!

I got to thinking how the printer default setting is similar to the default setting we all have. We have a default setting to naturally follow after Satan's ways and temptations. If—the first thing each day—we don't actively connect with God and choose Him to rule in our lives, we will, by default, allow Satan to influence what we say and do during that day. We don't have to actively choose to follow Satan for this to happen. We need only to neglect spending time with God to become easily tripped up.

I recently read, "It is not necessary for us deliberately to choose the service of the kingdom of darkness in order to come under its dominion. We have only to neglect to ally ourselves with the kingdom of light. If we do not co-operate with the heavenly agencies, Satan will take possession of the heart, and will make it his abiding place."* We may part company with Satan for a period of time, but if we don't have a daily vital connection with God, we will certainly fall into Satan's traps of self-love, self-indulgence, and sin. Jesus confirmed this fact when He said that even if someone has had a demon cast out but they don't fill the emptiness with Jesus, the evil spirit will return—with many more—to take up residence again (Matthew 12:43–45).

We don't have to be controlled by Satan "by default." We have the privilege and choice of connecting to Jesus, the true vine, through His Spirit each day.

Each morning we can pray, "I want to change my default setting today and yield myself to Your control, Jesus. I thank You for Your promised gift of the Holy Spirit to fill my life, connecting me to You as a branch to the vine, to produce fruit to Your honor and glory."

Merian Richardson

* Ellen G. White, *The Desire of Ages* (Mountain View, CA: Pacific Press®, 1940), 324.

No Light

Commit thy way unto the LORD; trust also in him;
and he shall bring it to pass.
—*Psalm 37:5*

The Africa journey was planned for two years. The whole family would travel from the Gambia to Nigeria, where I'd be a delegate to a women's congress. This would be our children's first visit with us to Nigeria.

As usual, we committed our road trip into God's hand. We got to the Gambia border late one evening. The last bus to the village across the border was empty, waiting for passengers. We waited till 9:00 P.M., and no other passengers came. We pleaded with the driver to proceed; he agreed, but only if we would pay for the vacant seats. Because of the situation we found ourselves in, we agreed. Before we left, another passenger did come, and we set out in the dark, rainy night. The rains came with strong winds, the interior bus lights went off, and we realized the vehicle lacked seals around the doors.

The bumpy road was full of gullies, and the roof and floor of the vehicle leaked. Soon we pulled through a big pool of stagnant water, and the vehicle's headlamps went off. A flood of water poured into the vehicle, soaking our feet. Visibility was almost nonexistent. I prayed, trusting God to see us through the journey. The vehicle attendants requested flashlights from the passengers. I had one and so did another woman. The attendant sat on top of the vehicle and shined the lights on the road so the driver could see. The attendant also removed his shirt to wipe the windshield because the bus had no wipers.

By this time, everyone was wet. We were cold and tense because we did not know what would happen. The children were afraid and clung to us. The whole family was now in God's hands; we had nowhere to go but to Jesus. We prayed for His intervention as the vehicle went through the windy, stormy, dark night.

The journey that should have taken about forty-five minutes took three hours.

Finally we saw a little light far off—our destination. I knew God had led and driven the vehicle. I praise Him for seeing us through to the end of the journey.

We may be going through storms on our journey through life. Everything may seem dark and foreboding. God, however, has promised to see us through. Be of good courage today!

Taiwo Adenekan

July 11

Sacrificial Offering

"Everyone who is willing is to bring to the Lᴏʀᴅ
an offering of gold, silver and bronze."
—*Exodus 35:5, NIV*

And everyone who was willing and whose heart moved them came and
brought an offering to the Lᴏʀᴅ for the work on the tent of meeting.
—*Verse 21, NIV*

Many stories have been recorded in the Bible of how the children of Israel willingly brought gifts to help with the Lord's work. When special gifts were called for by Moses for the building of the tabernacle, he ended up having to tell the people to stop giving because enough wealth had been accumulated for the designated project.

Today also, the benevolence of church members has enabled and promoted the spreading of the gospel to the far reaches of the world. As a result of our giving, many new churches have been erected in places where there would not have been any but for the sacrificial offerings of those to whose hearts the Spirit of God has spoken. God always blesses when His people bring a sacrificial and willing offering.

My local church has taken on several renovation projects. My husband and I budgeted for a monthly sum to be given for the construction of a new high school. Apart from this, there are renovation projects in the church that have been completed to which we have contributed, but there are others to be worked on. One Sabbath the pastor announced that the kitchen had to be renovated and needed to be done immediately because the city inspector would not allow us to continue to use the facility in its current code-violating condition. Therefore, each church member was asked to sacrifice $150. That amounted to $300 from our household. *Where are we going to get this extra money?* I thought. The still, small Voice that speaks so often to me told me not to worry because God would make a way.

Generally, our utility bill for the past five years had been between $350 and $550 for the months of November through February. However, we took some drastic measures to reduce this high cost, and as a result we paid a bill of $180 for November and $259 for December. The savings were enough to donate the $300 for the kitchen renovation.

God surely blessed us when we brought a willing sacrificial offering to Him. For what cause is He asking you to sacrifice today? He already has a blessing in store for you.

Eveythe Kennedy Cargill

Tending the Soil

There has never been the slightest doubt in my mind
that the God who started this great work in you
would keep at it and bring it to a flourishing finish
on the very day Christ Jesus appears.
—*Philippians 1:6, The Message*

The parables Jesus told when He was on earth some two thousand years ago have always fascinated me. One that captivates me the most is among those that Bible scholars insist was important enough to be recorded in all three Synoptic Gospels—the parable (Matthew 13:3–8; Mark 4:3–8; Luke 8:5–8) evoking the image of seed trying to grow.

While working online on a project with another writer, I received a message from her that pulled at my heartstrings. "I know you don't remember me. It's been years, and our encounter was very brief. I was only at school for four months. I never had any classes with you, but I saw you quite often, and the girls in the dormitory loved you. You made a positive impact on me." I was humbled by her generous words. Also, she was right that I could not remember her!

I scrolled down through her intriguing message and learned other ways my life had evidently touched hers: "You were always soft spoken, kind, and caring." Reading her words about an incident that had occurred thirty years earlier had me picturing a shy, yet eager, young girl striving to grow while soaking up the atmosphere of the rich soil around her. I praised God for the opportunity to be part of the environment that fostered her development.

Later when my new friend told me about the personal statement her daughter had written to append her residency application, I could tell that she had transferred that same nurturing philosophy to her child. "Her insatiable thirst for knowledge matches her equally unquenchable desire to help others."

Reflecting on her first message, I could almost hear that young girl's voice, but I focused on the vulnerability inherent in her final line: "Maybe one day I can tell everyone that you are my friend."

Master Gardener, thank You for allowing us to help as You take care of fragile souls. Thank You for remembering us as we attempt to enrich the soil around us. Thank You for the "flourishing finish" You allow those about us to experience—which encourages us in return.

Glenda-mae Greene

Building on the Rock—Jesus Christ

"When a flood came, the torrent struck that house
but could not shake it, because it was well built."
—Luke 6:48, NIV

While watching the news one evening, I saw that heavy rain had caused the collapse of a newly built library. The school's administration had applied for funds to assist in the building of a new library and also for buying library books. Until now one of the school offices had been used as the library. Many people contributed to the building project in various ways. After a few months the building was finished and inspected. The date for the opening ceremony was decided. This was the day the library books were delivered. The students anticipated growing academically with the aid of a new library.

One day, however, a storm struck, bringing heavy rain—and winds so strong that the new library building collapsed. All the joy and expectation came to an end. What a sad sight to see the bookshelves and the books rain-soaked and covered with debris! What had caused the newly built library to collapse? Further investigation revealed that the foundation had not been strong. Because of a weak foundation, all the financial investment, the book donations, the time, and the energy spent on this venture ended up as a total loss.

This experience reminded me of Christ's parable of the flood (Luke 6:46–49). Two structures, houses, were built on two different foundations. On the day of the great storm, the house built on sand collapsed while the one built on the rock stood firm against the storm. Pictures on the news of the faulty foundation caused a sudden fear to grip me, for I suddenly reflected on the foundation I had laid for my children. I know I have done well in showering them with different gifts on various occasions. Yet, did I give them the gift of Jesus? I have invested in their education, giving them a good academic foundation. But did I help them build on Jesus, the Rock? If I was not careful to help them build characters on the firm foundation, Jesus Christ, then I neglected giving them the best gift of all. Would they be able to withstand the strong winds of temptation and trial faced in this world?

Lord, forgive me where I have failed in raising the children You have entrusted to my care. May I be grounded in You and follow Your guidance as I continue to lay their foundation.

Gertrude Mfune

Combat Stress

For I am convinced that neither death nor life, neither angels nor demons, neither the present nor the future, nor any powers, neither height nor depth, nor anything else in all creation, will be able to separate us from the love of God that is in Christ Jesus our Lord.
—*Romans 8:38, 39, NIV*

I listened dispassionately to the routine portions of the service, quietly absorbed in a discussion with God about the spiritual crossroads at which I found myself. I was in church because I still believed, still trusted God, and knew that I needed to be there. I was there in spite of my uncertainties and strange feeling of dissatisfaction. I was there because of God's consistent demonstrations of love and goodness in my life. But I was weary of the journey and felt disconnected from the body of believers. Spiritually exhausted with trying to hold tenaciously to my commitment, I just couldn't shake the apathy born of fatigue.

Then the choir started to sing about a tired old soldier who wants to give up. The soloist, a tenor with an exquisite voice, admonished the tired old soldier to "hold on," "never give up," "keep the faith." I was startled out of my apathy, convicted that this was a direct and immediate reply to the questions I had been silently asking God. The choir repeated the admonition again and again: "Hold on, old soldier." It was as if there was nobody in the church but me, and God was speaking directly to me. Sometimes when I pray, the answer comes in quiet, unobtrusive ways that could be missed if one were not paying careful attention. God was not subtle this time. He saw how Satan had intensified his psychological warfare against me. God took immediate, direct, explicit counteraction to defend me. The words were not hidden in parable or a cleverly worded sermon. God simply said to me in song, "Hold on. I know what you're going through, and I've got it. Don't give up now. Keep the faith." I sprang to my feet in humble acknowledgement of God's instructions.

This old soldier *will* hold on—and will never give up. This old soldier will keep the faith and be victorious because God's grace is sufficient. The challenges that we face every day sometimes seem insurmountable, but God is big enough to carry us through to the end.

So regardless of the mountains that you face, rest assured that God is able and willing to sustain you. Soldier on, my friend. Keep the faith.

Beverly P. Gordon

When God Says No

Search me, O God, and know my heart;
Try me, and know my anxieties; . . .
And lead me in the way everlasting.
—*Psalm 139:23, 24, NKJV*

Seeking God to ask for various things or answers to life's problems is a daily occurrence for many Christians, including myself.

When I was a child I learned in Sabbath School that when we ask, God may answer Yes, No, or Wait. I must admit, the answer I have the greatest problem with is No.

One Sunday a dear friend of mine asked me to agree with her in prayer for an answer she needed. It was regarding something very important to her, and I gladly agreed to pray. The answer to her situation would come the following Wednesday. So we prayed and prayed, and my husband also joined in petitioning God for a positive answer to this request.

Then Wednesday arrived and I received a message from my friend saying she had not gotten the answer she wanted. It was evident that God had said No.

She was devastated. She had stepped out in faith regarding this situation and had even spent money in anticipation of a Yes answer.

I called her immediately.

While sobbing over the phone, she told me of her disappointment with God's answer and that she could not understand why He would say No. I listened and empathized and then in the end said, "I know this is not the answer you wanted. But when God says No, He knows why. He knows more than we do. Take comfort in that knowledge."

When I got off the phone, I thought of No answers in my life and the many times I was angry with the situation and disappointed in God for not answering as I had wanted. It was easy to tell my friend what I told her, yet these words were not so easy to apply to my own life.

Regardless of that fact, it's true. God knows the past, the present, and the future. He knows me—my life, my desires, my character. So when He says No, I need to trust that because of His knowledge, He is doing what is best for me. Yes, it's hard to accept, but it's the truth.

So I prayed and asked God that the next time He says No, to please also remind me of the words I told my friend—and to help me to be accepting of His answer and trust His knowledge.

Heather-Dawn Small

The Treasures of a Child

Jesus said, "Let the little children come to me, and do not hinder
them, for the kingdom of heaven belongs to such as these."
—*Matthew 19:14, NIV*

Climbing trees, making fake food, painting, playing dolls, drawing, joining a club, messing with clay, pedaling a bicycle: this list could go on. These activities, and more, provided fun that I enjoyed in my childhood and were part of the process of my maturing in healthy ways.

Certainly, remembering childhood provides several humorous memories that are fun to report in a circle of friends and relatives, usually resulting in an exchange of much laughter.

I remember a childhood day when my sister and I were playing. We were making fake food in our little wooden house for our cousin, Maikon. I tried forcing him to drink "hot chocolate." In reality, it was powdery soil that we had taken from the side of the road and mixed with water. Thankfully, Maikon managed to escape the ordeal with much agility!

When I reflect on my childhood, I remember that I always kept my curiosity level above normal, trying to figure out the unknown. People seemed to be a box of treasures to be opened, and every compartment of my house was a place full of strange objects ready to be unveiled. Therefore, each day was unique and full of discoveries to satisfy my childhood curiosity.

We adults admire children for their sincerity and, above all, for their not being limited by a single view of the world. They are open to new explanations that help answer their endless stream of questions. A major problem for most adults is that routine kills our desire for new discoveries each day. We make do with where we are. Having lost our sense of curiosity and wonder, we assume we have reached the top of Mount Everest—in our understanding—when, in fact, we haven't even achieved the first sixteen hundred feet (five hundred meters) of our climb.

When Jesus said the little ones should not be diverted from His presence, I read between the lines and interpret also that His will is that we never lose our desire to learn new and better ways to live our lives. He wants us to walk in those ways with a deeper understanding of His will for us. Jesus longs that, as a child trusts his or her parents, you and I also come to His lap and enjoy His protection, His perspectives, and—always—His love.

Mayla Magaieski Graepp

His Watchful Eye

The LORD watches over you—
the LORD is your shade at your right hand.
—*Psalm 121:5, NIV*

Some years ago I lived in a country where security was primitive, if not primordial. Houses had to be protected from thieves with iron bars on doors and windows, causing them to look like a prison. Craftsmen, however, transformed the iron into a beautiful work of art.

The two-story house where I lived had a backyard surrounded by a brick fence with barbed wire on top. I appreciated that kind of security because I often had to stay in that country alone for several weeks at a time. One day, however, I found out that the price of being secure could turn against me.

It was a Friday afternoon and my helper was washing my car in preparation for the Sabbath. I opened the house door and stepped outside to talk to him. While I stood there, a sudden gust of wind closed the door behind me. The door was locked, and I'd left the keys inside. I panicked. There was no way to get back inside, as all windows and doors were secured with iron bars. My helper was worried, so he went around the house to see if he could find a way for me to get in. He found none. I was in a terrible predicament: it was Friday, the sun was setting, and finding a locksmith in that country was very problematic.

My only recourse was to pray. I told my helper that I was going to pray to God. I stood next to the door and prayed silently to my all-powerful God. I told Him about the problem and that I needed to get inside before it got dark. I asked Him to open the door, and I proceeded to turn the doorknob by faith. And what a miracle, it opened! I stepped inside praising and thanking the Lord for His intervention. I firmly believe that He wanted me to know that it was He who opened that door because right then, another gust of wind came with a loud sound and shut the door behind me. I tried to open it from inside but couldn't. I used another door to get outside and tried to open that door from outside; it didn't move. The door was shut tight from inside as well as outside. For many days no one could open it until I was advised to replace the lock.

What a powerful God! What an experience and testimony for my helper! It was also a reminder that the Lord is always ready to answer our prayers, no matter how insignificant the requests may seem. We serve an awesome God.

Flore Aubry Hamilton

The Crumpled Bike

The Angel of the Lord encamps around those who fear Him [who revere and worship Him with awe] and each of them He delivers.
—*Psalm 34:7, AMPC*

Many years ago my husband, Cyril, and I lived in a rural village called Chipperfield.

Cyril had to cycle seven miles to school each day and, of course, cycle the seven miles home again after teaching all day.

One day—near the end of a school term when both teachers and students were tired—I kept waiting for Cyril to return home in time for tea. I was looking out the front door when I saw something rather unusual: a tall, pointed hat was moving along slowly on the other side of our high hedge. I could tell the hat belonged to a policeman because a policeman's badge was secured on the front of the helmet. A policeman was behind our front hedge.

A moment later a second policeman came through the entrance to the garden and walked straight down the garden path toward me.

He greeted me kindly and said, "Your husband has had an accident. He is currently in the Peace Memorial Hospital in Watford (ten miles [sixteen kilometers] away). Unfortunately, he crashed into a large petrol tanker." As I pictured my husband crashing into the lorry carrying petrol in its large, circular tank, I asked anxiously about his welfare. In response to my shock and questions, the policeman continued, "Your husband has no broken bones."

At this point in the conversation, a very tall policeman emerged from behind the hedge—the one whose hat I had seen move behind the top of it. He was carrying the remains of my husband's now-crumpled bicycle. In fact, it had broken into two halves.

I took one look at the tangled mess and wondered how my husband, riding that bike, could have survived the impact of the accident. Then I realized that the tall policeman had been hiding the remains of the bike so that I would not collapse with shock before knowing the rest of the story. Although Cyril had no broken bones, he did have a big bump on his head. After sleeping for fifteen hours, he awoke and was able to be propped up. A few days later he returned home. How thankful we all were for God's protection!

Aren't you glad His angels are encamped around each of us today?

Monica Vesey

Tough Love

"Those whom I love, I reprove and chasten;
so be zealous and repent."
—*Revelation 3:19, RSV*

I watched a documentary on tough love many years ago and found it quite interesting. Parents who loved their delinquent children, but would not tolerate their bad behavior, gave them an ultimatum. The child had to sign a document containing terms and conditions for the benefit of living in the family home, and they had to comply in order to stay. They sometimes tested their parents and reneged on the agreement, but were given second chances when they repented.

Our heavenly Father has had to practice tough love because of our rebellious nature. Since Creation He has laid out terms and conditions that will guarantee us a place in His home. He spoke directly to Adam and Eve and gave them specific instructions for living in Eden. They could enjoy all the benefits as long as they abstained from eating a certain fruit. They reneged, God applied tough love, and they were driven from their home.

The children of Israel, as they wandered for forty years in the wilderness, were also given terms and conditions through their leader Moses. These they repeatedly violated, and God again had to apply tough love. They constructed a golden calf and were struck by a plague. They complained about the manna, and God sent quail that made them sick. Miriam's rebellion caused her to become leprous. It seems they were in constant rebellion and violation of the terms and conditions given, never learning from previous mistakes, always testing God. As a result, most of those who started the journey were not allowed to enter the Promised Land, and those who entered made it because of Moses' intercession and God's grace.

Isn't it sad how we have perpetuated this tradition? We know that there is an eternal home for us to share with our Father, free from crime, terrorism, sickness, death, and all the other byproducts of sin. We have the terms and conditions for inheriting this laid out for us in the Bible, now available in many languages and versions to suit our taste. We have the benefit of learning from the experiences of those documented in the Bible. Yet we too continue to test God. Christ's intercession has been protecting us from our deserved rewards. May we daily renew our contract with God and, with His help, strive to avoid any violations so that we will be able to live in the heavenly family home.

Cecelia Grant

Canola Fields

It is the God who said, "Let light shine out of darkness,"
who has shone in our hearts to give the light of the knowledge
of the glory of God in the face of Jesus Christ.
—*2 Corinthians 4:6, NRSV*

My husband and I prefer overcast weather when we drive long distances in the summer—we don't get headaches from squinting into the sun for fourteen hours. However, when the day is gray, our spirits are never truly happy. Several years ago on a cloudy July day, we started on a long trip. Larry put the last bags in the back of the car and tucked a pillow behind the front seat in case the passenger wanted to take a nap. I packed sandwiches, carrot sticks, and water bottles into our cooler. We locked the door and headed north, hoping to be at our son's house in three days.

Three hours, 303 kilometers: Whitecourt, Alberta. We stop, stretch, eat breakfast, and change drivers. The gray weather continues. *Five hours, 59 minutes, 625 kilometers: Beaverlodge, Alberta.* We drive slowly past a 4.5-meter-high sculpture of a beaver. The clouds have turned to rain. We decide not to take a photo. *Seven hours, 1 minute, 714 kilometers: Dawson Creek, British Columbia, the start of the Alaska Highway.* The rain stopped an hour ago, but we feel dull and listless in the overcast weather. I doze as Larry drives. *Seven hours, 30 minutes, 765 kilometers:* Gray skies continue. We're almost at Taylor, British Columbia, when I awake. "I always like the deep valley as we descend to the Peace River," I comment to Larry. He suggests we picnic on the other side.

I nod my head as I anticipate our descent, but then I stare at the plateau. "Look!" I say excitedly and point to the canola fields in the distance. There is no break in the clouds, but the fields are golden. Shining. Despite the gray, overcast day, the mass of small flowers glows, brightening the countryside, clear to the horizon. They aren't reflecting light; instead, they somehow seem to create it from within.

Over the years, I've often thought about those canola fields. I, too, want to shine, not just when it's vacation time, but also when I have a stack of essays to grade. Not just when I'm with friends or celebrating the birth of a grandchild, but also when I'm grocery shopping, taking out the garbage, attending a committee meeting, or making a difficult decision.

I don't want to simply reflect joy; I want it to be so integral to my life that it shines forth from my soul.

Denise Dick Herr

July 21

Eye Contact

The angel of the LORD encampeth round about
them that fear him, and delivereth them.
—Psalm 34:7

It was laundry day at the missionary children's boarding school I attended in the Ngong Hills, Maasai territory, in Nairobi, Kenya. Because thirty-five girls would be doing laundry that day, I decided to get a head start. I got up at 5:00 A.M., said my prayers, organized my laundry, and went to the laundry room. As I had hoped, I was the only one in the room. The only *person*, that is.

As I began to load the machines, I had a sense of being watched. I dismissed my foreboding, but a few minutes later, I heard a whimper—and a gentle tug on the hem of my jogging slacks. When I looked down I saw the most beautiful bundle of fur I'd ever seen—in the form of a lion cub! Instinctively, I knelt down and began scratching the top of its head. The cub purred in delight and playfully grabbed my hand with its two front paws and nibbled on my fingers. "Aw, you're hungry," I said. "I can get you some warm milk from the cafeteria." The cub rolled on his back, allowing me to tickle his tummy. For a few seconds, I was in Eden.

Suddenly a deep growl jolted me back to reality, freezing my blood. The cub leaped on all fours, and with his tail set firmly between his legs and head down, the little traitor cowardly whimpered his way back to his mother—a golden-tan, 280-pound (127 kilogram) lioness. I stared at her at the laundry room entrance and recalled the caution of our Maasai guardians: "Never run from a wild cat; back away slowly and quietly, and keep your gaze on the ground." Capital advice, no doubt. The trouble was that I was trapped in the laundry room with nowhere to "back away." And I had just been staring into the hazel eyes of the lioness ever since her first growl!

Hot tears of terror and desperation welled up in my eyes. "Dear Jesus—" The words got stuck in my throat; maybe I'd asphyxiate before being torn to pieces by this enormous beast. Just then, the lioness grabbed her cub by the neck, turned around, and simply walked away.

I gasped for air! Tears ran down my cheeks now. *I was alive!* I could hardly believe it. Though physically still thawing out, I was emotionally thrilled! I thanked God that, once again, my guardian angel was closer to me than my foe. He always has been. And I praise God for allowing me to be a miraculous exception to the rule: never stare a cat in its eyes!

Evelia R. Cargill

God Is in the Details

"But the very hairs of your head are all numbered."
—Matthew 10:30, NKJV

We buried my sister, Lynne, seven years ago this month in Indiana. My dad brought home a stone plaque sent to her funeral, which he immediately set in the flower garden under the lamppost. It reads, "When someone you love becomes a memory, the memory becomes a treasure."

Once again, three years after my sister died, my mom and I stood watching a hearse drive away. This time it was my father, dead of leukemia. These words came to me: *No more pain, no more death, no more crying.*

Floyd Ernest Nudd / November 9, 1925–July 22, 2013. On Facebook that day, I wrote, "My dad was there when I came into this world; I was there when he left it." After his last loud gasp at 3:00 A.M., I tried to get his blood pressure and pulse. A sigh, then silence from both of us. At 3:00 P.M., final arrangements were made at the funeral home. Our family keepsake book is dedicated to Lynne and is entitled *3 PM* because that's the time my parents were married.

God is in the details. I knew Dad would never grieve over Lynne again. Neither of them could get out of bed or walk when they died, but they will run to greet each other on resurrection morning. I chose a wreath for my floral piece to symbolize my family's circle of love. The door on sorrow is closed for my dad. He has missed Lynne for the last time. At my sister's casket my dad had said, "I love you, I'm glad you were my daughter, and I'll see you when Jesus comes." At my dad's casket I said, "I love you, and I'm glad you were my father, and I'll see you when Jesus comes." The doctors said he had approximately six months to live, but he had survived only six weeks. Yet I was privileged to be there for fifty-eight of the sixty-three years of my parents' storybook marriage.

As we mourned my father's passing, we noticed that for July 22, my mom's day calendar read, in part, "hill and dale in slumber sleeping." Interestingly, her home here is in the Hills & Dales Subdivision. Yes, God is in the details.

Through details He gives us assurance of His presence in times of grief. God bless those of you who know this firsthand. And always God is in the details—of our entire lives—with a love so personal that He knows the number of hairs on our heads. Yes, details.

Diane Shellyn Nudd

Altered for a Purpose

"In his hand is the life of every creature
and the breath of all mankind."
—*Job 12:10, NIV*

You will take about eighteen breaths in the next minute, one thousand in the next hour, twenty-six thousand by the end of the day. In the past year, you took some 9.5 million breaths. For some of you, they were taken in moments of intense pain, grief, loneliness, fear, and loss.

Perhaps you were making plans to get married. The wedding never materialized, and so you learned to wear the mantle of singleness with grace and dignity. Some of you are parents or grandparents who watched Satan lure your son or granddaughter along the path to destruction. Today you have no idea where they are or what they are doing.

The day your cancer was diagnosed you were afraid. Afraid and uncertain if you'd be around to see your daughter mature into the beautiful young woman she would become. And no, it isn't easy to overcome the bitterness that springs from the discovery of a spouse's unfaithfulness or to find the courage to walk away from a poisoned relationship. But you have found that strength.

When your baby passed away, you cursed God. When you lost your mother unexpectedly, your world collapsed. But we who are left after a loved one's death must go on. God gives us those twenty-six thousand breaths each day for a reason. Our situations are not the result of chance or luck, good or bad. Either God has allowed them or He has ordained them.

You may be in a strange country far away from everything and everyone you hold dear, or imprisoned and struggling to survive in unimaginable circumstances. You might be consumed by rage, or sinking in the bleakest despair; whatever the circumstance is, though, God will never abandon you. Though it may not feel like it, our situations are opportunities, not catastrophes. Our lives have been altered for a purpose. No matter how our lives have been altered, the fact that we still have breath is a favor from God.

The psalmist declares, "Let everything that has breath praise the LORD" (Psalm 150:6, NIV). So, let's praise Him with the breath He so graciously gives us. Let's thank Him for our unique opportunities, and let's accept the peace He so freely offers.

Avery Davis

Spirit-Filled

Wine is a mocker,
Strong drink is a brawler,
And whoever is led astray by it is not wise.
—*Proverbs 20:1, NKJV*

When I was a teenager, most of my friends experimented with alcohol. Under its influence, several had unplanned pregnancies, and another unwittingly risked her life by combining alcohol with her medications. Another sustained serious injuries when his car hit a lamp pole at high speed.

Satan uses alcohol to degrade humankind. He ensures that it is widely available and socially acceptable, so much so that it is less socially acceptable to abstain! If that were not enough, medical science now promotes the moderate use of alcohol for heart health, while failing to mention its association with cancer, especially breast cancer. In reality, the veggies and water that young Daniel chose as his diet in Babylon—and regular physical activity—are more effective for cancer prevention, heart health, and cognitive function than any amount of alcohol.

Alcohol contributes to one third of all road fatalities and is a factor in much of the domestic violence and child abuse that destroy families and individuals. Recently our next-door neighbors got into a rage. We were shaken by the angry words they flung at each other as their emotions spiraled out of control. Alcohol had eroded yet another precious relationship.

With four times as many "problem drinkers" as alcoholics in the U.S., Audrey Kishline founded Moderation Management, a support group for those who want to moderate their drinking, rather than abstain. Six years after founding the group, she had a personal crisis, got drunk, and drove up the freeway the wrong way, killing two people. She was convicted of vehicular homicide and sent to prison. Alcohol impairs self-control, yet self-control is exactly what is needed to achieve moderation.

In Ephesians 5:18, Paul writes, "Don't get drunk on wine, which produces depravity. Instead, be filled with the Spirit" (CEB). The Spirit produces "love, joy, peace, patience, kindness, goodness, faithfulness, gentleness, and self-control" (Galatians 5:22, 23, CEB). The contrast with Proverbs 23:29, 30 is striking—those who have woe, sorrow, contentions, complaints, wounds without cause, and red eyes are those who "go in search of mixed wine" (NKJV). God's advice is for our best good. Seek to be filled with the Holy Spirit, not alcoholic spirits. Choose one or the other, for you cannot have both.

Nerida McKibben

My Will or God's Will

Father, if thou be willing, remove this cup from me:
nevertheless not my will, but thine, be done.
—Luke 22:42

I believe God has a plan for each person born in this world. Despite the circumstances, your birth was not a mistake. I always tell my students they need to discover the purpose for which they were born. "What makes you unique from others?" I ask them. When they find and work toward fulfilling their purposes, they find happiness. Through prayer, the reading of His Word, the voice of the Holy Spirit, and godly friends, God will reveal His will for our lives. God will reveal our special talents, big or small, that make up who we are.

However, God cannot always reveal His will while we are still clinging to our own will. Sometimes His will is right in front of us, though. I once said to a friend who was embarking on a trip: "I hope you find what you are looking for because sometimes you go around the world looking for happiness, and all along it's waiting for you to acknowledge it. Sometimes you need to find yourself first. Prioritize your life according to the Bible. Then you will find balance as you also come to know your likes and dislikes."

Trust that God has good plans for us. What an amazing assurance to know that even if we walk through the dark valley, God is with us. The Bible does not say we won't face challenges, but God will carry us through those challenges. All we need to know, as Christians, is that our Redeemer lives. He guarantees our destiny both in this world and in the world to come. What an amazing God!

In Christ's strength, let us submit our wills to Him. He will enable us to be a constructive force that reckons with the darkness of this world. A force that stands for the right, come what may. Living in His will shines His truth on others. Through us God brings hope to the hopeless and meaning to the lives of those who don't feel valued. Others will want to know more about His will for their lives. Souls can be won when we are living in God's will—not in our own.

Lord, let Your will be done in our lives today. Teach us, while we are still young, to acknowledge You. Don't let past experiences rob us of the inheritance You have promised to those who live within Your will. Give us courage to walk in the light You shed on our paths.

Deborah Matshaya

It Wasn't Mine

Commit everything you do to the LORD.
Trust him, and he will help you.
—*Psalm 37:5, NLT*

When my sister told me about an invitation from the author of the book she was reading, I was curious. The author invited readers to share stories of their pasts telling how God had changed their lives for His glory despite those pasts. I thought it was a great idea but wasn't sure about contributing. I knew I wouldn't have a story as interesting or as touching as the stories of many of the other contributors. I wondered if it would even be worth my effort.

As I read through the author's invitation, I came across the fine print. The paragraph explained that if your story were chosen, you would receive no compensation at all—not now, not in the future. No matter how much money the book made, I—as a contributor—would receive only a copy of the book. Nothing else. I hesitated. I don't have a problem using the gift God gave me to contribute to programs that will help others. Yet, in this case, the compiler of the book would most likely be paid—only the compiler.

As soon as I started to hesitate about writing for this book, my Friend—the Holy Spirit—impressed a question on my heart: "Exactly who are you writing for?" I had to seriously contemplate the question. If I were truly writing for God, the fact that there was no compensation would make absolutely no difference to me. The idea that I could potentially touch someone else's life with my story— and the fact that someone else would know of God's goodness—would be all I needed to consider. Yes, I would commit this work to God, and let Him have His way.

Because author submissions were due on May 31, I began to affectionately refer to my project as "May 31." When a few other surprise projects came my way, I had to put May 31 aside for a while. As this project was something I wanted to continue to talk to God about and commit to Him, I didn't mind the delay. By the time I was able to start working on the project, I realized, with happiness, that my attitude toward it had completely changed.

After I committed the work to God, He helped me understand that the May 31 project was not my work; it was His gift to me.

I was just grateful to have Him use my hands as a part of the work for His kingdom.

Maxine Young

Summer Evenings

When the cool evening breezes were blowing, the man and his wife
heard the Lord God walking about in the garden.
—*Genesis 3:8, NLT*

They settle down on a neighborhood with the gentle ecstasy of flying Frisbees and shared tomatoes. They cause a kind of intoxication, but a wholesome, allowable one.

They're perfect for sneakily putting bouquets on the doorstep of the woman who found and returned your dog countless times, and for taking said dog for a run in the field even though you have more important things to do—just because he needs his doggy dose of a summer evening to prevent more jailbreaks.

I love summer evenings. I always have.

The memories: fireflies in a jar. Treats from the ice cream truck. Unforgettable games of hide-and-seek tag with handsome boys much older than one would dare talk to in, for instance, a store.

And more memories: running like the wind. The smell of charcoal fires. Watermelon seed spitting fights. Family. Friends. God.

I'm wrestling with some deep, existential sadness lately. I'm a melancholic songwriter who has learned to expect my feelings to fall through the floor from time to time. They lie in a painful blob somewhere in the region of my solar plexus like a beached whale for about a week. Then finally the serotonin receptor-builders in my brain kick into high gear and the whale miraculously slips back out to sea.

I know this sadness will resolve, but right now it's sitting heavy in my soul. And the antidote, my therapy, is summer evenings.

I think God is trying to tell me, through the perfect weather, the simple pleasures, and the nice neighbors, that sometimes all I have to do for Him—and for anyone else—is enjoy His gifts.

To look up to heaven, and say, "Thank You." To be suspended in time, grateful that not all is sad, desperate, or disappointing.

That's what He wants for me tonight, in His company.

I think I'll take it.

Jennifer Jill Schwirzer

Civic Reward by Working for Jesus

"But from there you will seek the LORD your God, and you will find
Him if you seek Him with all your heart and with all your soul."
—*Deuteronomy 4:29, NKJV*

My husband has a multitalented niece, Melody, who loves children. Melody and her husband live on a fruit block in Mildura, Victoria, Australia. They raised four children and like going to a smaller church, so they cross over the mighty Murray River to Dareton in New South Wales to worship God.

Melody is musical; it's one of her many talents. She started a children's choir, and it was successful in many competitions. After a few years, and as the children grew older, the choir was disbanded. So Melody, who is also enthusiastic about vegetarian cooking, started giving healthful cooking demonstrations at the hospital where she works as a nurse. The hospital also asked Melody to give demonstrations on healthful living.

Another project of Melody's—a yearly one—is Vacation Bible School for primary-age children. She and her church reserve and decorate (a different theme each year) the Elderly Citizens Hall. So much preparation needs to be made. They collect and freeze donated bread and buns from a local bakery. Melody's team puts up posters around town each year, inviting the participation of children who live in that district. With the help of other men and women at her church, they gather up and cook food to give the children for morning tea and lunch. Games are prepared and crafts made to take home from the event. This Vacation Bible School has taken place for some years now, yet the team at Melody's church never tire of welcoming the children to the annual event as they ride in on a bus—the same bus that brings the aboriginal children into Dareton for schooling. Today a number of unchurched mothers now bring their children to the Dareton weekly Sabbath School programs. Members of Dareton's civic council have taken notice of the good work done by Melody and her church. As a result, they nominated her and the church for the Australia Day Award. God has blessed Melody and her church for using whatever gifts they have in spreading the love of Jesus in their community in ways that are needed.

Though small, the church is making a big impact in their town and receiving God's blessings. What talents do you have to use for Jesus? He will bless them when put to His service.

Joan D. L. Jaensch

July 29

From Camp Meeting to Christmas and Beyond

He who testifies to these things says,
"Yes, I am coming soon." Amen. Come, Lord Jesus.
—*Revelation 22:20, NIV*

Mommy, how long until camp meeting?" Jeremy asked yearly on some winter day shortly after Christmas (sometimes even the day after Christmas). And he asked every year until he understood how the calendar worked and could figure it out on his own. Katrina and Jessica, his younger sisters, followed in his footsteps, asking the same question several times during the winter and early spring months. All three of them looked forward to camp meeting every year. It was that special time when they were set free on the more than three hundred acres of land at Valley Vista, running anywhere and everywhere with friends, many of whom they only saw once a year. They went to their children's meetings, learned about Jesus, swam, played, slept, and did it all over again the next day. It was ten days of bliss. All too soon, it would end. We packed up and went home.

And every year, usually on that trip home, I would hear the question, "Mommy, how long until Christmas?" I would answer back, "Six months; that's one hundred eighty days." Then every so often throughout the summer months and on into fall, the question would come again. "How long?" All three of them looked forward to Christmas every year. It was that special time when they were able to visit faraway family. They played with cousins, anticipated gifts, learned about Jesus, played in the snow, *ooh*ed and *aah*ed over the pretty lights. Pure pleasure could be seen in their eyes. All too soon the day was part of history and we were packing up the lights and other decorations to store away until the next year. Then, within a few days, "Mommy, how long?"

These two questions have ever since been imbedded in my mind as pointing to the two most important events in my young children's lives. Special times that to this day my children (and my husband and I) look forward to every year (even though we're all much older now).

There's another question I have asked again and again. I hope my children have asked it as well. I even hope you have asked it. It goes like this: "Daddy, how long until we're all with You in heaven?" My prayer is that each of us anticipates that day with even more excitement than Jeremy, Katrina, or Jessica ever anticipated camp meeting or Christmas.

Kathy Pepper

Growing in Grace at Jesus' Feet

For by grace you have been saved through faith.
—*Ephesians 2:8, NKJV*

Mary Magdalene is my favorite person in the whole Bible; I believe that she was a woman "after God's own heart." In fact, I'm sure of it! You see, Mary spent every opportunity she had at Jesus' feet. We know her story by heart, but I'd like to make it practical for us.

Mary was transformed; she was saved through her faith. She grew in grace through her relationship with Jesus. She was no longer the person she used to be. Her old, sinful life was gone and her new life was formed at Jesus' feet. There are so many aspects of her life that are amazing, but the one that really speaks most to me is her place at the cross and at the empty tomb.

Nearly everyone had abandoned Jesus at the cross, but not Mary! Though she was heartbroken, she had made her choice to be close to Jesus—and that's where she stayed. Right from the beginning, that was the place to be for her (see Luke 10:39), and on that awful day, that's where you find her (John 19:25). She couldn't do anything to change the situation, so she decided to be as close as she possibly could. I can imagine that Mary cried herself to sleep that Friday night. Many of us women cry on many occasions. Being a woman, I can put myself in Mary's place—I definitely would have cried!

But to me, what's most interesting in her story is when Jesus speaks to her on resurrection morning. He puts on her lips, the lips of a woman—a transformed woman—the message of the Resurrection. Mary was the first person to receive the message and then commissioned to spread the good news!

What about you and me? Are we growing in grace? Are we spreading the good news? Do we allow Jesus to be in charge of our lives? "For by grace you have been saved through faith" is such an important statement. Salvation is a gift from God. It's not something we earn because of our good works. How we allow this grace to work through us is what's important. You and I need to be at Jesus' feet every moment of our lives. It's the *only* way to grow in grace.

I want to be found at Jesus' feet at the Second Coming. What a glorious day that will be, my friends! My prayer is that we continue to grow in grace through faith.

Erna Johnson

Little Ducks

And when he putteth forth his own sheep, he goeth before them, and the sheep follow him: for they know his voice.
—John 10:4

One summer morning my husband and I went to a park to enjoy some fresh air and the peaceful lake. We suddenly spotted a mother duck with fifteen ducklings waddling across a busy road. Cars stopped to let them cross. Children got off their bikes to smile in wonder. Entering a garden on the other side of the road, mummy duck jumped over a red brick garden border. Her ducklings tried to do the same but fell back onto the pavement. She quacked softly, waddling back and calling for them to follow her.

Soon she realized they were still too young and could not. She jumped back in their midst much to their wing-fluttering joy and excitement. Then mummy duck took another path until she reached the open entrance to the garden. Her babies soon lined up behind her and merrily followed her. Mummy had found a path with no obstacles that her babies could follow.

This incident made me think of God and how He asks us to follow Him. Yet sometimes while we are trying to follow Him, we come across obstacles that we cannot overcome. We fall back as Jesus stops and watches over us with loving eyes to see if we'll try again. When we finally cry out that we can't make it on our own and call for His help, He answers our pleas by coming to our level. Sometimes He leads us to a smoother path where there are fewer obstacles. He adapts Himself to our situation and He says to us: "OK, you've tried enough. You still need to grow to overcome these types of obstacles. Let's take another path. After you grow more, you can handle bigger challenges and overcome greater obstacles. Yet I will always be with you. I promise you that you will be able to make it."

Like the little ducklings, we stumble. We get up and try one more time to jump, but we fall. Often our obstacles are our taste for forbidden things, our disturbed emotions for wanting the wrong things. Those obstacles Jesus can help us overcome. He will give us strength to overcome our frailties and conquer our temptations. As with the little ducklings, the path may be long and full of danger. Yet He always walks before us, choosing and preparing the way. Amen.

Thank you, little ducks, for that inspiring morning and that helpful lesson!

Monique Lucile de Oliveira

Cultivate by Pruning, and Grow the Best Fruit—Part 1

But the fruit of the Spirit is love, joy, peace,
longsuffering, kindness, goodness, faithfulness.
—*Galatians 5:22, ASV*

A few years ago I took a trip by railcar from Düsseldorf, Germany, to Lisbon, Portugal. The trip provided wonderful cultural stops in the cities in between: Paris, Munich, Innsbruck, Rome, Barcelona, Madrid, and finally Lisbon.

The train sped through beautiful European valleys and mountainsides, and my attention was riveted by the fruit trees depicting the art of espaliering (a tree or shrub being trained to grow on a flat plain, often against a wall or trellis). The espalier technique produces both a beautiful and an efficient way of growing fruit trees. The training of an espalier tree depicts the art of precision, and it can take a few to many years. It is not for those who must have instant gratification! Espaliering is a gardener's delay in gratification.

A well-trained espalier lives longer and bears much more fruit in a much smaller space than an untrained tree. And it also becomes a piece of living sculpture, a beautiful testimony to the interaction of gardener and tree. First, the skeleton of the tree is formed through careful pruning to train branches in precise positions to become the rigid support—the skeleton of the tree. The result is a geometrically recognizable shape and optimization of the sap flow, which leads to more fruit from the tree compared to what can be expected from a tree that is unpruned or is pruned without the intention to maximize fruit production.

The aim of pruning fruit trees is not only to give the tree every opportunity to be healthy and to give a good harvest of fruit but also to allow the gardener to manipulate the trees into shapes that suit the space they grow in.

God reminds us that the best training of His children begins at the earliest possible moment, before any of our thoughts are out of alignment with His will. Hence, the importance of the mandate and promise contained in Proverbs 22:6: "Train up a child in the way he should go."

Prudence LaBeach Pollard

Cultivate by Pruning, and Grow the Best Fruit—Part 2

Keep your father's command, and do not forsake the law of your
mother.
Bind them continually upon your heart; Tie them around your neck.
When you roam, they will lead you; when you sleep, they will keep
you; And when you awake, they will speak with you.
For the commandment is a lamp, and the law a light.
—Proverbs 6:20–23, NKJV

The mandate and promise contained in Proverbs 22:6 are not just for parents; they are for all who respond to God's calling on their lives. Similar to the training of children, we are not to be left to the way we would naturally go. Psalm 51:5 reminds that "I was shapen in iniquity; and in sin did my mother conceive me." We naturally have corrupt hearts, which must be redirected in the way we should go—the way of God.

If we love our children and if we love ourselves, we will train our hearts in the way God desires. Meaning that, as soon as possible, every child should be led to the knowledge of the Savior, and daily we must seek knowledge of the Savior's will for our lives and for that day.

As the beautiful fruit-laden trees depicting the art of espaliering riveted my attention, I contemplated their geometrical shapes and the optimized sap flow that resulted in more and larger fruit than I had seen in any other orchard.

Forty some years ago God's calling on my life led me to the daily study of His Word, and He continues to show me what needs to be pruned from my life. This He will do for any of us who seek His will and cooperate with the pruning process.

For some, it is sexual gratification that needs to be delayed.

For others, it may be the habit of lying or telling partial truths that needs to be trimmed away.

For still others, it may be hatred towards enemies—the mean boss or coworker.

Today the decision is ours—the decision to grow a well-trained life capable of bearing the fruit of the Holy Spirit, a living sculpture, a beautiful testimony to the interaction of the heavenly Gardener and His human creations. Meditate on the words of Scripture for guidance because "the commandment is a lamp, and the law a light."

Prudence LaBeach Pollard

A Long Wait Home

Be still, and know that I am God.
—*Psalm 46:10*

Patience is something most of us struggle with. For instance, some of us may struggle with having to wait patiently in a grocery-store line or on someone to take us somewhere.

My husband, who is legally sightless, had an appointment for an outpatient procedure at the hospital. His insurance company supplies transportation for doctor visits, so I called to schedule a ride. The van came, and the driver was very nice. When we arrived at our destination, he gave me a card with the toll-free number to call when we were ready to be picked up.

The procedure took longer than expected, but I had informed the nurse that we were riding in the insurance van, so I needed to know when I should call for our return trip. She said she would come and let me know when my husband was in recovery.

While in the waiting room, to my surprise, I saw Kay, a church member, working at the desk. She saw me and came over and gave me a hug. I had no idea she worked there.

After a couple of hours, the nurse came and gave me the OK to call our ride. I went to the desk and called the number on the card but got a recording. I waited "patiently"; but after about seven minutes, I hung up the phone and redialed.

I was getting really impatient and frustrated as I continued to be kept on hold. The receptionist saw my frustration and tried to call on her phone but to no avail. I was getting really upset. I asked the receptionist if she knew Kay, who worked downstairs. She said, "Yes, do you go to the same church?"

"Yes."

"I'll call her, and she'll find you a ride home. Don't get upset."

Kay came, and we told her the situation. She said, "Not to worry." Because she had her church directory, she would call someone to pick us up. I praised God and relaxed.

The Lord places people in our paths, though sometimes we don't always know why. I had no idea that Kay worked there, but the Lord knew I was going to need help, so He allowed me to see her at that particular time. She called one of our church members, and the church member came and took us home. I had been so impatient and worried while the Lord was already working it out!

"Rest in the LORD, and wait patiently for him" (Psalm 37:7).

Elaine J. Johnson

He Is Ever Faithful

But my God shall supply all your need
according to his riches in glory by Christ Jesus.
—*Philippians 4:19*

It was six weeks since D-Day, or the day of my divorce hearing in court. The money I had received at the divorce settlement was quickly disappearing into back mortgage payments and back taxes. It was already mid-June, and I still didn't have a teaching job for which I had been searching for months. How could I care for my children? I had searched and searched for a job. I hadn't taught in eighteen years except for occasional substitute teaching.

One Friday afternoon I called a nearby school district in a neighboring state. Yes, they did have a job for an English teacher. Monday morning I hurried to turn in yet another completed application. "Actually, we don't have a job for an English teacher," the secretary told me. Another disappointment. Driving home, I tried to remind myself of how the Lord had always provided for all of our needs. I claimed Bible promises while asking, "How will my older boys be able to go back to college? How will we eat or pay the mortgage?"

That week I heard about three job possibilities. A friend called to say that the local academy had a job opening. My son's academy dean told him of a job opening at a boarding school in another state. The sister of my children's teacher said she'd tell me about several more.

I asked the Lord that only one opening would work out, so that I would know that the new job was His choice and not mine. The local academy had someone else they wanted to hire. The out-of-state school had asked another teacher to fill the position but would consider me if she declined. A couple of days later someone called from the education department of my church's local area. They had three openings, but only one fit my talents and family needs!

A week later two of my boys and I drove three hours to the school with the opening. At the interview, I was offered the job. What the Lord provided was so much better than anything I had thought of. My youngest son and I moved to a comfortable little house near the church school where I would teach. I didn't need a babysitter. My son stopped stuttering. The church community opened their hearts to us. "My God shall supply all your need." He did it over and over again for the next twenty-five years. Praise His name! His promises are true!

Kirsten Anderson Roggenkamp

Jesus Cares!

Behold the fowls of the air: for they sow not,
neither do they reap, nor gather into barns;
yet your heavenly Father feedeth them.
Are ye not much better than they?
—Matthew 6:26

In the city where I live, the capital of Ghana, it is not common to find a fruit-bearing plant. I was happy for the opportunity to get out into nature when the church territory where I live planned a weekend leadership workshop away from the city.

The Friday workshop program was rained out. I woke up early to hurriedly prepare to make up for lost time before the Sabbath activities began. On my walk to the local church where the meetings were being held, I had to descend into a valley. Suddenly, I heard a voice directing my eyes to the top of the ridges above me, which surrounded the church—the ridges of Kpando, a town in the Volta Region of Ghana.

What I saw was marvelous. I was overwhelmed. On top of the hill were pawpaw [papaya] trees bearing beautiful ripe fruits of a very vibrant yellow color. At first, I saw just a few birds, but soon they gathered in, calling others with whistles of praise. The aroma of the pawpaw brought them in great numbers. I had never experienced such a beautiful scene! The birds flew high and then higher, dived down, and took bites of the pawpaw, clapping their wings, chirping, dancing, and praising God for His goodness.

This scene reminded me of the hymn "Great Is Thy Faithfulness." God was meeting the birds' needs. Their happy singing recalled another hymn: "Let Us With a Gladsome Mind." Their songs took me, in my mind, to Matthew 6:25–31, especially the twenty-sixth verse: "Behold the fowls of the air . . . your heavenly Father feedeth them. Are ye not much better than they?"

If God so provides for the birds of the air that don't plant, reap, or store up in barns, will He not provide for us? What then is our worry? What then is our burden? He who said He cares about us is faithful. We are to respond to His promises and His blessed assurance, and we will experience the goodness of the Lord in our lives.

Jesus really cares for us. Jesus loves us so much that, while we were yet sinners, He died for us (Romans 5:8). Jesus is interceding for us, so that where He is, there shall we also be (John 14:2). In the meantime, He has prepared our table. He is faithful. Jesus really cares! Amen.

Charlotte Osei-Agyeman

The Present

She is more precious than rubies:
and all the things thou canst desire
are not to be compared unto her.
—*Proverbs 3:15*

It will be my grown-up daughter's birthday soon. She will be twenty-eight years old. I've been thinking about what to buy her for a birthday present. It occurs to me that she might not open or even accept the present I send to her. So should I not buy her anything?

There has been a division between us over the years, and we've become estranged. I can't even think of why the division came about. It seems to just happen in families these days more often than it used to. "It's just a sign of the times," some people say, but I disagree.

I think that problems in the family have been around since time immemorial. After all, there were problems in Joseph's family in the Old Testament. His jealous brothers even resorted to throwing him down into a pit!

So does that mean, then, in the case of my daughter, that I shouldn't buy her anything special? Of course, it doesn't. I will carefully choose something that I hope she would want.

After all, isn't that what our heavenly Father would want me to do and what He has done for us? He offers us a very special gift as an expression of His love— His Son!

Of course, it is up to us whether we accept or want His gift. I seem to remember that there was a falling out, way back in time, when we became estranged from Him. Didn't it begin with Adam and Eve and their self-serving choices in the Garden of Eden?

So, despite our being responsible for starting the family rift, does God then give us a gift that is less than His best? Not at all. We are still His children, and He loves us. He continues to favor us with many blessings. Most of all, He gives us the gift of unity with Him through Jesus. God created us, and He wants to give us life eternal through His Son. That is precious.

However, we seem to have this willful nature that wants to do its own thing and go its own way. Sometimes we want different things from what our heavenly Papa wants for us. However, unlike our earthly parents and earthly presents, God is our heavenly Father who gives us *the* perfect gift anyway.

May each of us accept His precious gift—abundant life in Jesus.

Laura A. Canning

Experiencing God Through His Handiwork

"For I know the plans I have for you," declares the LORD,
"plans to prosper you and not to harm you,
plans to give you hope and a future."
—*Jeremiah 29:11, NIV*

For ye shall go out with joy, and be led forth with peace: the
mountains and the hills shall break forth before you into singing; and
all the trees of the fields shall clap their hands.
—*Isaiah 55:12, ASV*

Walking outside on a late autumn afternoon, on the street, I noticed the beautiful colors of the leaves that had fallen from the trees. Hundreds lay on the ground in the church's parking lot where I had arrived for my scheduled walk around the church.

The wind began to blow, and I noticed the movement of the leaves. In slow motion at first, they appeared to be lining up as though waiting for instruction. Soon the leaves stood up on their sides and began racing, dancing, and leaping as though they were headed toward the finish line of an Olympic event. My heart thrilled that my God would do something so exciting for me. "Oh, how He must love me!" I exclaimed. I love the wonderful way my Lord allowed me to experience Him through His handiwork.

One morning recently I was summoned by that sweet, still voice as He said to me, *"Come to our special place; I want to speak to you."* Of course, I got up and prepared to meet my Savior. As I waited to hear His voice, I gazed outside my window where I could see lofty trees of different varieties and sizes. Then I heard that still, small Voice saying, *"Don't start your day being busy. Sit here and wait for Me to speak to you. After all, I know the plans I have for you today."* I saw the trees waving and "clapping" their "hands"! The fierceness of the invisible wind caused them to move, and the birds, nestled in their hideaways, to flutter and fly away.

As the wind causes the shaking and swaying of the trees, so the Holy Spirit breathes on us, admonishing us to arise under the influence of God's power when He says, "Go." The trees moved effortlessly through the force and will of the wind. So should we move by the will of our Holy Father, "for in him we live, and move, and have our being" (Acts 17:28, ASV).

Lenora Dorf

Off the Mic

For great is his love toward us,
and the faithfulness of the Lord endures forever.
—*Psalm 117:2, NIV*

As part of the immigration requirements to become United States citizens, my husband and I needed to have medical exams. We checked with all of the listed doctors and chose the cheapest one; however, it would still cost us about six hundred dollars. Being unemployed, we could not fund the exams unless we drained our limited pocket money. We put the problem aside and hoped that God would send help before the deadline.

A week before the deadline a man came to me in church and told me to see him after the service. I was unable to see him because I was preparing to lead the afternoon program for women's ministries. But Brother Twumasi did not give up; he went to see my husband instead.

I was standing in front of the whole congregation when my husband came to me with a smile and said, "Switch off the mic." I thought, *Why?* So he switched off the mic himself and told me, "Brother Twumasi has given me an envelope, and it is very thick!" Adjei could not wait for the program to end to tell me the good news. Because he did not want others to hear it, he had told me, "Switch off the mic!" We later found out that fellow church member had given us five hundred dollars. Even though he had been helping us a lot as a pharmacist with our prescriptions, that gift was a miracle. It was an answer to our private prayer to the Almighty. Now all we needed was just one hundred dollars more.

I was very happy and more than grateful to God. But, friends, I was not surprised because our awesome God has proved Himself faithful so many times for me. All I could say was that which the wise hymnist wrote, "Great is Thy faithfulness! Morning by morning new mercies I see." God is faithful, but that is not new. Even in Old Testament times, Jeremiah wrote, "Great is his faithfulness; his mercies begin afresh each morning" (Lamentations 3:23, NLT). The psalmist exclaimed, "For great is your love, higher than the heavens; your faithfulness reaches to the skies" (Psalm 108:4, NIV). I say with David, "I will thank you, Lord, among all the people. I will sing your praises among the nations. For your unfailing love is as high as the heavens. Your faithfulness reaches to the clouds" (Psalm 57:9, 10, NLT).

I think God is phenomenal. Don't you?

Mabel Kwei

Invitation to the Heavenly Feast

A certain man made a great supper, and bade many: and sent his servant at supper time to say to them that were bidden, Come; for all things are now ready. And they all with one consent began to make excuse. The first said unto him, I have bought a piece of ground, and I must needs go and see it: I pray thee have me excused. And another said, I have bought five yoke of oxen, and I go to prove them: I pray thee have me excused. And another said, I have married a wife, and therefore I cannot come.
—*Luke 14:16–20*

As often as I have read or heard this parable, I never thought I would be among those with an excuse not to attend the banquet supper. This was not an invitation to a simple meal; it was to a feast in a heavenly kingdom beyond human description. Who of us doesn't enjoy food, especially served banquet style? Perhaps my recent interpretation of this parable isn't as you would apply it, but it struck a meaningful chord for me. At the time, I was working toward goals that would benefit a condo association, a conference, and a university. Was I ready to drop them for a heavenly feast?

In the summer of 2013, I had a thymoma (tumor of the thymus) that needed medical attention. A biopsy was taken, and surgery was deemed too risky to perform. I was devastated when my doctor said, "There is nothing we can do for you." It took time to absorb the finality of my future. Would my departure be soon or delayed?

I wasn't ready to have my days numbered. I had many projects I wanted to complete. I had been recently appointed as treasurer of our condo association. I was replacing the manual method of accounting with computer programs that would be more informative. I was volunteering at the Burman University archives, scanning and recording all documents and photos in digital formats. There was much more to do. I thought, *I'm the one who can find answers quickly for those needing information on past history. Do I think I'm indispensable?* Then I began to think of more serious issues. It was at this time that the parable of Luke 14 flashed to my mind.

Was I declining the invitation to the heavenly banquet? Was I making excuses for not being able to attend?

God has been good. An army of prayer warriors continue to pray for me. My health challenges aren't encouraging, but I thank God continually for the blessings He gives.

When the banquet call is announced, I want to be there!

Edith Fitch

Disciplining With Gentleness

But the fruit of the Spirit is love, joy, peace, forbearance,
kindness, goodness, faithfulness, gentleness and self-control.
—*Galatians 5:22, 23, NIV*

Once while volunteering at a local school fund-raiser, I observed (though I couldn't hear) a teacher roughly reprimand a preteen in his mother's presence. The mother had also been volunteering when the teacher had signaled her to bring her son into his classroom. As they exited the private meeting, I saw the crestfallen face of the boy and noticed the mother wiping away her own tears with a tissue. They resumed their work at the fund-raiser, but my heart felt sad for them. I slipped over to the mother and gave her a quick hug without pursuing the reason for her tears.

A bit later I had the opportunity to approach the teacher when he was alone. "I have also been a teacher," I told him pleasantly. "And I've been the parent of a once-enthusiastic pupil who is now a prodigal." Since the teacher was giving me his guarded attention, I continued. "My son, from an early age, did his very best to be helpful. But a particular teacher in a Christian school mistook his helping other students as classroom misbehavior. Once she even pulled him into the girls' restroom to spank him and accuse him of disobedience. Then she refused to pass him to the next grade at the end of the school year. She talked to others about my son, but she never talked to me."

Because my listener showed no sign of disinterest, I elaborated. "So the next year I enrolled my son in a public school. I also wrote to a Christian advice columnist who, in a sense, became an activist on behalf of my son and others like him who had been mistreated by teachers. The columnist's efforts were rewarded—in the form of a new stipulation requiring prospective teachers in parochial schools to pass a child psychology course. Unfortunately, my son will always carry a deep scar inflicted by that teacher." I now pled earnestly with my listener to deal gently with his students and families. Later in the day I noticed him beckoning the preteen and his mother into his classroom for a second conference. This time they all emerged smiling.

Paul, in Galatians 5, listed gentleness as one of the fruits of the Spirit. On whose face can *you* put a smile today because you "grew" the fruit of gentleness and touched a heart?

Consuelo Roda-Jackson

Missed Grasp

When Jesus heard that, he said, This sickness is not unto death, but
for the glory of God, that the Son of God might be glorified thereby.
—*John 11:4*

Satan attacks when we make an effort to draw closer to God. Thankfully, God always wins in the end. I saw this play out once while on a hike during a spiritual retreat.

I was looking intently in front of me, trying to get a foothold on the side of a hill, when I heard screaming. I looked back to see what it was about. A student, coming downhill toward me, was gaining speed. She held out her arm to grab hold of something—anything—at the same time yelling desperately for help. I immediately extended my arm but missed her.

Suddenly, the screaming stopped. She lay still in the dirt; her head profusely bleeding after hitting it hard on a rock two arm lengths away from me. Then it hit me. If she had caught my arm, I would have been lying motionless or worse. I sent a quick prayer heavenward while rushing to her side. I called her name. No answer. Her pulse was quickly weakening. The thought that we'd lost her shook me violently. What now? Eerie silence. Everyone started praying for a miracle.

An ambulance responded quickly, but we needed to transport the student to the closest road. First-aiders attended to her while I went back to the camp to get blankets and inform the principal. The walk to the closest road seemed to last forever. Meanwhile, the girl regained some consciousness, but every slight movement made her throw up.

An hour later I was in the emergency room of Chong Hua Hospital, Cebu, Philippines, and requesting the girl's admittance. I was bloodstained, my bare feet soiled, and I had no cash on hand. This hospital was known for its excellent facilities, skilled staff, and very high fees.

I wish I had remembered today's text then—that when Jesus heard that Lazarus was sick, He said this sickness was for the glory of God, that He might be glorified. I did remember, however, that God would take care of us. I was confident everything would be all right.

This experience, which happened at a spiritual retreat, became a significant landmark in my journey of faith. How many times do we remember that God is in control as we are experiencing a life-and-death situation? Wouldn't it be wonderful to be reminded of John 11:4 when the going gets rough? For the record, the student did recover. Praise the Lord for His goodness!

Rojean Vasquez Marcia

Nothing Is Impossible for God

Your eyes saw my unformed body;
all the days ordained for me were written in your book
before one of them came to be.
—*Psalm 139:16, NIV*

It is wonderful to know that there is a God who knows everything, sees everything, and can do it all. I am impressed as I look back at my life and see what God has done.

I lived with my maternal grandparents until I was four. When I came to live with my mother, she was pregnant with my brother and lived with her second husband. I grew up knowing that my mother had been widowed, and I believed that. But when I was a teenager, I began to ask why my mother did not have my father's death certificate or a picture of him. She never wanted to talk about my father or the past, so my curiosity went away with time.

When I was eighteen years old, I married an extraordinary young man from the church. In our wedding invitation, beside my father's name, I had these words written: "In memory." I always wondered what he would have been like, how he died, and many other things about him. I never commented on my thoughts to anyone. I believed that I had these concerns because my mother did not want to talk about it, but God knew all the circumstances.

One day, when I opened a Web page of my network of friends on the Internet, I saw a message from a girl who claimed to be my cousin. She said that my father was alive and had been looking for me for more than thirty years! I was stunned. I could not believe what I had just read. I accepted the invitation to be an online friend with her, and she sent me pictures of my father. Then I called my sister, who lives next door to my mother. I sent her a picture, asking her to show it to my mother for confirmation. To my surprise, my mother confirmed it was a photograph of my father.

My father had not died. He lived 1,200 miles (1,931 kilometers) away from me. I finally had the opportunity to meet him, after thirty-four years of being separated. I was able to see him, my uncles, aunts, and cousins, who were excited to meet me as well. I gave each one a book, *Signs of Hope*.

I am sure that God brought my father and me together for a purpose—to win him for the kingdom of heaven. I know that nothing is impossible for God and that nothing happens by chance. Is there someone important in your life that you need to seek out for the kingdom?

Nilva de F. Oliveira da Boa Morte

God's Answer

"Before they call I will answer;
while they are still speaking I will hear."
—*Isaiah 65:24, NIV*

During my sophomore year of college, I was brought face-to-face with the accuracy of God's promise in Isaiah 65:24.

Juggling multiple roles and having financial and work worries due to a major accident involving my dad had affected our home life and resulted in many prayers. The only problem from my viewpoint was that God seemed to be saying, *"Wait,"* instead of immediately taking care of the situation as I had been praying He would.

On this particular day, I was walking to school. I arrived at the main road I had to cross. I could see that it was busy. From past experience, I knew it could be several minutes before I could cross.

God, have someone stop for me, I prayed to God in my mind. That was all. I had crossed this road for school five days a week, four times a day since August. It was now March. In all that time, I'd had fewer than five people stop for me. Two cars were passing as I was walking up to the intersection. After they were past, the very next car stopped, and the driver motioned for me to cross the road!

Thank You, God. I did not deserve this, I thought humbly as I crossed the road.

Later that day, as I was leaving class, my dad called to tell me that we needed to press forward on some important paperwork about which I had been praying. This information had also come in answer to part of our prayers. What I remember most though, is the answer to my thought prayer: *God, have someone stop for me.* A driver stopping to let me cross the road was unimportant compared to the major issue my father had referenced in his call. Yet God had reminded me that day that He was still in control and taking care of me and my family.

Does God always answer prayers as obviously as this? No. But we do know that Jesus is leading in the details of our lives, whether it is hearing from a friend we haven't heard from in a while or missing rush-hour traffic. God's little blessings in our daily lives evidence His care.

Today I challenge you to look for small blessings that you may have taken as a matter of course. Discover God's hand in the tiny details of your life.

Melinda Ferguson

This Is Your Time

He has made everything appropriate in its time. He has also set
eternity in their heart, yet so that man will not find out the work
which God has done from the beginning even to the end. . . .
For God has so worked that men should fear Him.
—*Ecclesiastes 3:11, 14, NASB*

Many of us would be much more comfortable if everything always stayed the same; yet it doesn't. Everything has its season, an appropriate time. I was reminded of that in a dramatic way as I saw my husband officiating at the marriage ceremonies of both of our sons. A season in the life of our family had changed, and a new season for new families had begun.

I am so thankful to God to be in this new season of my life; this time when I am enjoying two children in ministry, their spouses, one grandchild, my sweet friends who love the Lord, and especially my partner in ministry and the love of my life for thirty-three years.

This in no way means there are no problems to be solved, no more battles to be fought, no fears to be overcome, no challenges to be faced, no relationships to be fought for, or no sorrows to be borne. I suppose I could say I have never been so stretched beyond myself, so ashamed of my little faith, so lacking in knowledge, and so in need of mercy every morning. Yet this is still a great season—a great time in my life!

Though many of us enjoy nature's changing seasons, life's changing seasons may frighten us. Change can be difficult, but less so if we learn to go through each season with God. "There is a time for everything, and everything on earth has its special season" (Ecclesiastes 3:1, NCV). God has a purpose and a season for everything under heaven, and right now each of us is in one of His seasons. Perhaps it's the season of education or the beginning a first job. Perhaps the time of young love or the loss of a parent. Perhaps the time of a new baby or an illness. Perhaps the time of an empty nest or the fourth move in six years.

What is your season of life? Do not be fearful. Celebrate. Be thankful. This promise remains: "And surely I am with you always, to the very end of the age" (Matthew 28:20, NIV).

Whatever season you are entering, exiting, or in the midst of, choose to say, "This is my season, and a great place to be in God's timetable!" What are you learning, giving, or experiencing? Embrace it! With God's help, you can do it. With Him, this can be your best season!

Raquel Queiroz da Costa Arrais

Sometimes No

Once I was young, and now I am old.
Yet I have never seen the godly abandoned
or their children begging for bread.
—*Psalm 37:25, NLT.*

Sometimes God says *"Yes"* to our prayers. Sometimes God says *"Wait."* Other times God says *"No."* So why would a God who is eager to hear our prayers say *"No"*? God provides valuable lessons when His answer is *No.* Just reflect for a moment on three spiritual giants who all experienced *No* answers to their prayers.

Moses begged to enter the Promised Land. God said, *"No."* Why? God wanted Moses to understand that sin has grave consequences. When Jesus humbly prayed that, if it were possible, He be spared the bitter separation with His Father through death, God said, *"No."* The Father wanted to save us the only way He could—through the death of His Son, Jesus. When Paul requested that the "thorn" in his flesh be removed, God said, *"No."* The apostle needed more opportunity to grow through suffering and through faith. All three of these spiritual giants experienced—in Paul's words—God's grace being "sufficient" for them even when His answer was *No* (2 Corinthians 12:8). God had something better in store for all of them.

He does for you too. Perhaps you thought a certain someone was the man of your dreams, and if you did not marry him, you would never be happy. You prayed and God said, *"No."* You said to yourself, *I will never be happy.* But God has something better in store for you. He did for me when, in the midst of my sadness, He brought Trevor Fraser to my Bible study class at church. I looked into those big brown eyes and forgot all about that other fellow. God's *No* to me was an act of love!

Perhaps God's *No* involves a job position or some other dilemma. How do we live with the *No*? First, we remember Moses, Paul, and Jesus—and the end of their stories. "In the future life the mysteries that here have annoyed and disappointed us will be made plain. We shall see that our seemingly unanswered prayers and disappointed hopes have been among our greatest blessings."*

My dear sisters, wait patiently to see God's alternative for you. For I know that God's tomorrow will be better than today!

Edith C. Fraser

---

* Ellen G. White, *The Ministry of Healing* (Mountain View, CA: Pacific Press®, 1942), 474.

August 16

Worthy Friendship

A friend is always loyal,
and a brother [sister] is born to help in time of need.
—*Proverbs 17:17, NLT*

Having a mutual interest in writing, Lois and I decided to attend a writers' conference together. As a motley duo, we drove from Ohio to Michigan. Though she was driving with a disabled foot and I had a noncontagious infection, we were both determined to go.

We survived the trip and made new friends who would play roles in our futures as writers. After the writers' conference, Lois and I decided to form a writers' group, Dayton Christian Scribes, which grew quickly to about fifty members and maintains that same number after all these years. Some have moved on or passed on, and others have moved in to take their places. I was one who moved on, then returned, and moved on again. During the many changes, Lois remained and kept the group knit together.

My freelance career flourished as my husband and I moved across the country. Though Lois is a well-published author, her writing career took more of a turn toward mentoring other writers within the writers' group. I have benefited also; throughout our nearly forty-year friendship, Lois has remained my constant encourager.

My husband and I moved through six states with his job transfers and then retirement. It isn't easy starting over again—time after time after time. With each of my husband's job transfers, I had to go out and prove to my new world that I'm able to produce and meet deadlines.

As the daughter of a missionary physician, and someone who also held a long career in a medical office, Lois always offered me good advice. The apple fell close to her parental tree. She never let me think for a minute that I couldn't do whatever: write the toughest assignment or get through a malady's pain. She realized that it was the very newness of every transition that increased my abilities and provided me with new writing fodder.

The fact that Lois held faith in my ability to adapt, and her *insistence* that I can do it, led me to the attitude, "Yes, I can!" Our friendship has been mostly long distance, but it's one of the sweetest friendships a gal could want. We may not be next-door neighbors, but we virtually hold each other's heart—and the friendship keeps us young at heart as we age. In addition to all else, Lois and I are prayer partners. She's the stuff that makes friendship real.

Let's be that kind of friend to others.

Betty Kossick

Divine Deliverance

For the angel of the LORD is a guard;
he surrounds and defends all who fear him.
—*Psalm 34:7, NLT*

One bright, sunny August day in 1998 I was unusually excited, for in a few days my daughter would be formally starting school. That Friday, after completing my grocery shopping, my daughter and I stopped by the seamstress to collect her school uniforms. I was elated as I held the petite uniforms and inspected them. My daughter, too, could not contain her excitement as we did the final try-on with the seamstress. Satisfied that the uniforms fit perfectly, we left for home.

We arrived at about 2:45 P.M. My husband, a building contractor, greeted us from his office, which was on the same compound as our house. He indicated that he would join us in the house shortly. At about 3:00 P.M., he came into the house via the kitchen entrance. He kissed me goodbye and said that he was off to pay his workers their weekly wages. Generally, he left home on Fridays around 3:15 P.M. to pay his employees. However, on this particular Friday, he left fifteen minutes earlier for no explicable reason.

At 3:05 P.M., the kitchen door burst open. I thought that my husband had probably forgotten something and had returned to get it. I looked around expecting to see him. Instead I stared straight at a masked man toting a gun. Terrified, I screamed uncontrollably. He ordered me to stop screaming.

"Where's your husband, and where's the money?" he demanded, referring to the payroll. I told him my husband was gone and that we had no money.

The gunman made his way into the living room where my mother was caring for my daughter and four-month-old son. At the sight of the gunman, my mother screamed, "Jesus! Jesus! Jesus!" The more the man ordered her to be quiet, the more she screamed.

At that moment, I saw an opportunity to escape through the kitchen into the yard—where I saw another masked man in a vehicle! Because the vehicle wasn't blocking the entrance to the property, I was able to rush by and into the street for help. Very quickly traffic built up outside the house, while my mother and children also made their escape—with no injuries.

Let us truly trust the angel of the Lord to encamp around us today and to deliver us.

Gerene I. Joseph

The Power of Music

Speaking to yourselves in psalms and hymns and spiritual songs,
singing and making melody in your heart to the Lord;
giving thanks always for all things unto God
and the Father in the name of our Lord Jesus Christ.
—Ephesians 5:19, 20

I love good music, and I have developed this enthusiasm and fondness through years of listening to songs that put joy into my heart, whether morning, noon, or nighttime. I recall reading *The Desire of Ages* by Ellen G. White where she states that in Jesus' childhood He often expressed the gladness of His heart by singing psalms and heavenly songs.[*]

Memories of enjoying music during my early childhood years frequently come to mind as I recall going to church with my parents. In the children's department, I enjoyed singing as we acted out the words of songs that we sang. My enjoyment of music didn't end in the children's department, for there was a worship service that followed. I enjoyed listening to the church choir as they sang good, old gospel songs or hymns, exciting emotions in everyone.

At home, I became my parents' listening ears, knowingly and unknowingly, during early morning hours as I listened to my mother singing her favorite song while she prepared breakfast for the family. As a nosy listener, I discovered that my dad had his favorite song also because I heard him frequently singing. As he went about his daily activities indoors or out, he sang, "Amazing grace! How sweet the sound that saved a wretch like me! I once was lost, but now am found; was blind, but now I see."[†]

God's promises are true, and I thank Him for inspiring songwriters to write good songs expressing those promises. Good music has the power to inspire and heal when we're down. As we sing and listen to music, our minds are refreshed and invigorated, for good music is therapeutic. Through music, God helped me to carry on during and after the death of my husband of fifty-three years. Daily I'm reminded of the words of the song "God Will Take Care of You."

Let's join together trusting, believing, and singing God's promises and praises. Tomorrow will be better than today when He returns to take us to our heavenly home.

Annie B. Best

---

[*] Ellen G. White, *The Desire of Ages* (Mountain View, CA: Pacific Press®, 1940), 73.

[†] John Newton, "Amazing Grace," in *Christ in Song* (Washington, D.C.: Review and Herald®, 1908), no. 765.

Life Is Like a Bowl of Grits

Be kind to one another, tenderhearted.
—*Ephesians 4:32, ESV*

Stars still sparkled above as our family piled into the car for the trip to visit my uncle Francis. He was my mother's uncle, and once or twice a year we visited Aunt Ida and him. Two hours of travel brought us to a little park. My sister and I made good use of the playground while my mother and grandmother cooked breakfast over a fire, and our dad watched us play. Back in the car, three hours later we arrived, and I was glad we were staying the night. There wasn't much for kids to do, but our mother might go upstairs with us and let us explore the mostly empty bedrooms, or Daddy might take us for a walk into town.

Uncle Francis and Aunt Ida slept downstairs. I was fascinated by their nightcaps that hung on the bedposts. Outside the kitchen door was a well with a rope and bucket. Sometimes Uncle Francis would show us how they drew water from the well before they had running water in the house. And Aunt Ida made her own soap from leftover cooking grease. I'd seen the large blocks of grayish soap stacked in her pantry.

The next morning we sat around their big dining room table. Even the dishes looked old-fashioned. I didn't recognize everything. When I saw scrambled eggs and a plate of toast, I knew I'd be OK. But then, after the prayer, a steaming bowl of *something* was put in front of me. I took a bite. It tasted awful. Conversation flowed around me as I bravely ate one tiny bite after another until the bowl was empty.

Just then Uncle Francis looked my way. "Oh, you like grits," he boomed. "Here, have some more!" and he piled another load into my bowl. I could hardly breathe, but I was such a timid little thing that I bravely picked up my spoon. But my uncle's eyes were still on me, and he said in surprise, "Oh, you need butter and sugar on grits." With that, he added both to the bowl—and that made all the difference. Suddenly, I liked grits, and I still do.

I don't know if life is truly a bowl of cherries, but I do know that life is like a bowl of grits. Even the most unpleasant things go down better if someone adds the sweetness of a hug, kind words, and a smile.

I try to remember that.

Penny Estes Wheeler

Building for Eternity

*For as we have many members in one body, but all the members
do not have the same function, so we, being many,
are one body in Christ, and individually members of one another.*
—Romans 12:4, 5, NKJV

G od gave us eyes to see, ears to hear, a nose to smell, skin to touch, and a tongue to taste. As individual and different members of our body carry out different functions, so, too, are individual members of the church to carry out different functions. Each person is blessed with different talents, which, in turn, build up God's kingdom.

Romans 12:6 also tells us that "we have different gifts, according to the grace given to each of us" (NIV). This means that each of us with our various talents or gifts is asked to use them for the building up of God's kingdom. We are to sow these individual talents, gifts, and abilities as seeds into winning souls for eternity.

Creatures that borrow life from God ought to return to their Creator the honor, glory, and praise that are due His holy name. It is in so doing that we grow to reflect Him, His likeness, and His image.

We stretch forth our talents by virtue of faith and, with thanksgiving, trust that our Redeemer takes pleasure in assessing the measure of our talents sown to build up His kingdom.

With His help, we nurture these talents, believing that God will refine, cleanse, and perfect us according to His will, fitting us for His work.

One must never slight one's talent as unimportant, as God in His wisdom weaves together each individual talent to create a beautiful tapestry. Each talent is to be used in such a way that it draws our hearts intimately closer to God.

In addition, each talent rightly used gives men and women, boys and girls, a better glimpse of heaven.

When we surrender our lives to God's will, He equips us for His work. He enlarges our talents, time, and treasure into partnership with Him. We become co-laborers with God. In so doing, He sets us on the right path as we carry out our daily duties with an eye towards the glory of God and His soon-coming kingdom.

Samantha Bullock

An Angel in Her Path

Yea, though I walk through the valley of the shadow of death,
I will fear no evil;
For You are with me.
—*Psalm 23:4, NKJV*

For a few years, I was privileged to live in Cranbrook, British Columbia. Cranbrook is in the southeast area of the province in the foothills of the Rocky Mountains. It is truly a beautiful area with majestic mountains, forests, lakes, rivers, and an abundance of wildlife.

While living there, I had the companionship of my three dogs (two Newfoundland dogs and a German shepherd), and together we loved going for walks in the nearby forest. The forest trails went for miles, often intersecting other trails. While there was a leash law in this area, there were often unleashed dogs running free. My German shepherd was very protective of me, and my two Newfie males were only too happy to intervene if perceived danger came too close. The four of us experienced a couple of unfortunate encounters with other large dogs that were running free.

Because of my dogs, I developed a habit of pausing and asking God to send His angels to walk with us and found that when we paused for prayer, we never had an unfortunate encounter.

On our walks—just before we crested a hill to descend into a deep valley—we would arrive at a cross trail. Each time I gained courage to continue the walk into this valley by repeating Psalm 23. Shandy, my German shepherd, always liked to walk a few paces ahead of the "boys" and me to lead the way. On one particular day, after I asked God to lead and protect us, as we reached the cross trail and headed for the valley, my German shepherd stopped. She moved to one side of the trail as if peering around an obstruction, then to the other side, and back again. She looked up, turned around, and seemed to want to take the cross trail.

As we walked along the alternate trail, we had not gone far when up over that hill raced two large unleashed hounds that we had previously encountered with some unhappy results!

I am in awe every day of our loving Father's watchful care and how He wants us to invite Him to walk with us. I'm also convinced that my dog Shandy saw an angel that day.

I would encourage anyone who has not experienced God's closeness to "taste and see that the LORD is good; blessed is the man who trusts in Him!" (Psalm 34:8, NKJV).

Beverly D. Hazzard

A Good Name

Choose a good reputation over great riches;
being held in high esteem is better than silver or gold.
—*Proverbs 22:1, NLT*

I met my husband after officially giving up my search. I had thrown my hands in the air, sworn off dating, and told the Lord, "If You have someone out there for me, You better let me know loud and clear, 'cause I'm no longer looking." And just like magic, there he was two months later. Our romance was a whirlwind, and three months into our relationship we became engaged on a miserable, freezing-rain kind of day in December.

Almost everyone was shocked, though my best girlfriend said she had seen it coming when I was packing my belongings into a moving truck in Los Angeles to move closer to this guy I was dating who lived across the continent in a different country. The most shocked? My mother—she was blindsided. What was I doing? My whole life had been calculated. I'm the type of person who makes lists and values strategic planning. Besides how could I even know this guy in three short months? Perhaps it was hereditary; my grandmother had eloped one month after meeting my grandfather. My mother had married my dad only months into dating him (granted, they had known each other for a decade before they began dating).

The truth is I didn't need any more time. I had done enough dating and studying about relationships in my adult life to know exactly what I was *not* looking for, and to, in turn, know precisely what I *was* looking for according to God's standards for me. And Jordan was it! Every bit of "it." Now three and a half years into our marriage, I am more certain than ever that God truly designed us to be together from the very beginning. It was never a question. My mom has said time and time again she now sees God's great plan in putting my husband and me together.

Many times God can see beyond our own eyes to what is best for us. Jordan may not have been wealthy or lived in a prestigious city, but he had all the qualities that were important: a pure heart, a kind spirit, a strong work ethic, determination, and honesty. If I had followed the words and advice of so many around me, I never would have found my meant-to-be husband. It is easy to compare or place value according to the world's standards, but God's eyes are different.

Value what you have through His eyes, not comparing it to anyone else's.

Naomi Striemer

Another Day Closer to Paradise

Work together as a team for the faith of the Good News.
—*Philippians 1:27, ICB*

On March 15, 2013, the Holy Spirit urged me to pick up the phone and call my friend on the fifteenth day of working on the book I was writing: *Saints-in-Training.* Editor Penny Estes Wheeler thrilled my soul when she said that she'd be happy to assist me any way she could with my book project. I shared with her my dreams of someday having it condensed into a Christian sharing book. I mentioned that I feel Jesus has given me the gift of storytelling to help others see that, in our Creator God's eyes, we are all valued and loved.

We've actually been best friends for more than twenty years. She has been my mentor, my shoulder to cry on, and my sounding board when I needed to vent out loud! She has literally walked with me and my family in our journey with our child, Sonny, and his autism. I consider her a "mother in Israel" and a blessing to our church family. She has enjoyed a wonderful career as an author and editor; and, though officially retired now, Penny still has a servant's heart.

One day her purse "phoned" me. I remember it was on September 4, 2013, around 5:30 P.M. Just the day before I had given her an update on my book project. She advised me that I could improve my paragraph structure. I was working on this when my phone rang. Once we got straightened out who was calling whom, she said her phone must have gotten squeezed in her purse and subsequently dialed my number as she was just leaving a prayer meeting.

We laughed. She lives in Maryland in the United States, and I live in Alberta, Canada. "I think our guardian angels connected us for a reason," I told her.

After saying Goodbye, I bowed my head and prayed for some insight regarding the phone call. Then the cover image of a story, which took place in Russia, came to my mind. I remembered that, at the time, the Canadian prime minister was attending meetings in Russia. When I informed Penny of this insight, we prayed for God's will to be done during this tense time in our world's history.

What a blessing to pray with a friend who believes in the power of intercessory prayer! And each day that any of us prays is another day closer to Paradise.

Deborah Sanders with Penny Estes Wheeler

Appearances and Chocolate Chips

"Do not judge according to appearance,
but judge with righteous judgment."
—John 7:24, NKJV

Today I did a little research and determined something I have been wondering about for too long, concerning chocolate chips. (This may be where I lose those of you who disdain chocolate or perhaps have long since tossed it aside in favor of carob.) I am particular about chocolate, so particular that some people might think I'm a fanatic. I don't like it too sweet, and it must be fresh.

My daughter and her two teenagers were coming to visit. The grandson might be likened to the Cookie Monster, so Grandma was expected to have a supply of cookies on hand. I had a birthday coming up as well, so homemade ice cream was a possibility, which calls for homemade chocolate sauce. That being the case, I bought two packages of two different brands of chocolate chips. Upon coming home, I opened both packages and compared the taste and freshness. Revelation: the less expensive chips, which I have used for years, were, without a doubt, better than the more expensive brand. It may be that the price difference had caused customers to shy away from the more costly chocolate chips, but they did not seem as fresh as the less expensive ones.

What lesson might be learned from my experiment? The packaging, whether of chocolate chips or people, is not always proof of the quality of what's inside. The golden package and higher price made the more expensive chips seem more desirable, but I'd choose the others, hands down, any day.

My conclusion was this: judge not by outward appearances or first impressions. Get to know people. Give them a chance to prove who and what they really are. We aren't expected to be friends with every person who crosses our path, but each individual has value. Keep in mind that we are all in this world together, hoping to help each other reach the kingdom and to be there ourselves. Just as we enjoy chocolate, let us also indulge in a deeper enjoyment: "O taste and see that the Lord is good: blessed is the man that trusteth in him" (Psalm 34:8).

God's love never goes stale. His promises are as fresh as the morning dew on the blossoming rose—or as sweet as chocolate chips just off the assembly line.

Lila Farrell Morgan

Pray for His Children

*Arise, cry out in the night. . . . Lift up your hands
to him for the lives of your children.*
—*Lamentations 2:19, NIV*

It seemed like a typical April morning in the South Carolina Lowcountry with a warm caressing breeze and crisp blue skies promising a wonderful day. Yet I felt an urgent tug in my heart. As a mother, I have learned to breathe prayers for my children almost as continuously and subconsciously as breathing air. But now, for reasons I didn't know, a voice in my heart urged me to pray throughout the entire day for our youngest daughter, Karla.

In fact, this impression grew so strong that I asked Joyce, a sister prayer warrior from church, to join me in my intercession. "I will be praying," Joyce promised.

Karla is in college studying industrial design, and it is not unusual for her to work late hours in the studio. That evening she left school past 11:00 P.M. to make the approximately thirty-minute drive home. I had already gone to bed, but suddenly I was awakened by our son's unusually loud and anxious voice penetrating his bedroom door. "I am coming right away," Martin said. "Mom, Karla was in a crash. She tried to call you, but you were asleep, so she called me," he explained. "She is stuck on Highway 170. Police are on the way. Mom, she is OK. Don't worry." As soon as Martin left the house, I called Karla.

"Mommy, I should be dead. I should be dead." Her voice was filled with fear.

Later when I looked at the wreck of what was left of her car, I knew exactly what she meant. The car was twisted and bent on every side. The driver's side was so damaged that it seemed almost nonexistent. Yet our precious child walked away without a scratch. "Mom," Martin told me later. "This was a miracle." Before going back to bed, I quickly texted Joyce a short recap of the events and thanked her for her prayers. The next morning Joyce called me. "Ida, last night I went to bed, but for some reason I couldn't fall asleep. I was tossing and turning but just could not sleep," she said. "Around elven o'clock I heard a voice loud and clear, *'Pray for Karla one more time.'* So I did. After that, I closed my eyes and went to sleep."

Prayer remains largely a mystery to me. Yet I know one thing: God calls us to pray, and I will continue to pray—for the lives of His children.

Ida T. Ronaszegi

My Roommate

"Do not let your hearts be troubled. You believe in God;
believe also in me. My Father's house has many rooms; if that were
not so, would I have told you that I am going there to prepare a
place for you? And if I go and prepare a place for you, I will come
back and take you to be with me that you also may be where I am.
You know the way to the place where I am going."
—*John 14:1–4, NIV*

The registration deadline for the prayer retreat had passed. I knew that in all likelihood my health would not allow me to attend. But secretly I held on to a glimmer of hope that somehow the Lord would enable me to attend. Then the telephone rang. Francy's sweet voice said, "Flo, we have a room for you at the retreat. Your roommate will be Pele Alu." I breathed a prayer of thanksgiving. But I still had several tests to undergo that would determine if I had to travel out of the country for other medical opinions on my case. Again this meant that I might not be able to attend the retreat.

The sweet voice continued, "Don't worry, Flo; you'll be all right."

Three weeks remained till the retreat. Each day the sweet voice would call by phone, or my friend would visit me at the house to encourage me about going. However, I was scheduled for a barium meal test the week before the retreat, and I lost all hope of attending. Meanwhile my roommate Pele also got ill. Neither Pele nor I booked a room for the retreat. In a sense, we were putting up a barrier and making excuses rather than letting God decide and move.

On the morning of the departure to the retreat site, that sweet voice called once more, not to ask me whether I could go, but to ask me which bus I wanted to travel on. I could not resist now, as I had no excuses. My barium test was clear; my cousin Sulueti was available to be with my children. Pele, too, was available to be my roommate. We have been close sister friends since our high-school days but haven't had a chance in twenty years just to be ourselves and by ourselves. The retreat provided that opportunity. We thoroughly enjoyed the prayer, the scripture journaling, and the fellowship. Thinking about this experience, my mind goes to our heavenly home. Jesus promised us a room; it is already booked for us through faith. There will be a lot of space, lots of longtime friends, and best of all, Jesus Himself!

Fulori Sususewa Bola

How to Build an Altar

"He did this so that all the peoples of the earth might know
that the hand of the LORD is powerful and so that
you might always fear the LORD your God."
—Joshua 4:24, NIV

It was another exciting day for Israel. A younger generation had witnessed the miraculous wall of water holding back the Jordan River as their parents had seen at the crossing of the Red Sea many years before. Sure enough, just as God had promised, thousands of feet walked through the riverbed on dry ground! What a thrill to participate in such an awesome miracle!

God intended that even the next generation should know about this miraculous day, so He instructed Joshua to have a strong man from each tribe carry a huge stone from the middle of the Jordan River. That's where the priests had stood holding the ark as all the Israelites and flocks passed by. As soon as the priests with the ark and the men with the big rocks were safely on the west side of the Jordan, the wall of water broke loose and rushed downstream in flood stage again.

The Israelites camped at Gilgal, and there Joshua arranged the twelve large stones in an altar that would remain into the future. That permanent visual was there so the next generation could be inspired with the miracle God had performed to bring those Egyptian slaves into the Promised Land.

Does your home have some reminders of how God has led in your life, both to strengthen your faith and give your children something to encourage their faith journey? Here are some suggestions for building your personal altar.

1. Write out significant experiences you have had. List the sequence of events where you could see God's leading and how He resolved a specific problem. Or mark important encounters with God as you read your Bible. I read my Bible with a pen and ruler handy to underline special verses as the Holy Spirit impresses me. It's easy to look back and be blessed again.

2. Write names in the margin of your Bible when you're impressed to pray for friends and family members as an intercessor. Also look for objects in your home that remind you of a high spiritual experience, so when you clean or dust these things, your heart is warmed again.

Don't keep your "altar" hidden. Be sure to share your faith journey with your family and friends who will be encouraged by seeing the way God is leading in your life. And every remembrance will enrich your own experience!

Roxy Hoehn

Hatred, Hurt, Healing, and Forgiveness

For if ye forgive men their trespasses,
your heavenly Father will also forgive you.
—*Matthew 6:14*

Everyone I know has experienced hurt at one time or another. It may have come as the result of a divorce, death, tragedy, deceitfulness, poverty, or some other underlying cause. Hurt, as the result of a lie, is something that most of us have experienced. The tongue is a dangerous weapon. James 3:8 says, "The tongue can no man tame; it is an unruly evil, full of deadly poison." Scripture also tells me that "I can do all things through Christ which strengtheneth me" (Philippians 4:13); therefore, I am able to become victorious over all hurtful circumstances through Christ Jesus.

I have learned that if I fail to submit my grievances to the Lord and continue to dwell on them, I find myself enveloped with hatred. Hatred increases the risk of high blood pressure, strokes, cardiac arrest, and even the incidence of death. I once found myself sinking into a state of deep depression and recognized hatred as a contributing factor.

While attending nursing school, I learned that sometimes depression is anger turned inward. Once realizing the reason for my anger, with God's help, I began to counteract my thoughts by replacing negative thoughts with positive, healing ones. I now know the best treatment for hatred is forgiveness. Generally, the one who has caused your hurt is moving forward in life while you are having an eternal explosion. I speak from a personal experience from years ago. Thankfully, God has helped me grow since then.

Regardless of the challenges you may be facing today, peace surfaces when you find it in your heart to forgive. Forgiving on one's own is impossible, but "with God all things are possible" (Matthew 19:26).

In addition, forgiveness promotes healing. If your past hurt caused you to become angry, ask God to help you, so that your hurt and anger don't fester into hatred. He will take you through a healing process, and, over time, that whole situation will be largely erased from your memory. If, for any reason, flashbacks occur, you will find that they don't hurt so much anymore. God can heal completely. God has done this for me, and He will do the same for you if you will give Him that privilege.

My prayer today is that God will enable you and me to forgive as many times as necessary, so that, when Jesus comes, we can enter into, and live in, a sinless world for eternity.

Cora A. Walker

Lies, Lies, and More Lies

Saying, God hath forsaken him:
persecute and take him;
for there is none to deliver him.
—*Psalm 71:11*

Hold on to your seat, I have some wonderfully refreshing news! In Psalm 71:11, the writer's enemies are saying that God has forgotten about him, even though the writer has been faithful to God and is now aged. The writer's enemies are also threatening to come and get him.

Discouraging words can come from even familiar sources in our lives. Sometimes the words come from friends. Sometimes the words come from family members. At other times, our own brains can betray us. Yet our enemies' words are often not true. Their objective is to discourage us and cause us to fall into the pit of spiritual wreckage.

How can this tactic ever work on us? Well, here it is. We live in this sinful world, full of disease, distress, disaster, and dysfunction. We have been walking many years with the One who loves us best—God. Then the enemy of our souls comes to us in a time of discouragement and says, "God must not care so much about you because you didn't get that promotion." Or "You weren't healed when you prayed that you would be. Your prayer wasn't answered. God has forsaken you, and you are alone."

The longer one has been a Christian, the more of this kind of stuff the enemy of our souls can throw at us. Unfortunately, we sometimes halfway believe it. Perhaps even now you are sliding into this trap. In the process, you have been distancing yourself from God, and these lies are eating away at your faith.

"O God, be not far from me: O my God, make haste to help me!" (Psalm 71:12). Help me believe in You when I don't get what I want, when I don't understand, or when I am not healed. Disappointing events or situations in life are not a reflection on God. Rather, they are about living in a fallen world and on an alien planet. Ugly stuff happens here.

Don't buy into the lies of the enemy. Even though your life has not turned out as you had planned it would, God has not forsaken you. Everything is working out for your greater good or the good of someone else.

God doesn't want to be far from you now. Don't allow yourself to be far from Him.

Angie Joseph

Woman of Faith

In God I will praise his word, in God I have put my trust;
I will not fear what flesh can do unto me.
—*Psalm 56:4*

Some women in the Bible remain nameless, such as the widow of Zarephath, the woman at the well, and the widow of Nain. Therefore, the woman in this devotional shall remain nameless and be known as a woman of faith.

"May my two daughters and I stay at your house for a couple of days?" This query caught me by surprise when I answered the phone. I explained my housing situation. A lady from church was renting one of my bedrooms. The other small bedroom would not be adequate for her and two teenagers. She assured me it would be OK and that they would bring sleeping bags.

She faced a court date for divorce proceedings and custody rights. Her parents, siblings, and husband had all opposed her when she joined the church. The persecution of Christians is often keenly felt within our own family and households. After the proceedings, the girls were not with her. She tearfully explained, "They were taken away to live with my sister before transitioning back with their dad." She had no money for a lawyer, but prayers of faith sustained her defense.

G. K. Chesterton said, "Hope is the power of being cheerful in circumstances which we know to be desperate."* For income, this woman of faith began cleaning houses. Eventually, she was extended supervised visitation rights for a fee. Her extended family thought she needed psychiatric evaluation and proceeded in that direction.

Two policemen knocked at my door and inquired about my tenant. "Yes, she lives here."

As the woman of faith emerged from the bedroom, the police pushed into the house, taking her into custody. She asked, "May I take my Bible?" I was dumbfounded and asked the policeman, "How can you come into a residence and just take someone away?" He showed me paperwork that had been signed by a person unknown to me. They handcuffed her like a common criminal and transported her to a psychiatric care center for several days. Instead of experiencing depression, this woman shared the love of God with the people at the center.

What would I do in a similar situation? God sees and cares for His people, especially in times of trouble. We must remain faithful in every unpleasant situation we encounter in this life.

Retha McCarty

* G. K Chesterton, *Heretics* (New York: John Lane Co., 1905), 159.

"Where Can I Go From Your Spirit?"

Where can I go from Your Spirit?
Or where can I flee from Your presence?
—*Psalm 139:7, NKJV*

We cannot hide from God. We cannot evade His love. Have you ever tried hiding from someone in an effort to avoid them? Maybe, as a child, you attempted to escape a much-deserved punishment by hiding from your parent. Or perhaps you remember engaging in that classic game of hide-and-seek. We may have been successful in our attempts then, but we can never hide from God. There is no point in running; we can never escape His love.

This truth becomes increasingly evident as we search the Scriptures. Nothing can separate us from the loving care of our heavenly Father, not even our sins, for "He makes His sun rise on the evil and on the good, and sends rain on the just and on the unjust" (Matthew 5:45, NKJV). Romans 8:35 asks, "Who shall separate us from the love of Christ? Shall tribulation, or distress, or persecution, or famine, or nakedness, or peril, or sword?" (NKJV). Verses 38 and 39 answers, "For I am persuaded that neither death nor life, nor angels nor principalities nor powers, nor things present nor things to come, nor height nor depth, nor any other created thing, shall be able to separate us from the love of God which is in Christ Jesus our Lord" (NKJV).

God expresses His love to us in numerous ways. He sends heavenly angels to protect, help, comfort, guide, and direct us. Yet this is not the fullest expression of His love to us.

The fullest expression of His love is made manifest in Jesus Christ. God gave His only begotten Son, while we were yet in our sins. He did that because He loves us. He did that to save us from our sins and from our constant hiding. He did that to be with us forever (John 3:16, 17; John 14:1–3). No more hide-and-seek needed. Now that's love!

Oh, Father, where can I flee from Your presence? If I make my bed in hell, You are there. If I take the wings of the morning and dwell in the uttermost parts of the sea, even there Your hand will lead me, and Your right hand will hold me. Thank You for sending Jesus Christ to deliver me from my sins that I may live with You forever (adapted from Psalm 139:7–10).

Tricia Wynn

The Spanish Lesson—Part 1

"The word which you hear is not mine
but the Father's who sent me."
—*John 14:24, RSV*

I have taught Spanish language, literature, civilization, and linguistics for more than forty years. Although I was born in the United States, Spanish was my first language right up to the moment I walked into my English-speaking first-grade class. Spanish has remained a language that I have loved and nurtured through study and practice along with my other native language, English. I'm what you would call a true bilingual.

Over the years, and through my studies and travels, I have sought increasingly more effective ways of communicating the Spanish language to my students, both as a native language (I taught Spanish to native peakers for five years in Puerto Rico) and as a second language to English speakers. During my language teaching career, the second-language teaching profession has gone through a series of theories and methodologies that promised to bring our students out of our classes actually able to use the language. When I began my career, I, like most of my colleagues, inherited the grammar-translation method, a legacy of Europe's medieval method of learning Latin and Greek: read a passage, and translate it. Then it was the audio-lingual method, based on B. F. Skinner's stimulus-response theory. The idea was that if you repeated a word or expression enough times in the target language, you would come out of the class speaking that language—that rarely, if ever, happened.

It was Noam Chomsky's theory of universal grammar that finally broke the grip of grammar translation and endless repetition. He discovered that all humans come equipped in their brains with the capacity for language. The categories of language were already in the brain, waiting to be populated with the language used in the geographical area of the world where the individual was born and lived. Further brain research has helped second- and foreign-language teachers and learners. We have since learned that there are two areas of the brain that retain all the languages that one learns before the age of five: the Broca and the Wernicke. These are the languages you can speak without accent interference from another language.

In our Christian lives, may we not allow long-held methodologies and interferences to keep us from hearing and understanding the language God speaks from His heart to ours.

Lourdes Morales-Gudmundsson

The Spanish Lesson—Part 2

I will meditate on Your statutes.
—*Psalm 119:48, NASB*

Noam Chomsky—given his discovery that all humans come equipped in their brains with the capacity for language, along with subsequent brain research—concluded that a second language is learned in many ways, much like we learn our first language.

What this discovery meant for second-language teachers and adult learners was that usage of meaningful, contextualized language, *lots of it,* was the best way to learn and retain a second language. In other words, practice of meaningful language in a variety of meaningful contexts in which the language might be used by a student, tourist, nurse, or lawyer will lead to real second-language acquisition. It's not enough to teach *about* the language, but to actually engage students in *using* the language. In this mode of teaching and learning, practice and theory are two sides of the same coin. Ideally, practice is meant to reveal the grammatical principles behind usage, but grammar and usage always work hand in hand to help the student walk away with a working usage of the language in a variety of settings.

It struck me that there was a lesson to be learned here about the actions of faith and works in the Christian life. Faith and works complement one another and are actually ineffectual if one is without the other. You can learn *about* faith by studying the Bible and listening to sermons and reading books on the topic; but if you don't *apply it* in your life, it is worthless. Like practice and theory of second-language learning, if you don't use faith, you lose it. That is an axiom in second-language learning: use it or lose it!

Which comes first, faith or works, theory or practice? It's not entirely an idle question. Certainly, they must come together and operate in collaboration, one with the other. But, as with language theory and language practice, your practice of faith (the works of faith) will illuminate your understanding of faith (the theory of faith), and your understanding of the Word of God will feed into your works of faith.

I would go a step further here to apply another principle of second-language teaching and learning. *The more you practice and use the language, the more sense the principles behind that usage make and the more you want to study those principles.*

Lourdes Morales-Gudmundsson

The Spanish Lesson—Part 3

For as the body without the spirit is dead,
so faith without works is dead also.
—*James 2:26, NKJV*

Put into faith and works vocabulary, the more you act on your faith, be it ever so small (like a mustard seed!), the more need you'll feel to seek out the principles that sustain your faith. In fact, contemporary language teachers begin by practicing or illustrating, by a variety of means, a grammatical point or vocabulary and *then* explain the grammatical theory behind it (if it's not already obvious to the student). When we do it that way, students are already halfway to understanding the concept behind the usage, and we have to do a lot less explaining. If we explain the theory first, students think they already know the usage and are less motivated to see the need of actually using the language.

This same principle applies to faith and works and explains why there are avid Bible students who can recite texts and pray, as God would have it, and yet live quite a different life at home with their families. The double-life syndrome that has afflicted Christians since time immemorial is a problem of misunderstanding the intimate relationship between faith and works. It's not a matter of sending people to study the Bible more, but rather encouraging them to put into practice the little they do know and understand about God as revealed in Jesus Christ in every aspect of their lives, especially when they're *not* in church. The exercise of that little mustard seed's worth of faith will make Bible study not only attractive but deeply necessary.

Human motivation and persistence are what result in the delightful, hard-earned fruits of second-language learning. Since the Tower of Babel, foreign-language learning, in both its practice and theory, comes with the sweat of the brow. In the Christian life, however, the perfect coordination of faith (theory) and works (practice) can come only from the Perfect One in whom mercy and truth, "righteousness and peace have kissed" (Psalm 85:10). His perfect balance of theory and practice can bring similar spiritual balance into our own lives. Not so much intellectual theory that we forget how necessary practice is, nor so much practice that our actions and words become empty shells, devoid of life-giving truth and honesty. The seamless harmony of faith and works comes from inviting Jesus Christ into the daily life, allowing Him to seep into every nook and cranny of our existence, bringing life and light that no darkness can overcome.

Lourdes Morales-Gudmundsson

Will You Please Listen to Me?

I will instruct you (says the Lord) and guide you along the best
pathway for your life; I will advise you and watch your progress.
—*Psalm 32:8, TLB*

It was Tuesday morning. Snow had fallen the night before; not a lot, but enough to create a problem since the temperature had dropped significantly during the night, turning the snow to ice.

Tuesday—one of the days set aside to visit my ninety-five-year-old dad who lives in a nursing facility. Let me explain: I don't mind the cold or getting around in fresh snow, but when there is ice, I'm a no-go, no-show. *So what am I going to do today?* I wondered. *Maybe visit Dad a little later than usual in the day? OK. Maybe that's what I'll do.* Suddenly, I heard that still, small Voice say, *"Do not go outside today."* I kept on preparing breakfast, ignoring the Voice, and saying, *But it will warm up, and I can go this afternoon.* Again the Voice said, *"Do not go outside today."* Without paying any attention to the Voice, I continued mentally planning the day with *maybes.* Suddenly, the Voice came the third time, more loudly and emphatically: *"Didn't you hear Me say not to go outside today?"* This time I paid attention, laughed, and said, "OK, Lord, I heard You!"

But what will I do now? I'm not usually home on Tuesdays. Immediately some chores came to mind, and I had a satisfying day. I called the facility and learned Dad was comfortable.

On Friday afternoon, my neighbor's son came over, and I asked, "How are things going?"

He answered, "On Tuesday afternoon (yes, that *same* Tuesday I had stayed in), I did not realize how icy it was in the front yard. I went out, fell down, and hurt my shoulder. The doctor said nothing is broken, but I'm experiencing severe pain."

When he said that, my thought was, *Thank You, Lord, he did not break any bones. And thank You, Lord, for helping me to listen and obey.* As I reflected on this experience, I have thought of how God, in His goodness and love, speaks every day to warn us against hurting ourselves—spiritually, physically, and emotionally. But often we do not listen.

Now my daily prayer is, *May I be more willing to listen and obey You, Lord.*

Today let's listen and take our instructions from the One who knows what is best for us.

Maureen O. Burke

September 5

Colt Magnus

Train up a child in the way he should go:
and when he is old, he will not depart from it.
—*Proverbs 22:6*

He was just a furry black dot running across the street. I thought I had possibly run over him. I noticed two men on the corner with a sign: "Free bag of food and forty dollars for a puppy." At that moment, I was vulnerable. On the car seat were the ashes of my dog, Parra, that I had just had to put down due to old age and sickness. At home was Parra's only surviving sibling, Independence Day. But I had only twenty dollars left in my wallet.

I paused to make sure the puppy was all right as one of the men explained they couldn't keep it. The next thing I knew they were moving away from the car with my twenty dollars. And I drove away as the proud owner of a new dog and a partial bag of dog food.

In the weeks that followed, I named the two-month-old puppy Colt Magnus. About a year later, during a visit to the veterinarian, Colt misbehaved, becoming aggressive. I was perplexed and talked at length with the vet. He felt that Colt had probably been severely abused before I'd become his owner. Let's just say that Colt exhibited some social issues when strangers came around. The vet asked me what I planned to do with him.

Currently, Colt is a healthy four-year-old, jet-black, forty-pound dog. He still has some problems now and again. Yet I have learned so much from training him. For example, I must use a gentle hand and a calm but firm voice. If I am abrupt or even give him an unexpected tap, he becomes fearful.

Colt has learned that my being upset just means that he needs to do something differently. He now knows the difference between acting out of anger and acting out of love. Sometimes I just look at him and cock an eyebrow upward. He sits, hangs his head, and looks sorry for his misbehavior.

This training process makes me think of our heavenly Father. When we make mistakes and come to Him for forgiveness, He lovingly, carefully corrects us with kindness. He patiently shows us what we need to change. He does not speak harshly nor scream but, instead, speaks words of correction and guidance—in love. I am so grateful for this opportunity to learn.

Mary E. Dunkin

Joy of Bonding

Let brotherly love continue.
—*Hebrews 13:1*

My annual work leave in 2014 became a joy-of-bonding experience for me—my long-anticipated vacation to meet my sisters.

We had been separated for quite some time. In recent years, whenever we had vacations, we could not meet due to our busy schedules. On the third of May 2014, we finally got a chance to get together, thanks to our niece, Annie, who arranged everything. She had been able to buy our boat and airline tickets on the Internet well ahead of the get-together time. Even though these modes of public transportation were running at capacity, they had a place for us, thanks to our niece.

Praise God that all was well with good accommodations and advance preparations to visit our relatives and friends. We met our classmates, more friends, and, most exciting of all, every one of my siblings, nieces, nephews, uncles, and aunts. We visited the churches and schools in our hometown, eager to observe the furtherance of God's work.

We had great joy to see and learn how God prospered the work. The good time we had visiting with the church members was a complete joy for me. Together we ate, worshiped, encouraged each other, and talked about the progress of the church that we used to attend. (Back on December 21, 1961, my two sisters and I had been baptized together in the same church in Gabawan, Philippines.) There were fifty of us there that Sabbath afternoon. It was a joy for me to see many familiar faces in church; although some were missing, their children continue to serve the Lord in their place. All of us are eagerly anticipating their resurrection at Christ's return.

I look forward to another leave and joyful bonding time. Not my niece, but my Savior has made the arrangements for this journey—the transportation, the accommodations, and the itinerary. I know that this future get-together will be a time of unspeakable joy. We will meet our loved ones in heaven for an eternity of deeper bonding than we have ever experienced. We will see that our financial and personal sacrifices for the work of God will have resulted in many more souls for the kingdom.

Let us continue to bond with one another—in service and in joy—until He comes again.

Evelyn G. Pelayo

September 7

Fruit of the Spirit

But the fruit of the Spirit is love, joy, peace, longsuffering, gentleness, goodness, faith, meekness, temperance: against such there is no law.
—*Galatians 5:22, 23*

In our country, various fruits are grown. I'd like to compare these delicious, nutritious types of fruit to the fruit of the Spirit.

Love. To me, the all-nourishing apple represents love. Love for others is manifested in kindness. God said, "For he that toucheth you toucheth the apple of his eye" (Zechariah 2:8).

Joy. The mango, full of body-strengthening iron, reminds me of joy. What a delightful, juicy—and messy—fruit the mango is! "For the joy of the LORD is your strength" (Nehemiah 8:10).

Peace. The magnesium-packed banana, with its distinctive flavor, reminds me of harmonious relations, a product of peace. I love bananas. They contribute to sound sleep. "In peace I will lie down and sleep, for you alone, LORD, make me dwell in safety" (Psalm 4:8, NIV).

Longsuffering. Strawberries, full of vitamin C, come to us through the efforts of many who work the strawberry fields at minimum wage. The workers patiently endure difficulties and perform their backbreaking work under a hot sun. We should also be patient: "With all lowliness and meekness, with longsuffering, forbearing one another in love" (Ephesians 4:2).

Gentleness. Sweet, juicy figs, like the ones that grew on a tree of ours, represent the quality of gentleness. Gentleness produces compassion and consideration for others. "Whoso keepeth the fig tree shall eat the fruit thereof" (Proverbs 27:18).

Goodness. The kiwi, a small fruit packing vitamin C and big flavor, reminds me of God's generosity and goodness to us in even the smallest of blessings—which we are to share with others. "Surely goodness and mercy shall follow me all the days of my life" (Psalm 23:6).

Faith. A confident belief in solid truth makes me think of the stalwart pineapple. "The just shall live by his faith" (Habakkuk 2:4).

Meekness. "We remember . . . the cucumbers, and the melons," the Israelites complained to Moses, who was known for being meek before God (Numbers 11:5).

Temperance. Sweet grapes and their juice can turn to wine. "Every man that striveth for the mastery is temperate in all things" (1 Corinthians 9:25).

May our lives also exhibit the fruit of the Spirit.

Priscilla E. Adonis

Did You Take Your Medication?

A merry heart doeth good like a medicine:
but a broken spirit drieth the bones.
—*Proverbs 17:22*

Grandma, did you take your medication today?" my four-year-old grandson asked me one morning. Because of that question, I always smile now whenever I see someone taking their pills. Thinking about his simple question brings things to mind that I'd never considered before.

First, his question tells me that he is smart—grandmotherly bias notwithstanding. It also shows his overall concern for my well-being. He knows that I have problems with staying away from colds, and while he does not yet understand the medical reasons for taking the medication, he seems quite sure that taking it will help me.

Second, his question demonstrates the power of advertising. Obviously, the young child hears advertisements that often blare on the radio and television on our island nation even though we assume he is unaware of them. His question also tells me that he is applying my needs to what he has seen or heard. Now, whenever I move to the area where my pills are stored, he gives me a gentle reminder to take care of my health.

Thinking about my grandson's question reminds me of something else I need to do each day for *spiritual* health: praise God for His blessings in my life. I know that beginning and ending the day on a note of praise and thanksgiving can actually lengthen one's life and help one stay healthy. Maybe that is why I now hum praises all the time. I've heard that people who are thankful have greater resistance to common sicknesses and have better mental and physical well-being. Solomon, the wisest man who ever walked the earth, wrote, "A cheerful heart is a good medicine" (Proverbs 17:22, NIV). And praising God makes me feel cheerful.

My grandson's reminder also helps me remember that my words must guide those around me to better spiritual health (Proverbs 12:6). I long for that heavenly land where no one will ever need to ask, "Did you take your medication?" I long to go to the healing celestial gardens (Revelation 22:2).

Master Healer, You are my God! You have helped and protected me in the past. Help me choose words that give life and advertise healing to the nations. Thank You that the righteous will forever live and serve You, oh, God in heaven.

Nelly Thomas

Those Missionary Women

Who can find a virtuous wife?
For her worth is far above rubies.
—*Proverbs 31:10, NKJV*

Many women have sacrificed so much to travel far from their homes and loved ones to venture into unknown places, serving as missionaries with their young husbands. Some never saw their families again nor ever completed a formal college education. In remote places, they nursed the sick, delivered babies, and taught children in massive numbers. They learned to be horticulturists and farmers, so they could have enough food for their children. Others even helped to build their house or steered the mission boat through jagged reefs. Many walked long distances on narrow trails with babies in their arms.

One young woman left her parents in her safe family home and with her new baby traveled to meet her young husband waiting on a remote island in the Pacific. They traveled in an old truck far up into the highlands. There she was ushered into her new home—a grass and bamboo building supported by posts. She carefully walked into this house and placed her few treasured wedding presents on a shelf in the living area. She gently laid the baby girl in a crib her husband had made for the baby. The young couple cared for the scores of sick who came to the clinic on their veranda. They bandaged the wounds, sewed up torn flesh, treated lepers, and shared—with the use of a picture roll—about Jesus and His soon coming.

One cold, dark night a spark from their fire flew up into the thatched ceiling and burst it into flames. Instantly, the house became an inferno as red flames filled the sky. The husband screamed. The mother fled from the house, but the baby was still in her cradle where she had been laid. The father grabbed the baby and threw her out the window to the waiting neighbors who had heard the cry. That missionary wife was never the same again. In that fire, she lost every treasured possession and some of her adventurous spirit, and she almost lost her baby.

She lived on that island for more than twenty years, delivering babies, supporting her husband, and receiving little recognition. But God knew her heart. He also knows exactly where she lies waiting for Him to come and receive her to Himself. I want to meet her on resurrection day, along with the many other missionary women of worth who lived and sacrificed so much.

God calls each of us today to be a woman of worth in our own unique mission field.

Joy Butler

Holy, Holy, Holy. Amen!

Let me live that I may praise you,
and may your laws sustain me.
—*Psalm 119:175, NIV*

Joshua is the nine-year-old son of my sister-in-law. As a baby, Joshua suffered from cerebral malaria. This led to severe bouts of convulsions. Though his mother took him to different hospitals, the boy's condition did not improve. Several times the mother asked God to allow Joshua to die, but God remained silent. Then she asked God to let her to die in order to rest from her burdens. God still remained silent. Other women complained that she couldn't control Joshua's behavior in church when he would call out and run up and down the aisle, disturbing people. "Why even bring such a kid to church?" they would ask. Joshua's mother took him from church to church, but people always complained.

One day some church elders organized purposeful prayer and fasting on Joshua's behalf. Joshua remained silent in church for three weeks in a row. Women started asking again, "Where is that mother with the troublesome boy? For three Sabbaths now, we have not seen her. Perhaps she took the child to the hospital again." Joshua's mother overheard the women talking and replied. "I am here. The Lord did a miracle for Joshua after the elders prayed and fasted for him. For three weeks in a row, I have been able to sit silently in church."

The earlier convulsions had also rendered Joshua mute—unable to speak. But one evening, after the elders' prayers, Joshua called out with a loud voice, "Mama!" The whole night he kept on calling his mother and watched her intently. How my sister-in-law praised God for this second miracle! Several times nonbelievers had approached her about visiting witch doctors for help. She'd always firmly told them, "God knows why Joshua is still alive yet mute."

By December 2014, nine-year-old Joshua managed to utter a prayer: "Mtakatifu, mtakatifu, mtakatifu. Amen!" (Holy, holy, holy. Amen!) To date, that is Joshua's prayer every morning and evening.

Joshua's mother is thankful to the Lord for the miracles He has done for her son. Her faith and trust are strong, and she believes that one day Joshua will talk.

Yes, the Great Physician, the sympathizing Jesus, is at work for anyone whose life is challenging. Like Joshua's mother, we, too, can trust in His help and glorify His name.

Debbie Maloba

September 11

Don't Worry

Be anxious for nothing, but in everything by prayer and supplication,
with thanksgiving, let your requests be made known to God;
and the peace of God, which surpasses all understanding,
will guard your hearts and minds through Christ Jesus.
—*Philippians 4:6, 7, NKJV*

Overcome with sorrow and fear, I stood in my closet and contemplated my father's surgery.

Several months before, my sisters and I had received a phone call from our mother telling us that our father was gravely ill with polycystic kidney disease, a genetic disease that causes cysts to multiply in the kidneys. My father was given a two-month window in which to start dialysis or receive a kidney transplant. He was put on the five-year waiting list to receive a cadaver kidney; though, the best solution would be a living donor. My three sisters and I offered to donate our kidneys. After having our blood tested, we were given the news that all of us were blood-type compatible and had three out of six matching DNA markers. The last step was to get a sonogram of our kidneys to see if we had inherited the disease. Praise the Lord, none of us had it! The next few weeks flew by as more tests were performed to find the best viable candidate. I was given a 5 percent advantage. I was thrilled! I could help my dad.

As surgery day approached, I stood in my closet praying, consumed with "What ifs": What if my father's immune system rejects the kidney? What if I have complications? What if I can't sing anymore? All these questions swam in my head, making me worry,

I thought of Jesus crying out to God in the Garden of Gethsemane. I thought of how He sorrowfully fell on His face, prostrate in prayer, pleading, "O My Father, if it is possible, let this cup pass from Me" (Matthew 26:39, NKJV). Then I felt a peace come over me because my Jesus knew my worries. He knew my thoughts. He knew my fear because He had lived it Himself. God was with Him, and I knew that God was with me. Why be anxious? I fell more in love with Jesus after contemplating the great sacrifice He made for me. If He could give His life, I could donate a kidney and know that God was with me, no matter the outcome. Praise God, my father successfully received the kidney and is healed today!

Dear God, help me not to worry. With thanksgiving, I pray for Your peace today.

Margie Salcedo Rice

It Only Takes a Spark

"Let your light so shine before men, that they may see your good works and glorify your Father in heaven."
—Matthew 5:16, NKJV

I had an illuminating experience one day when my curiosity drove me into a newly found candle shop. I stood in the doorway for several minutes and took in the wonderful display of scents, shapes, and colors. I could have spent the whole day in there just deciding on what my purchases would be had my husband not suggested that there might be other stores in the mall.

Candles have always been a fascination for me, but I've often been chided that I never really take a lit match to any of them once I bring them home. They are just too pretty to melt. But aren't candles made for a purpose? To be lit? A lit candle enables it to set free a special scent while casting a warm glow on its surroundings.

People can be like candles—cold, hard, and waxy—with their wicks untrimmed, unlit, useless, and showy. Like candles sitting in their assigned places on a mantel or tabletop, collecting dust, some people do the same, taking years before realizing their potential. Then one day someone comes along with an encouraging word or a helping hand and lights a fire in the soul, freeing up goodness and talent that have been trapped inside for so long. Ladies, as with unique candles, you, too, are special! By your fragrance, your shape, your color, your warm glow, people will be drawn to you and to the God you serve. You can honor Him by using the talent He has given you to help those around you. Stand in the doorway of your home, in the foyer of your church, at the gateway to your community, and take pleasure in diversity.

I enjoy my candles even more now that I realize that it is OK to light them, enabling them to release their warmth, fragrance, light, and charm. And in opening the Word of God, I find my peace, courage, and wisdom to share with those around me as I let my light shine. So the next time you go shopping, purchase a scented candle, and let it be another reminder to live a Christian life. Be sure to light it often, and let the love of God melt and reshape your heart.

Dear Father, please light my life candle, so I can be on fire and be a good witness for You in my home, my church, and my community. Let me be warm, fragrant, and charming in all that I do today, so that the name of Jesus may be glorified. Amen.

Stephanie Arthur

September 13

"If You Knew . . . He Would"—Part 1

Jesus answered and said to her, "If you knew the gift of God,
and who it is who says to you, 'Give Me a drink,' you would have
asked Him, and He would have given you living water."
—*John 4:10, NKJV*

If you knew . . . She had come to the well at the sixth hour, probably around noon or so (hours were counted beginning at sunrise) to avoid the other women. Going to the well first thing in the morning wasn't just a chore to get needed water, essential for the day, but it was a social gathering. Women talked, gossiped, ignored her.

She knew why. They all knew. She was living with a man who wasn't her husband. She had had five husbands. Hoping that one man would stick around, protect her, provide for her, make her feel beautiful and loved. But she had gone through them, one after another. And still her heart longed to believe that she was loved and wanted, accepted and belonged. Yet the message from each relationship was that she was just not enough, that her need was too great and her heart too hungry. She would never find what she was seeking.

The women saw her as a sinner—used and worthless. No one wanted to be her friend. Going to the well in the morning was a painful reminder of who she was and how she just didn't measure up. She watched friends laugh and talk together while her heart ached for just one person who loved her, believed in her, wanted more for her.

So she came in the middle of the day when she knew it would be safe. No one would be there. No one would be pointing and whispering. She wouldn't feel the pain of being alone and unwanted.

When she saw the Man sitting at the well, she was surprised. She recognized from His clothes that He was a Jew. What was a Jew doing in Samaria? Jews avoided Samaria like the plague, going a two-day journey out of their way so they didn't become unclean and contaminated. But she knew she'd be fine. She could get in, get her water, and get out. He wouldn't speak to her. Not only did men not talk to women in public, but He was a Jewish man and she was a Samaritan. Jews didn't want anything to do with Samaritans.

Yet He did talk to her. And He will talk to you today as well. Be sure you're listening.

Tamyra Horst

"If You Knew . . . He Would"—Part 2

Jesus answered her, "If you knew the gift of God
and who it is that asks you for a drink, you would have asked him
and he would have given you living water."
—*John 4:10, NIV*

If you knew . . . She was thirsty—hungering for love and acceptance, to belong, be valued, be hopeful. Here she was at the well in the middle of the day, attempting to meet her own needs or at least avoid more pain—and the answer to everything her heart longed for was sitting right before her, but she didn't realize it. How could she? God didn't look like what she expected Him to. She never thought God would show up in Samaria and talk to her. She had learned to argue about what was right and wrong, but she hadn't learned about a God of grace and love who pursues even an outcast among outcasts.

If you knew . . . The same is true for us today. Our hearts are hungry and thirsty for love, acceptance, belonging, hope, courage, purpose, and joy. We try to meet those needs in many ways. We try to be thin enough, pretty enough, smart enough, educated enough, accomplished enough, *something* enough to finally feel like we are valuable and loved, like we make a difference. And while some of our efforts help for a while, nothing totally fills the hunger. Yet if we only knew God, if we only understood His heart for us, if we only believed that He so loved *us* that He did—and will do—anything for us, if we knew, we would ask Him to fill us.

He would . . . If we knew and trusted God completely and asked Him to fill those deep longings in our heart, He would. Not maybe. Not possibly. Not if we're good enough. Not if we measure up or do enough or get it right. If we asked, He would.

What are you thirsty for? Have you taken it to God? Talked to Him honestly about your heart and its longings? Do you really believe that He loves you completely and wants more for you than you can imagine? Do you really believe that He would go out of His way to pursue your heart because He wants to meet your deepest needs and make you whole? That He has a plan for you that will change the world?

If you knew . . . *He would.* Let's choose to trust God and His love for us and believe that in Him we are loved and valued. He's a God who went out of His way to pursue a thirsty outcast and transform her into the world's first evangelist. He's pursuing you too.

Tamyra Horst

Lessons From the Pecan Tree

"For the LORD does not see as man sees; for man looks at the
outward appearance, but the LORD looks at the heart."
—*1 Samuel 16:7, NKJV*

"So God, who knows the heart, acknowledged them [the Gentiles] by
giving them the Holy Spirit, just as He did to us."
—*Acts 15:8, NKJV*

One autumn morning I began to crack pecans from my tree in the yard. Some pecans had thick shells, and others very thin ones. Their shapes varied—long, short, round. I was looking for pecans whose nuts were meaty, nourishing, and satisfying to the palate. I never knew what I would find in the heart of each shell I cracked. As I opened them, I found some beautiful, tasty kernels. Others, however, were dried or rotten inside. Still others had not grown to full maturity. A few pecans had worms living in the very heart of the nutmeat. While cracking the various pecans, I began to think of how pecans illustrate several biblical principles.

First, as with the pecans, we cannot know the heart of another person simply by looking at the outer "shell." Though we have a tendency to judge by outward appearances, the Bible tells us that only Jesus can look at the heart. And when we—by spending time with others—allow Him to show us their needs, He will also show us how to deal with them.

Second, only God can see if someone's heart is spiritually dry from a lack of time-with-Jesus nourishment. God will show us which hearts around us are suffering spiritual drought with diminishing hope or courage. Often He will lead us to find words and ways to encourage these hurting hearts. We can invite them to pray with us or become part of a small-group Bible study.

Third, Jesus doesn't throw away the spiritually immature or the hearts that appear rotten to us because of their past sinful choices. Jesus knows that, more than anyone, they need acceptance, concern, tolerance, forgiveness, and love. And as they grow or heal, they need—more than ever—our patience. Both growth and healing take time. Jesus would have us treat them with the same mercy and grace with which He treats us.

I know Jesus would have us exhibit long-suffering with learning-curve mistakes and missteps. Our own too. He not only sees the heart behind the outer shell, He accepts and loves it.

Lord, help us to be like You—nonjudgmental, tolerant, compassionate, and loving. Amen.

Rebecca Crittenden Lowry Banks

Keeping Your Eyes on the Goal

So be careful to do what the LORD your God has commanded you;
do not turn aside to the right or to the left.
—*Deuteronomy 5:32, NIV*

am not a horse lover. Sometimes, on a vacation, I will try riding a horse, and it is not bad; but I am not out riding every weekend. My first two experiences with horses taught me much!

When I was about eleven years old, our school organized a festival. At the festival, one could actually try riding on a horse. I had watched other kids try it out, and the horse seemed really docile. She was probably picked for that very reason. So being adventurous, I decided to pay and give it a go. Well, the moment I got on the horse, it took off at lightning speed. I saw a fence coming into view, and, holding on for dear life, I thought, *This is it. I am going to fall off the moment this horse tries to jump the fence.* But apparently the horse didn't know how to jump, much to my relief, and somehow the owner was able to get the horse under control. It shook me up. There was no explanation for why the horse took off other than it wanted to go home, because, for the horse, it had been a long day.

My second experience with a horse happened when I was on my honeymoon. My new husband and I decided to take a ride at a nearby ranch. Many people came that day, and we were all paired with the horse the ranchers thought best matched up with us. We mounted our horses, and that was the last I saw of my husband. The horse I rode took off and headed for home, eager to get a rest and have something to eat. I was the first to arrive at the ranch. You can imagine how eager this horse was to get home. It had one thing on its mind: get home, and get there as quickly as possible!

These experiences reminded me a little of the text in Deuteronomy where we read, "Do not turn aside to the right or to the left" (5:32, NIV). We need to stay on track, obeying God and not letting anyone or anything get us to do something we shouldn't do. Just like the horse that was so focused on getting home, we need to be determined to stay on God's path, no matter what.

My prayer for each one of us is that we stay focused on God, His Word, and His purpose for us.

Clair Sanches-Schutte

The Laundry Lesson

Search me, O God, and know my heart;
Try me, and know my anxieties;
And see if there is any wicked way in me,
And lead me in the way everlasting.
—*Psalm 139:23, 24, NKJV*

Can Jesus use something mundane to teach us a lesson? Definitely!

One of my pet peeves is the stray tissue hiding in the laundry. One day while doing laundry, I thought I had checked every garment for any hidden tissues. Confident that I had rid the laundry load of any unforeseen disasters, I set all the dials for the wash cycle to begin. When all of the washer's whirring ended, I quickly opened the lid to transfer the load to the dryer. To my dismay, every item was littered with the remnants of someone's tissue.

I painstakingly shook everything and picked off lint from the garments before throwing them in the dryer. But the tissue had become enmeshed in the fibers of the clothing, making it very difficult to rid the entire laundry load of all the unwanted messy pieces.

As I worked at my task, Psalm 139:23, 24 came to mind. So I prayed for Jesus to search my soul. Since that day, I try to confess sin as quickly as it is brought to my mind. And because of this incident, I invited Jesus to do a more thorough search in me.

When I threw the last piece of laundry into the dryer that day, I hoped that the drier's filter would remove any remaining remnants of that stray tissue.

As I thought about this analogy between my life and the load of wash, I decided that Jesus is like our supreme Filter.

When Father God looks at us through Christ, He sees us only as pure and without the "lint" of sin marring our beauty.

As my load of laundry finished drying, I prayed, *Father God, I thank You for Your Son, Jesus, who forgives my sins. Search me today, so that I may become clean. In Jesus' name, amen.*

And yes, my load of laundry came out mess free, illustrating for me that Jesus can make me pure too.

Though my sins be as scarlet, I can become as white as snow (see Isaiah 1:18). *Thank You, Lord!*

Not only did I get my laundry done, but my soul felt lighter too!

Mary Louis

The Guiding Finger of God

And we know that God causes all things to work together
for good to those who love God, to those
who are called according to His purpose.
—*Romans 8:28, NASB*

I am never weary of watching God as He moves in the lives of His children. Yesterday I had a conversation with my friend, a sweet saint. What she shared touched me deeply and impelled me to record her story. She confided she had a serious problem that forced her to see a psychologist for weekly counseling. Though the psychologist listened to her with rapt attention, he one day blurted out, "How is it that you have so many problems, yet you are so happy?" My friend explained that, yes, she has problems, but God is the foundation of her life. Christ is the source of her joy, so even when she has problems, her wellspring of joy flows continually. After a couple more visits, my friend realized there had been a dramatic role reversal. Instead of the psychologist listening to her now, she was the one listening as the psychologist poured out her troubles to my friend. In one session, the psychologist blurted out, "I want to know your God!" From memory, my friend shared previously memorized Bible texts with the counselor, who asked, "How are you able to do that?"

A week ago when my friend arrived for her counseling session, the psychologist announced that she needs weekly Bible studies. The counselor not only wants to know my friend's God but also to know His Word as well as my friend does. So now my dear friend has the privilege of bringing to this precious soul the knowledge of God the Father and His plan of salvation through Jesus Christ. I hope, someday soon, the psychologist will say, as did the Ethiopian eunuch, "Look! Water! What prevents me from being baptized?" (Acts 8:36, NASB).

Yes, my friend thought she had problems that needed attention. Yet she had no way of knowing that her troubles would be the boat her Lord would use to row her across an ocean of despair to rescue one of His lost children, the psychologist.

Our awesome God doesn't always prevent His children from experiencing difficulties; instead, when we trust Him, He uses those tedious circumstances to show not only His glory, but also His grace. God permitted my dear friend's problems in order to show His grace to a wounded soul.

Jasmine E. Grant

September 19

In an Acceptable Time

This is what the LORD says:
"At just the right time, I will respond to you."
—Isaiah 49:8, NLT

Shortly before my graduation from the university, I prayed to God to get me a job sooner than later. I dreaded the thought of being unemployed. A friend called me the week after graduation to inform me of a job vacancy. I was hired. Finally, a job and a long-anticipated salary. However, the job proved to be a challenge from the onset. During the interview, I was asked about my religious beliefs and the effects they could have on my work schedule. The interviewer assured me my beliefs would be respected. After I was hired, though, my supervisor constantly pressured me to change my position. The work environment became extremely uncomfortable because of my unpopular Christian beliefs. I could now relate to individuals who gave testimonies of being reviled for their faith.

Eventually, the inevitable happened. I was terminated and, as a result, devastated. *Where is God in all of this?* I wondered. However, God reminded me of the Christian witness that He'd allowed me to exhibit on the job: "I form you and use you to reconnect the people with me" (Isaiah 49:8, *The Message*). I felt peace knowing God had used me. I believed I'd soon have another job.

Despite my earnest efforts, several months of unemployment followed my termination. I experienced ambivalence as I prayed and cried to God. These months taught me what it truly means to depend on God. I realized that He had me in the palms of His hands. Time spent at home with my parents gave me the opportunity to garden and volunteer in my church and community, which proved to be a real blessing. During this time at home, I discovered my father's slingshot, which God used to teach me an object lesson. A slingshot is used for launching. For it to be effective, the sling has to be retracted. The more energy used to retract the sling, the greater the launch and probability of it hitting the target. I realized I was the projectile in God's slingshot. My current setbacks are God's way of pulling me back as He prepared me for launching and landing. It has not been easy, as there are days when I ask God, "When will I be released?" His gentle response is consistent, *"In an acceptable time . . ."*

If you are in a pulled-back period of life right now; fortify yourself with God's unfailing promises. He will grant you favor and release you in His time!

Racquel Boswell

A Blessed Perspective

Blessed are those whose strength is in you,
whose hearts are set on pilgrimage.
—*Psalm 84:5, NIV*

D riving home with my young son, Dakota, in the backseat of our new-to-us car, my mind raced from one stressful thought to another.

It was March, a month that for us was more expensive than December. About half of the people in our family have birthdays in March, and that's when we typically go on vacation. Though the month was always a financial challenge, this year would be even harder than most. We had just cleared out our savings to buy a car. On top of this, things were busy at work, and juggling the needs of my office and my home was wearing me thin.

"Mommy," Dakota innocently interrupted my thoughts. "I'd like to pray to Jesus to thank Him for this car."

That's when it hit me that all the things I had been stressed about were really things to be thankful for! We were indeed blessed to finally have a second car. I was blessed to have a job, a home, and a family. I was also blessed to be able to take regular vacations. Most important, I was blessed by each person whose birthday we would be celebrating that month, not the least of whom was my precious son.

Over the years, I've cherished the lesson my son taught me that day, reminding myself that every situation in life has two ways to be viewed: through the lens of worry or the lens of gratitude. Some may say that we shouldn't use the word *blessed* to refer to the good things in our lives because that implies that those with less are not as favored by God. I disagree. Today I have less than I did on the day I learned that lesson in gratitude. Yet I would dare say that I am even more blessed now than I was then. I no longer have the health to work full time, but I am blessed that our needs continue to be met even with our reduced income. Our vacations may be simpler, our birthday gifts may be smaller (or more creative), and our cars are not likely to be replaced any time soon. But we are blessed to still have time together as a family, birthdays to celebrate, and cars that continue to run.

After all, blessings shouldn't be measured by the amount of the gift but by the gratitude of the recipient.

Lori Futcher

An Awesome Responsibility

And the LORD went before them by day in a pillar of a cloud, to lead
them the way; and by night in a pillar of fire, to give them light;
to go by day and night: he took not away the pillar of the cloud by
day, nor the pillar of fire by night, from before the people.
—*Exodus 13:21, 22*

Some years ago I was entrusted with a career responsibility. At the beginning of my tenure, I recognized my inability, inefficiency, and lack of knowledge to do the work, despite my availability. So, in humility, I went to my apartment, got on my knees, and bowed before my heavenly Father. I surrendered my life and will to the Lord, asked for a fresh consecration upon my life, and God's leading in my work. Gradually, my tasks became clearer, and I developed a work program. I thoroughly enjoyed the time spent in that capacity and experienced God's hand at work through the many developments, maturity, and results of our efforts.

This was an awesome responsibility I will never forget, even if I wanted to, because I still see the fruits of dedication and hard work, fruits for which I sought the Lord's help and guidance each day.

Some tasks are more challenging than others, and some tasks may seem to be too great until we come to realize that we have the knowledge and capability to do the work. We may also feel burdened by other tasks and can find relief only when we place them at the foot of the cross and ask for God's guidance. It is easy to get carried away with self when we feel we are doing well; but when we remain faithful to God and stay at the feet of Jesus, it creates a balance in our responsibilities. Having the Lord's involvement gives satisfaction, and we can rest assured because the fruits of our labor are in His care.

Added pressure can also arise in our responsibilities when we are conscious of the comments and actions of others regarding our work, and we get caught up in our desire to please. In these moments, our education and capability are so easily forgotten, and we become overwhelmed. Our focus on what we desire to achieve and our relationship with the Lord are very important and should be the center of our goals. Our heavenly Father gives us the opportunity to have and share responsibilities. I pray that God will grant us the wisdom to come to Him when we are faced with awesome responsibilities.

Elizabeth Ida Cain

Taking for Granted

Ye that fear the LORD, trust in the LORD:
he is their help and their shield.
—Psalm 115:11

One massive earthquake in September 2010 destroyed much of the inner city of Christchurch, New Zealand, and some of its magnificent historical buildings had to be demolished. Workers have been busy ever since demolishing, fixing, clearing sewage pipes, repairing power lines, reestablishing communication channels, and straightening up crooked roads. Many residents built makeshift toilets in their backyards, lived in tents, waited for their homes to be inspected, and tried to get life going back to normal as much as possible. As tremors continued, frustration, anger, hurt, and pain pooled together, tiring nerves and stretching the limits of patience.

No one expected what lay ahead as their focus shifted to rebuilding and repair. Another big quake struck Christchurch in February 2011, dashing confidence and hope and plunging people into despair. Two more major quakes, measuring 5.9 and 6.4 on the Richter scale, rocked the city again in June, shattering any hope that may have been left.

It was not just physical loss that had to be dealt with but emotional, psychological, and financial loss too. Unable to help themselves, the people turned to the government for answers: Which suburbs were going to be demolished? What was going to happen to our homes? When was the rebuilding, if any, going to begin? As much as the Canterbury Earthquake Recovery minister would have liked to provide answers, he couldn't because he didn't know what tomorrow held. How could he?

As I drove home after work, used the remote to open the garage, and then started the heater, it dawned on me that these were all blessings I had taken for granted. I had electrical power, a home that remained intact, heating to keep me warm during the winter, and decent roads to drive on. Going about my chores for the evening, I only started counting the blessings and quit as there were too many—blessings I had taken for granted until now. Now as I live each day, I am reminded of the many blessings around me and praise God for opening my eyes to them.

There are a lot of tremors and aftershocks that keep rocking the people of Christchurch. No one knows what tomorrow holds, and none of us ever will; yet we can rest in the thought that we know who holds tomorrow.

Praise God for the assurance we have in Him!

Grace Paulson

Hospitality

Offer hospitality to one another without grumbling.
—1 Peter 4:9, NIV

Recently, my church pastor spoke to the congregation about hospitality. After every illustration, he would say, "Are you practicing hospitality?"

To many of us, it was an embarrassing question. There was silence; nobody dared to say, "Yes, I am."

The pastor's repeated question reminded me of the hospitality shown to strangers by my seven-year-old son, Micky.

One hot day, tired of correcting examination papers, I lay down on the couch to have some rest. Soon I drifted off to sleep.

A couple knocked at our gate. Micky, who was playing outside, invited them into the house. He made them very comfortable by asking them to sit down. He shook me, but I was fast asleep. Maybe he was nervous to host the visitors by himself, but he offered juice to them. Later I was told that Micky asked the visitors several questions. He spoke like a big, grown-up boy.

Suddenly, my eyes opened, and I saw a couple seated on the couch with juice glasses in their hands. I was stunned. I didn't know who these people were. However, these strangers were obviously enjoying their conversation with my seven-year-old son.

Immediately, I sat up. Before I could say anything, my son said, "Mumma, this uncle and aunty, who live in our community, I see them every day, when I go for bicycle ride."

The couple stood up and said, "Hello, Sister. What a lovely son you have! We have enjoyed his hospitality." They related the whole scenario to me. In response, I smiled at them. They said, "We are new to this community. We are trying to make friends, and that is why we are here at your home." Thereafter they became our close friends.

I was relaxed and happy to know that my son had offered hospitality to strangers. Today he is married and continues to be hospitable. I praise God for him.

In the Bible, we see that Abraham also offered hospitality to strangers—not knowing they were angels. The Bible teaches the importance of being hospitable.

Let us be hospitable to one another and enjoy God's blessings in the process.

Premila Masih

Reunion

For the Lord himself will come down from heaven,
with a loud command, with the voice of the archangel and
with the trumpet call of God, and the dead in Christ will rise first.
After that, we who are still alive and are left will be caught up
together with them in the clouds to meet the Lord in the air.
And so we will be with the Lord forever.

—*1 Thessalonians 4:16, 17, NIV*

Not so long ago, I helped to organize a fortieth-reunion luncheon for my former high-school class. It was wonderful to get together again after all the intervening years. In particular, it was fascinating to have the opportunity to learn something of the life journeys of previous classmates—the careers and interests they had developed, the families they had established, and the achievements they had accomplished.

The conversations went on long after our group was supposed to have vacated the luncheon venue, so it was fortunate that no one came to hurry us out. When the venue actually closed, a number of us relocated to the foyer of a nearby hotel, where some of the group were staying. We talked for several hours more; then, all too soon, it was time to part again. Sadly, a subsequent, sobering footnote to our celebration was the news that one of the classmates who had attended the reunion that day unexpectedly collapsed and died just a few weeks later; a stark reminder of the fragility of life.

Some goodbyes are more predictable, though no less unwelcome. Recently, my parents enjoyed a visit from long-standing friends who had moved to the United States many years ago, but with whom they had regularly kept in touch. Now in their eighties, these folk had made the long flight to Sydney in the knowledge that this would almost certainly be their last opportunity to meet with friends and family in Australia. In fact, their parting words were, "See you in heaven."

What a blessing it is to know that Jesus is organizing the greatest reunion of all—one to which we are all invited. A reunion from which we will no longer experience separation, either by distance or death, from those we hold dear. A time when we shall see our Savior face-to-face and finally come to fully understand our own life journeys and see how God's plans for us have unfolded.

I'm definitely planning to be there. I hope you will accept the invitation too!

Jennifer M. Baldwin

A Wedding Sponsor

And while they went to buy, the bridegroom came; and they that
were ready went in with him to the marriage: and the door was shut.
—*Matthew 25:10*

My husband, Abe, and I were so happy to be invited as sponsors to our niece's wedding. In our Filipino custom, being a sponsor is an honor and a responsibility. The bride and groom had selected us to be their advocates, counselors, and guides as they traveled their uncharted journey in life as husband and wife and, eventually, parents. A wise sponsor guides the newlyweds to seek their parents' advice also. The more sponsors the bride and groom invite to their wedding, the bigger the wedding.

When my parents were invited to be wedding sponsors, burlap sacks—to be filled with rice as gifts to the bride and groom, their families, sponsors, and relatives—lined our kitchen and dining room walls. The bigger the upcoming wedding, the more burlap bags I'd see lining the walls. Slowly, day by day and week by week, these bags would be filled with rice as the harvest came in from the rice fields.

So for the upcoming wedding in Maryland, I decided to augment our gift of money with rice, not only for the newlyweds but also for both sets of their parents. I know rice does not go bad with time when kept dry, so I bought several bags ahead of time. I planned the rice as a surprise for all the potential gift recipients. I bought the bags of rice and loaded them in the van but did not tell Abe about them. He might not have understood the tradition of giving rice as a gift. I wanted to be prepared if something were to happen to me before the wedding day.

This wedding preparation made me suddenly think of the ten virgins in Matthew 25:1, 2: "Then the kingdom of heaven shall be likened to ten virgins who took their lamps and went out to meet the bridegroom. Now five of them were wise, and five were foolish" (NKJV). I thought, *I better tell Abe my plan for the rice bags in the van, lest he give them away to friends or move them into the garage, exposing them to moisture or rainwater. I don't want to be without a gift for the bride and bridegroom—just as I don't want to be without oil in my lamp like the five foolish virgins. I want to be a worthy sponsor for the heavenly Bridegroom.*

Let's tell others about Jesus, so they'll be ready when He calls us to the wedding feast.

Rose Eva Bana Constantino

We Must Pray

"If My people who are called by My name will humble themselves, and pray and seek My face, and turn from their wicked ways, then I will hear from heaven, and will forgive their sin and heal their land."
—*2 Chronicles 7:14, NKJV*

Prayer is a privilege. Not only is it a privilege, but for the people of God, it's not optional. In order to enter the heavenly kingdom, we must pray. To stay connected with divine power, we must pray. To invite the Lord into our lives and circumstances, we must pray. But before we pray, we must have humility.

Whether we are experiencing good times or difficulties in life, our response must be one of prayer and faith. For "without faith it is impossible to please" God (Hebrews 11:6), and faithless prayer is ineffective. The Word of God says that "the effectual fervent prayer of a righteous man availeth much" (James 5:16). Therefore, righteousness and faith are both essential to answered prayer.

We must pray for the Holy Spirit and the latter rain. We must pray for ourselves, our families, friends, neighbors, coworkers, and enemies. We must pray for the prodigal sons and daughters who have strayed away from the Savior's side. We must pray them back into the arms of Jesus.

We must pray for the leaders of each of our great nations, realizing that they will remain great only as long as they honor God. If we honor God, He will honor us and answer our prayers. He has lovingly laid out for us a seven-step process of prayer as seen in today's text.

The steps are to humble ourselves; because humility precedes prayer. Prayer leads us to seek God; and seeking God causes us to turn from wickedness. God hears our prayers. He forgives our sin. Finally, He heals our land. If the land is not healed or restored, perhaps it's because we need to go back to humble ourselves and unite in earnest prayer.

We must not crack under the pressures of life nor be distracted by the cares of this world; we must be vigilant. And the only way we can do that and be successful is, as it says in *The Message*, to "be cheerful no matter what; pray all the time; thank God no matter what happens. This is the way God wants you who belong to Christ Jesus to live" (1 Thessalonians 5:16–18).

We must keep the faith. We must work for the Master. Most of all, we must pray.

Tamara Brown

We Know Not the Hour

"Therefore you also be ready, for the Son of Man
is coming at an hour you do not expect."
—*Matthew 24:44, NKJV*

I'm a baby boomer, which means I'm young enough to have experienced a surge of technical advancements and old enough to have difficulties keeping up with them. I've seen the telephone go from a finger-dial system to a smartphone that talks to you, takes photos, and sends text messages. Written correspondence came in the form of a postal letter or a telegram, but now Facebook and e-mail reach us with the touch of a button. Yes, the world is moving quite rapidly with all of these high-tech wonders to behold and entice us.

There are some things I didn't experience while transforming into adulthood, which I find disturbing today: a significant, spiritual decline in the world, for one. I rarely heard of homicides. I didn't experience a fear of going to school or work because someone might bring a gun to kill innocent people. Hurricanes and tornadoes were common knowledge, but tsunamis, global warming, and polar vortices were unknown concepts to me! Though the Bible does mention earthquakes and famines, the global devastation in the last few years is unfathomable. Even the evil of man's heart is so evident that *terrorism* is a common word throughout the world.

All of these changes and events bring me to the conclusion that Jesus' second coming is near. People have characterized these worldly occurrences as common and not necessarily reflecting the end of time. "Because of advanced technology," they say, "we're just more aware of crime and disaster." Yet Jesus said, "And because iniquity shall abound, the love of many shall wax cold. . . . And this gospel of the kingdom shall be preached in all the world for a witness unto all the nations; and then shall the end come" (Matthew 24:12, 14). He also warned of wars and rumors of wars, famines, pestilences, and earthquakes. Signs, He said, of His return.

Does this sound depressing? Does this make you fearful? It shouldn't! Jesus promises a better place called heaven with eternal life. In this promise, we can take comfort. We Christians are commissioned to share the gospel and participate in the heavenly going-home celebration.

Heavenly Father, help us to remain faithful and keep our hope focused on You, so we can be ready for Your return and claim Your ordained promises!

Evelyn Greenwade Boltwood

The Double Blessing

*And my God shall supply all your need
according to His riches in glory by Christ Jesus.*
—Philippians 4:19, NKJV

Where could I have put it? How could it disappear?" I kept asking myself, frustration mounting.

As an elementary-school teacher, born deaf in one ear and with a partial loss in the other, I needed my hearing aid. Now it was missing, and I had to go to work. I combed through the house like a detective looking for any clue that would lead me to it but came up empty. I grabbed an old hearing aid I still had and drove to school. It didn't fit well and had less power than my present aid, but it would have to do.

After praying and searching for ten days without success, I resigned myself to the fact that I would have to purchase a new hearing aid.

After school the next day, I went to see Elizabeth, the audiologist who sold me my aid. When I walked into the office, several people were there celebrating her birthday. It happened to be my birthday, too, so they invited me to join them, which I did. After a while, the guests left and Elizabeth and I were alone.

I told her that I had lost my hearing aid and I needed to order a new one. She warned me that there would be a fee of seventy-five dollars that the company would charge should I cancel the order. She added, "I'm sorry, but I have no control over that." I said that I understood. Because I had no other options, I told her to go ahead with the order.

Grateful that I could get a new hearing aid but concerned about the cost, I headed home.

Dinner was the next item of the day. I took out a box of aluminum foil to line a pan. As I started to tear off a piece of foil from the roll, out popped my hearing aid! I could hardly believe it! I couldn't imagine how it had gotten in there.

I thanked the Lord profusely and phoned Elizabeth the next morning. When I asked her about the cancellation fee, she told me that because I'd ordered the hearing aid so late in the day, the request hadn't been sent yet. Therefore, there was no fee to pay.

I thanked the Lord again, this time for the double blessing as He supplied my need.

Marcia Mollenkopf

Jesus Loves Me

God is our refuge and strength,
an ever-present help in trouble.
Therefore we will not fear, . . .
though its [earth's] waters roar and foam.

—*Psalm 46:1–3, NIV*

We all encounter troubled water sometime; overwhelming, angry waves that threaten to pull us under and drown us. (So be gentle to fellow travelers, you can't know what raging torrent they may be trying to cross!) Your angry water may be a diagnosis of cancer. Perhaps death has snatched a loved one away. A job is lost, or a child is lost to drugs. Or relationships are broken. Everywhere we look, there's more water than dry land.

My particular river swept me away on a perfectly calm, cloudless morning. Betrayed. Unloved. Terrified. Running. Away! Away! I flung myself on the riding lawn mower, willing the engine's noise to drown out the sounds of despair my own ears could not bear to hear. *Alone!* my mind shouted. Slowly, the engine's throb began to beat out a different cadence. *No! Not alone—Jesus loves me!* I began to sing, faltering at first, then gaining in volume and strength with every sweep around the yard until I was shouting, "Yes! Jesus loves me! The Bible tells me so!"

"I am with you," He promised. "You can do this hard thing. Don't be afraid." Exhausted, as on the floor of Elijah's cave, the quiet finally drowned out the deafening roar of a Jezebel's anger with the assurance of *His* power to protect and save.

"When you walk through the water, I will be with you," He promises. Perhaps it is a Red Sea, and He will wall up the angry waves, piling the trouble close enough to touch, yet it cannot touch us; making a way through, walking on the very bottom of the sea. Maybe it is a roaring river in flood, a raging torrent that has swept away bridges made of concrete and steel. "I will be with you when you walk through the water."

Passing years have brought awareness that the other party had a river to cross, too, and God's matchless love was surely as great for him as it was for me. God's strong arm of mercy and grace was wrapped just as tightly around him as it was around me. His Son's agony on the cross was for him, just as it was for me. Perhaps in that better place, I will come to understand it all as our four-year-old did as he grappled to make sense of the senseless: "Maybe when we get to heaven Dad will see us and say, 'Hey, Mama and kids! Come on over!' " Maybe so.

Jeannette Busby Johnson

Guided Safely Into Harbor

For thou art my rock and my fortress;
therefore for thy name's sake lead me, and guide me.
—*Psalm 31:3*

Our cruise ship was scheduled to dock at Tortola in the British Virgin Islands. At first, Milton and I tuned in to the ship's television station, so we could watch the docking from our cabin. But we soon decided to go on deck to watch the spectacle. We headed for the highest point on Deck 12 but realized, after a few minutes, that a lower deck would provide the perfect vista to take pictures as we neared the harbor. As we stood and drank in the fresh morning air, we noticed a seagull perched comfortably on the bow of the ship, just above the ship's flag. One could easily mistake the gull for a fixture on the ship. It stood motionless as the ship inched its way to the dock. From time to time, it pecked at a loose feather, but other than that it kept its head straight and fixated on the land in sight.

From where we stood on deck, the ship looked much larger than the tiny berth into which it was to dock. Docking seemed impossible as our large ship, carrying more than thirty-five hundred passengers, steadily aligned itself. As soon as the ship drew alongside the first section of the dock, the seagull flew away. It had occupied the spot for quite a few furlongs* but now headed back out to sea. It was simply amazing. We were not the only passengers observing this special phenomenon. We heard many *ooh*s and *aah*s, along with comments of astonishment. It was as though someone had marshaled the bird to guide the ship to safety. Then when its work was done, it was off to find the next ship that needed its service.

Unaware of the events taking place on the bow of the ship, thousands of passengers had been busy in their cabins or had been about some other business. The gull, however, had done its job and had gone on its merry way. Even when we are not aware of God's guiding presence, He is right by our sides and is waiting to guide us safely into harbor.

Oh, God, so often You guide us to safety. You provide a safe place to take us home. You protect us from so much danger, and we are not even aware of Your presence. Today, oh, God, I want to thank You for protecting me, even when I am not aware of Your presence. My prayer is that I may live in the consciousness of Your presence.

---

* One furlong equals 201 meters or one-eighth of a mile.

Gloria Gregory

October 1

Your Father Knows

Your Father knoweth what things
ye have need of, before ye ask him.
—Matthew 6:8

May 13, 2009, was a very difficult day for me. After finding a lump in my right breast a few weeks earlier, I had just been told that my first ever mammogram was "worrisome." I had a core needle biopsy done and was told not to use my arm for the rest of the day. After spending the morning at the breast clinic and canceling the rest of my workday, I returned home to an empty house. I'd have the official test results in two weeks.

That afternoon, like many people in a crisis, I turned to God for help. I knew that I likely had breast cancer, even though no one had yet conveyed the dreaded words, "You have breast cancer." Years before, I had been given my grandmother's old promise box. I asked God to guide me in choosing a promise that would help me that afternoon. The first tightly rolled scroll I chose simply stated, "Your Father Knoweth." I burst out crying. God knew what had happened that day; He knew my fears, my need for strength and comfort, and whether or not I had breast cancer. He knew all of this before I even talked to Him. I spent the rest of the afternoon praying and reading my Bible. God also knew I needed this trial to bring me closer to Him and to slow down my hectic work pace in order to spend more time with Him. My Father knew I needed to trust Him and depend on Him more. God knew this trial would refine my character for an eternity with Him.

Now looking back over the past several years since my breast cancer diagnosis, there are many other things I know that God knew that day. God knew that this would bring me an even higher purpose in my career. He knew I would be able to help many other women going through breast cancer treatment. He knew that I would be able to give Him the glory for healing, strength, and wisdom. My Father knew that "all things work together for good to them that love God" (Romans 8:28).

At the time of my cancer diagnosis, I did not understand why this was happening to me, but I praise my Father in heaven for knowing what I needed and for providing this trial to bring me closer to Him for all eternity.

Your heavenly Father also knows what you need. You can depend on Him.

Karen Welch Dobbin

Disappointments

Though the fig tree does not bud and there are no grapes on the vines, though the olive crop fails and the fields produce no food, though there are no sheep in the pen and no cattle in the stalls, yet I will rejoice in the LORD, I will be joyful in God my Savior.
—*Habakkuk 3:17, 18, NIV*

Lady, you were not accepted for this job. We need someone with more skills since our church is very musical."

Hearing these words, I left the sanctuary of a small church in Michigan feeling very disappointed. I thought I was the perfect candidate for the position as pianist for the main service. Why did this happen after my many months of hunting for a much-needed job, one that would definitely help our family finances?

I was hurt and disappointed. Lying in bed that night, I asked the Lord to help me see His plans through my disappointment. God knew I needed a job. He knew I was praying about it.

Then He brought to my mind the story of Habakkuk. The prophet cried out to God because of corruption in Judah. When God answered, saying that the Babylonians would overtake them, Habakkuk didn't understand God's ways. He thought there could be a better solution. But when God justified His plan to Habakkuk, the prophet gave control of the situation into God's hands and trusted His ways. Not an easy thing to do when one is hurting, but this is the only way to have our perspective changed.

All of us have faced days of defeat or disappointment, but our responses can make all the difference. Frustrations can be either opportunities for spiritual growth or destructive blows. In these moments of deep disappointment, we must remind ourselves of those things about God that we know to be true, though they might not *feel* true at the moment.

After one month, a position opened at the Andrews University library, and I was accepted on my first interview. Working there provided some of my most enjoyable work experience—years when I could grow more than in any other place. Once again, God was faithful.

When we realize God is good and that He is in control of even the smallest details of our lives, we can look at our disappointments and say, "Yet, I still rejoice in the Lord."

God holds our destiny in His hands, and He knows what is best. Go in faith. Go rejoicing.

Raquel Queiroz da Costa Arrais

October 3

Lunch

The LORD is my shepherd, I shall not want.
—*Psalm 23:1*

The house was quiet. I sat in the hall looking at a brown paper-bag lunch. If you asked, I could have told you all its contents. *This was my lunch for today.* A knock on my front door brought me to my feet. My dear friend, Tracy, walked in, saw the bag, and said, "I have an idea."

Tracy had asked me to help her with her church's children's Vacation Bible School. The church needed volunteers to help during spring break and offered the program free of cost. Ninety-two children later, the Bible school was going well. I walked around, making sure each volunteer had the needed support. The hours of the day went quickly, except one: lunchtime.

During lunch, every child was given a brown paper bag. On the second day, I noticed little Anthony carefully examining the brown bag's contents, which he divided in two. He ate only half the lunch, stuffing the remaining brown bag in his backpack. I did not think much about it. Maybe he wasn't hungry or was saving it for later. That same day, while loading the bus for home, I saw Anthony turn away from the bus and start walking across the street. Concerned, I ran after him, making sure I didn't lose sight of him as he walked across the street to the back of a pharmacy garbage bin. A homeless woman sat next to the garbage bin. Anthony handed her the bag and explained how there was an apple *and* an orange in the bag today. The woman looked at me. She had three shawls on and torn shoes. Anthony turned around and simply said, "We share our lunch." He introduced us and then took my hand, and we left. On our way back to the bus, I felt like a parent, telling Anthony how dangerous that was, how he could get hurt, how important it was to stay close to one another for safety. He stopped walking and simply said, "I know. That is why I bring her food."

Two weeks later Tracy's church started distributing food to the homeless in the area. They plan to build a soup kitchen. As I help unload crates, I see Anthony. He walks up to me with a brown paper bag and extends it to me: "You missed lunch. Here. Half my lunch. There is an apple in there today." And with a smile, he walks away.

Anthony's friend was transported to the hospital and slept clean, calm, fed, for only one night before she died—but not before I sat next to her and watched her smile.

Dixil Rodríguez

My God Is Always on Time

"It shall come to pass that before they call, I will answer;
and while they are still speaking, I will hear."
—Isaiah 65:24, NKJV

I was having some financial problems, and I had fallen on hard times while waiting on my disability check to come.

Though I was working through a lawyer, he wasn't working as quickly as I hoped he would.

I prayed to God several times, still waiting on an answer.

On a Sabbath morning while waiting for my brother to pick me up for church, I got a call from a friend. I had told him the day earlier that I was having some financial problems. My friend told me that it was not fair for me to be suffering financially while he just sat by and watched. He asked me if he could help me out.

My pride almost caused me to say No, because I—as a woman—had been taught never to accept money from a man. I had been friends with this young man for several years, and he helped me through a lot of tough times. He had encouraged me to go back to finish college. I had done that and now had a college degree.

My friend had been a listening ear for me many times when I needed to vent. I took a moment to think and then told him that I would accept his offer. I told my friend that I could definitely use the money.

"Then I will send a money order," he said. I was very happy that he could help.

It's amazing how, when you need something, God knows exactly how to help. In trying times, when things get rough, it's good to know that we can rely on God to give us what we need. Even if things are rough, we must always trust and believe that God has our best interest at heart. We are His children. It is His delight that we should prosper in our walk with Him and be in good health. Anything that we need that will help us do those things, He is more than willing to provide for us.

God may not always act in our behalf in obvious ways when we want Him to, but He is always on time.

Kristen Hudson

October 5

Better Than My Plans

Trust in the LORD with all your heart and
lean not on your own understanding.
—*Proverbs 3:5, NIV*

I had only been with the state agency for about a year when a promotion opportunity in the superintendent's office arose that seemed too good to be true. Not only would it boost my salary and general schedule rating, it would also give me a bit of prestige.

Miraculously, I qualified for the position and was allowed to interview.

Each day thereafter I waited with bated breath until late one afternoon when the superintendent came to my cubicle. I was so excited! "We were impressed with your interview, but we are giving the job to someone outside the agency with more state experience. We're really not sure you could handle the stress of the job," he said. (From my observation, that office held little in the way of stress.)

Shocked and hoping the disappointment didn't show on my face, I replied, "I'm sure you are right. I will look forward to meeting the new person."

Not seeking to promote myself because I enjoyed my current position and coworkers, I did my best on a daily basis for the next several months. Then came the day I arrived at work wearing a wig, tired, and not feeling well—the effects of chemotherapy.

When the superintendent told me how sorry he was for my misfortune, I mentioned that the current cancer episode was my second, the first being twenty-seven years earlier. I added that each day since then I had known that I was a time bomb waiting to go off. I thought, but refrained from saying, *And you thought I couldn't handle stress!*

A few years later a foundation was established for the agency. We employees took part in a wonderful celebration during which awards were given.

Not only did I receive two notable awards, but I was shocked to receive the coveted Employee of the Year award!

Now happily retired and looking back at that time, I marvel at how the Lord had better things in mind for me—beyond prestige or money.

I also am reminded not to think of my own selfish ways but to be humble and trust that He has my best interest in mind.

Eunice Porter

White Peacocks

He has made everything beautiful in its time.
—*Ecclesiates 3:11, NIV*

I was meandering through my favorite store when I first saw the white peacock feathers. They were sandwiched between layers of glass, captured like snowflakes, creating a delicate chandelier. I paused to look at them, the moment of wonder pressing gently into my memories.

I didn't know white peacocks existed until that day. I searched the Internet to buy their feathers, but they were beyond my budget. Every now and then I remembered those feathers and imagined how awesome it would be to see a pure-white peacock displaying his tail.

Years later my parents were visiting. For some reason, we talked about white peacocks, and I remembered those feathers. A couple of days later we drove down a quiet lane close to my home. Suddenly, my dad's cell phone rang. He pulled off the narrow lane into the driveway of a house to take the call. Through the car window, I could see some small white feathers pirouetting gently in the breeze. I stepped out to gather a few. "Hello!" a lady called from the other side of a tall hedge. "Can I help?" I explained we'd pulled off the road to take a call and that I'd seen the white feathers. "Do you like them?" she asked. "They're from my white peacocks. Would you like to see them? They have four baby peachicks that just hatched yesterday!"

So I went to see seven pure-white adult peacocks and four creamy-colored chicks. I commented, "I love white peacock feathers! I think they're exquisite!" The woman asked if I'd like some as the ones that fall she just puts in a pail by her door. She told me to "just help yourself" and "take as many as you want." Overwhelmed, I thanked her and offered to pay, but she declined.

Life was busy. So I left the peacock feathers in a vase by the hearth. Later our church was planning a festival of flowers, each display celebrating poetry and creation. My friend Dorothy explained, "I'm doing a display about white peacocks, but I'll have to improvise as I'll never find any real white peacock feathers around here."

I smiled. "I have some real ones you can use. I think God's been guiding me to them for the last five years—for this very moment!"

Thank You, Father, for the gentle way You lead us, even taking care of the tiny and beautiful details of our lives.

Karen Holford

"Water Heater!"

And he said unto them, Go ye into all the world,
and preach the gospel to every creature.
—Mark 16:15

I went to pick up my son at the park where his school's class had an outing that day. Most of the children were playing all over the park, being supervised by various teachers from Drew's school for the handicapped. To one side of the park were picnic tables. Some parent chaperones and teachers were there cleaning up the remains of a picnic lunch. I saw Joyce, my son's teacher, by one of these tables and walked over to her. As Joyce and I spoke, I leaned against the picnic table. I did not notice the little boy, Benny, who climbed up on the table until he pulled on my sleeve. Startled, I looked at him. He said, "Water heater!" The words meant nothing to me, so I looked back and continued to talk to Joyce. Benny pulled my sleeve again, exclaiming, "Water heater!" I put my arm around Benny, afraid he might fall off the table, but continued to talk to the teacher. He again said with determination, "Water heater!"

I was upset. I wanted to talk with Joyce, but Benny's exclamations were interrupting us. To distract him, I said, "Yes, water heaters are useful."

As I turned back to Joyce, Benny said, "Water heaters are useful."

Suddenly, teachers, parents, and students surrounded us, all laughing and congratulating Benny with happy tears on their cheeks. Joyce told me, "This is the type of breakthrough we all live for! Benny is nine years old and has never before said anything but 'water heater.'" By the end of the school year, Benny was talking normally, was mainstreamed to public school the following year, and has caught up with his class, now being considered a normal student. My offhand attempt to distract the boy had put him on the path to recovery. Now, decades later, when I remember Benny, I wonder how many times someone has reached out to me, wanting to know more about my God's love, yet I simply made some offhand comment meant to distract the person so that I could continue with whatever I was doing at the moment.

Beloved heavenly Father, please make me less self-involved in my dealings with others. Open my eyes to those who reach out to me, so that I may spread Your truth to those seeking Your love and my attention. Thank You. Amen.

Darlenejoan McKibbin Rhine

Follow the "Preppers"

*"Therefore you also must be ready,
for the Son of Man is coming at an hour you do not expect."*
—Matthew 24:44, ESV

The island of Providenciales experienced a major power outage on February 9 some years ago. Because our island rarely experiences power outages, an outage that lasted for a day and a half was something to contend with. Islanders were caught off guard when they lost electricity for such a long time. No electricity for many of us meant no water, stove (for electric stove users), and refrigerator, not to mention no microwave, charged cell phones, computers, tablets, or Internet access.

The basic necessities were difficult to come by. Many of us scrambled to find solutions to meet our immediate needs, such as obtaining food.

This experience taught me a few lessons: the first of which is that just as the power outage took us by surprise, so will the second coming of Christ if we are not prepared. Like modern-day "preppers"—people around the world extensively preparing in advance for food, shelter, and personal security in the event of a cataclysmic event—we, as Christians, must be "preppers" for the Second Coming. Like the wise virgins in Christ's parable, we must be prepared and not be caught off guard when He comes (Matthew 25).

The second lesson that I learned from the outage that day was that crisis can strike at any time. On that February 9, no alarm sounded so we'd know to make last-minute preparations. At Christ's return, there will probably be no news flash, e-mail, or text message going out to declare the need to prepare for the King's return. We must be ready ahead of time.

The third lesson I learned was that as Christians, while we live in a technologically driven society, we must not become too attached to our technological devices. It is good to get off the grid sometimes. This means no e-mail, text messages, or online messages for a while. Instead let us take more time to focus on our soon-coming King. Doing this has the potential to help us not be so reliant on these other resources.

So let us follow the preppers. Let us be ready, not only for earthly catastrophic events, but especially for the great day when Jesus will come to take us home to heaven.

Taniesha Robertson-Brown

Recliner Chairs From Heaven

As for me, I will call upon God;
and the LORD shall save me.
—Psalm 55:16

Our son-in-law, Jerry, was in the intensive care unit (ICU) of a large hospital after being involved in a very serious automobile accident. My daughter and I traveled to the city where Jerry had been airlifted and took up residence in the ICU waiting room. Many family members of ICU patients were actually living in the waiting room.

A number of comfortable recliner chairs were available in the waiting room, and these were carefully guarded by those who obtained one. Straight-backed chairs, or even the floor, were the only other alternatives for those spending the long hours there. Neither my daughter nor I left the room unless we left our pillow or other personal item in our recliner chairs, and someone watched over them until we returned.

One day during the early morning hours, I noticed that someone had vacated a recliner chair. I was so excited! But just as I was about to notify someone about the vacant recliner, a teenager jumped up from the floor and plopped himself down in it.

I was exasperated! That kid should have been courteous enough to let an older person use that chair! I had personally appointed myself to the recliner chair police force and often checked with others around the room to see who would be leaving and vacating their chairs. It didn't occur to me to ask God to provide a recliner for someone who badly needed it. I guess I felt that I was the only person there who could solve the problem.

One morning about nine, a woman from across the large room approached me and said, "There is an empty recliner next to me. Do you know someone who could use it?" I thanked her profusely and went to tell another person about the vacant recliner. Not more than a few minutes later, the teenager vacated his recliner, taking his belongings with him. Wow, there were two recliners available in a matter of a few minutes!

As I pondered this situation, the Lord began to speak to me in my own language, which was Miss Take-Control-of-Every-Situation language. When I had finally realized that I couldn't do anything to help matters, God opened up two recliner chair vacancies, without any help from me! *Imagine that!* What can you trust Him to do for you today?

Terry Wilson Robinson

The Power of Personal Witnessing

"You will be my witnesses . . .
to the ends of the earth."
—*Acts 1:8, NIV*

Well into my senior years, I felt I was no longer of use to witness for God. Then the Lord brought to my mind memories from my youth, vignettes of small acts of persons unknowingly witnessing to my family.

When I was twelve years old, I was often home alone. One day an elderly neighbor came over, holding in her hand something she had made especially for my mother. It was a beautiful crocheted doily. Ladies of that era often did handwork—embroidery or crochet—to add to the decor of the home. I thanked her and told her I knew Mother would like it. The lady was known in the neighborhood as a devout Christian, and my mother was very pleased with our neighbor's thoughtfulness.

I remembered another time, when I was only six, that a neighbor witnessed without realizing it. It was a Sunday afternoon, and my mother was taking my brothers and me for a ride in the car. We passed our neighbor's house and saw him on his roof doing repair work. "Look, Mother," I said. "Mr. Smith is working on Sunday!" My brothers and I had been taught that it was wrong to work on Sunday because that was the Lord's Day.

My mother replied, "Well, perhaps he doesn't know any better." Later our family found out he worshiped on the seventh-day Sabbath. My mother had been a patient at a nearby Adventist hospital several times, and she respected the people and their beliefs. Now she thought differently of our neighbor.

I pondered these incidents through the years. When I was twenty, I accepted Christ as my Savior and also the seventh day as my day of worship. Those neighbors had witnessed to us without ever knowing it. When we get to heaven, I imagine we will be surprised at the number of people whose lives we have influenced—no matter which branch of Christianity we belong to. And we can witness no matter our age or station in life. "Let those who name the name of Christ remember that individually they are making an impression favorable or unfavorable to Bible religion, on the minds of all with whom they come in contact."*

Peggy Miles Snow

---

* Ellen G. White, "A Message of Judgment," *Southern Watchman*, January 17, 1905.

October 11

Waiting

Unto them that look for him shall he appear
the second time without sin unto salvation.
—*Hebrews 9:28*

The soft gray-and-black upholstered chairs provide adequate comfort. They match the muted gray of the carpet. On the walls hang colorful framed works of art depicting fresh pink-and-yellow wildflowers. The decorator of this room must have chosen them with a purpose—to distract the room's occupants from life's uncertainties. I am sitting in this hospital waiting room, while somewhere nearby, a surgeon with a scalpel is cutting my daughter open.

Though it's only 7:00 A.M., this large outpatient waiting room is crowded. Many people, like me, have come prepared for a long wait with books and magazines that we read or pretend to read. Others stare at their laptops. Some people simply tap their feet and look into space. We are doing what we can to endure the stressful wait.

Every now and then we hear a beep from some family's handheld monitor, signaling a message from one of the surgeons. Soon our monitor beeps. The news is good. "Your daughter has come through surgery just fine," the surgeon says. "I am pleased." And we are thankful. The next beep on our monitor will signal that our daughter is recovered enough for us to take her home. For others in the waiting room, the news may not be so good. Perhaps they'll hear, "The cancer has progressed too far." Or "There's not much more we can do."

I think of us as currently being in life's grand waiting room. Whether we realize it or not, we are all waiting for the good news that Jesus is on His way to take us to our heavenly home. Some of us are well prepared for the wait—full of the Holy Spirit, our lives a witness to His soon coming. Others are losing precious time, unmindful of the times in which we live as they "tap their feet" through choices that will not benefit them in this life or the next.

How are we spending our time in life's waiting room?

Do we share Jesus with others?

Through our prayers and witness, we can use this time to place our loved ones in the hands of the Great Physician and soon hear Him say, "You came through just fine. I am pleased."

Annette Walwyn Michael

Jesus, Our Life Saver

This day I call the heavens and the earth as witnesses against you
that I have set before you life and death, blessings and curses.
Now choose life, so that you and your children may live.
—*Deuteronomy 30:19, NIV*

It had been a difficult morning in our special school district classroom. It seemed as if every child had awakened on the proverbial wrong side of the bed. Shaun had gotten off the school bus in an angry mood and had planted himself in the middle of the floor, refusing to move or speak. Erica, normally reasonably cooperative, insisted she did not want to read as she slammed her book on the table. And then there was Brandon. He could not find his math paper, so he angrily pushed over his desk—books and papers scattering in every direction! Finally, after an hour or so of angry, uncooperative kids, the teacher I was working with looked at me and said, "I've had it. I can't take it anymore. I'm out of here!" And with that, she walked out the door. Well, of course, we couldn't both leave. I had no choice but to stay in the room and cope with twelve difficult kids.

About two hours later, when the other teacher finally returned, she handed me two packages of Life Savers hard candies and said simply, "Thanks for saving my life."

Fortunately, when God looked at our world, full of wicked, angry people, He didn't say, "Forget it. I've had it with these rebellious people!" Rather than "I'm out of here," Jesus said, "I have come that they may have life, and that they may have it more abundantly" (John 10:10, NKJV). Jesus has offered us a life saver—His life. First John 5:12 says, "Whoever has the Son has life; whoever does not have the Son of God does not have life" (NIV).

Jesus longs so much for us to have a relationship with Him. He wants us to spend time with Him every day in Bible study and in prayer. Jesus is our Example. Mark 1:35 says, "Very early in the morning, while it was still dark, Jesus got up, left the house and went off to a solitary place, where he prayed" (NIV).

If Jesus needed early morning prayer time, how much more do we! Jesus says that to know Him and His Father is eternal life (John 17:3, NIV). We need only to accept His offer, spend time with Him, and say simply, "Thank You, Jesus, for saving my life."

Sharon Oster

Vulnerable as a Child

"Behold, I send you out as sheep in the midst of wolves.
Therefore be wise as serpents and harmless as doves."
—Matthew 10:16, NKJV

Having grandchildren made me frighteningly aware of how vulnerable children are. When Silas was six and a half and Iris was two, they were both very much at the mercy of adults and of their environment. Once Iris's two little determined hands could turn a doorknob, her parents had to take extra precautions, as they learned the day she let herself out and wandered into a neighbor's yard but not, thankfully, into the street.

The children were also psychologically vulnerable. One day Grandpa shouted angrily at Silas, thinking it would make him more inclined to mind. Instead Silas fled to his room, now wary of Grandpa. Silas and Iris have good parents who love and affirm them, but their mother works daily with children whose parents are far more concerned with their own welfare than with that of their children. Whether they ignore the child's basic needs or belittle and verbally abuse them, such parents chip—or hack—away at the child's fragile self-esteem, unaware of the terrible destruction they cause.

When Jesus sent His disciples out to spread the good news, He noted their vulnerability. Today's Christians are not only vulnerable to worldly "wolves" but also to wolves clad in sheep's wool, who abuse Christians by misusing Scripture. Some of these wolves keep their Christian followers in a continuous state of childishness, causing Christians to be afraid to think for themselves or trust their own judgment for fear they will offend God by not coming "as a child." Insensitive and unspiritual Christians abuse others by harsh words of judgment or actions such as gossip or betrayal. Such wounds are rarely brought to light, salved, and healed. They are left to cripple the victim or fester with their attendant poison.

"Be wise," Jesus counsels us, as He did His disciples. Wisdom is a protection against false teachers. And He taught us to be careful in our relationships, treating others with love and kindness. When we allow God to place forgiveness in our hearts, when we bring healing care to the wounded, vulnerability is transformed into an opportunity for God to work in our lives and the lives of others.

Dolores Klinsky Walker

"Live Well, Live Blessed!"

"Daughter, you took a risk of faith,
and now you're healed and whole. Live well, live blessed!"
—Mark 5:34, The Message

I find myself constantly challenged by the invitation Jesus gave to a bleeding woman on a dusty road. As she reached out to touch His robe, she chose to exercise incredible courage and faith: a faith that was rewarded by the gift of healing. As she turned to slip away unnoticed, Jesus stopped her with His question, "Who touched Me?" There was so much more He longed to give her if only she would linger awhile in His presence.

Through her tears, and in spite of her fears, she shared the story of what Jesus had done for her. When she was through, she thought to leave, but Jesus had not yet finished the miracle. In a moment that was forever framed by grace, He blessed her. Though the crowd continued to press and the disciples tried to keep Him moving, Jesus took the time to pronounce a blessing on a woman no one had noticed. "Daughter," He said, "you took a risk of faith, and now you're healed and whole. Live well, live blessed!"

So, what does it look like to live well? Simply this. When we determine to live well, we ask ourselves an important question: What if? What if I dared to believe in beauty in spite of the pressing darkness? What if I chose to believe, even in the face of my unbelief? What if I chose to believe that which was dead within me could be raised to life? What if I dared to believe I will yet dance to the music of a little girl's laughter and discover that little girl is me?

When we receive Christ's blessing and accept His invitation to live well, it causes an irrepressible outflowing of gratitude within us. It is Zacchaeus repaying his debts fourfold. It is Mary breaking open her precious alabaster box. It is Paul, enduring shipwreck and prison and stoning. It is Peter whispering, "I am not worthy to die as my Savior." Christ's blessing brings with it the uncommon courage to live boldly for Him. And when necessary, it provides an uncommon courage to die for Him.

Best of all, His blessing was not for this woman alone but for all who would follow after her and find themselves in need of a miracle. His blessing is for you and me. Will you linger a while at His feet and receive it?

Karen J. Pearson

The Hero of Hard Times

For his compassions never fail.
They are new every morning; great is your faithfulness.
—*Lamentations 3:22, 23, NIV*

Recently, I ran into a friend who asked, "Heide, what are you doing these days? You've just fallen off the map!" Some might think so, but I've crisscrossed that map, coast to coast, four times in five years. Not for fun but to actually pack up and move. No wonder people wonder about my whereabouts! After four productive years of directing the Women's Resource Center, my husband and I moved back to Florida. I assumed that with a moderately impressive résumé I could easily get a job in a variety of occupations. Even with high-level connections, the only job that opened up was in a rural area where we'd lived twenty years before. I cried for two days and then submitted to God's will. God gave me special joys that year in that peaceful, slower-paced area.

God then did one of His miraculous, part-the-waters surprises, and I found myself back in California starting a chaplain residency—the fulfillment of a twenty-year dream. It was a double blessing because my husband, Zell, fulfilled his dream of completing a master's degree. After the year of residency, I was offered a chaplaincy job in Florida. Wow! Except for the stress of moving back and forth across the country, happy days were here again! Four months later it all fell apart. With the upheaval in health care, I was downsized with many others at the hospital. Stunned, I reeled in a thrashing sea of emotions but clung to my only Comfort.

The frustrating, discouraging roller coaster of job hunting ensued again. No doors opened in Florida for Zell or me. Just hints, hopes, and maybes. Finally, a job opened back in California. I moved back out, not knowing if this was just God's temporary solution. We had no idea we'd be apart for more than a year with job possibilities ultimately fizzling. I love my chaplain ministry, but there were many tears about the long separation and the uncertainty in our lives. When all leads dried up, Zell moved our belongings west. Though the most problem-plagued move we'd had in thirty years, we were grateful to finally be together again on the same coast!

Looking back, God again comes through as the Hero of hard times: ever there, ever caring; OK with tears, OK with weakness; spreading bits of beauty in the midst of trials. There are still uncertainties, but we know God is in control. Great is His faithfulness!

Heide Ford

My Journaling Journey

And then GOD answered: "Write this. Write what you see. . . .
So that it can be read on the run. . . . If it seems slow in coming, wait.
It's on its way. It will come right on time."
—*Habakkuk 2:2, 3*, The Message

What does a teacher do without a voice?
"Be still, and know that I am God" (Psalm 46:10, NIV). That is just what I learned in March 1995 when I totally lost my voice for three weeks. During January of that same year, I had received what has become one of my most treasured gifts. It was the third women's devotional that our church had published—*A Gift of Love*. I began to enjoy every moment with the devotional book each morning, but I had put the accompanying journal aside.

Journaling was not something I did.

The loss of my voice gave me some needed quiet moments with God. A few months earlier I had purchased a book titled *Prayer Country* by Dorothy Eaton Watts. That book, along with the gift of the journal, would change my prayer life forever. I read each prayer journey the author shares in that precious book, but none has blessed me as much as my journaling journey. I have also been able to encourage many women to join me on that journey. It has been one of the strongest areas of spiritual growth in our women's ministry. What a joy it brings to hear women testify of the miracles of answered prayers they had recorded in their journals!

Today, seventeen years later, I have seen God come through for my husband, my children, and many family members and friends. I praise God for the faith-building experience it has been for me as I see God come through again and again in response to prayer. I encourage each one of you who reads this to begin a journaling journey today, if you haven't already.

Just write in your journal the cries and desires of your heart for your children and for yourself as a mother or sister. Put your thoughts, fears, hopes, dreams, concerns, and prayer requests before God. Then wait to see Him work in His time.

As the prophet Habakkuk counsels in Habakkuk 2:2, 3, "If [the answer to your prayer] seems slow in coming, wait. It's on its way. It will come right on time" (*The Message*).

Claudette Garbutt-Harding

Dreams and God's Leadings

Who knoweth whether thou art come to the kingdom
for such a time as this?
—*Esther 4:1*

When I saw you in church," said Norval, "a dream I had three years ago popped into my mind. I saw the fulfillment of that dream." Later he elaborated on his dream, which he'd jotted on a piece of yellow notepad. The dream had come after he became a widower. He also shared more about his story. Two women had offered to help him raise his now-motherless children: a ten-year-old son and a twelve-year-old daughter. He welcomed their proffered help, especially from the tall, attractive young woman that he and his children had known as a nearby neighbor. All worked well except for one component: even after many invitations, the woman had not wanted to attend church with Norval's family. To him, that was a most important issue.

While working in Hinsdale, Illinois, in the hospital medical records department the hospital administrator shared that the hospital needed a qualified person to head the department, as the current director was retiring. He urged me to get the qualifications needed for the position. This required taking coursework in Danville, a smaller town nearby. After I was accepted, the school director helped me to find a room at the local YWCA. For the first few months, each Friday after classes, I returned to Hinsdale to attend church and work at the hospital Saturday night and all day Sunday.

One day the medical records department director, Mrs. McDole, encouraged me to attend church in Danville. "As a small church, they'll welcome you," she said. So one Friday I stayed put at the YWCA. Early that Sabbath morning I took the bus to the Danville church. Following the service, many members welcomed me. Among them were Norval A. Jackson and his two children. He offered to help with transportation for me. Later he shared his dream with me. Believing in the fulfillment of his dream, he added, "I need someone to help me raise my children."

One week our local church minister preached on Esther's obedience to God's leadings. He read Esther 4:14: "Who knoweth whether thou art come to the kingdom for such a time as this?" He repeatedly incorporated the verse in his sermon, reaching my heart.

Norval's family helped plan our wedding, and my physician brother flew from California to give me away. Ever since I can remember, Esther 4:14 has been my favorite Bible verse. And, throughout the ensuing years, the message has became a source of comfort to me.

Consuelo Roda-Jackson

Service—Not Applause

That you, being rooted and grounded in love,
may be able to comprehend with all the saints
what is the width and length and depth and height—
to know the love of Christ which passes knowledge.
—*Ephesians 3:17–19, NKJV*

My piano playing leaves a lot to be desired. However, it does suffice at church when more talented, gifted, and skillful players are not present. One day as I sat at the piano to play, someone asked the key of a hymn in order to accompany with the guitar. When I replied that I didn't know, the person was surprised. I could tell how many sharps or flats the hymn had but didn't know the key in which it was written. It was puzzling to the person that I could play the piano yet not know the name of the key in which the music was written.

I'd taken music lessons for years during my childhood and early adolescent years. It wasn't something I'd chosen to do nor was it something I'd always looked forward to doing. I usually balked at practicing. However, Mama wanted me to serve the church. Sure, she thought recitals and other musical pieces were nice, but it was the hymns that brought her real joy. For her, my music was all about serving God and not performing for applause.

Now, being more mature and appreciative of my opportunities, it became my desire to do a better job in this area of service for the church. I started taking piano lessons again. *Voilà!* I'd never comprehended music theory. Before my lessons, I wouldn't even attempt to play anything without the notes in front of me, not even simple pieces. I can actually play a few hymns now, not by ear, but by understanding and utilizing the notes that go with that key—though there is still room for a lot of improvement.

Mama, though, would be happy to know that more than sixty years later, her love for God, her desire to serve Him, and her faithfulness have been true blessings for me and others. God is still honoring her faithfulness to Him in more ways than I'll ever realize on this earth.

God gave His Son, His Word, and His Holy Spirit for us. Many times we fail to comprehend and appreciate the "width and length and depth and height" of the sacrifice made on our behalf and all that is available for us (Ephesians 3:18). *Father, give us the desire to sit at Jesus' feet, the Master Teacher, each and every day, so that we can serve You. Thank You, Father!*

Sharon M. Thomas

October 19

Make Yourself a List

I want you woven into a tapestry of love,
in touch with everything there is to know of God.
—*Colossians 2:2*, The Message

In my home office is a tattered box with no monetary worth. Into it, I tuck notes that I write to myself, and I store quotes from newspapers and magazines. It's valuable to me because those pieces of paper hold ideas for writing.

Today I found two pieces of paper at the very bottom: one, a yellowed to-do list written years ago. I'd listed thirteen promises to myself to accomplish that month. I'll share just three of them. *First, encourage the pastor's family.* The pastor is buried now, as is one of his daughters; but his wife and I remain close, though long-distance friends. *Second, plan a dinner for Ben. He'll be baptized this week.* That dinnertime provided happy heaven conversation, as we sat around the table with members of his family. They all became heart-tied friends to my husband and me. He, too, has passed now. *Third, give an unexpected gift, homemade if possible.* That was fun to do. The gift was a poem I had decoupaged on a slate, written for one of my college professors. She treasured it. I was an older college student, and our ages were close. When she vacationed, her trips were always somewhere in a far-off land. She'd post letters to me, which I treasured, with beautiful postage stamps from different countries.

Why thirteen promises? I don't know, yet I believe that they were nudges from God because, as I reread them, I recalled that every one of them resulted in lasting family-of-God friendships.

I don't know why I saved the list for so long, but I'm glad I did. It reminds me that even though I can no longer do all of those thirteen things, due to physical limitations, I can still encourage and love people. It also reminds me of a quote written by the Christian author Ellen White: "All our energies should be turned to the obedience of Christ."* That's passing on Jesus' love.

And guess what? I'd written that quote on a piece of scratch paper that I also found in the bottom of the box. Coincidence? I think not. It's one of those God things that Christian writers relish passing on to readers!

Betty Kossick

---

* Ellen G. White, *Testimonies to the Church*, vol. 4 (Mountain View, CA: Pacific Press®, 1885), 81.

Teach Me to Forgive

And be kind to one another, tenderhearted,
forgiving one another, even as God in Christ forgave you.
—*Ephesians 4:32, NKJV*

Forgive is one simple word, yet so complex to explain, let alone to practice. Watching the movie *Diary of a Mad Black Woman* made me realize how hard it is to forgive people who have wronged us. Yet we need to for our own sanity and happiness. We often pray, "Our Father in heaven, forgive us our sins as we forgive those who trespass against us" (see Matthew 6:9, 12). But how often do we practice what we preach? I now realize that when you forgive a person, you free yourself from anger. Anger can eat you up like cancer. It's good for neither soul nor salvation. You become a prisoner in your own body. When you forgive, however, you let go and ask God to take over. Let's simplify this with two opposite hypothetical situations:

1. Someone hurts you. What do you do? You kill him or her. You go to jail. You have taken away your freedom, and you suffer till you die. The question is, Was anger worth it?

2. Someone hurts you. What do you do? You let go and pray to God to deal with the person as He, in His wisdom, sees fit. Believe me, He never forgets.

We all want blessings, and we can experience blessings in our lives when we release anger and forgive people. This is not easy.

We need to pray for courage to acknowledge people who have wronged us as well as to follow Christ's example of love and forgiveness. When we do this, we allow God's mercy upon us.

Psalm 27:11 says, "Teach me Your way, O Lord, and lead me in a smooth path, because of my enemies" (NKJV). In this life, we will have enemies, but as Christians we need to find the power to forgive by depending on God. We are all sinners saved by grace. Who, then, are we to judge any person?

Psalm 30:5 says, "Weeping may endure for a night, but joy comes in the morning" (NKJV). We all have been hurt. Believe me when I say that God takes note of every tear that falls.

It won't be long; joy is on its way for you and me.

Deborah Matshaya

October 21

Drifting Away

I cried by reason of mine affliction unto the LORD,
and he heard me.
—*Jonah 2:2*

We disembarked for a day in Grenada, my first time on the island. The island tour included the option of a swim at a beach. At Grand Anse Beach, my cruise roommate and I changed into our swimsuits and ventured into the water up to our knees. I can't swim, so I splashed around with my feet firmly planted on the sand. A teenage boy swam over and made small talk. He had a flotation device and told us that he would be our lifeguard if we hired him.

Our new young friend was very engaging as we conversed about his family and life on the island. At one point, he asked me to hold his flotation device so he could show me some dives. I threw my arms over the tube, putting my weight on it, and raised my feet to float beneath me in the tropical water. I watched the boy dive, impressed at his confidence in the water. We continued to amiably chat, and I continued to float.

Suddenly, my roommate called out "Where are you going, Sharon? Back to the ship?" I didn't understand what she was saying, so I turned to look in her direction. To my dismay, I discovered I had drifted far from the shore. I extended a leg to get my footing on the sand again and walk back toward shore, but my toes couldn't touch the ocean floor.

I panicked. Would this nonswimmer drown in Grenada? Or would a lifeguard helicopter come to my rescue? Would my offshore rescue make the evening television news? Then I heard a still, small voice saying, "Calm down. Relax. Breathe." I immediately obeyed its instructions. Holding on to the floatation device for dear life with one arm, I gently paddled with the other arm. I approached slowly the shore. At long last, I got close enough to stand up. Relieved, I profusely thanked my roommate for warning me that I was drifting away from the shore. The outcome of my predicament could have been disastrous had she not noticed. My junior "lifeguard," however, had seemed oblivious to my danger.

This experience reminded me of how easily sin can cause us to drift away from God. Satan uses drugs, alcohol, domestic violence, sex, money, peers, jobs, fame, glamour, and sometimes even family members to lure us away from our Lord. We must hold on to Him as tightly as I clung to that flotation device. Only He can plant our feet safely on solid ground.

Sharon Long (Brown)

The Birthday Present

And he said unto them, The sabbath was made for man, and not man for the sabbath: therefore the Son of man is Lord also of the Sabbath.
—Mark 2:27, 28

Parenthood is an exciting experience. Long before a baby arrives, the parents, brimming with love for their little one, prepare everything possible for the child's health and happiness.

So, many, many years ago God started preparing for the arrival of His new son and daughter, Adam and Eve. Their happiness was uppermost in His heart of love, as He created a beautiful new earth just for them. The air was fresh and clean; the grass luscious, sprinkled with myriads of multicolored, delicately perfumed flowers forming a velvet carpet. Music from countless throbbing, feathered throats filled the atmosphere with praise. In a few days, everything was ready, and God brought into this breathtakingly beautiful world His newly created children. But something was missing—their birthday present, a tangible token of God's deep love for them. He held nothing back but freely offered them twenty-four hours of His precious time every week. He called this gift "Sabbath." Oh yes, God walked and talked with His children every evening in their Garden, but the Sabbath was something special. Their Father, Creator, and Sustainer of the vast universe was offering them the gift of quality time with Him as a present. To me, this is nothing short of mind-boggling.

There is no more mention of those evening walks later when sin built a barrier between God and His earthly children, but He never recalled His gift of the Sabbath. Sinful though we undoubtedly are, His love for us is no less than it was for Adam and Eve in their pristine perfection. Perhaps it would even be correct to say that His love today is greater still because our need of Him is even more desperate.

Finally, the Sabbath comes to us as well, gift-wrapped in a very special blessing. It is freely offered to each child of God and will continue to be until we celebrate it together with Him, face-to-face throughout eternity.

It is our privilege to enjoy the Sabbath as a date with our beloved Creator and Savior.

We can participate in this weekly opportunity to rejoice in His company, to bask in His love, and to express our own devotion and gratitude to Him.

Revel Papaioannou

Maranatha

If any man love not the Lord Jesus Christ,
let him be Anathema Maranatha.
—*1 Corinthians 16:22*

If anyone does not love the Lord Jesus Christ,
let him be accursed. O Lord, come!
—*1 Corinthians 16:22, NKJV*

In the Bible verse above, the New King James Version gives us the meaning of those last two Greek words, *Anathema Maranatha*. Certainly we do not want to be accursed. On the other hand, we who love the Lord Jesus Christ long for Jesus to come soon.

After serving the Lord in church work in many areas of India for forty years, we chose to live in Maranatha Colony, Hosur, India. It's very close to our church headquarters in that part of the world. There are about fifteen houses here in this colony where we retirees live. We all own our houses with a little garden or orchard. We enjoy tending our own gardens, and this helps us to be happy and healthy. Our colony is like a little haven with its comfort, good weather, and countless blessings from God.

Though a few of us have been laid to rest, due mostly to aging, the rest of us are still enjoying a normal life having reached the age three score and ten (seventy years as described in Psalm 90:10), with some of us even above fourscore and ten (ninety years of age). We are all of the same faith and enjoy going to church together on Sabbath. A vehicle comes to take us to church and brings us back home. We enjoy the fellowship at church and include it among the blessings that cheer us old people.

We ladies at our retirement community also conduct a prayer meeting each Wednesday for an hour. One of us presents a devotional talk, and then we all take part in a season of prayer for those in trouble or in need of help. God has answered many of our prayers. This ministry has kept us very close to each other like sisters in Christ should be.

Often we get invitations to functions such as weddings, house dedications, and birthdays. Being included in these events is a comfort to elderly people.

At our age, though, we are living on borrowed time and cling to Jesus' promise found in Revelation 22:20, "Surely I come quickly. Amen."

We in Maranatha Colony join with John in saying, "Even so, come, Lord Jesus."

Birdie Poddar

Socializing Angel

Judge not, that ye be not judged.
For with what judgment ye judge, ye shall be judged.
—Matthew 7:1, 2

I peeped through the curtain on the side window of our front door and anxiously watched the driveway. Soon a car would appear, bringing a new dog for us to evaluate for possible adoption. Recently, we'd had to say Goodbye to our German shepherd, which had left a huge hole in my heart. An SUV, bearing the logo for One Shep at a Time, pulled into our driveway. An attractive lady got out and opened the back door. A beautiful auburn-and-black German shepherd gingerly alighted from the backseat. The dog longingly looked up into my eyes as if to ask, "Will you keep me?" Soon the dog was lying at my feet and nudging my hand to pet her soft head. It was love at first sight. After a two-day trial period, we decided to keep Angel.

Soon after we had given Angel a home, we began to see that she had a few problems. She first jumped over the two-acre backyard fence with ease. Then, whenever I put her outside on the back porch, she would stand by the back door and shake for hours. She tried at every chance to chase our elderly cat, Moomba, but, with time and patience, they became friends. Angel was also overprotective. Whenever anyone came to visit, she leaned against my legs, shaking and growling if the person moved. Finally, after several months, I contacted a trainer to come to our house to help us.

After several visits and many practice sessions, we were delighted to see improvements. I decided to contact Angel's previous owner to find out more about her history. We were told that we were the fourth home she had been in during her two-year life span and that she had been abused. We then understood why she came to us with unresolved problems. We were happy that we had patiently hung in there and helped her to improve. She has become a wonderful pet for us.

Whenever I think back on Angel, I am reminded how quick we are to judge people. We look at their behavior as strange, bad, or inappropriate without taking the time to get to know and befriend them. Their pasts may well reveal severe scars, which cause their actions. Maybe these people are calling out because their hearts are lonely, fearful, or sad. Let us pray that we will not overlook an opportunity to befriend and patiently encourage their behavior to change.

Jesus surely has done this for each one of us!

Rose Neff Sikora

Potholes

For I know the thoughts that I think toward you, saith the LORD,
thoughts of peace, and not of evil, to give you an expected end. . . .
And ye shall ye seek me, and find me,
when ye shall search for me with all your heart.
—*Jeremiah 29:11, 13*

As a baby Christian, it seemed I could not avoid falling short of God's will. I knew what the Bible said and what was right and what was expected of me. But my mistakes and sins, it seemed, were eating away my glorious walk with my Lord until I felt as if they had little holds on my life.

I couldn't seem to get my work or shopping done before Sabbath, and I would put a load of laundry in the washing machine Sabbath afternoon. I couldn't refuse a cup of coffee, and I carelessly ate a sandwich with pork in it. I forgot to say my prayers and lost my temper with my husband. I didn't take back the pen that I mistakenly put in my purse at the insurance company. I spent six hours watching television and did not rise early and begin my day with the Lord. I told Mary I would pray for her but did not. I cheated on my income tax form and did not visit sick church members in the hospital. The list went on and on.

I was always doing something wrong that I really did not want to do and felt guilty afterwards. Though I'd been baptized, joined a church, attended it faithfully, and even held church duties, I still felt guilty.

Then one day I passed a sign that appropriately read "Grandview Bench, Pothole Capital of the World." The sign had a flat, torn-up car tire draped over it. That sign changed my perspective, because it depicted exactly how I felt—like the pothole capital of the world. Then I prayed some more about it. The Lord impressed me not to dwell on my mistakes but rather to keep looking up, up to the Son, not down at the potholes. "Ask Me," He says, "for strength to be made willing to change the potholes into flat, smooth ground."

Now I feel like putting a new sign that reads "Christian Under Construction" over the one on that road. It took Grandview a year to fix that road; but, at times, it may take longer to fix us.

Change this ratty, ragged tire of a human being into Your likeness, Lord, I pray.

Vidella McClellan

With All Your Heart

*Whatever you do, work at it with all your heart,
as working for the Lord, not for human masters,
since you know that you will receive an inheritance from the Lord
as a reward. It is the Lord Christ you are serving.*
—*Colossians 3:23, 24, NIV*

On my birthday, I received the news that I had lost my job in the publishing company where I had been working for eighteen years, ten of those years in management. A new manager had put another person in my place. I was devastated by the news, because I'd prepared myself (through business administration classes and other secondary courses) to perform the job well. Suddenly, it all went out the window. I lost everything I'd invested and at great expense to myself.

Desperate, I sought God. In less than two months, I had adapted to the new salary that now was my reality. Though humiliated and put aside by someone who does not fear the Lord, God fought for me and covered me with other blessings. Despite the disappointment, I continued to work with care and affection, because I understood that everything should be done for God and not for a flawed and sinful woman like me. Through tears, I clung to the verse that says, "And we know that all things work together for good to them that love God, to them who are the called according to his purpose" (Romans 8:28). So I found the strength to move on and to wait on God. He miraculously has supported me through these difficult times. And I grew through the trials.

Every day we are surprised by the events of life. Women are multifunctional beings who sometimes want to embrace the world. We work with attention and care at home, in church, and in companies. However, there come moments when we need to stop all the running and have some time for ourselves and for our special Friend. This pause causes us to gain strength to face the challenges or to enjoy the blessings. Jesus is waiting excitedly for our daily meeting and is happy when we sit down and start talking to His heart. When we share our joys, He rejoices with us. If we take our anxieties and sorrows to Him, our Friend cries with us and offers us His shoulder to rest on. This is the way we live with Him and He with us, a successful partnership.

Reflect on the words of Paul in Philippians 4:13: "I can do all things through Christ who strengthens me" (NKJV). And God calls us to persevere: "Whatever your hand finds to do, do it with your might" (Ecclesiastes 9:10, NKJV).

Sueli da Silva Pereira

The Great Change—Part 1

A new heart also will I give you,
and a new spirit will I put within you:
and I will take away the stony heart out of your flesh,
and I will give you an heart of flesh.
—*Ezekiel 36:26*

I am filled with wonder and awe as I contemplate the miracle of transformation that takes place in the life of a filthy, sinful person when Christ becomes a personal friend and Savior. My life is an example of this great change.

Just like the two "sons of thunder" in the Bible—Christ's disciples John and James (Mark 3:17)—anger was my problem.

This was very evident before I accepted Jesus as my Lord and Savior. I loved to have people around me, yet I could not tolerate nonsense from anybody. A little mistake from others set me ablaze. The anger arising from the mistake of another could be so great that it could result in my retaliating, insulting, and pronouncing evil words against that person. When I was faced with an unpleasant situation or my ego was touched, the anger rising up in me was like surging water—boiling water that bursts out and splashes on everyone close to it.

As I started studying the Bible and Ellen G. White's *The Desire of Ages,* a book on the life of Christ, I grew to know more about my new Friend, Jesus Christ. What fascinated me about Him was His meekness and lowliness. The manner in which He treated people impressed me deeply and caught my attention. He showed a constant love that never sought to hurt people. And when He spoke truth to them, He did so in love and with gentleness.

I developed a desire to be like Jesus. So I promised myself I would control my anger and be gentle to those who offended me. But the sad reality was that the more I tried, the more I failed. I was disappointed in myself. Yet I was ready to do whatever it took to overcome my anger and be like Jesus.

Then one day, while reading the Bible, I found the passage containing today's scripture: "A new heart also will I give you, and a new spirit will I put within you: and I will take away the stony heart out of your flesh, and I will give you an heart of flesh" (Ezekiel 36:26). God promised to do that for me!

Whoa! The work of transformation is the Lord's doing. I realized it is a miracle!

Omobonike Adeola Sessou

The Great Change—Part 2

Hide thy face from my sins,
and blot out all mine iniquities.
Create in me a clean heart, O God;
and renew a right spirit within me.
Cast me not away from thy presence;
and take not thy holy spirit from me.
Restore unto me the joy of thy salvation;
and uphold me with thy free spirit.

—*Psalm 51:9–12*

After learning from the Bible that God works change in our hearts, I asked Him to transform my heart and my feelings. I prayed for the grace to be sweet, kind, and forgiving of others.

As I prayed for this change of heart, I also learned that I would be transformed if I beheld Christ, keeping my eyes on Him. His invitation to me was, "Come unto me, all ye that labour and are heavy laden, and I will give you rest. Take my yoke upon you, and learn of me; for I am meek and lowly in heart: and ye shall find rest unto your souls. For my yoke is easy, and my burden is light" (Matthew 11:28–30).

One author's words about Christ's disciple John also described me: "Even John, who came into closest association with the meek and lowly One, was not himself naturally meek and yielding. He and his brother were called 'the sons of thunder.' While they were with Jesus, any slight shown to Him aroused their indignation and combativeness. Evil temper, revenge, the spirit of criticism, were all in the beloved disciple. He was proud, and ambitious to be first in the kingdom of God."*

Yet the great change that occurred in the heart of John also occurred in my heart and through the same process. "But day by day, in contrast with his own violent spirit, [John] beheld the tenderness and forbearance of Jesus, and heard His lessons of humility and patience. He opened his heart to the divine influence, and became not only a hearer but a doer of the Saviour's words. Self was hid in Christ. He learned to wear the yoke of Christ and to bear His burden."†

Dear sister, have you experienced this great change in your life since you have come to know Christ? If not, you can also be changed into His likeness by learning of Him and beholding who He is. Respond to His love for you, and He will give you a new heart.

Omobonike Adeola Sessou

---

* Ellen G. White, *The Desire of Ages* (Mountain View, CA: Pacific Press®, 1940), 295.
† Ibid., 295, 296.

Texting

> For it is the God who commanded light to shine out of darkness,
> who has shone in our hearts to give the light of the knowledge
> of the glory of God in the face of Jesus Christ. But we have this
> treasure in earthen vessels, that the excellence of the power
> may be of God and not of us.
> —*2 Corinthians 4:6, 7, NKJV*

I started sending Bible texts to my daughters, and my texting list has grown as a daily text can uplift someone. Texting quickly became popular when it was first introduced. And now many cell phone companies offer unlimited texting.

But it has its downsides; parents are concerned that their children are spending too much valuable time texting. They wonder, *What messages are being sent out?* People can be easily distracted as they are always on the lookout for, and are constantly alerted by, text messages. Texting has taken away from face-to-face communication and negatively impacted, in some cases, people's ability to write well. Texting doesn't portray facial expressions when sending messages and can sometimes serve to isolate us from one another.

As previously mentioned, I use texting as a source of encouragement for others. Daily I search for and find Bible verses that I am inspired to send out to family and friends. I have come across some unique texts containing meaningful promises from God.

The responses from my texting buddies include "Amen. Thank you. I remain faithful. Thank you for the blessing." "Amen, I believe it and claim this in Jesus Christ. This came in just in time. I needed it. He's awesome. Your prayers have kept me and my spirit rising to higher places in Jesus' name." My friends and family appreciate receiving the scriptural text messages, and I get to witness to them.

As Christians, we also use the word *text* as a biblical reference. Today we add *ing* to this ancient word to indicate the sending of a message to someone via cell phone. Texting is an opportunity to uplift and comfort each other daily, especially with the unlimited texting, for God's purpose.

Make texting a positive shout-out. Take texting to another level and reach someone. Text a text to someone from God's written and living Word.

Margo Peterson

Life's Puzzle

"For I know the plans I have for you," declares the LORD,
"plans to prosper you and not to harm you,
plans to give you hope and a future."
—*Jeremiah 29:11, NIV*

While visiting with my grandchildren, Brian and Mikki, this past Christmas, I noticed they had several puzzles. We sat at a table and attempted to put one together, but we had a hard time making much progress. "Let's stop doing this for now," said one of my grandchildren.

"Yes," agreed the other, "we can come back to it later." So we left the puzzle unfinished with unplaced pieces scattered everywhere. Soon we became engrossed in other family activities. Yet from time to time, we'd return to the puzzle and perhaps spot a piece that we could place. We were all thrilled with each of these additions to the puzzle. When we finally completed the puzzle, we were so happy with the outcome that we framed it!

My own life is like a giant jigsaw puzzle. Sometimes I have tried to force a piece to go where it didn't fit. Other times I've tried to fit in a piece before the others had been properly placed. Yet once one has begun assembling a puzzle, there is a drive to somehow finish it as quickly as possible. Over the years, I've learned that I needed to let God place my life's puzzle pieces in the correct order: college degree, marriage, home, children, now grandchildren and great-grandchildren. God had a plan for my life, and I needed to let it come together in His chosen progression—not unlike the outcome of a pregnancy. Once a baby is conceived, it starts to grow. But, ideally, it must fully develop before birth occurs.

Sometimes I haven't understood how all the pieces of my life were to go together and what order I should expect to have them assembled in. But God has promised that He has plans. He can see the whole, the completed puzzle, even though I can't.

With His help, following His example, and working in cooperation with Him regarding the pieces of my life, I will someday see the beautiful and final picture. I will understand His plan—despite the snags, curves, and detours along the way—for putting my life's puzzle together. I will see that the final outcome has been framed with hope and eternity with Him.

My life's synopsis is, If Jesus goes with me, I will go. I wouldn't trade anything for my life's sometimes confusing puzzle, for Jesus is leading me all the way.

Betty Glover Perry

Dump That Stuff

Therefore, get rid of all moral filth
and the evil that is so prevalent
and humbly accept the word planted in you,
which can save you.
—James 1:21, NIV

When we lived on Staten Island, the New York City Marathon began almost literally in our backyard. Fort Wadsworth, the U.S. Army post on which we lived, is situated right under the Staten Island end of the Verrazano-Narrows Bridge. The morning of the marathon, the fence between the army post and the bridge was removed; the cannon boomed; and the throngs of runners who had gathered on the parade ground behind our row house surged onto the bridge and the race began.

The first year we were stationed there, we were astonished at the stuff that the runners dropped as they began to run. Because the race begins very early and it is usually chilly on those October mornings, runners often used space blankets to keep warm before the race. When the cannon sounded, they dropped the blankets and lots of other stuff as well: toilet paper rolls, sweat suits, Thermos bottles, jars of Vaseline, Tupperware, and even a bottle of Kaopectate. We worried a bit about that runner! Our children took large garbage bags and collected bags full of loot. There were buses onto which runners could put things to be reclaimed when they arrived at Central Park, but few availed themselves of the service.

The second year the race managers brought in flatbed trucks onto which runners could deposit things, and those items would then be given to the Salvation Army or some other charity.

Paul often wrote about running the race of life. He wrote, "Do you not know that in a race all the runners run, but only one gets the prize? Run in such a way as to get the prize" (1 Corinthians 9:24, NIV). One cannot carry extra stuff and expect to win. And in Acts 20:24, Paul testified, "However, I consider my life worth nothing to me; my only aim is to finish the race and complete the task the Lord Jesus has given me—the task of testifying to the good news of God's grace" (Acts 20:24, NIV), and of course his final recorded testimony, "I have fought the good fight, I have finished the race, I have kept the faith" (2 Timothy 4:7, NIV).

We are all running the spiritual race, and we all have stuff—junk—that we need to get rid of and replace it with what will help us win the race: the Word planted in us.

Ardis Dick Stenbakken

Creation Mended

And he that sat upon the throne said,
Behold, I make all things new.
—*Revelation 21:5*

I was at the zoo, looking at a tiger that watched me intently through the bars of its enclosure. After a while, he rose to pace the boundaries of the confined yard and then went back to sitting and staring. I could only wonder what it must have been like when God created all these animals tame and free. When we consider the plight of God's creatures in the world, what hope of survival do many have? There are poachers after tusks, horns, teeth, fins, feathers, and skins. Habitats are destroyed by deforestation, a contaminated atmosphere, or a polluted sea. Land and sea creatures are becoming extinct, and many more are being traumatized by a changing environment. In a frantic effort to preserve some of these exotic species, open-range reserves and zoos with breeding programs are working hard to save them.

In comparison, what's so different with the human race? Not a lot, really, when we look at the condition of our world. Humans kill humans by the millions. Famines cause starvation. Earthquakes, cyclones, floods, fires, crime, and much more destroy human life on a daily basis. "For nation shall rise against nation, and kingdom against kingdom: and there shall be famines, and pestilences, and earthquakes, in divers places" (Matthew 24:7). Satan has made an utter mess of this planet, but the time is rapidly approaching when God will banish all evil. "Nevertheless we, according to his promise, look for new heavens and a new earth, wherein dwelleth righteousness" (2 Peter 3:13). Only our Savior can rescue us.

I'm so glad that God in His great love still provides enough for us to see beauty in His creative works. He is the Master Designer, and nature is His artwork. Consider the varieties, shapes, and colors of flowers, birds, and butterflies, and the breathtaking artwork in mountains, gorges, and valleys. Resting awhile in these sanctuaries brings peace and joy.

I praise God for the beauty I see now, but I eagerly anticipate seeing the earth made new. "For, behold, I create new heavens and a new earth: and the former shall not be remembered, nor come into mind. . . . The wolf and the lamb shall feed together, and the lion shall eat straw like the bullock. . . . They shall not hurt nor destroy in all my holy mountain, saith the LORD" (Isaiah 65:17, 25). Unspoiled.

Lyn Welk-Sandy

Count Your Blessings

*"Return home and tell
how much God has done for you."*
—*Luke 8:39, NIV*

Often in the paths of life we are tempted to become discouraged when difficulties arise and when everything seems to go wrong. We frequently forget to count the blessings, but it is amazing how the dark clouds dissipate when we count our blessings.

As I was thinking one day, I realized how many great things the Lord has done for me. Joy took hold of my heart, and difficulties became small. God took me from being a simple, extremely shy girl of meager financial means from the countryside of São Paulo to become someone who could be used in His work among children. As a teacher of children in their first years of education, I gradually learned how to work with little ones and teach them about God's love.

Over time, God gifted me with a wonderful husband and five precious children. (Today my five boys are adults; I have two granddaughters, and a third grandchild is on the way.) What else could I ask for? However, I must confess that I often was weak and tearful when facing the struggles involved in raising my children in the path of good. I also wanted to be the wife that the Lord wanted me to be. Many times I asked myself if I should have left my professional career behind in order to care for the family. I still have much learning and growing to do, but I feel the strong hand of the Lord has always been with me.

I dedicated myself to children's ministry in my church, always with the strong support of my husband. And I know that during the preceding years the Lord was preparing me for this work. He was shaping my temper and teaching me that only by His Spirit can we effectively do His work. And what greater joy can we feel than the assurance that we are instruments of the Lord?

Just as the Lord has blessed me, enabled my growth, and uses me for His service, He is using you as well. We cannot understand how He uses both the past and the present to shape us for service to Him. Nor do we understand how He turns dreams, both imagined and unimagined, into reality. Why not take a moment to count God's blessings in your life? By seeking Him through prayer and putting ourselves into His hands, we will experience even more.

Maria de Lourdes I. M. Castanho

Wedding Drama

Surely I come quickly. Amen.
Even so, come, Lord Jesus.
—*Revelation 22:20, 21*

Weddings in Africa are very significant and colorful affairs in every level of society. Weddings on our mission campus were always well planned and exciting events with many people involved. Usually all of the staff were included.

One Sunday two fine young people, related to mission workers, were married in the carefully decorated church on the campus. It was a beautiful ceremony, with the exquisite bride looking radiant and her attendants quite spectacular in their gorgeous dresses and plaited hair. The church service went smoothly— the flowers, music, singing, vows, and sermonette all entirely appropriate and obviously meticulously planned.

Following the ceremony, everyone gathered for the reception and celebration in white pitched tents, decorated with tulle, flowers, and beribboned chairs and tables. For a few minutes, the wedding party retreated to another part of the campus for photographs. In the meantime, the guests began to collect their food; but as soon as they sat down to eat, a sudden, freak mini-tornado ripped through the tents, hurling the canvas into the air before it crashed down on top of the terrified guests. Chaos instantly erupted. Guests screamed as tents collapsed on top of them. Poles ripped into people's legs and crashed onto their faces. Others found themselves covered in food, while piles of white plates were smashed. The beautiful many-tiered cake toppled to the ground amid the flowers and tulle in a jungle of twisted wires and ripped canvas.

For some, this was the end of an event that had been predicted to be the wedding of the year. They went home. Others were taken to the hospital or attended to by a doctor, the area Health Ministries director, or caring nurses and friends. The wedding event was eventually moved to the school gymnasium, and the proceedings went on. My thoughts and prayers went out to the bridal couple and especially to the mother who had planned it all so carefully.

How short lived are some of our hopes and dreams as well! We look forward to the final wedding celebration, the coming of Jesus when we will party together safely and securely, worries and calamities behind us. This world is not our home. As disasters and troubles, big and small, increase everywhere, we can only say, "Please come soon, Lord Jesus."

Joy Butler

Hot or Cold

"I know you inside and out, and find little to my liking.
You're not cold, you're not hot—far better to be either cold or hot!
You're stale. You're stagnant. You make me want to vomit."
—*Revelation 3:15, 16,* The Message

When I was growing up, I heard French spoken a lot in my extended family. My mother and grandmother often sat in our kitchen speaking French and then English (*anglais* in French) and sometimes a mixture of both, which is called *Franglais*. In high school, I naturally decided to take French for my language requirement. The first year I did pretty well. The second year I sat next to some boys who spent the whole class period interrupting me and blabbing, so I didn't learn much. I ended up not knowing much more than I did before my two years of French.

I've tried to learn on my own, many times and in many ways, over the years. I've bought French language courses but haven't studied them; I listen to French talk radio on the satellite radio in my car; and I get a French Word-a-Day e-mail, though I'm usually too busy to read it, much less learn it. I even learned some French lyrics verbatim so I can sing in French, but I don't always know exactly what I'm singing. For example, I learned an old French song that I thought was about a man's friendship with his beloved old cart horse only to later learn that the song was about him and his neighbor eating the horse. I would have more success becoming fluent in French if I got serious about it. If I took a class, read French books and translated them, listened only to French radio, watched French television or movies, and took trips to France or Quebec. French would become an actual part of me rather than something I knew a little bit about.

In the same way, reading the Bible a little here, praying a little there, listening to a bit of Christian music sometimes, going to church every now and then, are all good things. But they won't create a truly vibrant spiritual life. God doesn't want us to dabble in Him as if He were a hobby. He wants us to immerse ourselves in Him, to drown ourselves in Him. That's the only way we will ever have a vibrant, fluent relationship with Him. If you want the kind of friendship with God in which you finish each other's sentences, fill *every* part of your day with Him, not just certain parts. Surround yourself with God by every means possible. In that way, we will know Him and be known by Him in a way that won't make Him want to puke.

Céleste Perrino-Walker

Go on God's Errands

Also I heard the voice of the Lord, saying,
Whom shall I send, and who will go for us?
Then said I, Here am I; send me.
—*Isaiah 6:8*

Many years ago, when I was a preteen, I became a member of the Pathfinder Club, a church program for adolescents. Little did I know the lasting influence that membership would have on my entire life. I still fondly recall my varied experiences in those meetings, such as singing the Pathfinder song and memorizing the Pathfinder Law, Pledge, and Aim.

I still remember the moral and social values that were instilled in me during those training sessions. Any positive thing I have done, I believe, should be credited, to a great extent, to the Pathfinder Club. The Pathfinder Law has played a pivotal role in shaping my life. It reads like this. "The Pathfinder Law is for me to (1) Keep the morning watch. (2) Do my honest part. (3) Care for my body. (4) Keep a level eye. (5) Be courteous and obedient. (6) Walk softly in the sanctuary. (7) Keep a song in my heart. (8) Go on God's errands."*

I have found embedded in this law clear guidelines for successful Christian living. Inasmuch as I have embraced the law completely, there are two aspects of it that have become an integral part of me, guiding my daily actions—the last two: keep a song in my heart, and go on God's errands.

I have earnestly sought God to keep His songs in my heart, and God has faithfully awakened me each day with a song. That song usually stays with me throughout the day, creating a witnessing atmosphere for me. This experience has become so meaningful that I go to bed each night looking forward to a new song from God each morning.

To please God is my greatest desire. I am privileged to work in a Christian university. I conduct my work with the consciousness that I am on God's errands. I consider my work a ministry. So, as I interact with faculty, students, and staff members, I make deliberate efforts to present Christ to each one. Many students have expressed appreciation for the spiritual refreshment received from those experiences. I have been blessed in return.

Why not keep a song in your heart today and go on God's errands?

Jacqueline Hope HoShing-Clarke

---

* "Aim/Motto/Pledge/Law," GC Youth Ministries Department, accessed December 14, 2015, http://gcyouthministries.org/Ministries/Pathfinders/AimMottoPledgeLaw.

Are You Prepared to Evacuate?

Wherefore let him that thinketh he standeth
take heed lest he fall.
—*1 Corinthians 10:12*

For days, the weather forecasters had warned of the coming of the perfect storm, which they nicknamed "Frankenstorm," as Hurricane Sandy was expected to make landfall on U.S. soil a few days before October 31, 2012. According to the meteorologists, several factors were whipping the weather system into a superstorm: the storm would hit during a full moon, and a projected rain-and-wind combination would result in a sea swell of six to eleven feet (between one and four meters) and also bring probable sleet due to the lateness of the fall season.

President Obama signed emergency declarations, and all governors, mayors, the National Guard, and emergency personnel went into disaster-preparedness mode. Bridges, tunnels, and schools were closed. Airplane flights in and out of three airports were canceled, and other transportation services were suspended, as was trading on Wall Street.

Then came the call for the mandatory evacuation of zone A, comprising areas near the coastline and waterways. Some residents on Fire Island in zone A evacuated, only to return on the next boat, stating that they did not believe the storm would be that bad. Other areas that should have been included in zone A were mistakenly assigned to zone B. Those residents believed that they were safe. Then the historic storm hit and washed their homes away, as it did boardwalks, amusement parks, and whole communities.

Hurricane Sandy (which some said should have been renamed Jezebel) was deemed the second costliest hurricane in U.S. history. It claimed 286 lives—not to mention leaving millions of customers without power for days.

The Bible tells us that another storm is soon to burst upon us. This entire world has been assigned to zone A. Ready or not, Jesus is coming. Like some of the Fire Island residents, many people don't believe they need to be in a preparation-and-evacuation mode. For them, Christ's return will come with a vengeance that this world has never before experienced.

Those, however, who choose to heed the warnings and prepare—through a personal relationship with Him—Jesus will keep "in the secret place of the most High" until He comes to rescue them (Psalm 91:1). May we each be prepared for the coming of the Perfect Storm.

Vashti Hinds-Vanier

Construction on the Road

And I will bring the third part through the fire, and will refine them
as silver is refined, and will try them as gold is tried:
they shall call on my name, and I will hear them: I will say,
It is my people: and they shall say, The LORD is my God.
—Zechariah 13:9

Driving home from work yesterday, I noticed, on both sides of the road, blocks of metal frames wrapped in orange fencing material every sixty-six feet (twenty meters) or so. In this residential neighborhood, I could hardly see through the construction-material eyesores into the front yards with the beautiful flowers. Holes had been dug in the sidewalks and piles of dirt scooped out.

What could possibly be happening? I wondered, wishing for the materials to be cleared away. My son soon informed me that cables for superfast broadband service were being laid. Since moving back into this particular house, my family had been frustrated at times with poor Internet and phone connectivity and were hoping for improved service. Now that was happening. Although I was glad that the work was now in progress, I wasn't willing to put up with the mess that the construction workers were creating along my drive home. I wanted things to be intact but also to have the cables laid—two opposite and impossible desires. I'd have to put up with the mess if I wanted better connections. The construction transition was messy, yet necessary.

Suddenly, it occurred to me that I had the same conflicting desires regarding my relationship with Jesus. I was content with the way I was although I knew improvement was needed. Though I wanted to be "fixed," I'm not sure I wanted the mess that the process would create in my life. I just wanted a magical transformation without the ugly dirt being pulled out and thrown away first. That would be painful, shameful, and tarnishing to my self-image.

I knew, however, that cables can't be laid without dirt first being removed to make room for the cables. This was also true in my spiritual life. Unless I allowed God to dig out the clutter in my life first, He couldn't clean up the receptors so that I could hear His Holy Spirit speak more clearly to my heart and have better communication with Him.

The construction site in our neighborhood got cleared up in a few days. The road no longer looks messy and ugly. And I thank God for the spiritual realization that He brought to me through that messy site.

Grace Paulson

All of Those Branches!

That person is like a tree planted by streams of water,
which yields its fruit in season and whose leaf does not wither—
whatever they do prospers.
—Psalm 1:3, NIV

In 1903, my husband's great-uncle, Roy, moved with his parents to what is now our farm. Among other things they needed a fence to corral their livestock. Uncle Roy chopped down green willow trees and cut them into the proper lengths for fence posts. After digging the holes, he put the posts into the ground, tamping the dirt firmly around them so they would stand erect. As time went by, the moisture in the ground encouraged the posts to sprout branches and leaves. Uncle Roy's fence row grew into great trees where birds nested and under which small animals found shade. Children built tree houses in their sturdy branches.

The years went by, and Uncle Roy and his parents moved to a nearby town. In 1924, the parents of Darrell, my husband, moved with their firstborn son to the farm. Darrell was born the next spring as the row of willows continued to grow.

Now, on a windy day, we are able to hear the trees, some of massive height, creaking as they sway to and fro. It is rather a comforting sound. However, with every windstorm some branches break and fall to the ground. They then need to be gathered and hauled away. Looking out at our historic willows, we are reminded of the continuity of our family and happily continue to remove the fallen branches. This past summer an extreme windstorm roared through our countryside. Looking out after the storm, we were saddened to see that the willows had taken a real beating. Some of the larger trees were broken off near the ground. Looking at the stumps, we saw how much the trees had deteriorated— from the center on out. Today the beautiful branches that once were thick and plenteous are no longer there. Our row of willows looks rather bedraggled. We need now, with patience, to allow them to keep growing. In years to come, they will once again regain their original beauty. It may takes years longer than we will have on this earth, but grow they will.

Am I like the willows? Do I break apart with every strong wind and leave remnants of my life scattered about, an outward beauty hiding the rottenness within? My prayer is that I will be true to the core and live a spiritual life that is as healthy inside as it appears on my outside.

Evelyn Glass

Turn On the Light

The light shines in the darkness,
and the darkness has not overcome it.
—John 1:5, NIV

I spent last summer at home alone. My husband was at summer camp serving as the youth pastor. My teenage daughter enjoyed summer camp and other places with family and friends. Most of the nights that summer I spent in my living room, sleeping on the couch and keeping my cell phone and a small light close to me.

Honestly, I do not like to be in darkness. Everything in the dark looks different and bigger than in the light. If you have children, or you remember your childhood, then you know that a chair can be a big monster; a table lamp, some hungry animal; and shadows from the window, wicked wizards. One night-light or candle can take away the darkness, but it doesn't illuminate every corner of the room—especially not under the bed. With light, a child can sleep in peace.

Even God doesn't like darkness. One of the first things He created, using only words, was light, from nothing. "And God said, 'Let there be light,' and there was light. God saw that the light was good" (Genesis 1:3, 4, NIV). God never said darkness was good. From the beginning, through the entire Bible, darkness has always been the personification of everything that is the opposite of God. On the other side, light has always been of service to God.

Sometimes, with all that is going on around us every day, our world seems a very dark place. In fact, whether we are witnesses or victims, there are moments when our lives can seem so dark, even outside in the daylight.

Through Jesus Christ, God illuminated our dark world with unquenchable brightness: "When Jesus spoke again to the people, he said, 'I am the light of the world. Whoever follows me will never walk in darkness; but will have the light of life' " (John 8:12, NIV).

Jesus did not say, "I can bring or turn on light for you." He is very clear in His statement when He says, "*I am* the light of the world, the light of life." Jesus is the Light of life. It is important to remember that the light of Jesus doesn't take away every shadow from our lives, but He can bring enough peace for the children of God to rest.

Never hesitate to turn on Jesus, the Light of life. Do it today, and do not worry about your electric bill because the light of life in Jesus Christ is free.

Aleksandra Tanurdzic

Fantasy Island

"And if I go and prepare a place for you, I will come again and receive you to Myself; that where I am, there you may be also."
—John 14:3, NKJV

One day at our school, I was looking at a series of seven paintings depicting the human story from Creation week to the earth made new. The series portrayed Jesus in different activities with different people. As I was drawn into the visual experience, I could almost feel His joy as He will finally get to show us around heaven. I recalled an old television show, *Fantasy Island,* in which a short guy would get excited and call out, "Da plane, boss! Da plane!" every time he saw the private jet approaching the island with new visitors. Just imagine Jesus getting excited as He sees the end approaching, calling out, "Our children, Father, Our children!"

On the television show, once the plane landed, groups of people were whisked off as the island's host somehow made their secret dreams come true. Heaven will beat that! We each have a picture of heaven and the things we will do when we get there. Jesus is waiting to have us home with Him. After we meet our Father, it's hard to imagine what has been planned for us. After all, we're told that He "is able to do immeasurably more than all we ask or imagine, according to his power that is at work within us" (Ephesians 3:20, NIV).

He may take some of us to the animal kingdom and explain the animals—what they like to do and their characteristics. In heaven, I want to learn so much more about animals.

A fantasy some may have of heaven is perhaps to travel the Milky Way and have Jesus explain how light travels, where it comes from, why it never fades, how the stars keep spinning, and what the white dust is that we now see from the earth in the sky. For others, gardening in heaven may be a deep desire. Jesus can show us how to grow things we never imagined down here. Heaven will be the perfect place for bird-watching and from which to visit other planets.

Whatever our desire for heaven, Jesus will more than fulfill it. The most important part of this whole story, however, is the *reality*—not the fantasy—that Jesus loved us so much He came to earth to die for us. He did this so that one day we can be with Him in heaven forever. And the Bible records this as the desire of His heart. Let's choose to be there with Him!

Beth Versteegh Odiyar

God's Stronghold

"When you pass through the waters, I will be with you;
And through the rivers, they shall not overflow you.
When you walk through the fire, you shall not be burned,
Nor shall the flame scorch you."
—*Isaiah 43:2, NKJV*

After my husband and I were married, the Mountain Provinces Mission in the northern Philippines employed us. Heading up the health and temperance departments, we were part of the annual medical mission and evangelism-outreach planning. One of these medical mission trips took us to a tribal territory. A former colleague had returned to her tribal home as a public-health nurse. Her passion for positive change in people's lives was the impetus for her interest in returning to her community. Most of the people in that community still remained cannibals, though their children were receiving an education. The medical team from two church hospitals and the mission team journeyed to this tribal community where my colleague lived. A Japanese medical student resident, Itsuo, was also on our team. My friend housed us inside a small church of a local denomination—the only place that had a toilet bowl. We girls squeezed into one room, and the men on the team squeezed into another. Outside we could hear the sound of people cutting sticks. This made us so scared. Then the medical director was hospitalized with abdominal pain. We all came under the impression that the local people were preparing to kill us. We all knelt down and began to pray, remembering that the local residents were cannibals!

At 2:00 A.M., a primipara woman (a woman who has had only one pregnancy) was brought to us in difficult labor. Itsuo, a nurse, and I laid her on a table. Itsuo was assessing the fetal presentation when we noticed a part of a scrotum protruding. This indicated a breech presentation. We prepared whatever supplies we had for delivery, believing in God's help as we held hands together and prayed for His intervention. An hour later the baby was born without any complications. It was a boy! Exhausted but excited and happy, the woman named the baby *Itsuo*. News spread very quickly around the village, giving us favor with the local people.

Great is God's stronghold through prayer. He is our Refuge and Fortress. He made us friends of former enemies. Holding to God's stronghold brought hearts into unity with Christ's messengers of the gospel. Stay in that stronghold today and experience God's power in your life.

Edna Bacate-Domingo

Worry

The LORD is my shepherd;
I have all that I need.
—*Psalm 23:1, NLT*

We worry—a lot. Every day we uncover something new to be anxious about, whether small or significant. The unknown intimidates us, so we worry about a whole range of things. At least, I do.

Though we all have legitimate concerns, God tells us that we have no need to worry.

What peace we could enjoy if we would take this to heart daily and believe it! But how can we submit our worries? It is so difficult to let go and let God take them. Yet He is our true Shepherd. He knows the path we are on and the path that is in our best interest. He genuinely cares for each one of us in a special way. God is *for* us! What joy is ours! Jesus urges us in Matthew 6:25, "Therefore I tell you, do not worry about your life, what you will eat or drink; or about your body, what you will wear. Is not life more important than food, and the body more than clothes?" (NIV). He points us to His care for the birds and assures us He will meet our needs as well. "Therefore do not worry about tomorrow," He says, "for tomorrow will worry about itself" (v. 34, NIV).

What a promise! What a gift! When we set our sights on God, we are focusing on One that is so far above any storm that life may bring, and we find peace—God's peace. He will not leave us to our own efforts. If we trust in Him with all our hearts and give each day to Him, He will carry us all the way. After all, God will not invite us to be part of His perfect plan without equipping us. We may not have everything we *want* in abundance, but we always have everything we need.

Worry makes us forget who is in control. When I focus on myself, I worry and become anxious. Over time, I put my agenda before God's agenda for me. I become more concerned with presenting self than pleasing Him. I may even find myself doubting God's judgment. This is a dangerous pitfall. Besides, God has freely and graciously given us talents. If we concern ourselves with those of others, we neglect our own. But if we concern ourselves with ours, we can inspire both.

We are invited to shed all of our worries and give them to Jesus. We can then more freely serve and live for Him. What a blessing! Will you make that choice today?

Taylor Bajic

Leap of Faith

Now faith is the assurance of things hoped for,
the conviction of things not seen.
—*Hebrews 11:1, NRSV*

Late one November afternoon our family decided to ice-skate. We pulled our skates from the cupboard under the stairs and ran down the hill as the snow turned pink, reflecting the brief Alberta sunset. Although our son had been skating at the rink in town, the ice had just recently formed on the lake. "It should be OK," my husband announced. "It's been cold for a week now."

I thought he was right, but I would have preferred waiting another week—just to make sure. Still, I laced up my skates and joined my husband and son on the lake. In the fading light, I studied the ice—several inches thick and crystal clear. I saw the frozen fronds of lake weeds and bubbles encased in ice. Then my son shouted, "Look at this, Mom!" Through the ice, we watched as a muskrat floated on its back with its nose next to a little mound of weeds pushed up to keep open a small breathing hole. Seeing us, it flipped over, pushed with its webbed feet, and shot away. We tried to follow its path, but the inch of light snow on much of the lake obscured its progress.

"C'mon, Dad. C'mon, Mom!" Garrick called as he sped down the lake. The snow flew as his skate blades flashed in the last of the daylight. We followed our son, laughing in the cold, cold air as we skated the length of the lake. How good it was to be alive, to exhale and have the condensation freeze on eyelashes, to stop suddenly and watch the snow arc up and drift down.

"There's soup on the stove. Let's get some," suggested my husband as we skated through the darkness. I skated more slowly, enjoying the quiet for a moment. And then I caught my breath. Just a few feet away I saw a large, dark circle, a place where there was no snow. Had it just blown away, or was there a hole in the ice? Would I be able to stop my gliding skates in time to avoid it? Or perhaps I should just trust—the three of us had skated for thirty minutes with absolutely no indication that the lake wasn't completely frozen.

And so, on that dark but star-filled night, I made a leap of faith. I breathed deeply, stoked strongly, and glided across hard, clear black ice.

The evidence is there that God loves us. Our leaps of faith will land us firm; we can glide into our future, secure that we are His.

Denise Dick Herr

It Only Takes a Little

In the same way, good deeds are obvious,
and even those that are not obvious
cannot remain hidden forever.
—*1 Timothy 5:25, NIV*

Tackling paperwork at my desk is one of my least enjoyable chores. So when I could no longer put it off, I promised myself I would work until finished and would allow nothing to stop me. I was just beginning to see some results when one of my eyelashes escaped and landed in my eye. I usually think of my eyelashes as a set, if I think of them at all. However, it took only one tiny eyelash to cause everything I was doing to come to a complete stop. That's when I decided that little didn't necessarily mean unimportant. Small things impact lives more than we realize.

Eve took one bite of forbidden fruit and changed the world forever. One little stone in David's sling killed a giant no one else could conquer. Esau ate one bowl of lentil stew and lost his birthright. One little boy gave Jesus his lunch, and the Lord used it to feed more than five thousand people.

God entrusts us with power to change lives by what we do or say, even in a small way.

With that privilege comes a responsibility.

Many of us can recall at least a time or two when someone said a kind word, we've read a Bible verse, heard a sermon, or received a compliment that lifted our spirits and changed our outlook from bleak to better.

Even when we have seemingly little to offer, we can combine our gifts or talents with those of others to make a positive difference.

Years ago when someone in our church family was having a difficult time with finances, individual members would help by paying a bill, buying medicine, offering gasoline money, and performing other kind acts. Sometimes that took quite a sacrifice on the part of one person. Then someone suggested that if each family that was able would contribute one dollar per month, those contributions could go into a fund to help church members in such emergencies. We called it the Church Family Fund. Although it has changed over time, with different families each adding just a little, it's still helping people today.

God will bless the smallest kindness because it glorifies Him.

Perhaps He wants us to remember that little doesn't necessarily mean unimportant.

Marcia Mollenkopf

The Kernel of God's Word

Trust in the LORD with all thine heart; and lean not
unto thine own understanding. In all thy ways acknowledge him,
and He shall direct thy paths.
—*Proverbs 3:5, 6*

He shall call upon me, and I will answer him:
I will be with him in trouble; I will deliver him, and honour him.
—*Psalm 91:15*

I often struggled with retaining throughout the day what I'd read in my morning devotionals. One Tuesday, September 17, the day's text was Proverbs 3:5, 6. I read it, phrase by phrase, and earnestly asked God to divinely fulfill the true meaning of His words in my entire life.

At work that day, a lady approached, asking if she could leave an application letter. I affirmed she could. One hour before closing, a valuable staff member gave notice of her departure—too far and too expensive to commute to work. I was stunned and sad but understood.

That evening I pled with God, "Please fulfill Proverbs 3:5, 6 in my life and this work situation." The next morning's devotional text was Psalm 91:15. I did call upon God and was later impressed to open the application letter from the previous day. When I did, I was surprised to learn the woman was better qualified than the outgoing staff member. And she lived within walking distance. I praised the Lord and continued prayerfully to chew on these texts with their invitations and promises from our most understanding heavenly Father. He asks me to acknowledge Him in all my ways, and He will direct my path. So I pressed Him a little more.

For seven days, I tried to make contact with my aunt battling cancer. On the seventh day, I told God about my deep desire to speak to her. The connection was made. What a God!

On Friday, I was still contemplating the two devotional texts. As an entrepreneur, I evaluate monthly operational costs and then assign a value of minimum daily sales. Fridays are short days; achieving this target is harder. "*Please*, God, do this for us." At twenty-seven minutes to closing, the Lord did!

I am learning to stress less and to prayerfully, humbly, trust in—and call on—Him. For many years, I'd failed to eat the kernel of God's Word. How about you? In what ways can you trust God more? Have you cried to Him lately?

Keisha D. Sterling

"They" Are Following Me!

For I am not alone.
—John 8:16

Have you ever had one of those days where every fiber of your being aches from the challenges of the day? I recently experienced such a day. Exhaustion consumed me. Stress subdued my smile. Words took too much energy, and I could only sigh in relief that the day was finally over. As I was coming out of the building, I was greeted with a "Praise the Lord" from a gentleman whose endless energy brightens any day. Reading my face, he stopped me and said, "You know what I tell people? I tell them 'they' are following me." I was baffled.

What on earth is he talking about? I wondered. *Is he seeing things?* When he revealed *what* was following him, I could only praise the Lord with him!

The good news is that "they" are following each of us just like they followed those whose stories in the Bible inspire us with possibilities. "They" followed Mary Magdalene. She was the first to see Jesus after His resurrection. Paul persecuted Christians, but "they" were following him too. That is why he is known as the greatest preacher that ever lived. Rahab, a harlot, is listed in the genealogy of Jesus. Noah got drunk soon after being delivered from the Flood. David committed adultery and murder, yet was a man after God's own heart. These individuals were all being followed by "them." So are we. What is it that possesses such power in our lives on this Christian journey?

In the words of the gentleman that greeted me, the "they" that follow all of us are grace and mercy! Mercy does not render the punishment I deserve for my sins, and grace blesses me in spite of the fact I don't deserve the Savior's blessings. We are living this moment because of grace and mercy. What a mighty God we serve!

In the darkest times of our lives, when we feel forgotten and alone, grace and mercy are following us. When we feel like we have failed miserably, grace and mercy are lifting us. When illnesses consume our bodies, grace and mercy comfort us. Whatever our plight, grace and mercy assure us victorious lives in Jesus! Thank the Lord that "they" are following us. Be encouraged!

"Surely goodness and mercy shall follow me all the days of my life, and I shall dwell in the house of the LORD my whole life long" (Psalm 23:6, NRSV).

Deborah M. Harris

Praying in the Supermarket

Who comforts us in all our troubles,
so that we can comfort those in any trouble
with the comfort we ourselves receive from God.
—*2 Corinthians 1:4, NIV*

My favorite time of the day to do grocery shopping is early afternoon when the supermarket is quiet. One day while standing in the frozen goods section checking my shopping list, someone came around the corner and the person's cart bumped into me. I looked to see what was happening and saw a distraught young woman who began apologizing profusely. She asked if I'd been hurt, and I assured her I was all right and asked if she was all right. Quietly she said, "This is not my day. Things just are not going right." Then she went on to explain that she had lost her mother a few months earlier and some days were difficult for her. "Some days I'm fine; then other days the grief is unbearable." Her eyes welled up with tears as I told her I was so sorry. She continued, "My siblings are not very understanding of my feelings and tell me to get over it."

Quietly I said to her, "I understand what you are going through." I explained to her that I, too, had lost my mother sometime before and understood how unpredictable those feelings could be. Her response was one of relief that someone understood.

Then I felt impressed to tell her about Someone else who understands all we are experiencing, and asked if it would be all right for me to do so. She agreed and briefly I shared with her some thoughts about Jesus and how much He cares about us. Then, standing there in the supermarket (and grateful it was still quiet), I prayed for her comfort. She expressed her thanks for my understanding and intervention and said she felt much better. We wished each other a good afternoon and continued our shopping.

She completed her checkout transaction and left the store before I did, but when I came out, she was sitting in her car. She called out to me and asked if she could take me to my home. Because I live three-quarters of a block from the supermarket, she would have to drive around three blocks to get to my place. I thanked her and said I would walk.

That day I thought of the many people who are walking around with aching hearts and prayed, *Dear Lord, help me to come in contact with some of these people, so I can share Your love and be a blessing.* Will you join me in this endeavor?

Maureen O. Burke

Missing Passport

And all things, whatsoever ye shall ask in prayer,
believing, ye shall receive.
—*Matthew 21:22*

After putting all four of our kids through college, I convinced my husband to go with me on a no-hurry, no-planned-itinerary European tour. We would just go where destiny led us and accumulate memories we could treasure for a lifetime. We decided to invite our friend who was the best man at our wedding and his wife to join us in this adventure. We met at Heathrow Airport in London. From there, we boarded a Eurostar train that took us overnight to Paris. We visited the Eiffel Tower and other famous romantic sites in France, Belgium, and Switzerland.

I have a cousin living in Bonn, Germany, who invited us to visit with her family. They took us around to must-see places for tourists, and we experienced firsthand local customs and traditions. We were really impressed with German discipline, work ethic, and the modern infrastructure that they enjoy.

My cousin convinced us to go to Rome and visit the Vatican. Early the following morning we were up and ready for a new day's adventure. My niece suggested I carry, instead of my large handbag, a smaller one for safety and security reasons. After hours of sightseeing, we boarded the train, where we would sleep overnight. It would arrive in Rome the following morning. As soon as we got settled in our stateroom, the conductor came around, inspecting our tickets and passports. Frantically searching for my passport in my bag, I just could not find it. Then I remembered it was in my large handbag that I had left in Germany. The conductor was not amused and just snorted that Italian immigration may not let me in without a passport. That night I prayed, fervently claiming the promise that whatever we ask in prayer, believing, we shall receive. I asked God to give me a good night's sleep and that all would go well the following day. The next morning at the train station Roman immigration officials swarmed into assigned sections of the train to inspect passengers' documents. For some reason, our immigration inspector just passed me by and motioned us to pass through.

That experience strengthened my resolve to commit my ways to God and to believe that, if we are faithful to Him, He is faithful and just to deliver on His promises.

Zeny Marcelo

A Parallel

And unto the angel of the church of the Laodiceans write;
. . . I know thy works, that thou art neither cold nor hot:
I would thou wert cold or hot.
—Revelation 3:14, 15

Does anybody remember cold winters during the so-called good ol' days on the farm with no electricity and no central heating system? The potbelly stove, along with the kitchen cookstove, supplied heat during the day, but at night heated bricks were prepared to warm cold beds. Last winter I dressed in layers within the confines of my home when the temperature dipped below zero for many days and nights. Recorded temperatures in our area revealed we were experiencing the tenth coldest winter on record. The snowpack made it seem even colder. *Brrr!* The winter blues set in before I even recognized what was happening. The glistening snow was beautiful, especially when I looked out the window, observed the evergreens laden with white, and witnessed a brilliant red bird perched on a branch. God's nature is amazing, but the beauty of it all was not enough to satisfy my insipid state of mind. Even my craft room, laden with unfinished winter projects, no longer captured my interest. My warm bed seemed to be my only consoling factor.

A *Missouri Conservationist* magazine arrived the day that I felt most vulnerable to the winter blahs. The magazine always provided a nature cartoon. The January edition was no exception. I quickly located the cartoon and laughed out loud as I identified myself in its hilarity. It pictured two rabbits. One stood at the bedroom door, and the other rabbit stirred in bed with a very sleepy face that seemed to reflect the sentiment "do not disturb until spring." The caption read, "Rabbits don't hibernate. You're just lazy!" I giggled with amusement as the rabbits paralleled my dilemma and alerted me that I was leaning toward a hibernation outlook.

Silly? Yes, but when I reworded the caption, it brought me back to reality: "Humans don't hibernate. Your desires are reminiscent of Laodicea." At that time, my church was studying the book of Revelation at our midweek services. The Laodicean mind-set, a disease of the church, wants things comfortable and safe. But this lukewarm state can be overcome.

A personal relationship with Jesus, who stands at the heart's door and knocks, is the solution. Let's open the door and let Him in. Jesus will heal our maladies if we ask in faith.

Retha McCarty

The Sparrow

"So don't be afraid;
you are worth more
than many sparrows."
—Matthew 10:31, NIV

I was feeling unusually low that morning. I had some financial hardships and work challenges that seemed to be insurmountable. I had just started my morning devotional, hoping that God would speak to me and provide me with strength and comfort to take away my doubt and fear.

Suddenly, I heard a loud thud.

A bird had flown into my sunroom window. I quickly ran to the window to look for the bird. I saw a small sparrow that had fallen on to the deck just outside the window. It was just sitting there, looking stunned, and appeared nearly dead. I immediately prayed to God to take care of this innocent sparrow, to help it recover, and then to enable it to fly away and join the other sparrows in my yard.

Though I went back to continue my devotional reading, I frequently felt compelled to return to the window to see if the sparrow was still there. I found it difficult to focus on that day's devotional topic of God's forgiveness while I worried about my newfound feathered friend.

And then I noticed—no, it wasn't right away but within half an hour—the sparrow opened its eyes, stood upright, and, incredibly, flew off as if nothing had happened. I was amazed by this simple example of God's love and care for one of the smallest of His creatures.

This incident made me think of the words to the song "His Eye Is on the Sparrow."* That song asks why we should be discouraged when we encounter difficulties. After all, if God notices a sparrow, He certainly notices us. God tells us in His Word that not one sparrow falls without His knowledge and that we are of much greater value than many sparrows (Matthew 10:29–31).

That morning God showed me He cared for a small sparrow and that I could be confident He was going to take care of me and provide for all my needs. If we put our trust in Him, He will take away all doubt and fear. He will assuredly provide us with strength for whatever we are facing. We can be certain that He is watching over us and that He cares for us every day.

---

* Civilla D. Martin, "His Eye Is on the Sparrow," 1905.

Karen Welch Dobbin

A Shelter in the Time of Storm

He guides the humble in what is right
and teaches them his way.
—*Psalm 25:9, NIV*

On April 24, 2014, I sent a cell phone message to my friend Elsa about bringing her some food items. The sky was bright and clear as I went downstairs in the elevator.

When I reached the ground floor, rain was falling. I went back upstairs and got an umbrella. Again on the ground floor I saw that the thunderstorm was unexpectedly heavy with rainfall. I informed Elsa that I would not turn up at her place. I walked a longer route toward a hawker center, an open-air complex where food is cooked and sold from vendor stalls.

On my way to the hawker center, the rain gradually lightened. Finally, I reached the complex and ordered my vegetarian meal. As I was about to take my seat, there was another heavy downpour with thunder. When I sat down, protected from the storm, I remembered a song, "A Shelter in the Time of Storm."* The song reminded me that the Lord is my Rock and Shelter "in the time of storm."

When the food was served, I took my time munching my meal. I sent another message to Elsa about going to her place. After my meal, I went home to get the food items for Elsa. At first, I wanted to use a shorter route, but it was still raining. I remembered the intensity of the heavy rain and thunderstorms, so I took the longer route.

On the way to Elsa's place, I saw a lady carrying her eighteen-month-old toddler. A baby carriage was in front of her. A few ladies with umbrellas passed her by. The young mother seemed to be waiting for someone. She asked me, "Could we shelter under your umbrella for just three blocks?" Of course, they could. We had a brief chat on our walk together.

When she reached her destination, she thanked me. I said, "You're welcome!" Then I added, "You are fortunate that I decided to change my route today."

"God bless," she called as we parted ways. After I reached Elsa's place and gave her the food items, the rain stopped. My mission accomplished, I remembered how important it is to trust and obey. Romans 8:28 says that "God works for the good of those who love him" (NIV).

That day He had not only sheltered me but had also guided my steps so I could provide shelter for a young mother in distress. Truly "He guides the humble in what is right" (Psalm 25:9, NIV).

---

* Vernon J. Charlesworth, "A Shelter in the Time of Storm," ca. 1880. Yan Siew Ghiang

Finishing Strong—Part 1

Speak encouraging words to one another.
Build up hope so you'll all be together in this,
no one left out, no one left behind.
I know you're already doing this; just keep on doing it.
—1 Thessalonians 5:11, The Message

The annual Turkey Bowl, which occurs at a local Christian camp, is becoming a family tradition. Each year I join my sister-in-law, Melissa; her daughter, Kaleigh; and my cousin, Pam, in running it on Thanksgiving morning. It's not the only five-kilometer (5K) run the four of us do together during the year, but it is the coldest. And this year there were several inches of snow on the ground. The course is hilly in spots. Some of those spots quickly became muddy as several hundred people ran through them on their quest to finish the race.

I wasn't running the race for a fast time. My goal was to run with Melissa across the finish line. She wants to run and wants to finish strong. But between work and kids and school, training is just hard to manage. So I determined to push her, affirm her, encourage her, and not let her quit. While Kaleigh and Pam ran on ahead, Melissa and I made steady progress toward the goal.

There were several other women running right around us. Sometimes they'd pass. Other times we'd pass them. I attempted to speak words of encouragement and affirmation to each of them. One young woman stood out. When we'd slow to a walk to allow Melissa to catch her breath, she'd run and pass us. Once ahead of us she'd need to walk and catch her breath. Then we'd pass her. As we began our last mile, we were running next to her. As I talked to her, I learned that her name was Serena and this was her first 5K. Friends had encouraged her to run, but they had run ahead and left her behind. She was a young mom with a toddler and baby at home, and she was struggling to finish. I encouraged her to finish with us. We'd walk up the last hill, then run strong to the finish—just one-tenth of a mile downhill all the way. Another woman, Diana, joined our growing group as I encouraged her to pace with us and finish strong.

Pam and Kaleigh were waiting as we began our ascent up the last hill. They'd finished and were coming back to run us in. Together the six of us climbed our last hill and began our descent. I encouraged everyone to run and finish strong, "It's all downhill from here!"

Today, draw at least one person who is struggling in life's race into your supportive circle.

Tamyra Horst

Finishing Strong—Part 2

So encourage each other and build each other up,
just as you are already doing.
—*1 Thessalonians 5:11, NLT*

With three other women from my family, I was participating in the annual five-kilometer Turkey Bowl at our local Christian camp. My goal was to run with Melissa, my sister-in-law, across the finish line. Diana and Serena, a young mother, had fallen in with our group. My niece, Kaleigh, and my cousin, Pam, had already finished but had returned to run us in. Now we were beginning our descent down the last hill toward the finish line.

I ran every step next to Serena. She was going strong. Then halfway down the hill, she lost her fight and wanted to quit and walk. "We're almost there! You've got this! You can do this! The finish is just around that corner!"

"I feel nauseated. I can't do this," she cried as she almost slowed to a stop.

"No, you've got this! Your friends are just round the corner; let's run in together!" The words of encouragement seemed to give her the strength she needed. We began running again. We passed two more runners as I called out words of encouragement to each of them. "Good job! You've got this! Finish strong!"

The crowds near the finish line began cheering for us as well. "You're almost there! You're almost there!" We finished strong. Friends surrounded Serena, hugging her and cheering for her. One thanked me for running her in.

As I thought about the race later, I realized how much like life it is. We're all running. There are days when we just don't think we can go any farther, days when we want to give up. Quit. Sometimes even when the finish line is just around the corner. God knew there would be days like this. He never created us to run the race alone. He calls us to encourage one another and build each other up. "Speak encouraging words to one another. Build up hope so you'll all be together in this, no one left out, no one left behind" (1 Thessalonians 5:11, *The Message*). No one left behind. How? By speaking encouraging words. By building up hope in each other. By running together.

Look around. Who's running near you? What words of hope and encouragement can you offer them today?

Tamyra Horst

Daily Thanksgiving

Give thanks in all circumstances;
for this is the will of God in Christ Jesus for you.
—*1 Thessalonians 5:18, ESV*

I was at a worship meeting, and the topic of the day was thanksgiving. The speaker asked whether we had ever just jotted down the things we were thankful for, and challenged us to try to think of a thousand things or situations for which we were thankful. I thought, *Wow! That will take a lot of pages! Where can I start?*

A thought occurred to me: *I'll start from my head to my feet. So thank You, Lord, that I had this thought. This is number one on my list. But then, not really. If I hadn't come to the meeting, I wouldn't be thinking about things for which I'm thankful. But that's not number one either. If I didn't have a job, I wouldn't have had the privilege of attending this meeting. Ah, but if my parents hadn't sent me to school, I wouldn't have my job. If my grandparents hadn't instilled the importance of education in the minds of my parents . . . And if . . .*

I concluded that truly every breath, every second, and every moment bring a lot of things to be thankful for. A list of a thousand thankful thoughts would be just the beginning because, if we take the time to open our hearts and explore with our minds the blessings for which we are thankful, the list is endless.

As I went through the exercise of jotting down things for which I was thankful, it gave me an opportunity to think of how great and awesome God is.

Every situation, every experience, every detail, and every person that I could think of gave me countless reasons to be thankful. Even those situations or experiences that were not very pleasant gave me reasons to be thankful, and I had to smile. "Give thanks in all circumstances; for this is the will of God in Christ Jesus for you" (1 Thessalonians 5:18, ESV).

Now I understand better why it is the will of the Lord for us to exercise thankfulness. It is not for Him to feel good. Rather, it is for us to feel His closeness. It is for us to feel loved and to know how rich our lives are because He is there.

So let our thanksgiving be a daily thanksgiving.

Jemima Dollosa Orillosa

A Relay Race

Wherefore seeing we also are compassed about
with so great a cloud of witnesses, let us lay aside every weight,
and the sin which doth so easily beset us,
and let us run with patience the race that is set before us.
—Hebrews 12:1

As I was handing out church bulletins one Sabbath morning, I heard children's voices from one of the classes singing, "When the sun goes down on Friday, it's Sabbath." That started me thinking about how all the children, in their Bible study classes, are still singing the same songs that we used to sing when I was a child.

This reminded me of a relay race where each team member runs in only one designated part of the race. Several members make up each team, but only one baton is passed from team member to team member during the race.

The song and its message, which I heard the children sing, are like a baton that is passed from one generation to another. This passing on of the legacy of faith will not end until this life's race is done and Jesus comes.

Proclaiming the gospel message is very important. Along with that come other important responsibilities. For example, how is a person who spreads the message living and planning her life? Children observe their parents and families to learn how to structure their lives. If the older generation doesn't model living the message, what will the children have to pass on when the time comes for them to spread the message? If the lifestyle and choices of the older generation show children they are living for things, instead of for the hope of eternal life, what will the children have to pass on to the generation after them?

We need to bless our children and pass on to them a strong faith in the hope that Jesus is coming to save them.

We need to pass on God's promises in the Bible and the assurance that He will not let us down. Sing their songs with them. Pray with them. Love them as Jesus does. Prepare them to run well in the relay race of eternal life.

Then many others will have the opportunity to be prepared as well.

Donna Sherrill Lewis

Comfort Blankets

"Blessed are those who mourn,
for they will be comforted."
—Matthew 5:4, NIV

When you're feeling really sad, what's the best thing I can do to comfort you?" I asked each of my children.

"Make me a big mug of hot chocolate with whipped cream and chocolate sprinkles!" "Just listen to me, and then give me a big hug." "Give me a really good back rub!"

"And what about you? What do you like when you're sad?" my daughter asked.

"Let me think. A bit of extra help, a hug, doing something fun, having someone pray for me. But usually I just imagine I am sitting in God's lap, and He is giving me the biggest hug ever, and His tears are all mixed up with mine. I pretend I am lying against His chest, and I can hear His heart beating with love for me and everyone else in the whole world."

As a family therapist, I often see families who are going through really difficult times. Everyone is feeling sad, and sometimes lonely, because no one has the emotional energy to comfort anyone else. So we make "comfort blankets." Each person in the family has a stack of paper squares, and each person's squares are a different color. Everyone writes on their colored squares some of the ways they like to be comforted. Then we stick them all on to a large sheet of flip chart paper to make a poster they can take home. Hopefully, it will remind them to comfort each other in the ways the other person most appreciates. We also talk about the things people do that leave us feeling *more* sad and alone—talking about their own problems, criticizing us for not being more positive, not really listening when we tell them what we're experiencing.

Who are the people you know that may be going through a sad time right now? What could you do that would be comforting? Listening with a warm, understanding heart; being sad with them (Romans 12:15); making some meals for their freezer; taking them out for the day; doing something with them that they enjoy; sending a card; or calling them up. What would you write on your own comfort blanket? What are the Bible verses and stories that comfort and encourage you? How can you let other people know how to help you to feel happier and less alone?

Dear Father, please help me to share the comfort You have given me with another person who needs to experience Your love and comfort today. Amen.

Karen Holford

The Gray Refrigerator

"Before they call I will answer;
while they are still speaking I will hear."
—Isaiah 65:24, NIV

We built our home twenty years ago when most cabinets came in varying shades of brown, but we wanted ours to be gray. The people who installed the cabinets were surprised at how well the gray cabinets, baseboards, and wooden doors looked when finished. When we went looking for a refrigerator that would blend with our gray cabinets, we found nothing. So we painted our refrigerator gray.

After many years, our refrigerator suddenly quit working one day. Buying a new one would not only be expensive, but we would never be able to have it painted. We needed to find some color that would work as well as possible with our kitchen color scheme. At the appliance store, we selected a refrigerator, which we were not terribly excited about because it was our only option. On the scheduled day, our new refrigerator was delivered. The plan had been for the deliverymen to remove our old refrigerator and dispose of it.

At the time of the delivery, a television satellite repairman, a friend of ours, was working on our Christian television satellite system in the kitchen. He was there when the deliverymen took out the old gray refrigerator and plugged in the new one—which didn't work! How strange!

Our repairman friend suggested that a switch may have been thrown in the fuse box. Sometimes one will automatically shut off if water gets near it. A tiny switch also can be turned off when trying to plug in something else. And, yes, the switch had gotten turned off. When we switched it on, the new refrigerator came alive.

"Do you suppose," someone asked, "that the same switch might have gotten shut off *before* the old refrigerator stopped working? If so, then the old gray refrigerator might still work."

Once again the deliverymen went into action. They removed the new refrigerator, brought the gray one in from their truck, and plugged it in. It hummed to life!

Isn't it amazing how God works through situations of everyday life for our benefit? If our repairman friend hadn't been there, we might not have thought to check in the fuse box and then be spared the expense of a new refrigerator. God answered a prayer I hadn't even prayed.

Lana Fletcher

Twenty Strokes for Worshiping

In God is my salvation and my glory;
The rock of my strength,
And my refuge, is in God.
Trust in Him at all times, you people;
Pour out your heart before Him,
God is a refuge for us. Selah.
—*Psalm 62:7, 8, NKJV*

A friend of mine got married in 1999. With the first love of newlyweds, she and her husband met day-to-day challenges. Eventually, they were blessed with four children. Unfortunately, her husband was a drinker, and the stress of raising four children gradually caused his drinking to increase. In addition, he began to beat her: twenty strokes with a cane every night that she attended church, a seminar, or a church meeting.

My friend gave her life to Jesus and was baptized in 2003. As she grew in Christ, she was eventually chosen to be a children's teacher in her local church. This responsibility she accepted despite the twenty strokes with a cane every Sabbath night.

And so it went for my friend for years: attend a church meeting, and get twenty strokes with a cane. In April 2012, my friend decided to attend a children's ministries teachers' convention. One of the sessions was about the power of prayer and how God works miracles through prayer.

So my friend started praying for her husband to stop beating her and to cease his drinking.

When she went back home after the convention, she received her usual twenty strokes with a cane. This time, however, the beating ignited in her a sense of urgency to never miss any kind of church gathering, despite the persecution.

In December 2012, she went to a women's ministries congress and joined other women in prayer bands. There she gave her testimony, and all the women began praying for her. A year later this woman's husband reduced the twenty strokes to sixteen strokes a beating. Eventually, he reduced his drinking and stopped beating her completely.

In January 2013, the man was baptized. His wife is now free to worship and attend church services without any fear of punishment.

God remains my Refuge and yours, an ever-present help in trouble.

Debbie Maloba

Stain

"Though your sins are like scarlet,
they shall be as white as snow."
—Isaiah 1:18, NIV

Ohio can have harsh winters, and this past winter was no exception. Salt had to be sprinkled, almost daily, on roads and walkways to make them safe. The salt helps to melt the snow, but it can leave a stain of chalky residue on surfaces. If you have ever rubbed up against your car in the winter and discovered salty residue on your clothes, then you know what I am talking about.

One winter morning, with my hands full, I picked up the newspaper, which was delivered in a plastic bag to protect it from the elements, and added it to the rest of the stuff in my arms. When I got ready to leave work that day, I put on my black coat and noticed a white substance all over my coat. I had errands to run before I went home and did not want to go into the store looking like a mess. So I grabbed my purse and lunch bag and headed to the restroom to remove the salt stains.

After wetting a few paper towels, I started wiping my coat off, but it seemed that after cleaning one spot, another would appear. Then I noticed that my black purse had white stains on it also. I grabbed more paper towels and started cleaning them off. *Oh, no, more stains on my lunch bag also! Where did this all come from?*

From the newspaper! Yes, it had been shielded from the elements. Little did I know, however, that when I picked it up that morning, its plastic sleeve must have been stepped on earlier by someone with the slushy salt mixture on his or her shoes. Then the salty slush transferred to my clothes and belongings when I touched it. Earlier that morning the stain from the residue was not visible. As the day went on, though, it dried and became unsightly.

As I was vigorously scrubbing my coat, purse, and lunch bag in the restroom, I thought about sin and how it rubs off on our lives. Though sometimes unnoticed at first, sin is sure to leave a stain unless daily prayer and communion with our heavenly Father scrub it out.

Lord Jesus, I pray that You will wash me and make me whiter than snow.

Angèle Peterson

Little Becomes Much

And when he had taken the five loaves and the two fishes,
he looked up to heaven, and blessed, and brake the loaves,
and gave them to his disciples to set before them;
and the two fishes divided he among them all.
—Mark 6:41

It's snowing here today. The soft white substance looks beautiful on my patio, covering the furniture, ground, and plants that have hibernated for the season. It's delightful seeing this winter wonderland come to life right before my eyes. Sitting in my sunroom, I get an excellent view of God's handiwork in nature. Looking at the sight from a warm shelter feels wonderful. But out there somewhere are many who have no such luxury. They may be under a bridge or maybe in a mall or store trying to stay warm as long as possible before braving the cold. What does God expect us to do with so many homeless people?

That's the question the disciples asked when faced with feeding five thousand men, plus women and children. Instead of sending the people away, Jesus commanded the disciples to feed them. With what? Five barley loaves and two fish? Yes, with five barley loaves and two fish—and the blessing of God the Father. So the disciples took what they had, Jesus asked God to bless it, and all were fed.

In Acts 2, the people faced a similar challenge. The Word says that everyone had things in common, and they sold their possessions so that no one lacked anything. They, too, took what they had, and God blessed it so that everyone was taken care of. I know the Word of God says we have the poor with us always, but sometimes that is used as a cop-out to neglect doing something for others (Mark 14:7). As Christians, we have a responsibility to bear one another's burdens and so fulfill the law (Galatians 6:2). It has to be more than giving a beggar a dollar or so at a stop sign.

As I contemplate these truths, I ask God to show me ways I can do more for those in need, both those who are homeless and those destitute of the Word of God.

Father God, help us to feel the burden of those around us and offer what we have. We know You will multiply it to meet the needs of Your children under the bridge, in prison, and in our communities. In meeting their needs, we show them Your love and invite them to become heirs with us. Thank You that little becomes much when we use it to help and win others for You.

Shirley P. Scott

Taking Care of Daddy

For the Lord Himself will descend from heaven with a shout. . . .
And the dead in Christ will rise first.
—1 Thessalonians 4:16, NKJV

My father had been very ill and was now leaving the hospital. "When an older person is this sick, their brain takes a real chemical hit," his doctor told us. "Your father will be different, but he will still be your father." She added that he must have twenty-four-hour care. He and my unmarried sister shared a house, but she worked full time, as I did, so we would have to find daytime care for him. He had a horror of nursing homes, so that would be our last option.

That's when our daughter Noelle and our son stepped in. Both were out of school, and both lived at home. Noelle said she could quit her job to take care of Poppie, while our son, who worked from home, said he would help too.

And that's how Daddy came to spend the last months of his life with us. He was ninety-one and until then had been in fairly good health. In fact, he had started cooking, and his specialties were homemade vegetable soup and potato salad. The soup was every bit as good as Grandmother's had been, and his potato salad even better than my mother's, for he added tiny bits of raw garlic.

Home health care came on a regular basis, as did someone to help with his personal care. Noelle was his main support and worked hard to make meals he would enjoy while our son helped in other ways. With the passing months, Daddy grew weaker. He ate a little less. His steps were uncertain. It took more effort to get him in and out of bed.

Early one morning our doorbell rang. Puzzled, I ran downstairs to open the door. It was our youngest daughter. "Bronwen! What are you doing here?" I asked, tears in my eyes.

"I just decided to come." She had finished her night shift (she's a registered nurse), had her car serviced, took a nap, and then hit the road. It was six hundred miles from her place to ours. She'd spent a few hours sleeping in a motel and then driven on in. We were *so* happy to see her. Early the next day I came down to check on Daddy. "How does he look to you?" she asked. "He looks like a man dying." She nodded a "to me too." Less than twenty-four hours later, with most of his family around him, he drew his last breath. During his last moments, we were singing to him. As Dad fell asleep in Jesus, Noelle said, "We sang him to God."

Penny Estes Wheeler

343

December 2

Wait on the Lord

Your eyes saw my unformed body;
all the days ordained for me were written in your book
before one of them came to be.
—*Psalm 139:16, NIV*

You saw my unformed body inside the womb. You knew how long I would live even before I was born. Unlike us, God doesn't wake up one morning, is surprised, and says, "Oh, Pat Everson has cancer: What am I going to do?"

In 1974, I started a job that I worked for the next thirty-three years. My little girl born during that time grew up. Upon graduating from medical school, she met and married the son of one of the top cardiovascular surgeons in the state of Nevada, going into practice with her father-in-law.

In September 2013, I had what I thought was a bad cold and called the doctor's office to make an appointment. No doctor appointments were available, and I opted to see a physician assistant. She gave me a round of steroids and antibiotics. One week later I was no better, so she gave me a stronger dose. She suddenly decided to send me for a chest X-ray. It showed a mass on my right lung. *"Be still, and know that I am God,"* my heart and head cried out (Psalm 46:10, NIV). In October, I was sent for a CAT scan. The mass was confirmed and appeared to be cancer. *"Wait, I say, on the LORD"* (Psalm 27:14). In November, I was sent for a PET scan. "Yes, the mass is cancer, but we just don't know what kind." Again I comforted myself with, *"Be still, and know that I am God."* In December, I went for a breathing test to determine if my heart and lungs were strong enough for another test. All test results were sent to my little girl, now grown up and eighteen years into an established practice. I went to see her. She confirmed that I indeed had cancer and wanted to go straight for surgery because the needle biopsy would be too dangerous. Still it was not certain what kind of cancer I had. No, I did not pursue a second opinion. *"Be still,"* my heart continued to cry out.

So I underwent surgery on the day God had ordained—according to His plan—before I even existed. And I survived. I learned my cancer was common to nonsmokers, very slow growing, and concentrated in the upper lobe of my right lung. The entire lobe was removed and there was no need for chemotherapy or radiation. I thank God for strength to overcome challenges in every area of my life. I know that He has equipped me with everything that I need for health of mind, body, and spirit—including my doctor.

Pat Everson

G'bye Pawade

Accept one another, then, just as Christ accepted you,
in order to bring praise to God.
—Romans 15:7, NIV

E ach year in early December both hospitals in our area put on the annual Christmas lights parade. Hundreds of people gather to watch the procession march past in the early evening. My young friend Gracie told me that she took her two-year-old to see the parade for the first time. The little girl loved everything about the show: the multicolored lights, the floats, the marching band, the costumed people, the animals, and the candy. When they had to leave before the huge crowd dispersed, the young child turned around and whispered softly in her baby voice, "G'bye, pawade."

That same evening a middle-aged friend paid me the visit that we'd scheduled earlier. "It took forever to get here," she explained apologetically. "I had to make several detours because of the parade. But I'm so glad I missed the blaring sounds of the band because my head used to ache each time it passed."

Contrasting the poignant farewell of the little child with the displeasure of my older friend sent my thoughts swirling. Both parties had totally different perspectives on the same event due, I suspect, to the differences of human nature, life stages, tastes, attitudes, and perceptions, which were poles apart. How we deal with situations and other people, however, is a personal choice and often dependent on our backgrounds. Ellen G. White addressed this more than a century ago when she wrote, "We differ so widely in disposition, habits, education, that our ways of looking at things vary. We judge differently. . . . There are no two whose experience is alike in every particular. The trials of one are not the trials of another."*

The next day, as if a Spirit-inspired reiteration, I got a card with today's text embossed on the cover. It reminded me that the best way to handle the differences we face is by accepting the fact that we are different. A tolerant attitude motivates us to show love, and that, in turn, moves us to praise God. It's a beautiful God-powered cycle of love and acceptance.

Thank You, loving Lord, for reminding us all that our purpose in life is showing the world through our love how great You are. You have the last word, and I praise You.

Glenda-mae Greene

---

* Ellen G. White, *The Ministry of Healing* (Washington, DC: Review and Herald®, 1905), 483.

December 4

Secret Enemies and Trust

Trust in the LORD forever, for the LORD,
the LORD himself, is the Rock eternal.
—*Isaiah 26:4, NIV*

One Christmas we played a game called "secret enemy." Everyone brings a present appropriate for either a man or woman. The presents are placed together. The individual who begins the game chooses any present and reveals who his or her "secret enemy" is. Then this person selects a gift and gives another name. In this particular game, a person opening a present he or she doesn't like can exchange it with another present that someone else has already opened—whether the other individual wants to or not. This rule in the game generates many interesting situations.

For example, I received a nice tray with bread figurines. However, I noticed my father had just opened a raw cotton rug with a fish painted on it. The rug was lovely. I was tempted to exchange my tray for his rug. In fact, I told him this. Then he stated, "If I were you, I wouldn't make the exchange."

For a second, I thought about ignoring his advice, but then another thought crossed my mind. I almost never did what my father suggested, except in professional areas. *Perhaps he knows something that I don't,* I thought. Reluctantly, I accepted his suggestion.

At the end of the game, my father called me and said, "Because you decided to accept my advice, I am going to give you the rug."

I was speechless. My father did not realize the tremendous lesson that he had just provided for me. However, the enormity of my new discovery terrified me: when I need to make important life decisions, I am not able to believe that other people have better solutions than mine! I carry out my own decision, break, and fall to pieces.

How difficult it is to go against my own determined will. I want to do what I want, in the way that I want, and when I want. If it is so difficult for me to accept the opinions of other people, whom I can see when they're speaking to me, imagine the difficulty of accepting the will of God, whom I do not see! I have a great deal to learn about faith and trust. A Bible verse states that "in quietness and trust is your strength, but you would have none of it" (Isaiah 30:15, NIV).

Help me, Lord, to trust totally in You.

Iani Dias Lauer-Leite

Saved in an Accident!

For he will order his angels
to protect you wherever you go.
—Psalm 91:11, NLT

One foggy December morning I drove out to the main road, stopped, and carefully looked at both sides of the road to make sure there were no other cars coming, so I could make a left turn to go to work. It was a two-lane road, with a speed limit of forty miles per hour. After making sure that there were no other cars around, I proceeded to make the left turn. As soon as I made that turn, I heard a sudden and loud bang, which greatly shook me up. In fact, only as I looked in my rearview mirror did I realize that I had run into a car, which spun three times and stopped on the side of the road. To this day, I have no idea where that car came from.

Because it was foggy outside and the small Honda was gray, I had not seen the car. In total shock, I stopped my car on the shoulder, terrified. I kept praying aloud, not knowing what to do. Just then I saw the driver of the other car, a young man, walk up to my car window and ask if I was OK. The man was nice, courteous, and did not exhibit any anger or irritability over the accident. I thanked God that no one was hurt—not even a scratch!

A police officer came and checked the young man's car and found that it was not drivable. Only the right side of the front bumper of my car was broken, and the car was drivable.

After exchanging insurance information, I learned that the other driver had the same insurance company as I did, so it would be much easier to settle this claim. Of course, I got a ticket because I had made a left turn without making sure the road was clear. However, I was very grateful to God that we were not hurt. Since nothing else was wrong with my car, I was able to go to work that morning. With that strong impact, this accident could have proven fatal.

I know my guardian angel protected me and that young man in this accident. An oncoming car could have easily hit him because his car had spun in the opposite direction of the flow of traffic. Also, if he had been injured, my insurance company would have had to pay a lot more, and my insurance rate would have risen.

In every way, my loving God protected and helped both of us in this horrible accident.

I love to claim the promise in today's Bible verse. Truly God's angels do protect us, for God has told them to do so. Doesn't that give you reassurance as well as courage for today?

Stella Thomas

Longing for Home

Even the sparrow has found a home,
And the swallow a nest for herself,
Where she may lay her young—
Even Your altars, O LORD of hosts,
My King and my God.
—*Psalm 84:3, NKJV*

Have you ever wanted to reach your destination after a long time of travel? Well, I have. I began my long journey home because of civil unrest in Rwanda, where I was serving as a student missionary. I was sad to leave my new friends and the new culture I was just starting to experience after only eight months of mission service. I spent my first night of travel in the neighboring country of Burundi before boarding a cargo plane the next day headed for Kenya.

I felt relieved after arriving in Kenya, though I wouldn't be home until I reached Bermuda. As I waited—a whole week—before receiving word of my travel itinerary from my parents, I longed for the familiarity of home. *Great,* I thought upon receiving my travel plans. *Mom and Dad, I'll be seeing you soon!* But my parents were afraid an uninterrupted trip would be too long for me, so they'd arranged for a weekend stopover in England. I learned I'd be spending the weekend with a family there who had Bermudan connections.

What? Another stop? Why can't I just fly straight home? I didn't want to spend the weekend with anyone, even if it was in England. But because my parents were the ones who were paying for my ticket, I had no choice in the matter. Off I went to England, not realizing I'd be there for the weekend with a wonderful family (Dr. Jeff and Patti-Jean Brown) and attending church at Newbold College. What a great experience!

From England, it was on to New York, where I was joyfully reunited with my parents. Yet I still wasn't home. Finally, we arrived home in my own country, welcomed by a crowd of friends and family who had come to celebrate my arrival. It had all been well worth the wait!

Sometimes I find myself longing for my heavenly home. I want to see family and friends again, those familiar faces that death has separated from me. I want to see the patriarchs of old who have encouraged me along this journey. I want to be free of sickness, war, and death.

And I know that if I persevere to the end of my journey, my patient wait for my heavenly home will be well worth it! It will be for you too.

Dana M. Bean

Powering Up

But if we walk in the light as He is in the light,
we have fellowship with one another,
and the blood of Jesus Christ His Son cleanses us from all sin.
—*1 John 1:7, NKJV*

I was sitting in an airplane for a lengthy amount of time, awaiting takeoff after an even longer wait in one of the country's busiest airports. It was even more crowded after a series of storm fronts had delayed the entire airport's operations.

Making phone calls to reschedule meetings, hotel rooms, and connecting flights was a priority. Everyone on the plane seemed to have the same needs, and every cell phone in the plane seemed to be running low on power.

It's lucky I took the time to charge my extra battery pack, I thought as I plugged in my portable charger to renew my cell phone battery. I did not have enough battery to share with everyone in the plane, of course. Yet I did have enough power to share with my seatmate after I saw her helplessly holding her equally depleted cell phone and looking longingly at my charger.

What if I had not planned ahead? I mused. *What if I had not made time to charge and bring my extra battery?*

Both my fellow traveler and I needed to contact family and business associates. With no power, we would have been cut off from them with no way to communicate. Taking the time earlier to be fully charged now allowed me stay in communication at the time I needed it most.

How about my spiritual batteries? Am I as careful to take the time to keep them fully charged?

How many times in my life do I rush out the door without powering up in my spiritual life? How many times am I powerless to communicate with my heavenly family? How many times have I left another person in need of God's power because I had little or none to share?

We may not be able to share with the entire world, but taking the time to be fully charged lets us share that blessing with our closest neighbors.

Lord, help me to fully power up with You each morning, so I will have Your light and Your power in my own life. Let my spiritual battery be fully charged so that I may share You with others who also need to be in contact with You. Amen.

Suzanne Blaylock

Miracles in Plain Wrappers

They shall walk, and not faint.
—*Isaiah 40:31*

Sustaining grace is one of the most powerful answers to prayer, one of its greatest miracles. It may not look or feel like a miracle, but, in my opinion, it is one of the greatest and most rewarding joys of Christianity. Sustaining grace is the ability to *press in* to Christ, *press through* a difficulty, and *press on* to victory. It is God-planted hope, determination, and perseverance that enable us to move forward instead of backwards in the Christian life.

"Man was originally endowed with noble powers and a well-balanced mind. He was . . . in harmony with God."* I want that back—all of it. Do you? It takes serious time with God, lots of prayer, and hard work to experience this type of miracle, and it is a battle. This work is not speedy, but it is sure. It is not glamorous, but it is glorious. Exciting miracles are great, but they do not mature us. The miracle of growth in Christ does not feel like one. God delivers us as we listen to His voice, take His hand, resist our inclinations, and do what He says.

The flesh is strong. "For the desires of the flesh are against the Spirit" (Galatians 5:17, RSV). I come from a very violent, unstable background and started running away from home at the age of five. I ran the gamut of evil for many years, including a serious eating disorder for twenty years. God knows what He is getting into when He gets ahold of us, and we are no problem for Him.

Miracle 1: Getting my attention, not just once, but daily. You can thank Him for that too because you are reading this, so He has your attention!

Miracle 2 (just as amazing): Whereas I used to run toward evil and sin, now I run from it. If I stumble, I get back up, and keep running in the right direction. If you are wholly invested in Christ, you know this process. If you don't, I invite you to take that step of full surrender.

Miracle 3: Perseverance. Perseverance says, "I don't care how long it takes; I don't care how hard it is; I am going to believe the promises, do what I know instead of what I feel, and move forward by faith." Faith is not the victory that *avoids* the problems of the world, it's the victory that *overcomes* the sin problem in the world.

Vicki Griffin

* Ellen G. White, *Steps to Christ* (Washington, DC: Review and Herald®, 1908), 17.

Cat Head Biscuits

But our citizenship is in heaven,
and it is from there that we are expecting a Savior,
the Lord Jesus Christ.
—*Philippians 3:20, NRSV*

I have always been thankful for having married into a kind and loving southern family. I admired my mother-in-law, who could make the best biscuits ever! Each biscuit was individually kneaded to perfection. My husband and I looked forward to going back home to enjoy those large, fluffy biscuits, served with gravy. Shortly after moving into our first apartment, I decided to make my husband some biscuits that would be as fine as his mother's. I kneaded them until I was sure they were perfect! When I removed my first batch from our oven, they looked anemic and knotted, but they smelled delicious. I knew my husband would be proud of my efforts! As I eagerly carried my biscuits to our small dinette table, one of the biscuits rolled off the baking pan, hitting the floor with a firm bounce! I apologized repeatedly as I watched him saw the biscuits in half. He kindly remarked, "Dottie, anything that comes from your oven will always be good!" After fifty-six years, he continues to be generous and kind regarding my domestic failures. Over the years, I have wondered why his mother's biscuits were so tender and delicious, absolutely perfect every time. Could the lowly biscuit take any credit for its perfection and availability upon her table? The biscuit gets no credit for its existence, appearance, or delicious taste, for each biscuit is handcrafted by its maker.

So it is with humanity. We can claim no credit for our physical existence or spiritual fitness. Each person must be fully surrendered while being handcrafted and molded individually by our Creator. He alone knows how light His touch must be. He will never overwork me in His hands to where I may become hardened. He knows the exact ingredients needed to prepare me for serving Him and others. He, too, controls the heat in life's oven, so that one may retain a tender heart for others.

My favorite Christian writer, Ellen G. White, says, "The formation of character is the work of a lifetime."* As we move forward in life, surrendering to God's will, we will begin to experience a change in personal taste, finding delight in meditating on that which is noble. We will also become a greater blessing to others we meet on life's journey.

Dottie Barnett

---

* Ellen G. White, *Child Guidance* (Washington, DC: Review and Herald®, 1954), 162.

Mother's Diary

And the LORD said unto Moses,
Write this for a memorial in a book.
—*Exodus 17:14*

Marie Jansen was my mom. She passed away on April 5, 2015.

I remember her helping people. There was the time in the 1960s that two of my younger cousins spent a summer with our family. Then the time my parents invited a young girl named Pam to live with us while her family situation was getting straightened out. These times were sometimes frustrating for my brother and me, but I believe we learned how to be less selfish.

I remember Mother spending countless hours baking bread for fund-raisers for the local church school. She served her church as the treasurer for thirty-five years.

At Mom's funeral, many folks related to us their stories about her. Time after time my mother had impacted people's lives in so many different positive ways. Again and again people told my brother and me, during the hours of the pre-funeral viewing, that when our mom told people she would be praying for them, they had the assurance that she really *would* be praying for them.

In this context, the words from a page in Mother's diary—read during the funeral service—held even deeper meaning for those of us who were given a peek inside of her heart. The following journal excerpt is what she had written twenty-eight years earlier.

"I'm only a speck, a small, small speck of humanity, and have never thought of making any impact in words or deeds on my fellow man. But I guess, when we look around, we all are just that [little specks]. Look at the influence that all these little specks are making upon humanity. Maybe [specks of] love, peace, joy, patience, and giving. I would love to think [these are] what I will leave to mankind. I would surely feel very sad to leave hate and ugliness as a remembrance to friends and fellow acquaintances and family. I would love to have a small impact on my [fellow man] for good. My little speck of humanity is only that. But please remember me as a little speck of good and love. By Marie Jansen, Dec. 27, 1987."

I believe that Mother did leave in this world a little more love, a little more peace, and a little more joy—through the lives of those her life sweetly touched.

Today what legacy will you choose to leave with those in your sphere of influence?

Karen Jansen White

God's Mercy for a Workaholic!

But because of his great love for us,
God, who is rich in mercy, made us alive with Christ
even when we were dead in transgressions—
it is by grace you have been saved.
—*Ephesians 2:4, 5, NIV*

I had been hard at work planning my busy schedule two weeks before Christmas. I had been ignoring how I had been feeling all weekend. On Saturday night, I began feeling excruciating pains in my lower back. I blamed the mattress for being too soft and spent the remainder of the night sleeping on the floor. Early on Sunday morning I had the responsibility of conducting Bible studies for incarcerated juveniles. I drove to the facility and completed the Bible study while hiding my pain. I only had enough strength to drive back home and crawl back on the floor in pain. I remained there until it was time to go to work Monday morning.

As I walked, my steps were slower, and the pain was stronger. It became clear that I needed to go to the urgent care clinic and see a doctor. I prayed for God's mercy as I drove. I was so weak driving just twelve miles that I had to stop and rest.

When I arrived in the clinic examining room, the nurse took my blood pressure. It was 90/54 and falling. The doctor immediately came, and I was placed in a wheelchair and taken to triage. After blood tests revealed I had sepsis (a life-threatening blood infection) and an abnormally large kidney stone, I was taken by ambulance that night to the hospital. Upon arrival, I was told that a urologist was waiting in the operating room to insert a stent into my kidney. As the nurses and anesthesiologist prepared me for surgery, the doctor looked at me and said, "Do you realize this can be fatal? What took you so long to call the doctor?"

I had the most calm, peaceful feeling. Yes, I knew I had been foolish to put my job and ministry before my health. Yet God loves us so much that He saves us even though we don't deserve it. As they wheeled me into the operating room, this verse came to mind: "Thou wilt keep him in perfect peace, whose mind is stayed on thee: because he trusteth in thee" (Isaiah 26:3).

The infection cleared after a week of medication and hospitalization. The day after Christmas the kidney stone was surgically removed. Although I had to take nearly two months off from work, God's mercy saved me, and I am so grateful for another chance to serve Him.

For what are you grateful during this season?

Charlene M. Wright

December 12

The Suitcase Containing the Tools

Give all your worries and cares to God,
for he cares about you.
—*1 Peter 5:7, NLT*

How we enjoyed the month that our son, Tony, spent with us before he flew to Cambodia to serve as a volunteer teacher. Christmas Eve was the start of his four weeks with us at home. The days that followed, filled with a New Zealand heat wave, blue skies, and fishing trips with my husband, passed quickly. At the end of that month, with heavy hearts, we drove the 217 miles (350 kilometers) with Tony to the international airport at Christchurch. He was catching the next morning's first flight to Auckland, then on to Singapore, and finally to Phnom Penh, Cambodia. From there, he would travel to Siem Reap, another 199 miles (320 kilometers) farther.

That night as I lay in bed unable to sleep, God told me He would look after my son. An immense feeling of peace came over me. After a quick breakfast the next morning, we repacked the car and drove the very short distance to the airport. Tony had a bag of clothes, another bag containing literature, and a third bag full of tools he would need but which, he'd been told, would be impossible to purchase in Cambodia. He checked in for his flight. We said our goodbyes and prayed together before my husband and I left.

The first e-mail I received from Tony was sent at the Singapore airport. The next day he was safely at his destination. But one suitcase was missing—the one containing the tools. Because Tony had given me the bag's tag number, I phoned the airline. The next day I phoned and the next and the next. Before long, the airline's lost property staff and I were on a first-name basis!

Many times I was asked to describe the suitcase: color, approximate size, any identification stickers or ribbons on it. I thought of all the luggage areas in so many airports being checked and rechecked. So many flights all around the world! So many people traveling to so many destinations! Had Tony's suitcase left Christchurch? Yes. Had it left Singapore? Well, we were told yes, but that airport is immense, with four terminals. Maybe it was in Phnom Penh. The week slowly passed while our prayers continued. Then on Friday—what joy! The suitcase had been found in Singapore and had been flown to Siem Reap, where Tony soon retrieved it.

There is no doubt God was looking after it, though the lock was now gone. Yet nothing was missing. All of Tony's tools were intact. What an answer to prayer! Surely, God cares about details.

Leonie Donald

Christmas Reflections

Weeping may endure for a night,
But joy comes in the morning.
—*Psalm 30:5, NKJV*

I spent Christmas at my sister's house in California one year. One morning while there, I sat in her family room, looking at the pictures of my nephew that she had on display. I noticed that each picture showed him at a different age in his life. In all of the pictures, he was smiling, but his face looked a bit different in each picture as he had aged. I could see the subtle changes in his features from one picture to another. My sister has one child, a son, and he is precious to her and to each of us siblings. We love him dearly, and as he has grown to adulthood, we have prayed him through life's challenges, mistakes, and joys.

As I continued looking at the pictures, I smiled, but some deep thoughts also came to mind. I looked back at my life, and I could see myself at the different ages and stages in my own growth to adulthood. I recognized physical, spiritual, and emotional changes. Reflecting on each stage, some memory surfaced and brought a smile to my face. Yet I also remembered many difficult times in my life. In certain seasons of life, it seemed, the difficult times had outweighed the good times. And though that may be true, I could still remember times of joy in each stage. Small though they may have been, there was joy.

Looking back at our lives can be depressing, depending on our point of view. Yet that day my point of view changed.

Now as I look back at life's trials and mistakes, I also look for times of joy—and I always find them. Life is difficult. That's a given. But life with Jesus means that, no matter the difficulties, there is also joy. And that gives me hope for the future.

Difficult times will come, and I may yet make some mistakes I will regret, but God will also give me times of joy that remind me that in this life there is hope. There is something to look forward to, something to keep me moving on.

I'm not sure where you are in life today. Maybe you've been looking back, and you are harboring feelings of anger and sadness over your past. I challenge you today to look for the moments of joy in your past. As you find them—and you *will* find them—praise God that no matter how dark the night, He always gives a light to cheer our way.

Heather-Dawn Small

Life's Turbulence

And call upon me in the day of trouble:
I will deliver thee, and thou shalt glorify me.
—*Psalm 50:15*

On December 14, 2013, I traveled home with my mother and one of my daughters for my oldest daughter's traditional marriage. As we were waiting to board the plane, we noticed how happy the passengers were, traveling to join their families for year-end celebrations.

A few hours into our flight, however, we started experiencing turbulence. In a matter of minutes, the turbulent air currents were tossing the plane up and down and from side to side. I closed my eyes and prayed, *Lord, is this how the three of us are going to die?* You can imagine the frantic shouting, crying, and praying going on in that passenger cabin!

My favorite Bible texts came to mind during that time. I remembered God's counsel to "call upon me in the day of trouble: I will deliver thee, and thou shalt glorify me" (Psalm 50:15). I also claimed, "He shall give his angels charge over thee" (Psalm 91:11). I reminded my God that we had committed this journey into His hands before departing, and I believed He had sanctioned it.

As the prayers of the desperate passengers continued, a woman stood up and began sharing the Word of God. A few minutes later the turbulence ceased, along with the noise in the cabin. The same woman who had been sharing God's Word faced us and said, "To all of you that just gave your lives to God during that turbulence, don't take it back now that the storm has stopped. For you will encounter much more turbulence as you travel through life!" We all laughed, but she did give us words to think about.

Life's turbulence comes in different forms: illness, financial hardship, and emotional pain. When problems strike us, we can seek God's face by the prayerful claiming of His promises. And when the trials ease off, let us continue to remember His promises and pleadings with us. We should fulfill those promises we have made to Him.

We must faithfully keep open our communication line with Him at all times. Let us continue, in His strength, to be faithful to the One who has promised never to leave nor forsake us.

You may be experiencing turbulence in your life right now. If so, God has made provision for it. Hold Him to His promises. Hold tightly to His hand—for He has hold of you.

Victoria C. Nwogwugwu

Heritage of the Lord

Children are a heritage from the LORD,
offspring a reward from him.
—*Psalm 127:3, NIV*

Every day when you turn on the television or spend time on the Internet, you can see terrible news, driven by the uncontrolled impulses of violent people. In the last decade, the number of homicides, suicides, and rapes we hear about in the news has increased. Newspapers and television news show this reality every day to parents who wish to provide a healthy upbringing for their children. We live in difficult times. The outside influences on children are stronger than ever before, and there have never been so many places of distraction, so much information given out over media, and so many children who spend hours on the Internet and watching television programs that are inappropriate for them.

Raising healthy, free, and successful children is a challenge. Parents hide their emotions, and children hide their tears. According to the writer Augusto Cury, children do not need giant parents, but human beings who speak their language and are able to penetrate their hearts and understand their emotions.

Psychologist Daniel Goleman, who researches and writes about emotional intelligence, says that the current generation of parents has to work more and more to maintain a standard of life better than the generation of their parents. This means that they have less free time for their children and that those children often live far from their relatives, especially far from the grandparents, and the children do not play outdoors. They get stuck in their apartments or homes for fear of violence. But you can see the result: nervous, angry, grumpy, aggressive, and depressed children. Can you reverse this situation with your children? Maybe you feel insecure. But know that you are not alone!

You have the Father of love and mercy who can help you. Seek divine guidance for working with your child's emotions and channel them to the joy of a happier life. May Jesus be in your home and may you share with Him your joys and anxieties. Hand in hand with Him, may you feel safe while leading your children along the path of good.

Meibel Mello Guedes

The Words

*"The grass withers, the flower fades,
But the word of our God will stand forever."*
—Isaiah 40:8, NKJV

I sit in my home office, my desk stacked with thick parchment paper and small envelopes that will all end up in a manila envelope. I begin to cut the parchment paper into smaller pieces, open my Bible, and pick up my pen. A small lamp shines over the Bible, and I transcribe the verses selected. Twice I stop to pray that these words will shine their light on the dark, just like they did for me. I remember the despair.

I look at my dining-room table and see what I wish would disappear: medical bills, more medical bills, insurance bills, and the envelope that was delivered today—divorce papers. My life on a table, overflowing with nothing but despair. I stack the medical bills by categories. Then I pick up the manila envelope with the stamp of a law firm. *This arrived quickly.*

Newly wed I followed my husband twelve hundred miles away from my family for his dream job. In a week, after we sat with the oncologist, I was told a "sick wife" would interfere with his new job, and that same day he moved me out of our home. That night in a new apartment, boxes all around, I remembered what I had inherited: faith and strength. No tears had been shed. I called my family. A week later I opened the mailbox to find a manila envelope. Inside were smaller sealed envelopes. I carefully picked one out and recognized the writing: my mother's. The envelope read, "For when you are sad." Inside there were more than twenty small pieces of paper with quotes from the Bible. The second envelope: "Promises of healing." I shook the manila envelope and more than fifteen smaller envelopes fell out, all of them with handwritten Bible verses my mother had picked for me: "For when you have doubt," "Praises to God," "For when you feel alone," "God's love for us." The last envelope: "My prayers." As with all of the others, it had handwritten words, my mother's penned prayers, placing my life at God's feet.

Now my transcribing is done. I address the envelope to my friend who has lost both her daughter and husband in a car accident. I hold the package in my hands and pray. God's Word is powerful. Anything and everything we ever need to live a better life, a blessed life, is there. The light we seek in the dark is there. I glance at the envelope one last time before I turn off the lamp, knowing how heavenly light resides in the words inside.

Dixil Rodríguez

Marinating in His Words

Let your speech always be with grace,
seasoned with salt, that you may know
how you ought to answer each one.
—*Colossians 4:6, NKJV*

Some years ago I single-handedly attempted to prepare my first vegetarian dish using tofu. This was in keeping with my lifestyle change of eating healthier. I started dinner preparations with no prior research on the required process to transform plain tofu into a flavorful dish. After all, how hard could this be? With the other dishes completed, I hurriedly prepared the tofu by adding a little salt, natural seasoning, and coconut sauce. The aroma was inviting. I felt proud as I put some of the food I'd prepared on my plate.

I sat down to eat, but the first bite of the tofu was distasteful. What had gone wrong? I became discouraged. Would I be able to go through with this lifestyle change? After consultation with others who had previously given me sumptuous dishes of prepared tofu, I learned the secret for adding flavor to this bland, high-protein meat substitute: marinade! Tofu is somewhat like a sponge; it has no flavor. For best results, marinate it. As years passed, I learned various preparation methods for tofu, all of which helped to enhance the finished product. I was recently introduced to seasoned tofu, which makes life easier for the busy vegetarian cook.

Not only was I learning a practical lesson about the preparation of tofu, but also, in retrospect, I realize that tofu is sometimes like our Christian lives. How can we "taste and see that the Lord is good" if we don't spend time marinating in His Word (Psalm 34:8)? This marinade of the prayerful study of His Word keeps us from becoming bland, unenthusiastic Christians. We cannot hastily read through His words and neglect our relationship with Him, thinking we can wait until the last minute to season our lives with His grace. A day is coming when we all have to go in to the "pot" of afflictions. Some of us have experienced trials already. They have made us realize that only through ongoing faith in God's Word and time spent with Him in prayer and study—the marinating process—can we remain encouraged and faithful.

In God's mercy, He has given us enough information to become seasoned in and by His Word, prepared to share it with others as we prepare for the Second Advent. Let us prayerfully marinate in God's Word, so we can bring His saving flavor to those around us.

Racquel Boswell

Encounter at the Intersection—Part 1

"What I'm trying to do here is get you to relax, not be so
preoccupied with getting so you can respond to God's giving. . . .
Steep yourself in God-reality, God-initiative, God-provisions. . . .
Don't be afraid of missing out. You're my dearest friends!
The Father wants to give you the very kingdom itself."
—Luke 12:29–32, The Message

I sat at the intersection, waiting for the light to turn green. The sun was shining through the treetops on the hill ahead. The scene evoked a deep longing in me, and a prayer welled up from deep inside and drifted silently toward heaven.

Father, I feel like You have so many things to show and tell me—so many ways You want to bless me. I don't want to stand in the way of what You are trying to do in me by being too slow at recognizing and making the choices I need to in order to let You have Your way. I don't want to miss out on any of Your blessings.

I gripped the steering wheel as if to squeeze a response from it. I looked again at the trees on the hill beyond the light, but this time my mind's eye saw oak trees covered with acorns. Then my mind opened up, and the Lord began speaking into my thoughts:

"Do you see all of those acorns? They could never all become oaks. There are too many, and that's just from one season. If every acorn became an oak, the whole world would be filled with nothing but oak trees, and soon there would be no room for anything, including oak trees. My blessings are like that! There are too many for you to ever receive them all. I have too many dreams, too many thoughts of blessing you— there is no way in this life you can ever fulfill all the dreams that I have about you. Even if you started making all the right choices from birth until the day you died, you'd still experience only a fragment of My blessings. Rachel, there are too many for you to ever have them all!

"But at the same time, there is no way you could ever mess up so badly that I have no blessings left for you. No matter what choices a person makes in life, there is no way to go beyond the reach of My blessings. When a person has gone as low as they can go, when they turn to Me, I am still only at the beginning of My blessings for them. No one can ever out-sin My infinite grace. The only thing that can keep Me from blessing you is your refusal to come to Me."

Rachel Williams-Smith

Encounter at the Intersection—Part 2

*"If God gives such attention to the wildflowers, most of them
never even seen, don't you think he'll attend to you,
take pride in you, do his best for you?"*
—*Luke 12:28, The Message*

Your thoughts and plans are treasures to me, O God! I cherish each
and every one of them! How grand in scope! How many in number!
If I could count each one of them, they would be more than all the
grains of sand on earth. Their number is inconceivable!
—*Psalm 139:17, 18, The Voice*

While pondering the lesson of the acorns and God's abundant blessings, for a moment, I worried about not receiving all the blessings God had for me. But He wasn't finished.

"Think about all the flowers that have bloomed since Creation in all of the countries of the world until now," He said. *"My primary purpose for making flowers is to delight the senses of humankind. Yet every season so many flowers bloom that no human eye sees.*

"My love is like that! I have so much of it to express that My blessings are everywhere—just in case.

"You see, I think of you every moment, and My thoughts about you alone are as the grains of sand on the seashore. Yet can you count all the grains of sand that are in just one small sand pail? And I think of every human being as intensely as I think of you. I have more love than anyone can ever comprehend! That's why I can be God and still allow you complete freedom of choice. No matter how you've used that power, I can still turn things into a blessing if you give yourself to Me. But I want you to choose My way because I love you and want you to be happy.

"In a way, that's all I do—dream of ways to make you happy! I only get to see a very small portion of My dreams ever come true for you or anyone, but I don't want you to be anxious about this because you will never receive all the blessings I have! So relax in My love and know that I can't help but bless you if you let Me. Just let Me have My way. I love you," He said. *"With an everlasting love, I love you,"* He finished with a whisper to my heart.

The traffic light changed. I drove up the tree-covered hill, the sun still shining through the treetops, setting them on fire. And my heart was aglow with the wonder of God's love!

Rachel Williams-Smith

I Don't Ever Have to Be Afraid

Behold, I send an Angel before thee, to keep thee in the way,
and to bring thee into the place which I have prepared.
—*Exodus 23:20*

A friend recently shared, in these words, her powerful story of loss—and hope.

"Mike, my physician husband, had not been feeling up to par on a trip to Southern California after the new year to help our children and grandchildren pack for a weeks' long trip to the Middle East. Mike insisted on being admitted to the hospital (after I dropped the children off at the airport) for further tests to pinpoint his issues. A week later we learned the results: pancreatic cancer. Back home, his references to peace and confidence in his relationship with His heavenly Father encouraged us. I hated to watch Mike slip away but didn't want him to suffer.

"During the recent Christmas holiday shared with our children, I had thought ahead of a theme for my new year. I remembered planning a children's Sabbath School program when my eldest was a toddler. I'd titled it 'I Don't Ever Have to Be Afraid—Angels Watch Over Me.'

"Our next year's Christmas tree with its hundreds of tiny white lights will be covered with white angels, many crocheted or made of fabric and lace. Now, with Mike's passing, how I will need the constant reminder of this new year's theme: Even in difficult times, I am *never* alone. Jesus and His angels *do* watch over me. God's promises bring me comfort. My 'heritage from the Lord' comforts me as well (Psalm 127:3, NIV). After Michael died, I felt so tired and overwhelmed. Then my youngest grandson, Prentiss, began a campaign: 'Grandma, please come to our house, and we'll all go to Disneyland.' We did. A few months later I flew to Nebraska to spend time with my son, Jason, and his family. The day before what would have been my fiftieth wedding anniversary, Jason took me for a surprise manicure and pedicure—a super treat for me.

"Yes, my life is changing. I have left the 'us' of my life. I will carry with me cherished memories of living many years with someone special. I will especially cherish the fact that I don't ever have to be afraid—angels watch over me. Just as they watched over Mary and Joseph traveling in search of shelter. The birth of the Christ child that night still fills us with Heaven's love and hope for the future, just as the angels' song reminded shepherds they were not alone."

My friend, neither are we alone. May God's care through His angels bring us peace.

Carolyn Rathbun Sutton

Fasting at Christmas

"Is this not the fast that I have chosen:
to loose the bonds of wickedness, to undo the heavy burdens,
to let the oppressed go free, and that you break every yoke?"
—Isaiah 58:6, NKJV

Our home is getting emptier—our children have grown up. One daughter has her own family with three children, and they have decided to spend Christmas this year with her husband's family. My mother, who lived with us for years, died twelve months ago. Our other two daughters are still single, and it looks like we will spend Christmas this year with just the four of us. We like the idea of celebrating Christmas quietly, for once, with little to prepare.

Today I read Isaiah 58:6–11. These verses made me think. For some time now, we have been hearing the call for revival and reformation in our church. Many believers long and pray for change. They realize that even though they pray and fast, have their quiet time, and go to church regularly, something—somehow—is still missing. What could that be?

In reading this Bible passage, I realized what real fasting is. It is not renouncing eating; rather, it is *giving* food to others. It is not abstaining from something, but rather giving something.

Even the Israelites did all that God asked them to do. They sought God, they fasted, they prayed, and they kept the commandments (see Isaiah 58:1–5). Yet their actions toward others were wicked, abusive, and selfish. They did not care about the poor and the lonely; they only thought about themselves.

In order to fast, we don't need to refrain from food and pleasures, but we do need to be at peace with our neighbor, to forgive where needed, and to be an encouragement to others. We need to do the right thing and stand in and lift up our voices against injustice, abuse, and wrongdoing of all kinds. We need to show our appreciation and love to others.

It seems to me there is a clear relationship between revival and reformation and how we treat our neighbors—especially the weak ones and the ones who are marginalized in society. Let's change that. By the way, I just told my two daughters and husband that for Christmas Eve this year, I am going to invite people who are lonely and who have nowhere to go. My family is supportive of this idea. Who knows? We might benefit from this arrangement too!

I wish you a merry Christmas and a happy New Year!

Denise Hochstrasser

The Christmas Gift

And this is his command: to believe in the name of his Son,
Jesus Christ, and to love one another as he commanded us.
—*1 John 3:23, NIV*

D o not open until December 25" was written on the Christmas card tucked inside the gift bag. It was Christmas morning, and I decided this would be the first gift I would open. My gift was a coffee mug intended for music lovers. Musical instruments, a grand piano, quarter notes, eighth notes, treble and bass clefs decorated the outside of the mug. Inside, near the rim, was a line of music. For Christmas, my friend always found something unique and special. As I looked at this gift, tears came to my eyes. This would be the last gift I would ever receive from her. You see, she had died the day before following a prolonged illness.

Upon earlier notification that she had been admitted to the hospital, my husband and I decided to drive the two hours to visit her. We were welcomed into the hospital room by her family. When her son heard my name, he immediately found the gift that was intended for me.

"This is for you," he said. His mother had been suffering from a lot of pain, but she still thought of others.

Fifteen years earlier my husband had been her pastor. That's when our friendship began. Now as she lay in bed, she turned to my husband and asked if he would conduct her funeral and then asked me if I would play the organ.

Over the years—and despite our many moves—our friendship remained intact. Occasionally, I would fly to visit one of our sons and have a two-hour delay at the airport. My friend and I would have lunch together. All too soon it was time to catch my plane. She would give me big hug, a gift bag, and a stack of church bulletins. Phone calls kept us connected: who got married, who had a baby, who had a shower, who got baptized, who had died and had a funeral. She was a friend that could be trusted.

Now she was resting.

After her funeral, a mutual friend told me that he found a Christmas card in the church mailbox from her. "She loved everyone unconditionally" was his way of describing her.

What a wonderful way to be remembered!

Vera Wiebe

Gina's Induction

A wrathful man stirs up strife,
but he who is slow to anger allays contention.
—*Proverbs 15:18, NKJV*

I t was December 23, and Gina's labor was scheduled for today! She was so excited as she made her way to the hospital where labor would be induced. But the birthing unit was busy. Gina was advised that no midwives were available to care for her, at least not today. She was disappointed and a little anxious about her unborn child, hoping another day would make no difference. On Christmas Eve, expectations again ran high when Gina phoned in to see if we had room. I had to apologize and tell her that we were again too busy. Her anxiety and disappointment began to spill over into anger. I could hear her mother in the background, stirring up strife. I invited Gina to come see me that afternoon, so I could check the baby and find another date. She was welcome to bring her mother with her.

The birthing unit staff advised me not to see them alone as two days before they had been vocal and abusive with my tall male colleague. The staff thought that I, a small woman, didn't stand a chance! I knew it was irregular to arrange an induction on Christmas Day with fewer staff on duty, but I sensed the staff's empathy toward me. So I asked if they would be willing to make an exception for Gina. They kindly agreed.

I began to pray for grace to deal with Gina and her mother in a kind and loving manner. It was intimidating when Gina, her husband, mother, and father all arrived that afternoon, bristling and ready for an argument. Praying silently, I sat and listened to all they had to say. The still, small Voice prompted me not to react when they raised their voices and made threats. God's grace was clearly at work when I was able to smile and reflect His love to them, apologizing for the delay and reassuring Gina that her baby was still quite safe. They accepted my offer of a Christmas Day induction, and we parted amicably.

The induction was unnecessary, for the next morning Gina arrived in early labor! And a few hours later, when her baby got into trouble from the umbilical cord wrapped round its neck, God had me right outside her door, able to deliver her without delay. As the baby arrived, safe and well, her room was filled with tears of joy, encouragement, and gratitude.

I think the miracles God works in our hearts are the greatest miracles of all.

Nerida McKibben

He Thought of Me Above All

In the beginning was the Word, and the Word was with God, and the Word was God. The same was in the beginning with God. All things were made by him; and without him was not any thing made that was made. In him was life; and the life was the light of men. . . . And the Word was made flesh, and dwelt among us, (and we beheld his glory, the glory as of the only begotten of the Father,) full of grace and truth.
John 1:1–4, 14

The Christmas season seems to be, at times, the rehearsed story of Christ's birth. But tonight the story really resonated with me. Our God, our mighty Creator, became part of humanity, His creation—a poor, vulnerable human baby. Oh, how the inhabitants of heaven must have held their breath. His arrival was announced not by an earthquake or lightning-streaked thunder and howling winds, but by the beautiful sound of an angel choir singing praises. A bright star (possibly an angel) guided the wise men in their search of the Holy God, born to save us and give us salvation. Not just for those in His lifetime, but for us centuries later.

My thoughts then went to His death; for He was born to die. When He died, the earth quaked ferociously, winds howled, lightning streaked across the sky with blinding flashes while thunder roared loudly. Dead people arose from their graves (Matthew 27:52, 53). Again, the inhabitants of heaven must have held their breath. God the Father was, for the first time, separated from His only Son by sin. Yet Jesus conquered death and the grave through His resurrection. The plan of salvation was fulfilled. Soon He is coming again to take us to heaven until, as Revelation explains, we settle in the New Jerusalem for eternity. I'm completely humbled by the thought that my wonderful Creator decided to become a human baby as part of the plan to save my life! And He loves me so much He took the risk of stepping down from heaven and coming to earth to live a life of hardship. He went toe-to-toe with the devil just for me. Why shouldn't I be willing to give my life to Him? Why am I not more inclined to do His will? Woe be unto me if I only meagerly attempt to follow Him.

I challenge you to take a deeper look at Jesus Christ and His first advent. Let's not simply repeat the story. Let's allow ourselves to really take in the depth of His actions on our behalf.

I challenge you to join me in pursuing a closer walk with the Savior.

Kelli Raí Collins

You Prepare a Table

You prepare a table before me
in the presence of my enemies.
—*Psalm 23:5, NIV*

The fragrant scents of Christmas dinner drifted from our kitchen to mingle with the fresh pine branches and fire. Spiced cranberry candles flickering throughout the house blended with the aromas of onion and sage, mulled cider, pumpkin pie, freshly baked rolls, roasts, and casseroles that composed the festive meal we would soon share with friends and family.

Now my favorite part—setting the large dining-room table with an elegant combination of thrift-store treasures and beautiful family heirlooms: a gold damask tablecloth so large that it draped gracefully nearly to the floor; heavily monogrammed oversize napkins from France; antique gold plates and ninety-nine-cent cranberry crystal goblets; a centerpiece of pink-and-red apricot parrot tulips, cream poinsettias, rich green fir branches, and clusters of pepper berries; candles glimmering in the tall gold candelabra at either end of the table—a special birthday gift from my mother. As I place the napkins into filigreed silver rings, my thoughts turn to Bible stories about celebrations. God loves celebrations! The first miracle of Jesus occurred at a wedding feast and made it even better. David gives me another favorite picture: "You prepare a table before me in the presence of my enemies" (Psalm 23:5, NIV). I contemplate God preparing a table for me, knowing intimately what I will find beautiful and delightful. He and I sit down together to a gourmet meal of fresh and delicious flavors so rich, intricate, and deeply satisfying that I can't even imagine it all.

We dine in the "presence of my enemies." My enemies aren't human. They are the thoughts that steal my peace. My enemies are worries over unresolved situations: conflicts still percolating at church, work, or in my family; piles of bills and a meager bank account; an illness not yet healed. Yet God comes right into the middle of these unresolved, messy, troublesome situations and invites me to sit down and relax in His care. He knows my anxious humanness that wants to find resolutions and action plans, so I can feel that I have the right to rest a brief while. But He wants me to learn that it's possible to rest even without seeing resolutions. He wants me to sit at His beautiful table of blessing and see *Him* instead. He invites me to find fresh strength in quiet enjoyment of His present provision, confident hope that all of my current uncertainties will have future resolutions to glorify the same God who prepares a table before me today.

Kelly Mowrer

December 26

The God of the Impossible

I love the Lord, for he heard my voice;
he heard my cry for mercy. Because he turned his ear to me,
I will call on him as long as live.
—*Psalm 116:1, 2, NIV*

Some time ago three people in my family, people whom I love very much, got involved in a foolish fight. Because all thought themselves to be right, I noticed that making peace would be very difficult, almost impossible.

I suffered a lot with this situation; yet from the beginning, I trusted in God and knew that only He could reverse it. In my prayers, I constantly asked Him to at least restore the situation a little bit and to help me endure the pain of seeing loved ones not talk to each other. Those were difficult months—months of heartache and waiting on God for a miracle.

Then one Christmas Eve God made the reconciliation. It was as if a broken vessel had been completely restored. God responds wonderfully to our prayers. He always gives more than we ask and always surprises us.

When writing this devotional, I remembered that, about a week ago, I asked God to show me if it would be worthwhile to continue praying for one of those people involved in the family fight. This person's heart seemed unreachable. However, God has shown me that Yes, for Him nothing—nothing—is impossible, so I must continue to pray for this individual.

Yesterday, God turned a dream into reality. I am sure my other two dreams will also be fulfilled, which will happen when the remaining two individuals give their lives to Him.

God is faithful. We can place on Him all of our anxieties and fears. We can trust Him with our dreams and desires. The time when we will see our prayers being answered may not come fast, but God's responses will be worth the wait. Every minute of prayerful wrestling with God, pleading with tears, and looking for strength at the feet of the Father, will be worth it. The more arduous the path, the more valuable the reward.

In Romans, Paul tells us that "we also glory in our sufferings, because we know that suffering produces perseverance; perseverance, character; and character, hope" (Romans 5:3, 4, NIV).

Thank You, Father! This was the best Christmas that I could have received!
For which of God's blessings are you thankful this Christmas season?

Adriza Santos Silva Barbosa

The Gift of a Name—Part 1

A good name is more desirable than great riches.
—Proverbs 22:1, NIV

Growing up, I repeatedly heard the disappointing story behind my chosen first name. It seems no one had thought about choosing a name for this brand-new baby girl—me! When the nurse entered Mother's hospital room to say the doctor would need my name before he could sign the birth certificate that day (because he'd already waited a week), family members, including my father (who wanted to name me, his firstborn, Polly) and my aunt Marva suddenly entered into a heated controversy regarding what my name should be.

As the story goes, the television was on in the midst of all of this verbal commotion, and *The Gale Storm Show* was airing. Someone came up with the bright idea to name me *Gail,* with my middle name being Loréss (accent on the *é,* please) after one of my grandmother's sisters.

For years, I felt as if I'd been an afterthought, not planned for, not even down to my name. How careless of my family to put off something so important! It left a hole in my soul, a scar, for many years to come. Names are important. They point one's way in life—a destiny of sorts. Your name is your identity mark. It prepares the way and gives signal to your purpose-driven being. That is what I believed.

Through the years, I have come to believe that a name should be purposefully given. Names suggest a prayer answered. A name denotes a celebration and gives permission for that child to grow and become all that the name entitles that child to be. It is the salutation of the highest honor we can bestow upon a child!

Since moving to the continent of Africa, my early fascination with the naming process has turned into a deep appreciation for this particular tradition steeped in the culture here. My South African family and friends give names to their children that will help to serve as a roadmap for life. If the children should lose their way or themselves on their paths in life, then they should go back to their names—their names will lead them safely home.

In God's time, I would learn the significance of my given name. Meanwhile God was preparing my heart to understand the gift that my name truly is. After all, it is He who said, "You will be called by a new name that the mouth of the LORD will bestow" (Isaiah 62:2, NIV).

Gail Masondo

The Gift of a Name—Part 2

To be esteemed is better than silver or gold.
—Proverbs 22:1, NIV

After my birth, a whole week passed before my family chose a name for me. This knowledge made me feel like an afterthought for much of my life. Eventually, I married a South African musician. At a Johannesburg concert welcoming me to South Africa, one of the guests handed me a small piece of paper on which a name had been written. My heart jumped a couple of times in anticipation because here I was, an American of African lineage and heritage, on African soil in the land of my ancestors. And now, in my hand, was a South African name given to me by an African woman. Was it really a name? I would ask someone.

My Caucasian South African host and then my husband, Victor, the musical director for the evening, steered me back to the woman, Sibongile Khumalo (a renowned South African singer, I learned), who had given me the slip of paper. I approached her respectfully and requested, "Please pronounce this for me, and would you mind sharing the meaning?" She pronounced my new name, "Busisiwe." Then she said, "Gail, it means *blessed*!" When she repeated my new name, it brought a smile to my face as broad as the stage on which she and the other artists were about to perform.

Then, a few years back, a pharmacist of Jewish heritage, newly returned from maternity leave, shared the name of her new baby girl: Janet Gail. "What exactly does *Gail* mean?" I asked.

"Well," she explained, "in Hebrew *Gail* means 'Father's joy.' " Tears filled my eyes. For so many years, I had longed for some explanation—from a name's perspective—of my worth. Now I learned (in a pharmacy!) what Heaven had always known, that I was known and would be always known as my "Father's joy." He had chosen *Gail* for me. He had brought me to my adopted homeland to set the record straight, and I would be now and forever known as "Blessed [Busisiwe] by being the Father's joy [Gail]"! My name had not been a mistake, after all, no matter how it was derived. It was the truth of who I was called to be—my Father's joy!

Perhaps you, like I, have struggled with self-worth issues through the years because of things you didn't understand about your life. Yet each of us has a divinely ordered identity and purpose for which the Father created us. Ask how you can bring Him joy today; then, be blessed.

Gail Masondo

Are You Excited About Seeing Jesus?

For now we see only a reflection as in a mirror;
then we shall see face to face. Now I know in part;
then I shall know fully, even as I am fully known.
—*1 Corinthians 13:12, NIV*

It was my seventy-fourth birthday, and I was flying with Morris, my husband, on our way to Barbados for our family reunion and the celebration of my mom's ninety-eight years of life. We experienced frightening turbulence during the flight between Charlotte, North Carolina, and Miami, Florida. Fear filled the plane and I found myself holding tightly to the armrests while praying, *Lord, please don't let anything go wrong with this plane; help us to arrive safely.* The young woman in the window seat leaned toward my husband and mentioned that this was her first time traveling in an airplane. She was visibly nervous.

Finally, the rough weather subsided, and the pilot announced that we were preparing to land. Minutes later, fear struck again when he said that we would have to wait fifteen more minutes because of eighty-five-mile-per-hour winds in Miami. Then he announced that our wait had been extended another forty-five minutes as we might have to refuel in Fort Lauderdale.

Anxious thoughts about unfavorable weather conditions and our connecting flight created deep concerns for me. When we booked our flight, we had a three-hour layover in Miami; it had seemed like a long wait then, but not now. My anxiety was quickly replaced with joy when the pilot announced we were cleared to land. As the plane descended, the young woman at the window became very excited. She told us it was her first time to see beaches and palm trees, and she couldn't wait to go to the beach. Thank God, we landed safely. We hurriedly checked the listings for flight departures to learn which gate we would depart from. Based on previous experiences, I was prepared for a long walk, but God had gone ahead and worked it all out. Our gate was right across from where we'd landed. What a great relief! God is so merciful.

Sitting at the departure gate, I smiled as I recalled the excitement of the young woman seeing beaches and palm trees for the first time. Thoughts of the grandest reunion flashed through my mind. What joy will be ours when we see, for the first time, our beloved Savior face-to-face. We'll be home at last! What an awe-inspiring and spectacular moment that will be! I can hardly wait. Fellow traveler, are you excited about seeing Jesus?

Shirley C. Iheanacho

Creating SMART Goals

Forgetting those things which are behind and reaching forward
to those things which are ahead, I press toward the goal
for the prize of the upward call of God in Christ Jesus.
—*Philippians 3:13, 14, NKJV*

As an occupational health nurse for a global corporation, I am challenged every year to set goals for purposeful improvement in my career. If you have not set a goal for which to aim, you will not know when you have accomplished what you desire. Without a direction, a destination, or a goal, how can you pick a direction, choose a road, or plot a course to get there?

Just as we set goals in our work environments, we need to set purposeful goals in our spiritual and outreach lives. Jesus has given us a mission statement: "Go ye therefore, and teach all nations" (Matthew 28:19). To fulfill this God-given mission statement, we need to set goals. When we set goals at work, they must be SMART goals and need to include at least one goal that stretches us. A SMART goal has these qualities: Specific, Measurable, Attainable, Realistic, Timely.

Specific. To set a specific goal, we must answer six *W* questions. Who (is involved)? What (do I want to accomplish)? Where (will I do this)? When (do I plan to reach the goal)? Which (requirements and constraints must I take into consideration)? Why (am I doing this)? A *general* goal would be, "I want to win souls for Christ." But a *specific* goal (encompassing the six *W*s) might state, "My church Bible study class will mail out flyers to all Colbert County mailboxes by August 30 to generate interest for our church's evangelistic series next year."

Measurable. Measure your progress as you reach target dates and deadlines. Experience the exhilaration of achievement along the way.

Attainable. Figure out ways to reach goals, looking for opportunities to bring yourself closer to fulfillment. You will grow and expand to match the goals you have set.

Realistic. Laboring toward your goal, in love, can make even the hardest job seem easy.

Timely. Ground the goal within a time frame, or there will be no sense of urgency.

Do you listen to the news and believe Jesus is coming soon? If you want to do something to win souls for Christ before the door of probation closes, then you need to set a goal for your own personal outreach. Maybe your New Year's resolution will result in the salvation of souls.

Sandi B. Cook

Beauty From Imperfections

And what does the LORD require of you?
To act justly and to love mercy
and to walk humbly with your God.
—Micah 6:8, NIV

Tonight I gaze in wonder for the last time at the most beautiful Christmas tree I have ever decorated. Tomorrow, being New Year's Day, I'll take it down. Until now, my Christmas trees had been Douglas fir, but this year I found a great price on a more expensive noble. I picked out a lovely (or so I thought at the time), bushy tree.

Push, pull, tug, strain. I sawed the thick trunk again, wondering why a retired senior even bought a live tree, let alone refused help in putting it up. But come on, this is Oregon where lush evergreens dot the countryside—an artificial one is out of the question! Not until I put the tree in the stand, though, did I notice what I term *scoliosis*.

What to do now? The tree obviously dipped to one side! I would certainly need to use my resourcefulness to create something that covered the defect. For that step, a big gold ribbon with a large bow to cover the spot and cascade down the front of the tree. The color scheme—gold and silver? Yes! Silver balls topped with bows from recycled gold ribbon. White lights. The final touches—plastic snowflakes from the dollar store.

Voilà!

At this point, I was beginning to see an exceptional tree, but it wasn't until I turned on the lights later in the evening that I saw a tree as equally beautiful as those professional ones in current women's magazines. Needless to say, visitors marveled at its beauty.

Aren't we humans much like that tree? We all have imperfections, visible and invisible. Yet Jesus chose ordinary men to be His apostles. He mingled with ordinary people and used anyone for His kingdom, warts and all. To feel we must be perfect is incorrect. God is able to make something beautiful from each of us.

Are imperfections keeping you from becoming all that you can be in God's kingdom? Instead of what you don't have, concentrate on ways to use the gifts you do have.

As the new year opens up before us, why not trade your insecurities for a bold step of faith?

Eunice Porter

2017 Author Biographies

Taiwo Adenekan is a teacher by profession and a local women's ministries leader. She is married to an elder and has four children. She currently resides in the Gambia, West Africa. **July 10**

Priscilla E. Adonis writes from Cape Town, South Africa. She likes writing, card making, and working in the flower garden. She has two daughters and two grandsons that live in the United States. As a widow, she thanks God daily for keeping her safe and for His blessings on her. **Jan. 20, Sept. 7**

Mofoluke I. Akoja is happily married to Olalekan Akoja. They have a fifteen-month-old daughter named Esther. The author works as senior development officer at Babcock University in Nigeria. She enjoys inspiring people and also serves as a church clerk. **Mar. 10**

Ginny Allen, a retired school nurse, lives in Vancouver, Washington, USA, with her husband, David. She has mentored women around the world and is best known for her interest in prayer. She has spoken for retreats, seminars, prayer conferences, church weekends, and camp meetings. She founded Joy! Ministries and has authored *God's Love Song*. **June 1**

Dorett Alleyne lives in Palm Bay, Florida, USA. She and her husband are parents of three wonderful young adults. She is a senior laboratory technologist who loves to sing, cook, organize and plan, watch old movies, and play puzzle games. She is currently a member of the praise team, the choir, and a female quartet in her church. **Apr. 20**

Deniece G. Anderson is a registered nurse living in Atlanta, Georgia, USA. Her motto is, "If I can help somebody as I pass along, then my living shall not be in vain." **May 13**

Rosana Nieton Andrade is a nurse technician. She has always been very active in church, working in the areas of the Beginner and Junior Sabbath School classes as well as in the Adventurer and Pathfinder Clubs. She worked at the Center for Healthy Living and developed evangelism work for eight months in the Fundação Casa de Praia Grande, Brazil. **June 2**

Raquel Queiroz da Costa Arrais is a minister's wife who developed her ministry as an educator for twenty years. Currently, she works as the associate director of the General Conference Women's Ministries Department. She has two adult sons, two daughters-in-law, and one adored grandson, Benjamin. She enjoys music and traveling. **Feb. 21, May 20, Aug. 14, Oct. 2**

Stephanie Arthur is the treasurer at Lawai Valley Seventh-day Adventist Church in Hawaii, USA. She is also the director for the Bags of Love ministry. She and her husband, Martin, have two adult children and four grandchildren. She enjoys walking, gardening, sewing, and cooking. **Sept. 12**

Edna Bacate-Domingo lives in Loma Linda, California, USA. She is an associate professor and serves as an elder, Sabbath School teacher, and superintendent in her church. She has three adult daughters and is blessed with one granddaughter. **May 3, Nov. 11**

Yvita Antonette Villalona Bacchus writes from the Dominican Republic and currently serves as a music director and violinist for her church. She loves writing devotionals. She has been greatly blessed by them over the years. Writing devotionals is her way of forwarding on blessings to others. **May 27**

Taylor Bajic grew up in Chattanooga, Tennessee, USA. After her first year of college, she ventured to Newbold College in England, where she met her husband. She stayed in the United Kingdom for six more years. Her husband, Filip, is a pastor. They recently moved back to Chattanooga, where they hope to continue their ministry. **Mar. 21, Nov. 12**

Carla Baker is the director of Women's Ministries for the North American Division of Seventh-day Adventists. A native Texan, she thoroughly enjoys living in Maryland with its abundance of flowers, trees, and lovely weather. She also likes flower gardening, walking in nature, traveling, and spending time with her grandchildren. **Apr. 5, July 7**

Jennifer M. Baldwin writes from Australia, where she works in risk management at Sydney Adventist Hospital. She enjoys family time, church involvement, Scrabble, and crossword puzzles. She has been contributing to the devotional book series for more than seventeen years. **Sept. 24**

Beatrice Banks is a retired principal and teacher in Pooler, Georgia, USA. She served the South Atlantic Conference for thirty-nine years and also served for eight years on the board of education. She loves gardening, desktop publishing, traveling, the classroom, and home decorating. She has written and published several poems. **May 18**

Rebecca Crittenden Lowry Banks, a retired nurse, has three adult children. She serves her community as a volunteer and enjoys writing, camping, and tending her one hundred-plus houseplants. She volunteers at a multi-denominational help center in Florence, Alabama, USA, where she lives. **Sept. 15**

Adriza Santos Silva Barbosa is a pediatrician who lives in Brazil. She has two treasures: her husband and her beautiful daughter. She likes being with family, hiking outdoors, and participating in the ministry of intercessory prayer. **Dec. 26**

Dottie Barnett is retired and lives in a beautiful country setting in southeast Tennessee, USA. For more than fifty years, she has served in children's and adult Sabbath School leadership. She has written a devotional blog, *Whispers of His Wisdom*, for the past several years. She loves photographing flowers, mowing her large lawn, and camping with her family. **Dec. 9**

Dana M. Bean is an educator from Bermuda. She loves God, food, the color orange, photography, writing, children, and granola. She works for the Lord as a church clerk, Beginner Sabbath School teacher, and leader of the Adventurer Club. **Jan. 2, June 5, Dec. 6**

Annie B. Best is a retired teacher in Washington, D.C., USA, a widow, a mother of two adult children, and a grandmother of three. She enjoys reading and listening to music. Working as a leader in the Beginner and Kindergarten departments of her church years ago inspired her to compose a song, which is published in *Let's Sing Sabbath Songs*. **Apr. 3, Aug. 18**

Cynthia Best-Goring lives in Glendale, Maryland, USA, where she is the principal of an elementary school. Her passion lies in helping children learn, teachers teach, and all become acquainted with our heavenly Father. She is a wife and also the mother of two adult children. Cynthia's hobbies include writing, playing the piano, and reading. **June 21**

Moselle Slaten Blackwell is a retired widow. She has two adult children and one granddaughter. In her church she serves as a deaconess, Sabbath School teacher, and choir member. Her favorite interests are working in the yard, listening to religious music, watching beautiful sunsets, and enjoying a clear, moonlit night sky—all of which speak of God's sovereignty. **June 19**

Suzanne Blaylock is a practicing physician in Muscle Shoals, Alabama, USA. She enjoys providing service for her community as part of her service to God. **Dec. 7**

Fulori Sususewa Bola is a senior lecturer with the School of Education at Pacific Adventist University in Papua New Guinea. She has two adult children, and, apart from teaching, she coordinates a practicum for education and theology students to engage in service to the community for people living with disabilities. **July 4, Aug. 26**

Evelyn Greenwade Boltwood is a mother of two and grandmother to two. She is coordinator for the Western New York Area Adventurers and Master Guides. She is a member of Akoma, a women's community gospel choir that raises scholarship funds for young women matriculating into college. She loves youth ministries and the Lord. **Sept. 27**

Racquel Boswell hails from Jamaica, where she is active in youth ministry. She is a medical technologist who dreams of one day having her own lab. She enjoys a good book on relationships. She also loves singing, preaching, and planning celebratory functions. Racquel has a passion for soul winning. **Sept. 19, Dec. 17**

Tamara Brown lives in Murfreesboro, Tennessee, USA, with her husband and son. She enjoys writing and supporting her spouse in health and couples ministries. She is a U.S. Army veteran who aspires to become a successful Christian author someday. Her favorite Bible text of hope is 1 John 1:9. **Jan. 23, Sept. 26**

Vivian E. Brown is a retired educator residing in Huntsville, Alabama, USA, with the love of her life, Jimmie. She remains active by teaching computers at a senior center and giving private piano lessons in her home. Her favorite pastimes include traveling and photography. She and her husband enjoy a close-knit family of three adult children and six grandchildren. **July 3**

Samantha Bullock lives in the island country of Saint Vincent and the Grenadines in the Caribbean. She is an economist and is actively involved at church with the Sabbath School team. In her spare time she enjoys sightseeing and writing. She is delighted to contribute a devotional to this year's book to help win souls for God's kingdom. **Aug. 20**

Maureen O. Burke was retired and lived in New York, USA. She served her church in many capacities. She enjoyed music, reading, writing, and nurturing new church members. She especially loved engaging in a ministry of encouragement to those who needed it. Maureen died in April 2014. **Sept. 4, Nov. 17**

Joy Butler was born in New Zealand but has lived and worked in many parts of the world. She is a woman of courage and conviction who was profoundly influenced by her grandmother. Joy is a devoted wife, mother of three adults, and doting grandmother of four. Her interests are writing, public speaking, piano playing, bush walking, and meeting new people. **Sept. 9, Nov. 3**

Elizabeth Ida Cain is administrative assistant at a motor vehicle dealership in Jamaica. Active in women's ministries at her church in Saint John, she also teaches floral arranging art design. She appreciates the women's devotional books and those who make them meaningful. As a contributor, she is happy to be part of this journey. **Feb. 3, Sept. 21**

Hyacinth V. Caleb was born and raised in Antigua, West Indies, and attended Seventh-day Adventist universities in Trinidad and Jamaica. She presently resides in Saint Thomas (United States Virgin Islands). She is an educator at the Ivanna Eudora Kean High School in Saint Thomas. **Apr. 17**

Florence E. Callender is a published author, speaker, and speech-language pathologist. She is also president of DaySpring Life Options. She lives in New York, USA with her teenage daughter. Florence's goal is to help others live better by being prepared, passionate, and purposeful every day. **Jan. 7**

Laura A. Canning lives, and was born, in what was the extensive acreage of Windsor Great Park (in England), where, among other varieties of trees, a few very old, tall pine trees stand! In addition to enjoying the company of her pets, she enjoys tinkering about in her garden, writing, and, as time allows, venturing out to find new and interesting places. **Aug. 6**

Ruth Cantrell is a retired teacher and counselor from the Detroit public school system. She is a wife and also the mother of two adult sons. Residing in Belleville, Michigan, USA, she enjoys women's and prayer ministries, reading stories, music, organizing programs, and encouraging others. **June 4**

Evelia R. Cargill lived in Africa as a missionary during her adolescent years. She holds a master's degree and has worked as an early childhood educator for more than ten years. A few of the many activities she enjoys include singing, swimming, and decorating. **July 21**

Eveythe Kennedy Cargill lives in Huntsville, Alabama, USA. She teaches at Calhoun Community College. Eveythe presently serves on the board of elders at the Oakwood University church. She has been married to Stafford for forty-two years. They have two adult children and one grandchild. **July 11**

Raquel Carrera is a member of the Calimesa Seventh-day Adventist Church in California, USA. She is married to Obed, and they have two children, Samuel and Leila. Raquel has a passion for serving God and for education. **Feb. 19**

Cynthia Case-Walters is a registered nurse who loves working with young adults in a community college in Jamaica. She is the mother of three lovely children and has three golden granddaughters. Through the years one of her greatest joys has been working as a volunteer in community services for her church. **Mar. 27**

Maria de Lourdes I. M. Castanho lives in Brazil with her husband; five sons; three daughters-in-law; and granddaughters, Julia and Luisa. She loves working with children and is coordinator for the children's ministries in her church. Her favorite pastimes are making crafts, reading, and being with her family. **Nov. 2**

Marialva Vasconcelos Monteiro Chaussé is married and active in church as a music director. She likes art and painting. She lives in Canavieiras, Bahia, Brazil. **Mar. 20**

Suhana Benny Prasad Chikatla is originally from India but now lives in Alabama with her husband, Royce. She works at Wallace State as an online teaching consultant and trainer and is an adjunct professor at Auburn University. She volunteers as an executive council member for women's ministries. Her passions include making new friends and recycling. **June 30**

Caroline Chola lives in Pretoria, South Africa. She is currently the Women's and Children's Ministries director of the Southern Africa-Indian Ocean Division. She is married to Habson, and they have four adult sons and two grandchildren. She enjoys gardening, but her passion is to see women discover their potential and use it to the glory of God. **June 14**

Rosemarie Clardy writes from Candler, North Carolina, USA, where she and her husband enjoy the blessings of country living while raising their three teenage sons, along with many family pets. They volunteer at church and school. **May 30**

Ella Clark-Tolliver is a retired college dean, counselor, and professor. She provides seminars and training throughout the United States and is an author of one book and a variety of articles. She is an active member of her local church in northern California. **June 7**

Kelli Raí Collins grew up singing with her sisters in church. She loves writing poems and songs and periodically sends out devotional thoughts via e-mail to friends and loved ones. She is currently working on a bachelor of arts degree in English. She lives in Suitland, Maryland, USA, with her husband and three children. **Dec. 24**

Rose Eva Bana Constantino is the widow of Abraham A. Constantino Jr. She is the mother of Charles, Kenneth, and Abraham III. She serves as a faculty member at the University of Pittsburgh School of Nursing. **Sept. 25**

Sandi B. Cook is married to Tim and has a daughter and a granddaughter. She lives on a farm in Alabama, USA. An occupational health nurse, Sandi loves helping people and serves as church clerk. **May 8, Dec. 30**

Maria Raimunda Lopes Costa resides in Bacabal, Maranhão, Brazil. She is a teacher, a writer, and a poet. She is involved in missionary work and is an avid reader of the women's devotional books. She has a published book, *Vivências* (Experiences). She enjoys walking and reading good literature. **May 9**

Patricia Cove writes from Ontario, Canada. She is a semiretired teacher and enjoys all outdoor pursuits, especially sailing and hiking. She has published two books. Her greatest desire is to see her family in heaven. She is actively involved in her local church and community. **June 20**

Sabrina Crichlow resides in Clifton, New Jersey, USA, with her husband and two children. She is a Christian woman who loves the Lord and shares this love through her actions to those in need. Loving people beyond their pain is what she aspires to do daily through her time, talent, and resources. **Mar. 19**

Marsha-Jay Dallas is a Jamaican poet and teacher of Spanish whose fascination with writing began at an early age. She enjoys reading and traveling and is passionate in her support for Adventist Christian education. She is grateful to God to be able to use her talent to His glory and to help others. **Feb. 17**

Avery Davis lives in England. She has a passion for women's ministries and loves to write. She considers it a privilege to be able to record and share these stories and thanks God for the support of her husband and children. **July 23**

Lisa DeGraw lives in New Mexico, USA, with her fabulous husband (John) and their two homeschooled children. Recently, she was published in *Backyard Poultry* when she won an essay contest about life stories with poultry. Her hobbies include bird watching and photography. **May 11**

Bernadine Delafield and her husband moved to Florida after her retirement from the North American Division Office of Communication. She is currently doing contract work for that division. Her love for travel and family makes life lovely! **May 12**

Karen Welch Dobbin, a physiotherapist, recently completed a master of science degree in cancer rehabilitation. She passionately provides rehabilitation for those diagnosed with cancer. Karen is director of health ministries at her local church in Winnipeg, Canada. **Oct. 1, Nov. 20**

Leonie Donald thanks God every day for the beauty of Queen Charlotte Sound, New Zealand, where she lives. She enjoys long walks, "devours" books, and admits to spending more time in her garden than doing housework. Leonie and her husband of more than forty-seven years attend the Blenheim Seventh-day Adventist Church. **Dec. 12**

Lenora Dorf lives in Huntsville, Alabama, USA. She became an Adventist through the ministry of a literature evangelist. She herself has had a very successful career in literature evangelism. She desires to continue giving Bible studies to share the good news of Jesus and to bring lost souls to Him. She is mother of three adult children and four grandchildren. **Aug. 7**

Louise Driver and her husband, Don, are retired but have been retreaded with different part-time jobs. They travel around the state preaching and leading out in singing at various churches. She volunteers as an elementary school librarian. She enjoys living in Idaho, USA, where her three sons and their families live. Her hobbies are music, gardening, and traveling to historic sites. **June 27**

Mary E. Dunkin is a daughter, sister, aunt, cousin, friend, caregiver, home economist, Pathfinder, teacher, seamstress, concierge, business owner, writer, and daughter of God. She is most proud of being God's daughter and eagerly waits for Him to come back. Until then she'll keep working. Her home state is New Mexico, USA. **Mar. 9, Sept. 5**

Pauline A. Dwyer-Kerr is a native of the beautiful island of Jamaica. She resides in Florida, USA, where she is currently a professor. In her church she has served as elder and in several other positions. She loves to travel and enjoys the outdoors. **Mar. 17**

Peggy S. Rusike Edden is a mother of three and a grandmother to one lovely little girl. In 2014 Peggy married her loving sweetheart, Robert Edden. She now attends Redditch Seventh-day Adventist Church in England. **Apr. 25**

Ruby H. Enniss-Alleyne writes from Guyana, South America. She serves as youth elder and family ministries leader at her home church, Mount Carmel. She lost her spouse, Ashton, in January 2011. She enjoys spending time with her three adult children, daughter-in-law, and adorable grandson, Alaric. **Feb. 7**

Pat Everson writes from Las Vegas, Nevada, USA. This is her first submission to the General Conference Women's Ministries devotional book project. **Dec. 2**

Mona Fellers is a pharmacy liaison helping people with mental illness. She is the women's ministries leader in her church. She lives in Colorado, USA, with her husband and has two lovely daughters and one grandson. She loves animals, birds, and serving the Lord. **June 15**

Melinda Ferguson At the time of this writing, Melinda lives in Rapid City, South Dakota, USA, and works as a registered nurse. She enjoys helping with various church programs, especially music. She keeps busy assisting family and, in her spare time, enjoys catching up with friends or reading. **Aug. 13**

Carol Joy Fider is a retired educator from Mandeville, Jamaica. She and her husband have two adult daughters. She is an elder, family ministries leader, and Sabbath School teacher in her church. The yearning of her heart is to go with Jesus when He gathers the saints of all ages. She enjoys mentoring young people, cooking, and gardening. **Feb. 27**

Edith Fitch, before her death in 2016, enjoyed a forty-one-year teaching career. In 1993 she found her second great joy in life—volunteering—which she did in the archive department at Burman University in Lacombe, Alberta, Canada. **Feb. 10, May 28, Aug. 9**

Lana Fletcher lives in Chehalis, Washington, USA, with her husband. They have one married daughter and two grandsons. Their younger daughter was killed in a car accident in 1993. She is grateful for her computer. It allows her to enlarge things, and she still enjoys reading, writing, and proofreading the church bulletin. **Nov. 27**

Heide Ford is a licensed Adventist minister serving as a hospital chaplain in California. She has served as a registered nurse, pastoral counselor, cofounder and associate editor of *Women of Spirit* magazine, and director of the Women's Resource Center in Southern California, USA. She loves dolphin and whale watching; walks with her husband, Zell; and *real* conversation. **Oct. 15**

Edith C. Fraser is a retired university professor in social work. She was in education for more than thirty years and speaks nationally and internationally about issues for women, families, and spiritual growth. She has been married for more than forty-five years and has two adult children and two grandchildren. **Aug. 15**

Lori Futcher is a freelance writer and editor. She has written for the *Adventist Review, Guide, Insight,* and the *Journal of Adventist Education.* Her son (mentioned in her story) is now a teenager, and she has also been blessed with a precious daughter. **Sept. 20**

Claudette Garbutt-Harding, originally from Belize, now lives in Orlando, Florida, USA. She has been an Adventist educator from kindergarten level through college for more than forty years. She has worked in Belize, Jamaica, and now Florida. She has been supporting her husband, Dr. Keith Harding, in ministry for more than thirty-six years. **Feb. 28, Oct. 16**

Georgina George is from the Caribbean island of Dominica. She is a teacher and completed her education program at Burman University in Lacombe, Alberta, Canada, where she now lives with her three teenage daughters. She is actively involved with children's and women's ministries and enjoys singing and coordinating musical programs in her local church. **Mar. 30**

Yan Siew Ghiang is a Singaporean Seventh-day Adventist Christian who works as a temporary in-home caregiver. The hawker center, an open-air complex where food is cooked and sold from vendor stalls, is her "evangelism network." She loves to read and write and do indoor exercises. **Apr. 12, Nov. 21**

Evelyn Glass and her husband, Darrell, live on their family farm in northwestern Minnesota, USA. Their greatest joy in life is spending time with their children, grandchildren, and their families. Evelyn keeps busy writing, serving her church, and quilting. Life is good. **Nov. 8**

Beverly P. Gordon lives in Pennsylvania, USA, with her husband of thirty-five years. She is a college professor and mother of two adult sons. She is active in ministry to families and youth. She enjoys gardening and writing in her spare time. **July 14**

Mayla Magaieski Graepp is a first-year student of architecture in Brazil. As a scholarship student, she works at the White Center as a research assistant. She likes to focus on studies and to research the history of her family. She also likes to run. Her aim is to reach others for Christ through her published articles. **July 16**

Cecelia Grant is a Seventh-day Adventist medical doctor retired from government service and living in Kingston, Jamaica. Her hobbies are traveling, gardening, and listening to good music. She has a passion for young people, to whom she is always giving advice. **Jan. 25, July 19**

Jasmine E. Grant is a retired social worker who worked as a senior counselor for eighteen years among pregnant addicts and addicted mothers in Jamaica, New York. She attends the Springfield Gardens church and is actively involved with hospitality and women's and family life ministries. As an avid reader, she enjoys autobiographical, self-help, and natural-cure books. **Sept. 18**

Glenda-mae Greene, a retired university educator, writes from her wheelchair in Palm Bay, Florida, USA. She enjoys meeting people and sharing in the narrative of their lives. She is a member of her church's disability ministries team. **July 12, Dec. 3**

Gloria Gregory currently serves as dean of the College of Education and Leadership at Northern Caribbean University in Jamaica. Through health and leadership presentations, she seeks to lead others toward positive life choices. She and her husband, Milton, a church administrator, have been involved in ministry for more than thirty-five years. **Jan. 18, Sept. 30**

Vicki Griffin is the director of the Lifestyle Matters Health Intervention series, the director of Health Ministries for the Michigan Conference of Seventh-day Adventists, and the editor of *Balance* magazine and the *Balanced Living* tract series. She has authored numerous books, and she lectures worldwide, sharing the lifestyle link to better mental, physical, and spiritual health. **Dec. 8**

Meibel Mello Guedes is a retired pastor's wife. She was one of the pioneers of women's ministries and AFAM (Shepherdess) in Brazil. Today she is dedicated to writing books and articles and lecturing at church events and educational institutions. She coordinates a graduate course on family therapy and counseling. She lives in Curitiba, Paraná, Brazil. **June 25, Dec. 15**

Maria Bellesi Guilhem worked as a secretary in an Adventist organization in Brazil for thirty years. A pastor's wife with three children and four grandchildren, she is now retired and lives with her husband in São Carlos, São Paulo, Brazil. She enjoys visiting the elderly. **Feb. 9**

Diantha Hall-Smith is a daughter of God. She is the wife of a devoted Christian husband who serves in the U.S. Air Force. They have two beautiful children. She was born in New York City and has had the honor and privilege of living in, and visiting, interesting places, domestically and globally. She enjoys writing, traveling, and spending time with her family. **Feb. 11**

Flore Aubry Hamilton loves the Lord. She lives in Huntsville, Alabama, USA, with her husband George T. Hamilton, and is the mother of two adult daughters. **July 17**

Deborah M. Harris, PhD, is CEO of Deborah Harris, Inc., an educational consulting business. She is known for her inspirational messages and is the founder of Praying for Our Children (prayingforourchildren.org). Deborah has two adult children and four grandchildren. **Nov. 16**

Marian Hart-Gay is a retired elementary teacher and nursing home administrator living in Avon Park, Florida, USA. She and her husband enjoy traveling, mission projects, and volunteering. Their greatest desire is to exemplify Jesus and to share His love with others. Between them they enjoy five children and seventeen grandchildren, counting spouses. **July 1**

Beverly D. Hazzard is the daughter of medical missionaries. She was born in England and grew up with her two brothers in Jamaica, Ohio, and British Columbia. She is a retired nurse administrator and lives in Kelowna, British Columbia, Canada. Mother of two adult children and grandma to five, she enjoys time with family, her dogs, travel, sailing, and mission trips. **Aug. 21**

Helen Heavirland, an author, speaker, and encourager, lives in Oregon, USA. For more information or inspiration, go to www.helenheavirland.com. Helen's latest book is titled *My God is Bigger*. **Mar. 18**

Marge Vande Hei is the mother of three and a grandmother. She has always lived in Green Bay, Wisconsin, USA, and is married to her high school sweetheart. She enjoys reading, walking, and bicycling. Her friends say she is fun loving, has a great sense of humor, and always sees the glass half full rather than half empty. She is always ready to pray with her friends. **Feb. 2**

Muriel Heppel enjoys nature and wildlife (from a distance). She is involved in church and community activities. She likes keeping in touch with her many friends and making new friends. She has a prayer ministry and enjoys bird watching, reading, traveling, and playing Scrabble and Upwords. **Jan. 13**

Denise Dick Herr teaches English at Burman University in Lacombe, Alberta, Canada. She agrees with writer C. S. Lewis that "you can never get a cup of tea large enough or a book long enough to suit me." She enjoys reading, writing, traveling, and the potential that each day brings. **July 20, Nov. 13**

Vashti Hinds-Vanier, born in Guyana, South America, recently celebrated her fiftieth anniversary of entering the nursing profession. She is widely traveled throughout Europe, Africa, and the Caribbean. Her hobbies include cake decorating and gardening. She enjoys spending time with her grandson, Jaden, and resides in Brooklyn, New York, USA. **Nov. 6**

Denise Hochstrasser is the director of Women's Ministries for the Inter-European Division and lives in Switzerland. Her vision is that all people would have the same possibilities in life and be free to accept a calling without restriction. **Feb. 1, Dec. 21**

Roxy Hoehn lives in Topeka, Kansas, USA, where she loves it when any of her eleven grandchildren join her at her squeaky rocking chair and read God's Word together! **Feb. 5, Aug. 27**

Karen Holford is a freelance writer, communication project manager, and family therapist living in Crieff, Scotland, where her husband is president of the Scottish Mission of Seventh-day Adventists. She enjoys writing, creative worship, sewing, and teaching recycled crafts at a local community recycling project. **Oct. 6, Nov. 26**

Tamyra Horst writes from Paradise, Pennsylvania, USA, where she lives with Tim, her husband of more than thirty years. An author, speaker, and communication director for the Pennsylvania Conference of Seventh-day Adventists, she loves being a mom to her two young adult sons and being a friend to an amazing group of women. **Sept. 13, Sept. 14, Nov. 22, Nov. 23**

Jacqueline Hope HoShing-Clarke has served in education as a principal, an assistant principal, and a teacher since 1979. She currently serves Northern Caribbean University as chair of the Teacher Education Department. She is married and has two adult children and one grandson. Jackie enjoys writing and gardening. **Feb. 20, Nov. 5**

Kristen Hudson is a graduate of Oakwood University. She enjoys writing, reading, and listening to good music. She lives in Huntsville, Alabama, USA, and likes to use the gift God gave her to encourage others. She hopes one day to publish a book. **Oct. 4**

Barbara Huff, a grandmother and freelance writer, attends the Seventh-day Adventist church in Port Charlotte, Florida, USA, with her husband. She loves to grow orchids and watch the birds at her feeder. **Apr. 30**

Patty L. Hyland is a retired teacher from Oregon's Rogue Community College as well as having taught elementary and secondary school in the mission field. She has been a pastor's wife for more than forty-five years and served by his side as a missionary in Sri Lanka and the Palau islands for fourteen years. She is chaplain at Asante Three Rivers Medical Center in Grants Pass, Oregon, USA. **May 29**

Shirley C. Iheanacho enjoys visiting shut-ins and going on Maranatha mission trips with her husband, Morris. She likes to encourage women to write and share their stories. She also speaks at churches, visits her children and grandchildren, and shares devotional books with strangers. She and Morris have been happily married for more than forty-six years. **Apr. 28, Dec. 29**

Merrilou Wilder Inks is a Christian musician and singer. She and her husband, Skip, live in Texas, where they continue her music ministry as well as run their family businesses. **Mar. 12**

Ericka J. Iverson and her husband, Jeff, are parents to two children, and they live in the sticks in northern Minnesota, USA. Ericka loves being a homeschooling mom and getting to see all the little "aha" moments in teaching her children! They greatly enjoy traveling, camping, and visiting waterfalls as well as Lake Superior and Lake Michigan. **Mar. 25**

Avis Floyd Jackson lives in Pleasantville, New Jersey, USA, and is a mother of five. She does business out of her home and is a party planner. Avis is active in her local church and is an Adventist by calling. **Apr. 23**

Joan D. L. Jaensch lives with her husband, Murray, in Murray Bridge, South Australia. They have two married sons, four grandchildren, and two great-grandchildren. Gardening and potted plants are her hobbies. **July 28**

Greta Michelle Joachim-Fox-Dyett is a wife, mother, artist, potter, writer, and teacher. Most of all, she is a child of the Most High God. At the time she wrote this devotional, she was earning her second degree in fine arts. She lives in Trinidad and Tobago. **May 17**

Elaine J. Johnson lives in Alabama, USA with her better half of more than forty-six years. She is active in her small country church. She has four children, twelve grandchildren, and three great-grandchildren. She enjoys reading, writing, and "computering." **May 21, Aug. 3**

Erna Johnson was born and raised in Iceland. She is director of Women's Ministries for the South Pacific Division. She is married to a pastor, Eddy. They have two adult children, and she loves being a grandmother. Her passion is helping women reach their potential in Jesus. **Mar. 7, July 30**

Jeannette Busby Johnson lives in Maryland, USA, which has many of the same letters as "Montana" (where she grew up) but none of the mountains. She has three adult children, six grandchildren, and a dignified coon hound named Ludwig. **Jan. 30, Sept. 29**

Angie Joseph is a pastor's wife, codirector of lay evangelism in the Iowa-Missouri Conference, and a Bible instructor. She speaks at women's retreats. **Aug. 29**

Gerene I. Joseph is married. She and her husband have two teenage children. Presently, she is director of Education at the North Caribbean Conference. She enjoys writing poems and playing the piano in her spare time. **Aug. 17**

Mukatimui Kalima-Munalula, MD, is training as an obstetrician and gynecologist in Lusaka, Zambia. She is married to Themba and blessed with three children and a nephew. She enjoys new recipes and running for charity. **Apr. 14**

Carolyn K. Karlstrom is a Bible worker for her home church in the Pacific Northwest, USA. She gives Bible studies, teaches, and preaches. She is also a freelance writer. Her articles have appeared in a variety of magazines. She is married to Rick, and they have a sweet black cat named Minuet. **Jan. 11**

Sonia Kennedy-Brown lives in Ontario, Canada. She is a retired nurse and teacher. She is presently working on her autobiography. She likes to read and dabble in writing poetry. "Service to others" is her motto. To those in need of them, she is ready to offer a listening ear, a Bible promise, and a hot cup of soup. **Feb. 4**

Iris L. Kitching enjoys writing poetry and creating children's picture books. She worked at the Seventh-day Adventist Church world headquarters: ten years in General Conference Women's Ministries, and more than ten years in General Conference Presidential. She and her husband, Will, delight in visiting family and friends, whether near or far. **Jan. 22, Apr. 24**

Kênia Kopitar is Brazilian but now lives in Florida, USA. She enjoys gardening, writing, reading, teaching music and piano, and taking care of animals. Her greatest desire is to meet God and her loved ones at Jesus' second coming. **June 6**

Betty Kossick A freelance writer, Betty has been part of seventy-seven books. She has authored three of her own: *Beyond the Locked Door, Heart Ballads,* and *The Manor.* For more information, e-mail her at bkwrites4u@hotmail.com. **Aug. 16, Oct. 19**

Patricia Mulraney Kovalski lives in Collegedale, Tennessee, USA. She loves to travel and enjoys her visits with her family in Michigan. She has many hobbies and has been doing English teas for family and friends since 1997. **June 22**

Andrea Kristensen lives in Vail, Arizona, USA, where she is a retired college and academy English teacher, a former editor for the General Conference, and a former copy editor at the Review and Herald Publishing Association. Currently she edits for her local church. Her hobbies include reading, writing, hiking, and, most recently, off-roading. **May 23**

Kay Kuzma, EdD, the president of Family Matters Ministry and a retired university professor, is still helping families by writing and producing television and radio spots from Kauai, Hawaii, USA. **Apr. 4**

Mabel Kwei, a retired university and college lecturer, did missionary work in Africa for many years with her pastor husband and their three children. Now living in New Jersey, USA, she reads a lot and loves to paint, write, and spend time with little children. **Jan. 19, Aug. 8**

Sally Lam-Phoon is a retired Women's, Family, and Children's Ministries division director with a new mission—to grandparent her four grandkids. Living in Singapore, she still enjoys challenging women to unleash their potential and use their gifts for the Lord. **June 23, June 24**

Janet Lankheet, a mother of four, was a news reporter before entering editorial work for the church and traveling worldwide as a minister. She lives in Michigan, USA, and is a local church elder. Her delights are her husband, Roger, her grandgirls, her CKCS (Cavalier King Charles spaniel) puppy, her betta fish, and her violets and orchids. **June 12**

Iani Dias Lauer-Leite lives in Bahia, Brazil. She is a college professor. At church she likes to help in music and prayer ministries. **Dec. 4**

Wilma Kirk Lee currently directs the Center for Family Wholeness (CFW) located in Houston, Texas, USA. She serves as codirector of Family Ministries for the Southwest Region Conference along with her pastor husband. She is a licensed clinical social worker. **Mar. 23**

Donna Sherrill Lewis lives in Caldwell, Idaho, USA, and enjoys gardening. She and her husband volunteer for community services two days a week and are involved in their church. She is finding it a bit hard to make a change to town living instead of country living. But she feels it was in God's plan. **May 6, Nov. 25**

Jan Hooper Lind enjoys being involved with music at the Coeur d'Alene, Idaho, USA, Seventh-day Adventist Church. She is married, a mom to five adults, and a grandmother to five grandchildren. Retirement from the nursing profession gives her time to knit. **Apr. 1, Apr. 2**

Sharon Long (Brown) is retired from her social work career with the government of Alberta in Canada. She is putting her training—as an associate certified coach (ACC)—to good use and is enjoying the fruits of her labor. She and her husband, Miguel Brown, love to travel and shop. Sharon likes to entertain, write, and work for her Lord and Savior, Jesus Christ. **Jan. 10, Oct. 21**

Mary Louis is a retired social worker. She and her husband live in California, USA, where she is active in visitation of the sick and the homebound. She has had several articles published. Additionally, she volunteers by writing memoirs for veterans of World War II. **Sept. 17**

Lynn Mfuru Lukwaro was born and raised in Tanzania. She and her husband live in Sharjah, United Arab Emirates, together with their two beautiful daughters. They serve the Lord in their church. Lynn enjoys traveling, stories, nature walks, teaching, and reading. **May 5**

Jeanene MacLean is married and lives in California, USA, where she enjoys birding with her husband, as well as reading, playing the piano, cooking, and baking. She is the mother of one young adult son, with whom she enjoys spending time whenever possible. **June 26**

Rhona Grace Magpayo is a retired optician who has a passion for helping people see better. She and her husband participate in annual mission trips to the Philippines with Operation Hope International. She has two adult children. She loves photography, traveling, and singing with the Sligo Friends. **July 8**

Debbie Maloba is the director of Women's and Children's Ministries for the East-Central Africa Division of the Seventh-day Adventist Church. She and her husband, Jim, have been blessed with five children. Debbie loves to train women in leadership and to make ministry proposals. **Sept. 10, Nov. 28**

Nokuthula Maphosa-Mutumhe is the first child of seven. Her father died when she was six. Her uncle took her in while her mother held a job in the city. Her life was not easy. These life challenges brought her to the knowledge of God quite early. She is now married with two children and is working toward a nutrition degree, as she has always aspired to do. **Feb. 12**

Zeny Marcelo and her husband live in California, USA, but have spent the last ten years as self-supporting missionaries to the Philippines. They are involved with the Adventist World Aviation Foundation. Both are active in church. They have four children and six grandchildren. Zeny enjoys playing the piano, quilting, and floral design. **Apr. 6, Nov. 18**

Rojean Vasquez Marcia writes from the Adventist International Mission School in Thailand, where she is teaching. Prior to this, she taught kindergarten through high school in the Philippines. She attends church at the Asia-Pacific International University (AIU) church and is involved in prayer ministry and community outreach through visitation to the AIDS hospice in Lopburi. **Aug. 11**

Marilyn Thompson Marshall is a teacher from Trinidad. She is also the mother of two adult children and grandmother of two girls. She is active in her church and served as women's ministries leader in 2013. She is presently pursuing a bachelor's degree in education. God has kept her in the palm of His hand, and He won't let her go. **Jan. 27**

Premila Masih serves the Southern Asia Division as director of Women's Ministries. She is married to a pastor, and they have two children. She has worked as a teacher for twenty-six years and served as a Shepherdess coordinator in her union. Her passion is house decorating, reading, and making friends. **Sept. 23**

Gail Masondo is a wife, mother of two adult children (Shellie and Jonathan), women's and children's advocate, songwriter, chaplain, Life in Recovery coach, and international speaker. She has authored *Now This Feels Like Home.* A New York native, Gail now resides in Johannesburg, South Africa, with her musician husband, Victor Sibusiso Masondo. **Dec. 27, Dec. 28**

Deborah Matshaya writes from South Africa, where she is a teacher. She enjoys gospel music and has contributed many times to the General Conference Women's Ministries devotional books. **July 25, Oct. 20**

Retha McCarty is retired and lives in Missouri, USA. She enjoys reading, crafts, poetry, crocheting, and birding. She has made numerous quilt tops for the Bags of Love ministry. She has been a church treasurer since 1977 and publishes a church newsletter each month. She is the author of a poetry book: *Rainbow of Rhymes.* **Aug. 30, Nov. 19**

Vidella McClellan is retired and lives in beautiful British Columbia, Canada. She is married, has children, and is a grandmother and great-grandmother. She loves to work in her garden among the flower beds. She is active in church and the community. She loves cats. Her current hobbies are crossword puzzles, Sudoku, Scrabble, and miscellaneous crafts. **Feb. 13, Oct. 25**

Nerida McKibben, an obstetrician and gynecologist from New Zealand, has a strong interest in lifestyle medicine as evidenced on the daily television show *Go Healthy . . . for Good,* which she hosts for the Hope Channel. She now lives in Silver Spring, Maryland, and shares a love of evangelism with her pastor husband, Dan. **May 4, July 24, Dec. 23**

Vicki Mellish is an occupational therapist who lives in Ontario, Canada. One of her favorite ways to study Scripture is to explore the analogies between its teachings and nature and the human body. Vicki is actively involved in prayer meetings at her local church. **Jan. 15**

Gertrude Mfune is a native of Malawi. She has been married to her pastor husband, Saustin, for more than thirty-seven years. She has three boys, one daughter, and two granddaughters. Fulfillment comes in mentoring young pastors' wives, helping in children's Sabbath School, singing in the choir, and gardening. Her hobby is learning new skills. **July 13**

Annette Walwyn Michael writes from Saint Croix, United States Virgin Islands. She is a retired English teacher and a published writer of Caribbean literature. Three adult daughters, three sons-in-law, and seven grandchildren are beautiful additions to her family. Her husband is a busy retired pastor. **Jan. 16, Oct. 11**

Quilvie G. Mills is a retired community college professor. She and her husband are members of the Port Saint Lucie Seventh-day Adventist Church in Florida, USA, where she serves as a musician and Bible class teacher. She enjoys traveling, music, gardening, word games, reading, and teaching piano. **June 29**

Marcia Mollenkopf, a retired teacher, lives in Klamath Falls, Oregon, USA. She enjoys church involvement and has served in both adult and children's departments. Her hobbies include reading, writing, music, and birding. **Sept. 28, Nov. 14**

Esperanza Aquino Mopera is founder and president of Polillo Life Enhancement Organization, Inc., a civic organization with the purpose of assisting families in finding trades or livelihoods to enhance their living conditions. **Feb. 26, July 6**

Lourdes Morales-Gudmundsson, PhD, is a university professor of Spanish language and literature and has been published widely in Seventh-day Adventist publications. Though living in California, USA, she has presented her seminar, *I Forgive You, But . . .* , on three continents and in most of the United States. She can be reached at lmorales@lasierra.edu. **Sept. 1, Sept. 2, Sept. 3**

Lila Farrell Morgan, who writes from North Carolina, USA, is a widow with five adult children, five grandchildren, and one great-grandchild. She attends the church where she and her physician husband were charter members more than fifty years ago. She enjoys her grandchildren, reading, baking, table games, observing nature, and keeping in touch with family and friends. **Aug. 24**

Valerie Hamel Morikone works for the Mountain View Conference in West Virginia, USA, and leads out in the Communications and Women's Ministries Departments. She loves to read, cook, bake, and do Internet research. **Mar. 29**

Nilva de F. Oliveira da Boa Morte lives in the state of Mato Grosso, Brazil, with her husband, Jucinei Claudio C. da Boa Morte. She teaches art, works in the state health department, and acts as secretary at church. She enjoys reading, painting, and witnessing about what Christ has done in her life. **Jan. 28, Aug. 12**

Kelly Mowrer is a speaker, writer, and concert pianist. Kelly founded and heads Live at the Well, a ministry encouraging others in the joy of practical, vital friendship with God. She lives with her husband and two sons in Tennessee, USA. **May 25, Dec. 25**

Dianne Murphy writes from Corner Brook, Newfoundland, Canada. She is a wife, mother, and grandmother. She enjoys the outdoors and likes to walk the hiking trails. She enjoys Bible studies with her friends and sharing Jesus' love whenever the opportunity arises. **May 26**

Judith M. Mwansa is originally from Zambia but currently lives in Laurel, Maryland, USA. She works for General Conference Women's Ministries and enjoys reading, music, traveling, and meeting new pastors' wives. She and her husband have adult children. **May 22**

Samantha Nelson loves serving alongside her pastor husband, Steve. She is CEO of the Hope of Survivors, an organization that assists victims of clergy sexual abuse. In her spare time (which is minimal!), she and Steve enjoy traveling, researching family history and genealogy, hiking in the mountains, and spending time with God in nature. **Mar. 1, Mar. 2**

Flore Njiki received a scholarship from General Conference Women's Ministries and decided to write a devotional to help other women achieve their dreams of obtaining a higher education. She writes from Cameroon, and this is her first submission. **Jan. 9**

Judith Fletcher Norwood, RN, has been her local church's children's ministries leader for more than thirty-five years. She is mother of Joey, wife of David, and grandmother of two. **June 8**

Linda Nottingham lives in Florida, USA, and teaches an adult Bible study class at her church. She is semi-retired but serves as a mentor to women business owners. She was also a 2012 honoree who was recognized by the Florida Commission on the Status of Women. **Mar. 31**

Diane Shellyn Nudd lives in the south of the United States. She is currently telecommunications advertising producer at Life Care Centers of America's corporate headquarters in Cleveland, Tennessee. She has served as a board member for the Chattanooga Chamber of Commerce and has produced a call-in talk show. **July 22**

Victoria C. Nwogwugwu is a registered nurse by profession. Vicki has a bachelor's degree in nursing and lives in New York, USA, where she works as a nurse administrator in a psychiatric hospital. Vicki is a wife, is mother of four children, and loves to tell people about the Lord Jesus. **Dec. 14**

Beth Versteegh Odiyar writes from Canada, where she has managed the family chimney sweep business since 1985. She has three children and delightful grandchildren. She enjoys mission trips, road trips, and creative homemaking. She hopes to become a writer and a painter. **Apr. 11, Nov. 10**

Daniela Santos de Oliveira was born in São Paulo, the capital of Brazil. She is married and teaches music. She likes singing, cooking, and going to the beach. She loves animals and being with her family and friends. **Mar. 3**

Monique Lucile de Oliveira lives in the United Kingdom with her husband, who is a lay preacher. They have two sons. She attends Newbold College, enjoys teaching Bible stories to Kindergarten children, and makes her own crafts to accompany the Bible lessons. **July 31**

Rosângela Carniato Camargo de Oliveira lives in Marília, Brazil, where she is an educator. Her favorite pastimes are reading and playing with her son. In church, she teaches the Beginner and Kindergarten classes. She is also director for women's and youth ministries. **Apr. 19**

Jemima Dollosa Orillosa lives in Maryland with her husband, Danny, and is a proud grandmother. Jemima's passion is organizing mission trips. She also loves to travel, visit her daughters, and see places with the family and her "golden girls" friends. **Nov. 24**

Charlotte Osei-Agyeman writes from Ghana, where she is the director of Women's Ministries for the South Ghana Conference. **Aug. 5**

Sharon Oster is a retired teacher assistant living in Evans, Colorado, USA, with her retired pastor husband. She enjoys day car trips in the nearby Rocky Mountains. She and her husband have three children and seven grandchildren. **May 16, Oct. 12**

Hannele Ottschofski lives in Germany. A speaker for the Hope Channel she organizes women's events, has compiled several women's devotionals, and has published a book, *My Father's Shirt*. **Jan. 21**

Bev Owen resides in Acworth, Georgia, USA. She has two adult children and four grandchildren and is married to Wayne. Currently, she and her husband own an assisted-living home and feel blessed to continue their ministry through serving the elderly. One of her hobbies is writing, and she has had numerous articles published. **Apr. 18**

Sharon Michael Palmer, a medical doctor, is married to Army Specialist Matthew Palmer. They reside in Fort Benning, Georgia, USA. **Mar. 16**

Revel Papaioannou works with her retired-but-working pastor husband in the biblical town of Berea, Greece. They have four sons and fourteen grandchildren. She is very active in her church, and her free time is filled with visiting, Bible studies, mountain hiking, and—whenever possible—reading and hobbies. **Jan. 3, Oct. 22**

Carmem Virgínia dos Santos Paulo graduated in languages and literature. She is a specialist in linguistics and teaching as well as a health and socio-educational agent. In her free time she likes to read, sing, and speak of God's love to others. At church, she is the youth director and the associate music director. **Feb. 6, June 16**

Grace Paulson, originally from Sri Lanka, now lives in New Zealand with her family. She works at Massey University and is the worship leader at her church. Her hobbies are painting, sewing, classical music, and gardening. She is writing her first book. **Sept. 22, Nov. 7**

Karen J. Pearson is director of publicity and public relations at Pacific Press Publishing Association in Nampa, Idaho, USA. Her favorite activities include writing and speaking of Jesus. She and her pastor husband have two adult children. **Oct. 14**

Evelyn G. Pelayo helps to finish God's work at the Adventist University Zurcher in Madagascar. She loves, and enjoys sharing with, orphans and needy people. Originally she is from Odiongan, Romblon, Philippines. She is married to Roger Zulueta Pelayo, and they have two sons. **Sept. 6**

Kathy Pepper is a pastor's wife and a teacher in Charleston, West Virginia, USA. She and her husband have three children and two in-laws. She enjoys graphic designing and uses this creativity in her teaching and pastoral ministry. **Feb. 23, July 29**

Sueli da Silva Pereira is a business manager and works in city hall. She has held various positions in the church—currently as a teacher of teenagers and as secretary of the Pathfinder club. She has a handsome and wonderful husband and three beautiful children. Her big dream is to someday go to her Father's home and live eternally with Him. **Feb. 8, Oct. 26**

Céleste Perrino-Walker is a much published Vermont author. News about her most recent books and upcoming releases can be found on her Web site: cperrinowalker.com. **Jan. 26, Apr. 22, Nov. 4**

Betty Glover Perry is a retired anesthetist. She and her husband are parents, grandparents, and great-grandparents. Her hobbies are playing piano and organ, researching and writing, and also mentoring and counseling. In addition, she composes articles for the devotional book and for a healthy living cookbook. She writes from North Carolina, USA. **May 31, Oct. 30**

Diane Pestes, international speaker and servant of God, is known for her commitment to Christ, memorization of scripture, and life-changing prayers. Her encouraging messages include Bible truth, life-changing stories, and practical applications. Diane resides in Oregon, USA. Her ministry is profiled on her Web site at dianepestes.com. **Mar. 28**

Angèle Peterson lives in Ohio and enjoys taking everyday occurrences and relating them to her spiritual life. She is eagerly, patiently, and faithfully awaiting Christ's soon return and proclaims the promise of Hebrews 10:37. **Nov. 29**

Margo Peterson writes from Eagan, Minnesota, and is a program assistant in special education. She has three children. She tutors reading and mathematics. Besides studying at school, she works with the young people of her church and spends time reading, traveling, walking, and enjoying her family. **July 2, Oct. 29**

Birdie Poddar is a retiree and comes from northeastern India but has settled in southern India. She has two adult children and five grandchildren. She enjoys gardening, cooking, baking, telling stories, writing articles, and composing poems. She is doing a handcrafted card ministry for those who need comfort and encouragement and does so to glorify God's name. **Feb. 15, Oct. 23**

Prudence LaBeach Pollard, PhD, MPH, RD, SPHR, is vice president for Research and Employee Services at Oakwood University, USA. She is also interim director of the Dietetic program and professor of Management. She has authored the book *Raise a Leader, God's Way.* It is available at www.adventistbookcenter.com or as an eBook at amazon.com. **Aug. 1, Aug. 2**

Eunice Porter is a retired Oregon, USA, state worker who is active in continued learning at Willamette University and involved in community, church, and philanthropic endeavors. She has had devotional articles published. She is a mother of three and grandmother of five. She enjoys sewing, tutoring, and playing piano and organ. **Oct. 5, Dec. 31**

Donna Reese, a retired speech and language pathologist, is a wife, grandmother, and private airplane pilot. She enjoys an active lifestyle in the California foothills, where she bicycles, hikes, swims, and skis. Donna enjoys freelance Christian writing and has been published in several magazines. **Mar. 15**

Darlenejoan McKibbin Rhine, born in Nebraska, raised in California, and educated in Tennessee, has now retired from the *Los Angeles Times* to the "soggy" state of Washington, USA. She is a widow with one son. She belongs to the North Cascade church and supports the Anacortes Adventist Fellowship company. **Mar. 11, June 18, Oct. 7**

Margie Salcedo Rice is a Christian recording artist who regularly appears with 3ABN and Family Reunion Music projects. She is a vocalist, violinist, composer, and music teacher living in northern California, USA. She is married to Geoffrey, an ophthalmologist, and is the mother of three musical daughters. **Apr. 7, Sept. 11**

Merian Richardson is a pastor's wife from Australia. She and her husband have three sons. She is a registered nurse and a radiographer who currently enjoys working part-time as a nurse in an aged-care nursing home. She spent fourteen years in Africa and Papua New Guinea, and enjoys music and sewing. **July 9**

Marli Ritter-Hein was born in the city of São Paulo, Brazil, married an Argentinian doctor, and worked with him as a missionary in Nepal and now Paraguay. She is a teacher by profession who loves music that points to heaven. She also enjoys nature, flower arrangements, and interior decorating. Most of all, she loves Jesus Christ and wants to spend eternity with Him. **Apr. 26**

Jenny Rivera lives in and writes from Brisbane, Australia, where she is a registered nurse. She is active in church, where she plays flute in the orchestra, sings in the youth choir, and serves as a deaconess. Every day she is overwhelmed at how God blesses her. She loves spending time with her family and friends, traveling, reading, and looking after her cockatiel, Luigi. **Jan. 12**

Taniesha Robertson-Brown is a teacher living in the Turks and Caicos Islands. She enjoys reading, writing, and spending time with family and friends. Her ministry efforts are supported by her dear husband, Courtney. Taniesha is the author of *Godly Families in an Ungodly World.* **Oct. 8**

Terry Wilson Robinson lives in Hendersonville, North Carolina, USA, with her husband, Harry. She is active in teaching the subject of disabilities awareness to elementary schoolchildren, as well as presenting seminars in churches and other organizations. She also loves to help her husband in teaching Revelation seminars. **Oct. 9**

Consuelo Roda-Jackson writes from Tappahannock, Virginia, USA. She is a widow and, most recently, became a volunteer at the Tappahannock Junior Academy library. She feels fortunate for having worked with kind and wonderful professional librarians, especially at Union College. **Aug. 10, Oct. 17**

Dixil Rodríguez, PhD, is a rhetoric professor and volunteer chaplain in Texas, USA. **Mar. 13, Oct. 3, Dec. 16**

Sayuri Ruiz Rodriguez is a daughter of the King of kings. She is also the daughter of the best parents on this earth! She is a pastor's wife who always prays to be joyful in hope, patient in affliction, and faithful in prayer. She believes that the best is yet to come— Jesus! She writes from Grants Pass, Oregon, USA. **Jan. 8, Mar. 8**

Kirsten Anderson Roggenkamp considers herself to be primarily a mother and grandmother, and, secondarily, a teacher. She is a retired teacher now living in Loma Linda, California, USA, with her new husband, Clyde. Though they were classmates in college, both had been alone for twenty-five years or more and now cherish their new life together. **Aug. 4**

Ida T. Ronaszegi teaches the art of composition and rhetoric and English for speakers of other languages (ESOL) at Savannah Technical College. She is also a freelance writer. Her work has been published in several articles. Ida also has a passion for prayer and women's ministries. She lives with her husband, Arpad, in Bluffton, South Carolina, USA. They have three grown children. **Aug. 25**

Kollis Salmon-Fairweather is originally from Jamaica, West Indies, but now lives in

Florida, USA, with her husband. She has served in different departments in her church. Though retired from the practice of nursing, she still remains active. Her hobbies include reading and singing. **Mar. 14**

Clair Sanches-Schutte is the mother of two sons and is married to John, a pastor and psychologist. At present, she serves in the Trans-European Division (headquartered in England) as director of Women's, Children's, and Family Ministries. The Lord has been good to her, and she thanks Him every day for His love. **Sept. 16**

Deborah Sanders lives in Alberta, Canada, with her husband, Ron, and her son, Sonny. In 1990, God blessed her with a successful writing and prayer-outreach ministry, Dimensions of Love. In 2013, she selected the best stories and compiled a book of sacred memories titled *Saints-In-Training*, a book she hopes Sonny can use in his witness for Jesus. **Mar. 6, Aug. 23**

Christa White Schiffbauer lives in Florida with her husband, Dan, two children, two cats, and many fish. She loves to send cards of encouragement to people and enjoys scrapbooking and praising God in song. She has also recorded a CD of encouraging songs and hymns titled *He Cares for You*. **Jan. 4**

Jennifer Jill Schwirzer resides with her husband, Michael, in Philadelphia, USA, where she conducts a private counseling practice and a speaking, writing, and music ministry. They have two daughters, Allison and Kimberly. Her latest book is *13 Weeks to Love*, available through Pacific Press® Publishing Association. **Feb. 14, May 15, July 27**

Shirley P. Scott serves as the director of Women's Ministries and Sabbath School for the South Central Conference of Seventh-day Adventists. A native of Baton Rouge, Louisiana, Shirley resides in Huntsville, Alabama, USA, with her husband, Lionel, a fellow Oakwood University retiree. She has three adult children, and two granddaughters. **Nov. 30**

Jaimée Seis was born in Germany in 1964. Even in childhood she was happy to know that Jesus was with her. Therefore, she would like others to experience God as a loving Father too. As a freelance writer, she has written articles, sermons, and books to make His abundant love known. **Apr. 8**

Omobonike Adeola Sessou is director of Women's and Children's Ministries for the West-Central Africa Division in Abidjan, Ivory Coast. She is married to Pastor Sessou, and they are blessed with three children. Her hobbies include teaching, counseling, making new friends, and visiting with people. **Oct. 27, Oct. 28**

Martha Shields is a native of Belzoni, Mississippi, USA, where she has lived most of her life. She has a wonderful husband. Together they have four beautiful adult children and fourteen grandchildren. At her church, Martha serves as prayer coordinator and deaconess in addition to assisting with women's ministries and Community Services. **Jan. 14**

Rose Neff Sikora and her husband, Norman, call the beautiful mountains of North Carolina, USA, their home. She retired from a forty-five-year career as a registered nurse. She enjoys walking, writing, and helping others. Rose has one adult daughter, Julie, and three lovely grandchildren. **Mar. 22, Oct. 24**

Heather-Dawn Small is the General Conference Women's Ministries director. She has been Children's and Women's Ministries director for the Caribbean Union Conference, located in Trinidad and Tobago. She is the wife of Pastor Joseph Small and the mother of Dalonne and Jerard. She loves scrapbooking. **Jan. 6, May 1, July 15, Dec. 13**

Thamer Cassandra Smikle lives in Spanish Town, Saint Catherine, Jamaica, with her husband, Wayne, and four beautiful children. She works as an auditor at Jamaica Customs Agency. She enjoys reading, singing, watching documentaries, and laughing. **Feb. 25**

Tamara Marquez de Smith writes from Florida, USA, where she lives with her husband and two daughters, Lillian and Cassandra. A native New Yorker who misses home, Tamara is looking for a new opportunity to use her talents for God. **July 5**

Peggy Miles Snow is retired from the Adventist Health System, having worked at Adventist hospitals in two states, Tennessee and Texas. Then she became administrator of skilled nursing facilities in Florida, Illinois, and Texas, USA. Peggy enjoys reading American history and writing poetry. Peggy has four children, four grandchildren, and four great-grandchildren. **Oct. 10**

Belinda Solomon is the wife of her dear husband, Lincoln, and has two children. She is a newly appointed teacher at an Adventist school in South Africa and is the children's and family ministries coordinator at church. She enjoys cooking, tending her vegetable garden, walking, learning to play the piano, and sewing, of course! **May 2**

Sylvia Stark is an artist living in East Tennessee, USA, at the foot of a small mountain. Her artwork is displayed in several states and in South America. She has also been published in *Guide*. Her passions include hiking, camping, backpacking, and contributing to the worship experience at various area churches through her singing and autoharp playing. **Apr. 21**

Ardis Dick Stenbakken edited these devotional books for many years after retirement from being the General Conference Women's Ministries director. She and her husband, Dick, live in Colorado, USA, and love spending time with their family. **Feb. 16, Apr. 15, Oct. 31**

Keisha D. Sterling works as a registered pharmacist and an entrepreneur. Fueled by the resolves to be saved (by God's grace), to be used by God, and to be thankful for blessings, she lives life believing that all things are possible when within His will. She serves women, young people, and the church while also supporting health and leadership ministries. **May 24, Nov. 15**

Naomi Striemer lives in Franklin, Tennessee, USA, with her husband, Jordan, and dog, Bella. She is a best-selling author, a chart-topping Christian singer and songwriter, and a sought-after speaker who tours around the world singing and speaking. In her spare time, she enjoys baking, board games, and the outdoors. **Feb. 24, May 14, Aug. 22**

Carolyn Rathbun Sutton, wife, mother, and grateful grandmother, lives in Alabama, USA. She enjoys being on the team that produces these devotional books, the proceeds of which go to provide scholarships to college-age women globally. **Apr. 13, June 28, Dec. 20**

Frieda Tanner is a retired nurse who moved to Eugene, Oregon, USA, more than twenty-four years ago to be near her daughter and family. She spends most of her time making nice Sabbath School items for children all over the world. So far her items have gone to ninety countries. Frieda is over ninety-five years old. **May 10**

Aleksandra Tanurdzic was born in Bosnia. She worked as a pastor, a dean of women at a seminary, and an assistant editor at the Seventh-day Adventist publishing house in Serbia. Currently she lives in Chicago, Illinois, USA, with her beautiful teenage daughter and husband. She also works there as a chaplain for Adventist Midwest Health. **Feb. 18, Nov. 9**

Charmaine N. Williams Tate is a woman whose rich history of trial, restoration, and renewal has set the foundation for her passion to inspire others to live for God. A native of Jamaica now living in Toronto, Canada, she is a mother, wife, friend, confidante, singer, writer, and Christian motivational speaker. She embraces each day as an opportunity to make a difference. **Mar. 4**

Arlene R. Taylor recently retired from health care after decades of working with Adventist Health facilities. Still living in the Napa Valley of northern California, USA, she devotes her time and energy to brain-function research, writing, and international speaking. **Jan. 17, June 9, June 10**

Tumusiime Betty Tenywa is a student at Bugema University in Uganda and has done research on psycho-social issues affecting children brought up by stepfamilies in her community, where she also volunteers as a counselor. At church she teaches young children and loves to sing. She thanks God for her marriage of more than fourteen years and for her eight children. **Mar. 26**

Nelly Thomas lives in Westmoreland, Jamaica, and has ten grandchildren. Seeing them flourish in their various seasons, along with the orange, mango, soursop, and June plum trees on her farm, brings her much joy. **Sept. 8**

Rose Joseph Thomas is an educator with the Florida Conference of Seventh-day Adventists, USA. She is married to her best friend, Walden. They have two children: Samuel Joseph and Crystal Rose. **Apr. 29**

Sharon M. Thomas is a retired public school teacher in Lacombe, Louisiana, but still enjoys working part-time and has had a variety of jobs. Her other interests include quilting, reading, walking, biking, and piano. She is always grateful for the omnipotent, omnipresent, and omniscient God of love whom we serve. **Oct. 18**

Shirley A. Thomas is a registered nurse who works at Tillamook Regional Medical Center. At present she is head deaconess, communications secretary, greeter, wedding coordinator, organist, and pianist at her church. She organizes the greeters and the teachers for her husband's Sabbath School class. She has six adult children, fourteen grandchildren, and four great-grandsons. **Jan. 1**

Stella Thomas works at the General Conference of Seventh-day Adventists as an administrative assistant. She has a passion to share God's love by distributing the book *Steps to Christ* through a lay outreach ministry in New York. **June 11, Dec. 5**

Bula Rose Haughton Thompson, first of fraternal twins, writes from Mandeville, Jamaica. She was a dental assistant for thirty-seven years and recently worked for the Southern Regional Health Authority. She is now enjoying her pre-retirement and is married to Norman. Her hobbies are sewing, singing, reading, and meeting people. **Apr. 9**

Rebecca Timon is an administrative assistant to the General Conference Women's Ministries director. She has one married son and a lovely daughter-in-law who are beginning a family. She belongs to several small groups, and her mission in life is to encourage her friends to study the Bible deeply. **Apr. 16**

Joey Lynn Norwood Tolbert is the administrative assistant to the director of the Samaritan Center in Ooltewah, Tennessee, USA. She is also an adjunct professor in the Humanities Department at Cleveland State Community College. She has been married to Matthew Tolbert for twelve years. They are the parents of Lela and Charlie. Joey sings with Message of Mercy. **June 17**

Gloria Turcios is not only the daughter of a pastor but also the wife of a pastor and the mother of one. She hopes that her grandson will someday be a pastor as well. Gloria has served the church as administrative assistant at mission, conference, union, and division levels. At present, she serves as a missionary, along with her husband, on the island of Palau. **Jan. 29**

Charlotte Verrett is a family practice physician who writes from Whiteville, North Carolina, USA. She and her husband, Leon, are parents to three grown sons whose families include three grandchildren. She is active in her church and enjoys writing and teaching children's Sabbath School classes. **Apr. 27**

Monica Vesey writes from England. When she was young, she lived in Aba, Nigeria, where she developed a passion for teaching. Until her recent retirement, she taught and helped children with dyslexia. She loves telling stories. **July 18**

Donna Voth, a retired teacher and health educator, lives in Angwin, California, USA, with her husband, Al, and dog, Lola. She enjoys volunteering at a hospital and at church. In her spare time she likes to watercolor paint and travel. **May 7**

Barbara J. Walker is a native of Jackson, Mississippi, USA, where she serves as clerk and elder in her local church. She is the South Central Conference Women's Ministries director for the state of Mississippi and serves as the president of a community choir. She also coordinates Morning Manna, a prayer ministry of her conference's Women's Ministries Department. **Mar. 24**

Cora A. Walker resides in Atlanta, Georgia, USA. She is a retired nurse, editor, and freelance writer. She enjoys reading, writing, sewing, swimming, classical music, traveling, and spending quality time with her family. **May 19, Aug. 28**

Dolores Klinsky Walker is discovering joy in "enhanced adulthood." Limited physical activity provides time for her to ponder God's ways, to write, and to pass on His love to others. She is married, and her family includes three children. Dolores writes from Walla Walla, Washington, USA. **Oct. 13**

Anna May Radke Waters, a retired administrative secretary from Columbia Adventist Academy, USA, has served at church as an ordained elder and greeter. Her greatest joys are her eight grandchildren and her husband, with whom she likes to travel and make memories. She likes doing Bible studies on the Internet and responding to prayer requests for Bibleinfo.com. **Apr. 10**

Elizabeth Darby Watson, PhD, MSW, is an associate professor of social work with a wealth of experience in the field of social work. She is a freelance author whose talents include creative writing, motivational speaking, and children's ministry. Dr. Watson is a successful single parent of three adult children (and their spouses) and has five wonderful grandchildren. **Jan. 24**

Lyn Welk-Sandy lives in Adelaide, South Australia. She has worked as a grief counselor, plays the hand chimes, and has spent many years as a pipe organist. She enjoys nature, photography, and caravanning around Outback Australia with her husband, Keith, serving where needed. Lyn is mother of four, grandmother of nine, and great-grandmother of four. **Jan. 31, Nov. 1**

Penny Estes Wheeler is a retired writer and editor who loves to travel. She recently visited Australia, where she held a koala and hand-fed kangaroos. She and her husband have four adult children and five grandchildren with another one on the way. They live in western Maryland, USA. **Aug. 19, Aug. 23, Dec. 1**

Karen Jansen White considers her three sons—Sean, Aaron, and Isaac Sinnett—to be her life's greatest accomplishment. She teaches piano and English as a second language (ESL) at Wisconsin Academy, USA, where she also accompanies the school's singing groups. **Dec. 10**

Sandra Widulle is married and has two children. She loves to express her thoughts in writing. In her local church, she is engaged in the children's division and uses her creativity to decorate the church. She lives in Germany. **Feb. 22**

Vera Wiebe has been involved in ministry with her husband for more than forty years. She has enjoyed organizing music in local churches and for camp meetings. For nine years, she was the Women's Ministries director for her conference. She is now retired in Lacombe, Alberta, Canada.. Her two sons and four grandchildren bring her pleasure and enjoyment. **Dec. 22**

Rachel Williams-Smith is a wife, mother, writer, and speaker. She has a bachelor's degree in language arts, a master's degree in professional writing, and a doctorate in communication. She serves as chair of the Department of Communication at Andrews University, USA. She authored *Born Yesterday*. **Dec. 18, Dec. 19**

Bronwyn Worthington lives in Spokane, Washington, USA, where she writes devotionals, teaches students, and cares for her family. Find out more about her at bronwynworthington .com or e-mail her at bronwor@gmail.com. **June 3**

Charlene M. Wright is an elementary special education school administrator and has worked in the school system for forty years. Her passion for prison ministry takes her into Washington, DC, and Maryland prisons. She provides Bible studies for both juveniles and adults. Currently she is secretary for the Allegheny East Conference Federation for Prison Ministries, USA. **Dec. 11**

Tricia Wynn serves as the pastor of a two-church district in the Lake Region Conference, USA. She is a graduate of the Andrews University physical therapy program and of the Seventh-day Adventist Theological Seminary. Tricia enjoys spending time with family, friends, and those with whom she has previously served. **Mar. 5, Aug. 31**

Maxine Young is a writer from New York City, USA. She is currently creating the e-book version of her booklet about God's promises to sufferers of chronic illness. **July 26**

Shelly-Ann Patricia Zabala writes from Syracuse, New York, USA, where she is a registered nurse. As a minister's wife and a mother of two energetic boys, she enjoys children's and women's ministries. Her hobbies include singing, gardening, and entertaining. **Jan. 5**

Leni Uría de Zamorano and her husband have two adult children and two grandchildren. She plays the piano and the organ and teaches a Sabbath School class in her church. She likes to travel, do handwork, read, and translate from English to Spanish. **June 13**